THIRD EDITION

STREETSENSE

Communication, Safety, and Control

Kate Boyd Dernocoeur, B.S., EMT-P

Laing Research Services
Laing Communications Inc.

Library of Congress Cataloging-in-Publication Data

Dernocoeur, Kate Boyd.
 . Streetsense: communication, safety, and control / Kate Boyd
Dernocoeur.—3rd ed.
   p.   cm.
  Includes index.
  ISBN 0-938106-21-X (pbk.)
  1. Medical emergencies. 2. Communication in medicine.
 3. Interpersonal relations. I. Title.
 RC86.7.D47   1996
 362.1'8—dc20   96-31540
                                                                 CIP

Published by Laing Research Services,
a division of Laing Communications Inc.
16250 NE 80th Street
Redmond, WA 98052
(206) 869-6313 • Fax (206) 869-6318

Copyediting: Elaine Yoder
Cover Design: Sandra J. Harner
Design & Production: Kelly C. Rush
Editorial Coordination: Laura Dickinson

It is the intention of the author and publisher that the care procedures presented
here represent accepted practices in the United States. They are not a standard of
care. People needing emergency or interfacility care should receive care by EMS
providers who work under the authority and guidance of 'a licensed physician. It
is the reader's responsibility to know and follow local protocols. Also, it is the
reader's responsibility to stay informed of emergency care procedure changes.

This edition of Streetsense is dedicated

to Jim and Melody
who are such good teachers to me,

to my brother, Tom Boyd, who has been a kind supporter,

and to hundreds of thousands of field providers in EMS
who provide a noble and important service to humanity

Contents

Foreword to the Third Edition

It's hard to believe that 1996 marks the 30th anniversary of the infamous White Paper, the document that introduced the modern concept of Emergency Medical Services. One could argue that EMS actually began in biblical times when the Good Samaritan stopped to render aid. However, hundreds of years would then pass before the National Academy of Sciences published the White Paper in an attempt to formalize the process of rendering care to trauma victims. It laid out a plan to bring together the resources necessary to create a *system to save lives*. It could also be said that with that landmark document came the first attempt to define EMS from a scientific perspective.

With that effort to describe the *science of EMS*, it was only a matter of time until someone took the time to describe the other side of the coin: the *art of EMS*. The year was 1985, and that someone was Kate Dernocoeur. The book she wrote bore the name of *Streetsense*. It was filled with ideas, suggestions, pearls of wisdom, and lessons from the school of hard knocks. It filled the massive gaps left by textbooks, whose focus was on the transmission of medical knowledge and the teaching of skills. *Streetsense* talked about how to do a better job of taking care of people, and taking care of yourself, too.

With this anniversary of the White Paper comes the Third Edition of *Streetsense*. It is appropriate that these two publications should share an anniversary. As the brief history of EMS has evolved, we have increasingly realized that the fusing of both the art and the science of EMS was necessary, not only for EMS to survive, but more importantly, for EMS to flourish.

As with the first two editions of *Streetsense*, the Third Edition is a living, dynamic document. It is a book to be read, and put away, and then read again. The timeless nature of *Streetsense* makes it at once a book for the novice EMS provider as well as for the seasoned veteran.

I have always been fascinated when I have picked up my tattered copies of the first and second editions how *Streetsense* has meant different things at different times in my own EMS career. Previously un-learned lessons are presented in a logical, straightforward approach, and forgotten lessons are retaught. The reader can polish his EMS craft to a shining hue with the bounty of information found within.

In the short time modern EMS has been around, a mere handful of documents have emerged as milemarkers for our profession. *Streetsense* is one of them, and should be required reading for anyone who aspires to step beyond the technician mentality, and truly touch the lives and souls of the people we are entrusted to care for: our patients.

—Mike Smith, EMT-Paramedic Director of EMS Programs,
Tacoma Community College (Washington)
"Tricks of the Trade" columnist, *JEMS* May 1996

Preface to the Third Edition

Whether you are a novice EMS provider or a veteran, there are lessons within this book that will help on a very practical and relevant basis. My goal as author has been to provide a work that can make a difference to the quality of your life as it is shaped by your experiences in EMS at the same time it impacts the quality of work you do on behalf of people needing help.

There are times when I am sure *Streetsense* has been the most misunderstood book in the history of publishing. Many people regard it as a book about safety. Others see it as a source for interpersonal communication tips, or for good information on stress management, or documentation, or scene control. It is all these things, and much more. Although this may make it difficult to "pigeon-hole" for the convenience of marketing, I was convinced that it would be worth the effort of creating this third edition because of how the book touches people. Many times in the past decade (and more), people have come up to me with statements like, "It's the most important book of any that we read in our entire paramedic class." and "Your book is what has kept me in this business—thank you!"

Streetsense is indeed eclectic. That is, it contains information about a wide variety of topics. It speaks to the safe and effective delivery of prehospital care from many varied points of view. The amount of "other" stuff you need to know in order to take your medical knowledge and skills to the streets is immense, and *Streetsense* addresses this information head-on. I wrote it because when I was first on the streets, in 1976, I had precious little streetsense, and there was no reference like this one to help me. It all came by the seat of the pants. Maybe that's why I remain steadfast in my belief in this little book. It is filled with good and important information.

Each element of streetsense covered in this book matters. If you use the information to improve your ability to connect effectively with others, you will meet their needs more fully. There is a whole array of strategies for improving communication simply by being aware of your own interpersonal style, and how you can consciously alter it. If you don't take time to understand other people, even for a few minutes, you could be hurt, or your agency's community relations could be shattered. Logistical savvy, such as how to approach a building or a parked car, is part of streetsense. Self-care and wellness are, too. So are the traits of tolerance and patience, and the habit of not acting on your prejudices. Attention to the various facets of streetsense matters to you, as an individual EMS provider. It also matters a great deal to others: your patients, bystanders, colleagues, other health professionals, and the general public. Many people have told me that each EMS provider ought to read this book at the outset of a career in EMS, and then again every few years. And if you've been an EMS provider for years and haven't read it yet, there's still a lot here for you, according to many seasoned veterans who thought they knew it all—until they read *Streetsense*.

Old friends of the book will notice some changes. Throughout the book, the writing has been polished up. The infection control chapter has disappeared, although parts of it remain in the chapter now titled "Stress and Wellness." The rest of the information for that chapter is abundantly available in other books. The two chapters on weapons have been blended into one. I believe the effect is much improved. The last chapter is renamed "After The Streets." The subject matter has shifted to a perspective intended to broaden your view of life both after a busy day and at the conclusion of your EMS career. Much of the information from the final chapter of the second edition is sprinkled throughout the book. Finally, there is a new chapter titled "Service Orientation and The Nature of Routine." With so much traditional emphasis on the "emergency" aspect of EMS, it seemed time, in this era of system status management and managed care, to address these topics. I hope this chapter will help create a positive way to perceive what are important and necessary—if quite unexciting, in the traditional sense—EMS activities.

The lessons within really do bubble to the surface differently each time you read the book. As such, then, *Streetsense* has served as a touchstone in the careers of many fine EMS professionals. Maybe it can provide the same service to you.

—Kate Dernocoeur, B.S., EMT-P
Grand Rapids, Michigan
June 1996

The Human Component in EMS   1

"The more you see of people . . . the more you realize that the whole world's like a play. You can change the costumes and some of the lines, but the characters are the same all over."

—Peace Corps volunteer

Chapter Overview

A fundamental principle of prehospital care is that it involves work-ing with human beings. You will meet all sorts of people: every age, sex, race, religion, socioeconomic level, and ethnic background. You name it, and chances are, you'll see it if you stick around long enough. You will witness living conditions that are far different from those you are used to seeing. You will encounter various ways that people cope with crisis and tragedy. The human component in EMS is what makes it so frightening—and so fun, frustrating, and rewarding. For those who can keep an open mind and an open heart toward the people who summon help, the experience will indeed be rich.

"Variety is the spice of life," and nothing varies as dramatically as people, particularly those involved in out-of-hospital[1] medical situations. It's ex-citing! To enter a scene of chaos, interact with many people at once, co-ordinate and facilitate a common direction for all that energy, and to do all of this with a clear mind and an effective, efficient style—that's streetsense. It is interesting that the mechanics of medicine can lose their significance

---

[1] The term "out-of-hospital" is used just this once. The reason this awkward term evolved is reasonable: to acknowledge that much of the work done by EMS providers will increasingly not result in the transfer of people to in-hospital care. Strictly, then, the term "prehospital" is less accurate. However, the word "prehospital" will be used from here on because it will probably always be the more familiar term, and because it doesn't twist one's tongue!

1

if you cannot communicate effectively, maintain your own safety, or control the situation. These are the three major components of streetsense.

Emergency medical services (EMS) is a people business. A big part of streetsense is "people skills." It's knowing how people tick; how they are likely to react in stressful situations. It's knowing when to push and when to yield. Knowing about people is the root of the difference between straight academic ability and a high-quality, efficient, effective prehospital worker. The EMS provider with that intangible umbrella of humanistic capability is the one to whom others on the scene—coworkers, the patient, and bystanders—inevitably will look for competence and control.

The notion of being well-rounded in this way may sound pretty grand. But everybody can strive to be the very best, most capable prehospital worker possible. The chance to develop these skills in school may be missing from many EMS education programs because of time constraints. That's fine; learning streetsense is an ongoing process anyway. Simply passing the exams and getting licensed does not mean there is nothing more to learn.

> Being in EMS isn't difficult. The real challenge lies with being *really good* at EMS.

Continuing education, both formal and informal, is vital. Every EMS call, whether routine or emergency, has something to offer, something for you to learn.

Being in EMS isn't difficult. The real challenge lies with being *really good* at EMS. It isn't easy to excel, especially when you are at the bottom of the seniority heap. It is frustrating to have to obey questionable orders. Every person in a leadership role at prehospital emergency medical scenes needs to be a student of streetsense. So do the people on their way up through the ranks.

Recognize and develop the three components of streetsense, no matter your level of involvement:

- *Communication.* People skills are the "soup stock" that you use for cooking up answers to the full range of the human emergency spectrum, from critical trauma, to medical problems, to routine transfers. Good interpersonal communication skills are a must. You may not be in a position to say a single word out loud. But as a member of the team that has come to help, you can still "say" a great deal. Wiping your shoes as you enter demonstrates a sense of consideration, and other nonverbal behavior will speak just as clearly. Verbal communication brings an even greater opportunity to employ effective, interaction-enhancing strategies.

To develop and maintain an accurate sense of self-awareness is essential. Know yourself! With that as a starting point, learn how to interact effectively with others. This includes patients, their families and friends. It also includes the rest of the EMS team, and other emergency and medical professionals. Failure to get along with first responders, firefighters, police, doctors, nurses, and most significantly, partners or other close coworkers, can be a career-wrecker.

- *Safety.* In the name of self-preservation, every prehospital worker needs to know how to protect numerous aspects of personal and team safety. The streets can be hazardous, no matter where you work. Inner cities may have a violent reputation, but people are people everywhere. The principles of safety go beyond self-defense in the face of violence. Many simple, daily safety measures are included. Some may seem downright mundane. But heeding the principles of safety could save an important life—yours.

Even very experienced people don't know it all (although there are many in the EMS ranks who would like to believe they do). Prehospital professionals with good streetsense know many practical tips and techniques that can reduce or eliminate the risks inherent to the prehospital environment. Many of these things have been learned traditionally by the "seat of the pants" method. This is hazardous and unnecessary. This text provides a solid foundation for practicing EMS safely. It offers a basis for making smart decisions about personal safety and control. This could prevent unnecessarily jeopardizing the whole EMS team. Anyone who is truly wise to the streets knows that there is always more to learn. In many instances, a single moment of overconfidence has resulted in a resounding slap in the face—metaphorical or real!

- *Control.* You aren't in charge, so you have no control, right? Wrong! For starters, you need self-control, and that's not always easy. Also, whoever is in charge may ask you to care for someone else, such as a patient's relative, or someone with minor injuries. Each person who represents the emergency services at a prehospital scene has some control responsibilities.

The principles of "control" extend past the obvious, too. They include control over your response to stress, your attention to your own wellness, your understanding of legal matters related to EMS, and your control over your life after the streets (both daily and once you retire).

Seniority and Professionalism in Streetsense

Each prehospital worker begins with no seniority, and has to achieve a certain degree of seniority before getting to be in charge of an emergency scene. During that time, a person might have the chance to observe excellent providers—or to endure a horrible "apprenticeship" with poor role models. Unfortunately, some people with a lot of street time don't have much streetsense. Tenure in EMS is no guarantee that a person is a good EMS professional, or wise about the streets. The time prior to becoming the senior person at a scene might be lengthy, or far too brief. Leadership slots in some EMS systems seem to be filled forever; the chance to "take charge" might take years. On the other hand, others have been forced to handle scene control before they were ready.

Doing prehospital work is mostly a matter of experiential learning, to gain "people" skills. This is true in both paid and volunteer systems, in rural, suburban, or urban areas. Each call provides new tips about how to do the work (assuming the EMS provider is willing to notice them). Some have learned street survival and developed their own personal style at the School of Hard Knocks. Although experience can be a very good teacher, it can also be a problem. Without guided training, many EMS providers have developed ineffectual and often insensitive methods for coping with the environment and the people in it.

Many may insist that streetsense cannot be taught, that it can only be developed over time. They have a point. Nothing can completely prepare a person for what will happen out there. But guidance in ways to approach a problem can help. Reading and hearing about the mistakes and successes of others is a start. This book is intended as a basis for the development of streetsense. It can make the School of Hard Knocks easier to endure and appreciate. Even people with decades of field experience can benefit, especially when they decide to notice and replace certain bad habits that have interfered with practicing paramedicine at its best.

Prehospital workers have notoriously strong and independent personalities. This is why the concept of professionalism plays a major role in streetsense. On one hand, prehospital workers are tremendously autonomous. The work of EMS is done independent of direct supervision. Without a strong sense of professionalism, there are times when it is tempting to behave inappropriately out on the streets. An EMS provider may give unsound advice or act inappropriately on emotional impulses, such as anger or frustration. On the other hand, EMS providers actually depend a great deal on each other. The umbrella of EMS covers us all. We are part of a team that includes on-scene professionals from other agencies, as well as those who await us at the emergency department doors. When everyone on the EMS team understands and appreciates the various roles, and behaves professionally within their own roles, the overall streetsense of the team is enhanced. It is a sign of system maturity. Without cohesive and steady intra-personal and intra-agency streetsense, the elements of communications, safety, and control are jeopardized. This is to everyone's detriment.

Streetsense and EMS Education Programs

EMS education is forced, by the curriculum and a limited schedule, to concentrate on essential medical knowledge and the skills necessary for stabilizing and saving lives. These are obvious priorities over learning how people tick, or ways to gain their trust and cooperation. However, this emphasis results in an unfortunate gap in EMS education. This is not the fault of hard-working educators, or their students. It is an un-avoidable reality. With so much to learn, there isn't enough time to absorb everything during initial training. Much remains to be mastered when the student begins working on the streets. Many areas worthy of further skill development are subtle enough that students may not recognize their limitations until they have been in the field for awhile—if ever.

Education programs, by their very nature, cause a phenomenon called the "technical imperative." That is, when a person learns some-thing, particularly a manipulative skill, the natural inclination is to want to try it. There is an urge to find a situation that justifies the application of a knowledge or skill, simply to determine whether it really works and how it feels to do it.[2]

Actually, one other thing overrides the technical imperative. At first, the rescuer's greatest challenge is to survive the calls without killing anybody! When the tones and beepers go off for the first few dozen runs, the excitement of direct patient contact on an actual emergency call stimulates unusual, sometimes inordinate, levels of adrenaline in anyone new to EMS. Soon, though, the technical imperative steps in. The desire to handle more challenging calls arises, so you can try out the things that you learned in school.

---

[2] Peter Rosen et al. "The Technical Imperative: Its Definition and an Application to Prehospital Care," *Topics in Emergency Medicine* (July 1981), 80.

Eventually, the calls blend. You have done enough IVs and handled a sufficient number of serious situations to trust your ability to cope with emergencies. You understand the basic rules of the game. Your definition of what constitutes a "good" call has narrowed to those situations that pose a "real" challenge to your experience and abilities. This is an unfortunate trap. At this point, some people feel that EMS has little left to offer, and quit. For those who stay, it becomes easier to identify areas to improve, while the compulsion of the technical imperative fades. Often, a desire arises for continuing medical education about the psychosocial aspects of the business. People realize that their initial education focused very little (or no) attention on the most common and far-reaching elements of EMS. They realize that their knowledge about such things as behavioral emergencies, suicide, stress management, or death and dying is lacking. "What about handling people in crisis?" they ask. "What about handling *myself* in crisis?"

A psychosocial emphasis is obviously secondary when a life depends on quick, appropriate medical intervention. In no way should these concerns override the obvious need for lifesaving skills. But lifesaving skills are needed in a very small percentage of cases, and psychosocial and interpersonal skills are required on *every* call. Students often discover that what they assumed to be the most exciting aspects of EMS during their initial training are not the most encompassing or even inspiring after all. Expectations set during training that led them to believe that they'd be constantly needed (and wanted) to save lives have to be adjusted.[3]

> Students often discover that what they assumed to be the most exciting aspects of EMS during their initial training are not the most encompassing or even inspiring after all.

In the long run, prehospital workers who are curious about the total spectrum of skills needed for EMS realize that education about the "people skills" is not only valid, but usually sorely needed. This is when the human component of EMS comes alive. Visionary initial training courses include the components of streetsense. Others perhaps make these topics available in continuing medical education classes. Either way, information about interpersonal communication and the other el-

---

[3] Kate Dernocoeur, "The 'We Save Lives' Myth," in *The Best of JEMS: Timeless Essays From the First 15 Years* (St. Louis: Mosby Lifeline, 1996).

ements of streetsense is needed by EMS professionals everywhere. Even the most brilliant prehospital technicians won't make it if they fail to respect the ongoing lessons offered in the prehospital environment. The School of Hard Knocks is there. It's one way to learn. But those who heed the voices of experience via their classroom and ride-along practicals will find the going less rough.

Responsibility of the EMS Organization

There is a certain amount of identity that stems from one's EMS affiliation. Your ambulance corps is visible in the community, and in communities with more than one ambulance service, it's natural to want yours to be considered the "best." This has resulted in an interesting phenomenon: there are innumerable "best in the nation" ambulance services, and the judges tend to have a highly biased viewpoint!

This is not all bad. Pride in affiliation is a natural, human trait. A company is a collection of individuals spending time in the same place, under the same logo, with the same purpose. There is a sense of united purpose. Field personnel predominantly view that purpose as "patient care," and they are correct. But there is more to it.

To bring excellent patient care to the community, members of a company (or agency, or volunteer group) must realize that the word "company" simply defines a framework. The human component, the *people*, in each company create its personality. Company personality is an important factor in the success of any organization. If you observe any industry, it is easy to discern a range of company personalities. Some organizations are friendly, some in turmoil, some angry and defensive, others falsely self-assured. All (or none) may be competent, but each has a different flavor. Why? The reason is because of the *people* who work for that company, at every level of the hierarchy.

Field personnel contribute to company personality in EMS through individual attitudes and efforts to help the company succeed. Perhaps this is a different way of viewing your job, but your personality does influence the company's. The relationship is symbiotic, which means that it is a relationship of mutual dependence. The company needs you; you need the company. Feeling content with your EMS agency is influenced by the way you integrate your approach to life, and how you work with the stated and implied philosophies of the company.

Therefore, EMS organizations, including volunteer groups, have certain responsibilities to their field personnel that transcend pay scales

7

and benefit packages. To get top-level work from employees, good companies recognize the relevance of a positive, healthful, realistic, and humanistic attitude toward workers. How else can workers be expected to "buy in" to company philosophies? Yet, while turnover is blamed on many causes, the number one complaint of those who answer numerous stress questionnaires has often been "administrative insensitivity."

EMS personnel certainly are not in it for the money or the hours! The emotional and physical demands of EMS require unusually enlightened management for optimal employee satisfaction. Agencies that fail in this area will experience unnecessarily consistent (and rapid) turnover. Great companies already know the value of adequate support systems for personnel. Employee Assistance Programs and the availability of help after particularly difficult EMS situations (known as Critical Incident Stress Debriefing, see Chapter 12) are a good start. Managers who take to heart their responsibilities to their field workers can generate an environment of success for field personnel, and thus for the company as well.

How to Develop Streetsense

Where to begin? A musical conductor does not begin by stepping onto the podium of a world-famous orchestra. A surgeon does not start out with open-heart cases. A prehospital worker who wants to strive for excellence in streetsense should start with a very familiar face: his or her own.

The need to understand yourself is a high priority in EMS. Yet many people are oblivious to who they really are and how they interact with their world. Maybe this is one explanation for the less-than-optimal treatment some patients receive. When rescuers do not understand their personal needs, how can they understand the needs of other people?

A good place to start is to ask yourself: "Do I have what it takes to do this job? Can I handle crisis?" There is a story that is told of an EMT fresh out of training who went to a very gory auto accident. There were several critically injured patients, and all on-scene resources were stretched toward their limits. The EMT's paramedic partner came around the back end of the ambulance in the midst of the fray and discovered the EMT sitting on the back bumper, obviously unable to function.

"What's the matter?" asked the paramedic.

The EMT looked up and said, "I never knew that blood smells."

Do you have the internal grit to do the work? How do you feel about death or dying? Is it possible to help other people grapple with tragedy when you cannot recognize your *own* feelings?

Everyone arrives at his or her first day of EMS training with a certain degree of innate streetsense. To a certain extent, the way you use your life experience as a learning tool will help formulate the kind of EMS provider you are. Few would argue with the fact that an older person with additional years of living usually brings a broader perspective than a younger person. An awareness of your strengths and weaknesses is a great start for further developing streetsense.

Once some self-understanding exists, try to understand other people. EMS workers have a unique opportunity to encounter the gamut of the human condition, on its own turf, in crisis. Every time EMS services are summoned, someone has perceived the need for help handling a situation beyond their control. Each encounter can provide the opportunity for professional and personal growth. Something can even be gained from ambulance system abusers. These people have needs, too. You are the vehicle of their efforts (misguided though they may be) to meet those needs. Other people are cursed with revolting or frightening diseases, such as infectious diseases or hideous skin ailments. These situations may cause some "helpers" to shrink away. There is a lot of negativity generated about many out-of-hospital scenes, and it can be hard to avoid having negative feelings in response. But by conducting each call in as positive a manner as possible, you will learn self-preservation, an essential component in learning to enjoy this work. By maintaining a positive outlook, even on the least desirable calls, you are putting streetsense to work. By viewing people as individuals and heeding the nature of individuality, you need never feel burned out from the "drudgery" of crisis.

Education programs, from the most basic level, teach the best ways to react to environmental hazards, such as avalanches, fires, explosives, electrical hazards, and so on. Your personal safety comes first, then the safety of others. An incapacitated rescuer cannot help those who need assistance. Yet the most common, everyday hazards are seldom addressed in EMS training. Your personal safety is far more likely to be threatened not by fires or floods, but by people. In the rescue role, you must consciously assess whether the people at each scene pose a threat. You must continue to assess that potential throughout the course of the call. Guns and knives are not hazardous by themselves. But they do become hazardous in the hands of people with malicious intent. So do nail files, baseball bats, tire irons, scissors, and scores of other everyday objects within easy reach. The real dangers behind these objects are moods and emotions, because these are the springboards for aggression.

Closely linked with safety is the element of control. Self-control is an acquired art, the natural outgrowth of maturity and personal understanding. The capacity for guiding or controlling, in a positive sense, comes later. The ability to control whole scenes comes still later. Too many people, as a result of the way their agencies are organized, have been made to conduct the full orchestra without first learning the tune.

> A person who consistently demonstrates forthright and responsible efforts to do tasks well (both on and off emergency scenes) will be rewarded with the respect of co-workers and a good reputation in the EMS community.

This is not only hazardous to everyone involved, but can be devastating to the prehospital worker who is forced to cope with unrealistic expectations from the management. Everyone deserves the chance to build some self-confidence in his or her ability to handle situations before having to be in charge. Optimally, people are allowed to learn about scene control over time, with good role models, and in manageable increments of magnitude.

Developing personal competence in EMS takes time. But a person who consistently demonstrates forthright and responsible efforts to do tasks well (both on and off emergency scenes) will be rewarded with the respect of co-workers and a good reputation in the EMS community. This is pertinent because a person with a good reputation is often the one who ends up with the responsibility, and opportunity, to manage scene control at prehospital situations.

The Challenge of the Human Component

One who keeps the human component in mind can never find EMS routine or boring. Certain variables are always present. The people—patients, relatives or friends, and bystanders—are always new. The time of day, the weather, and other contributing factors change from call to call. These things make each scene different. Rescuers change, too. Moods, emotions, levels of exhaustion and patience, and perceptions about the scene will vary. Larger social changes have influenced the evolution of the prehospital world dramatically. EMS offers you a front-row seat to witness era-to-era transitions. True, much of what we see is difficult: increasing violence, rampant substance abuse, unwanted pregnancies, communicable diseases, gangs, and the public hysteria surrounding them. But the variety of social changes alone can lead to an appreciation of the quality of life you may seek, or have attained. This, too, is a gift given to EMS personnel by the streets.

One way to retain the challenge of EMS through the years is to keep learning. A highly respected prehospital worker said he would quit when he stopped learning something new every day. He's retired now, but not because he stopped learning; he worked full time for a high-volume, urban EMS system for more than 30 years. He kept up with the changes, too, progressing from being an "ambulance driver" to a paramedic. When he left he continued to express his appreciation for the things EMS had taught him about life and the people in it.

A Word of Caution

No one is perfect, and no one can expect to be. Everyone who has worked in EMS can recall certain field actions that cause them, in re-membering, to cringe. Each person who engages in this important work has to understand that it is precisely because we human that we can do the work at all. It doesn't always go smoothly, or well. People seem to die in spite of our efforts. But it's just as important to recognize that sometimes they seem, too, to live in spite of our efforts! It's important to make a personal commitment to learn from your failures instead of dwelling on them—and also to be sure to take the time to celebrate your successes. Your internal critic will often speak up, if you're listen-ing. But be sure to listen for the internal "attaboy" or "attagirl," as well. Keep it balanced. You have an important job to do, but it's worth say-ing again: No one is perfect, and no one can expect to be.

Summary

Solid street savvy is an intriguing and intangible quality. Developing it is a lifelong challenge. It transcends mere technological capability. The medical basis for the care of sick and injured people, and the skills of IV therapy, airway control, CPR, splinting, and so on, are but the mechanics of EMS.

Streetsense is the art. To be able to encounter complete strangers and know within moments how to interact with them effectively, to dispense care safely and efficiently, to take control of each situation, and to ac-quire the respect of your peers; these are the true challenges we face.

Know Yourself

"The biggest single gift we can give ourselves . . . doesn't come in a pretty box. . . .
It doesn't cost a lot of money, and it may never impress the neighbors.
It's a quiet, readily-available commodity known as self-awareness. . . ."

—Herbert J. Freudenberger

Chapter Overview

Many people develop an interest in EMS because they are curious about themselves. They want to discover the limits of their personal capability "under fire." But at the same time, the demands of EMS require self-knowledge that will allow you to deliver emotionally unencumbered prehospital care. This results in a conflict, because the outlook EMS needs from its workers is the sort usually found only after lengthy street experience.

To know when to step in and when to back off is a trait of self-knowledge. No one handles every type of emergency call perfectly, and a good team knows its players well enough to recognize who should handle a specific situation.

Thus, each member on the EMS team at least needs to consider his or her capabilities for self-control. When emotions such as fear, anxiety, frustration, anger, sadness, grief, or guilt arise, your effectiveness is decreased. Because your capability for self-control will change from time to time, it is also important to keep a close eye on yourself as you continue to learn and grow.

There are specific techniques for raising personal awareness. You can develop a sense of objectivity, learn to listen to your senses and intuition, acknowledge personal views on death and dying, and learn how to view the tragedies of other people in a caring but personally nondraining fashion.

Another consideration in knowing yourself is to be able to recognize when physical force is your only recourse. Prehospital situations rarely require physical restraint of patients, or self-defense.
Most explosive circumstances can be defused with effective communication. But when aggression cannot be managed any other way,
you need to be ready to respond appropriately.

Personal understanding can happen only when we ask ourselves a lot
of difficult questions and try to find acceptable answers. Many people
are intrigued by the challenges of prehospital care. Yet it isn't until they
are well into it that they appreciate the extent of the demand for
self-understanding. People who acknowledge the value of streetsense
components early will benefit by applying the principles of good, healthy
interpersonal interaction right away.

Understanding yourself may sound easy. Perhaps it is for some
people. For most of us, though, it's deceptive. Even people who claim
to understand themselves well are sometimes surprised by the unexpected pockets of their personalities that emerge at odd moments.

Personal understanding is a continuous process. We are assaulted
by millions of new stimuli every day. It helps to have contemplated
certain predictable things before you encounter them. For example, it is
difficult to encounter death for the first time without anticipating your
feelings about it. This is also true of the other difficult EMS "predictables":
suicide, pediatric calls, psych cases, hysteria, squalor, poor personal
hygiene, urine, vomit, feces, and so on. Sometimes, EMS providers have
inappropriate reactions to their work. This is unsettling for the person
having the reaction, and it is unfair to others on the scene. One aspect
of self-awareness is learning how to delay certain reactions temporarily.

The obvious advantage to the teamwork inherent to EMS is that
co-workers often have complementary capabilities for handling the
various things that happen out there. Some workers are good at helping survivors begin appropriate grief processes, yet are poor at coping
with skid row drunks. If you handle psychotic people well, but not
children, and your partner is just the opposite, the capabilities of your
team are greater than its individual parts.

You cannot, and should not, try to be all things to all people. Everyone has limitations. Trouble begins when prehospital workers feel that by
virtue of having studied basic or advanced life support, they are expected

to cope with everything they encounter. That expectation may be established, incidentally, either by other people or by your own unrealistic perceptions of what an EMS worker should be. We are only human, and while the principles espoused by the streetsense concept are lofty, they are also intended to help you to remain self-aware enough to acknowledge your natural human shortcomings.

Your Unique Style

The nature of individuality gives each of us a unique way of being in the world. If there were a spectrum of style, one end might be extremely soft, gentle, and perhaps timid, and the other end extremely tough, hard, and unyielding. Neither is right or wrong, good or bad. The purpose of the spectrum is simply an assessment tool, a way to realize the way your style might impact other people. Conscious familiarity with your half of the interpersonal equation can have a positive effect during the variety of interactions that occur when assisting strangers in crisis.

Style assessment can begin with the obvious: physical presence. The size, shape, and other elements of your physical body will carry a powerful message to other people. Someone with a large, imposing body will have a different impression on others than someone who is slight-statured and petite. The first might be construed as "tough" while the second might be construed as "gentle." Other traits, such as gender, age, race, and other physical traits carry different tough-soft spectrum perceptions as well. These might include less tangible elements, such as the way you typically stand, how you move, everyday facial expression, and tone and volume of voice. All the factors that combine to say "this is me" constitute your natural presence. Interestingly, rescuer-type personalities have been found to share a constellation of traits. These traits give EMS providers

---

GENERAL PERSONALITY TRAITS OF RESCUERS

Need to be in control

Obsessive (desire to do a perfect job)

Compulsive (tend to repeat the same actions for similar events; traditional)

Highly motivated by internal factors

Action oriented

High need for stimulation

Need for immediate gratification

Easily bored

Risk takers

Rescue personality

Highly dedicated

Strong need to be needed

[Source: Jeff Mitchell and Grady Bray, *Emergency Services Stress* (Englewood Cliffs, NJ: Prentice-Hall, Inc., 1990.]

Figure 2.1

14

a tendency toward the tough side of the style spectrum. Assess the trait list (Fig. 2.1). Which are prominent in you? How a person uses these traits has an impact on interpersonal interaction. A strong-willed, control-oriented person has a different impact than a more yielding person. Whatever your natural style, it will be an asset at times, and a liability at others. The variety of EMS situations may call for a low-key, soft approach, or anything across the spectrum of possibilities, to situations demanding a powerful, commanding presence.

If you assess your natural style accurately and really understand your starting point on this tough-to-soft spectrum, you can learn to adjust your style to meet the needs of various situations. If you know you have a big, imposing presence, you can consciously soften it when you encounter a scene requiring a gentle approach, such as with a child. If your style wouldn't scare a flea and the events at hand call for a commanding presence, there are strategies one can employ to appear more in charge (see chapter 4). A person might want to have access to a variety of interpersonal roles (complete with congruent style) to meet the needs of different situations. Part of understanding yourself is knowing where the "real" you started the shift, and being able to return to that place at the end. This self-awareness has big implications both in terms of interpersonal communication and stress management.

Recognizing And Understanding Emotions

"Half our mistakes in life arise from feeling where we ought to think and thinking where we ought to feel."

—John Collins

Emotions are an integral and valid ingredient of being human. Sadly, many people have never learned much about their feelings. This may be true for many reasons, such as alcoholism, abuse, or neglect in the family, or other dysfunctional childhood experiences. People who learn to deny or ignore their emotions, who do not learn to honor and understand feelings, are emotionally handicapped. To ignore or squelch feelings is unhealthy. To acknowledge them is to open pathways leading to a better understanding of our reactions to life experiences.

Many people, both in EMS and in the general population, are out of touch with their emotions. Health care workers in particular need the extra awareness that emotions generate, because other people depend on us for emotional support and stability. Although those may seem to be unfair expectations, prehospital workers with excellent emotional understanding and control tend to be especially capable of providing all-around patient care. Those who make the effort to learn about emotions will find their patient care dramatically enriched.

On the other hand, a lack of understanding about emotions can result in regrettable reactions, including abusive behavior. Unfortunately, despite the good intentions of the majority of prehospital workers, some people in EMS have admitted to covertly or overtly abusing their patients. One story tells of two exhausted, angry EMTs who were called to transport "just another drunk" in the middle of the night. They decided to give the man a ride he wouldn't forget, so he would never call them again. He couldn't; he died of the heart attack he had been having instead.

Because the streets can be so volatile, several emotions warrant specific attention: fear, anxiety, frustration, anger, sadness, grief, and guilt. Of course, there are positive emotions as well—joy, pride, contentment—and EMS gives us these occasionally. But because of the nature of crisis, we more frequently feel the negative emotions. By studying their nature, we can understand the responses they evoke, both in the people we meet and in ourselves.

Fear

Fear involves a feeling of distress, and is typically considered a negative emotion. People generally do not like feeling afraid. Fear can be aroused by threats (real or imagined) of impending danger, evil, or pain.[1] Sometimes fear is sensed more as if trouble is "brewing." Impending trouble can serve as a red flag, for those who are sensitive to it, leading to an extra degree of caution. At such times, fear may be considered an ally in the quest for safety on the streets. Although we cannot jump at every shadow, we cannot throw caution to the wind, either.

Fear-based trouble might arise when others sense it in you. For example, animals recognize fear in people quite easily, and this awareness can lead to an attack. Similarly, certain patients who can sense fear in their EMS providers are more likely to act belligerently because they know they have the upper hand.

---

[1] *The Random House Dictionary* (unabridged), 2nd ed. (New York: Random House, 1987).

When you feel afraid (as everyone does, occasionally), determine as quickly as possible the source of that fear, then deal with it appropriately. If an angry patient is waving a gun at you, the appropriate action is to get out, take cover, and summon law enforcement officials. If a more subtle pit of fear lodges in your stomach because you are phobic about snakes and your patient is the victim of a rattlesnake bite, calm yourself with the mature reassurance that the snake is long gone. This is an imagined threat, and you should not allow your fear to break your attention.

Anxiety

Anxiety is a complex emotion. It combines the emotion of fear with one or more of the fundamental emotions: anger, distress, shame or shyness, guilt, or even interest and excitement.[2] Anxiety is common in rescuers new to the field, who have not had the chance to discover how capable they really are, or whether the information they have learned will actually do any good. They are anxious about the unknown, about "losing" a patient, about personal safety. They are anxious to please their preceptors, and they are anxious to appear professional to their patients. Some EMS providers never stop being anxious. Those who remain in EMS usually learn to handle everyday anxieties.

It is essential to recognize anxiety in yourself because your level of personal control contributes to the way you conduct yourself on the scene. Anxiety interferes with self-control. Some people in EMS are handicapped by chronic anxiety, and unfortunately, they cannot recognize it. For example, one paramedic with excellent intellectual medical knowledge never dealt effectively with his anxiety. Predictably, his voice got louder and louder, until he yelled at everyone on the scene! He always looked panicked. He seldom inspired much confidence in his patients, among bystanders, or in coworkers.

Once you recognize anxiety, you can take steps to control it. One EMT handled the anxiety of those first few emergency calls by closing her eyes en route, taking slow, deep breaths, and repeating the priorities of EMS in her mind: "ABCs . . . ABCs . . . ABCs." This focus on the early on-scene activities helped settle anxieties about whether she would be able to handle the job.

---

[2] Carroll E. Izard, *Human Emotions* (New York: Plenum Press, 1977), p.93.

Frustration

Frustration is common in EMS. It happens when, despite your best efforts, you are thwarted or otherwise disappointed by something. It's frustrating to encounter hostile patients, to miss a crucial IV, to find out you've been driving in the wrong direction for the last five minutes. Frustration pops up when workers are expected to handle calls in unsafe vehicles, when on-scene "helpers" don't cooperate, and when a patient who "should have lived" failed to respond to your treatment. It's frustrating to wait all day for a call, only to have the tones go off just as you sit down to dinner. Simply feeling frustrated can be frustrating!

Challenge yourself to learn something from each frustrating experience.

Frustration happens largely because people allow the things that are going badly to overwhelm them. There is no need to be consumed by it. First, be aware of the potential for frustration to arise, and then name it for what it is. Unacknowledged frustration interrupts your sense of perspective. You can minimize frustration by learning to view obstacles to your efforts objectively—even positively.

Challenge yourself to learn something from each frustrating experience. It does no good to let frustration eat at you. Frustration that is allowed to fester becomes explosive, and increases the tendency toward aggression. Carrying such a debilitating emotion from one call to the next is unfair to the new set of people you are meeting. They don't deserve to be the brunt of your response to a previous, frustrating experience.

Anger

Anger is closely related to frustration. Everyone gets angry at times. It's where and when you vent that anger that matters. Anger is stimulated by the feeling that you cannot do something you'd intensely like to do.[3] It is easy to get angry when a patient spits on the ambulance floor (or in your face), or when the same patient calls at 4:00 a.m. every day for a week. It is easy to get angry when people hurl every expletive at you, when they are self-destructive, when situations were poorly handled, and when you don't perform up to your own (realistic or unrealistic) expectations.

---

[3] Izard, *Human Emotions*, 329.

Anger can also be activated by "prolonged, unrelieved distress."[4] The hours in EMS can be brutal and the situations unrelenting. Even the way some EMS workers are notified that a call has come in can generate anger: "Sudden visual perception of light, if unexpected and particularly when changing a stable situation (sleep, meditation, concentration), may also serve as a stimulus of an anger response."[5] This happens all too often when the alarm tones go off and lights go on during the night!

Some people control their anger appropriately; others do not. Control of anger reaches its limits in everyone, once in awhile. But a professional *never* responds to anger by acting on it at a prehospital scene. Learning to recognize and defuse the stressors that generate anger (and other emotions described here) is a major reason for knowing about and practicing good stress management.[6] In most cases, when confrontations between patient and rescuer result in physical blows (and sometimes injury), cooler heads could have averted the fight. A person who has a tendency to act on anger would be smarter to learn ways to avoid such behavior. This will lead to much-enhanced prehospital effectiveness.

Sadness

The things people in EMS see affect them, often deeply. Feeling sad is normal, even healthy, since it's an honest response to many of the situations we witness. These feelings of sadness should not be squelched in order to appear to be unaffected. If you feel sad, express it. You may need to wait until after the medical demands of a call are through, but at some point give yourself the outlet.

Accept the fact that crying is part of sadness. Crying is nature's relief valve against sadness. Males and females both need to cry sometimes. One paramedic with nine years of experience claimed that he no longer "ever felt anything," good or bad, about the things he saw on the job. Not only was this person deceiving himself, but it is likely that he will pay a big price later, when a seemingly mountainous emotional backlog erupts, releasing the stress of internalizing his feelings for so long.

Sometimes it is not possible to pinpoint feelings of sadness. Sadness does not always arise in direct association with the offending experience.

---

[4] Izard, *Human Emotions*, 330.
[5] Frederick R. Stearns, *Anger: Psychology, Physiology, Pathology* (Springfield, Ill.: Charles C Thomas, 1972), 11.
[6] See Chapter 12: Stress and Wellness

Sometimes it is a nonspecific accumulation of little things that finally overflow your emotional reservoir. If you learn to recognize your own emotions, you can address them when the problem is small rather than letting them become an emotional obstacle that requires lots of work later.

Grief

There are other things besides death to grieve. Grief comes with all sorts of losses—minor, major, real, imagined, temporary, or permanent. Grief may be as fleeting as a twinge of regret for misplacing your favorite pocket knife. Or it can grip so tightly that there's room for little else and normal functioning ceases.

When we have tried to help others and failed, we suffer a loss. How anyone in EMS mourns such losses depends on his or her personal background. But whether your style is stoical or overtly emotional, and whether you consciously recognize it or not, you still grieve. The underlying distress that accompanies grief can combine with other emotions, such as fear, anger, guilt, or shame, to alter the exact nature of the grief.[7] If a patient dies because you give inappropriate medication, your grief will be compounded by a sense of guilt. If your patient dies and you feel you weren't working as well as you could have on that call, your grief may contain a component of shame.

A major source of grief for some is the loss of high ideals. For example, many people get involved in emergency medical services because they are altruistic. They want to help people and, by doing so, help make the world a better place. However, they have unrealistic perceptions of medical science. They eventually discover that mistakes do happen, that people sometimes die as a result, and that no one, including EMTs, paramedics, nurses, or doctors, is perfect. Yet, they grieve the loss of their ideals, and some are discouraged enough to quit. Others, who are able to, adjust, and continue in EMS with a new outlook.

For EMS providers who live in small towns or rural areas, the potential for losing a friend or acquaintance is very high. Grief is usually more intense when you knew the person involved. Since you're the one "into all this emergency stuff," others often expect you to have a stiff upper lip. This is a dangerous assumption on their part, and you should be careful not to fall into this trap. Acknowledge your grief and let it run its course. It is unfair and unhealthy to squelch your feelings in order to meet the

---

[7] Izard, *Human Emotions*, 308.

inappropriate expectations of others. Sharing the grief is healthier for everyone. Grief and mourning are discussed in more detail in Chapter 5.

Guilt

Guilt can eat you alive. It is the result of a feeling of responsibility or remorse over being part of a wrongful or even illegal act. These situations may be real or imagined. Of course, everyone in medicine dreads causing harm to patients. And because perfectionist tendencies are common in rescuer personalities, it isn't unusual for an inappropriate sense of responsibility to occur. Thus, because it is always possible to find something "wrong" with the way a scene was handled, it is easy to become guilt-ridden. One healthy answer to this tendency is to place responsibility for misfortune on the people experiencing it. Our role is to help, to the best extent possible, but not to assume responsibility for others' mishaps. Recognize that *no* scene runs perfectly. Errors and accidents happen. And health care workers are people, not gods. "If only I had . . ." should initiate a learning process, not a breeding ground for guilt.

If you have participated in a situation that clearly involved committing an offense, such as hitting and killing a pedestrian, or injecting the wrong drug by accident, an emotional burden may be generated that requires professional psychological intervention. Get help when you need it. Guilt can be disabling because it can haunt you long after the events that generated it are past. Don't let it get the emotional upper hand.

Emotional Carryover

No matter which emotions arise over the course of a day, be sure to "wipe the slate clean" between calls. If the last call made you feel angry, is it fair to carry that anger to the next scene? Emotions are contagious, and your anger could ignite the next scene when a calmer approach would have avoided a confrontation. If you are feeling sad about the last situation, will you be dangerously preoccupied by that emotion at the next address? If you let emotions simmer inappropriately, it is relevant to safety and effectiveness to change that tendency. There are techniques, to be discussed, for doing this. Despite our human imperfections, the more we strive to deal with emotions professionally, the better our field capabilities will become.

Acknowledging Your Past

Developing personal awareness is a continual process throughout life. It demands adjustments along the way, as we integrate new views of the world. Some people are remarkably lacking in self-awareness; for example, there are many people who do not even know how to find their own pulse!

The bridles of carriage horses are fitted with blinders next to their eyes, so that they can only view the road straight ahead. To learn self-awareness is to experience what these horses must feel when their blinders are removed. The world opens up, offering new perspectives and choices. Self-awareness cannot be bought and does not happen by magic. It requires personal effort and commitment—and the rewards are worth it.

Self-awareness cannot be bought and does not happen by magic. It requires personal effort and commitment—and the rewards are worth it.

Self-awareness is especially vital to EMS providers, because if you aren't in touch with the person you know best—yourself—how can you truly understand the strangers you'll regularly deal with? To recognize personal strengths is to polish them. To know weaknesses is to have the chance to eliminate or compensate for them.

Self-awareness lets you develop an effective interpersonal style and adjust aspects of that style that are inefficient or ineffective. For example, if you know you have a difficult time with certain personality types, you may choose to find alternative approaches rather than continue to use those that have failed in the past. You may let your partner try where you have failed, instead of stubbornly forcing the issue. If you know you are barely functional in the early-morning hours, you will be extra cautious as you approach scenes at that time of day.

Much of "knowing yourself" implies the need for day-to-day self-awareness. But just as Rome was not built in a day, neither were our personalities or behavioral patterns. There is much about us that comes along through the years—good and bad—that we carry into our work. The more you can learn about why you are the way you are, the better. Some people spend years in therapy or counseling trying to unravel their past. Although this has been or may be helpful to many, it is not what this section is saying we must all do. But to gain personal awareness through some introspection is important.

It is also worthy to note that one does not attain "self-awareness" in one fell swoop. It is a lifelong process of checking in with yourself now and then. Everyone is better able to see different things in themselves as they age. A person at twenty may feel confidently self-aware, and yet may look back from the vantage point of twenty-eight, or thirty-five, or fifty, and realize how much more there was to learn and acknowledge! There may be differing degrees of openness to self-scrutiny during different stages of life. Major life events, such as loss of a spouse or parent, or the threat of illness or death, often stimulate personal reflection because they create a sense of vulnerability. This is good, in a way, but don't wait for such moments to engage the sort of reflection that leads to self-awareness. Touch on it every day, a little, and the chance to be in tune with yourself will become a healthy habit (see chapters 12 and 15).

Hopefully, somewhere along the line, you received a foundation of qualities such as honesty, kindness, compassion, gentleness. Certainly, a sense of altruism (the unselfish desire to help others) is common among prehospital workers. Why else would we be willing to work ungodly hours, providing highly technical help to strangers, often putting ourselves in harm's way, for relatively little (or no) cash compensation—not to mention spending many hours a year in meetings and training?

Among the traits common to rescuer-oriented personalities is a desire to have control and authority. People join the EMS ranks for various reasons, such as a feeling of social responsibility. For many, care giving is second-nature because they have done it all their lives. A firstborn child from a large family inevitably has developed large degrees of responsibility at a young age. A child from the tough section of town will have to learn to manage his environment so that it will not "manage" him or his family. Adult children of alcoholics are well accustomed to taking care of their siblings or inebriated parents in the absence of a responsible adult. During childhood, crisis was a normal circumstance for many; they are accustomed to it and even thrive on it. Whatever the roots of rescuer traits, the ability to acknowledge them (and how they aided survival) will bring the chance to understand the sharper edges that can cause problems. Educating yourself about your past (and what it "did" to you) can help you understand your reactions to what you see in EMS. Why are you compassionate with kids, but utterly contemptuous of people who are intoxicated? Why does violence so deeply anger you? Why do you keep talking back to belligerent people? Why do you have a short fuse with people who are abusing themselves with drugs or unhealthy relationships? Certainly, such current events as the weather, the time of day, and your degree of exhaustion and hunger play a role in how anyone interacts. But maybe certain "emotional baggage" also helps shape your responses to prehospital events. The more you know about these things, the better and more professional your approach to the streets can be.

GENERAL ATTRIBUTES OF ADULT CHILDREN OF ALCOHOLICS

1. Adult children of alcoholics guess at what normal behavior is.

2. Adult children of alcoholics have difficulty following a project through from beginning to end.

3. Adult children of alcoholics lie when it would be just as easy to tell the truth.

4. Adult children of alcoholics judge themselves without mercy.

5. Adult children of alcoholics have difficulty having fun.

6. Adult children of alcoholics take themselves very seriously.

7. Adult children of alcoholics have difficulty with intimate relationships.

8. Adult children of alcoholics overreact to changes over which they have no control.

9. Adult children of alcoholics constantly seek approval and affirmation.

10. Adult children of alcoholics usually feel that they are different from other people.

11. Adult children of alcoholics are super responsible or super irresponsible.

12. Adult children of alcoholics are extremely loyal, even in the face of evidence that the loyalty is undeserved.

13. Adult children of alcoholics are impulsive.

[From *Adult Children of Alcoholics*, by Janet G. Woititz (Deerfield Beach, Fla.: Health Communications, Inc., 1983). Reprinted with permission.]

Figure 2.2

Adult Children of Alcoholics

It is estimated that there are more than twenty-five million adult children of alcoholics (ACOAs or ACAs). This makes it inevitable that there will be many EMTs and paramedics in that group. In fact, there may be a disproportionate number of ACOAs among the EMS population because ACOAs and people in EMS share many attributes. Is there a relationship? Possibly. For example, one source describes the common ACOA approach toward life as "don't talk, don't trust, don't feel."[8] How many paramedics and EMTs choose this approach in the wake of a difficult call? Such attributes can contribute to a self-destructive (or at least overburdened) attitude toward EMS, which is already challenging enough as it is!

Another ACOA researcher and counselor has witnessed certain generalizations in numerous groups of ACOAs that could affect delivery of prehospital care and how we react to our work. Although not every prehospital worker is an ACOA, you

---

[8] Claudia Black, *"It Will Never Happen To Me!"* (New York: Ballantine Books, 1981), 24.

likely work with someone who is. Therefore, the behavior of an ACOA can affect you, too. These generalizations are outlined in Fig. 2.2.

It is exhilarating to see an adult child of an alcoholic lay aside the years of denial and unload the emotional baggage of the past. Similarly, people with other secrets from the past—everything from learning disabilities, illiteracy, a history of child abuse, or other problems that may have interfered with an emotionally and mentally healthy adulthood—can benefit from learning why those events have affected them.

Values

Everyone has a value system. What is yours? There are generalizations about value systems that correspond with age, in that each generation develops general rules of conduct based on the existing social environment during the values-forming stage of childhood and adolescence. A classic example is that of Depression-era people, who tend to be highly conscious about their financial, logistical, and physical security. There are also value systems that develop as a result of religious education, socioeconomic background, role-model influences, and parental guidance.

Being able to assess your values clearly will enable you to maintain your professional conduct while interacting with people who may not agree with you. If you value honesty, and you're dealing with someone who is obviously lying, consciously recognizing this incongruency will help you bypass that sticking point if it's not relevant to the medical issue at hand. Someone without self-knowledge might instead act out on a sense of righteousness and be unnecessarily sidetracked.

How to Develop Self-Awareness

"Those people who are uncomfortable in themselves are disagreeable to others."

—William Hazlitt

Some people never engage in self-reflection, preferring instead to adhere to the thought that "I am who I am, that's the best I can do." Others, once they reflect upon their past, identify things they'd like to change. Self-imposed behavior modification is a challenging and life-changing effort. You *can* learn to have feelings. You *can* learn to touch other people compassionately, and to trust them. You *can* learn to control your stronger emotions (such as anger and sadness) until you reach an appropriate place to vent them. It requires awareness of your personality and behavioral traits, and then the willingness to modify them.

There are many ways to become more self-aware. But the hallmark quality required is patience. As one writer said: "Develop the quality of patience. Not patience as a waiting for something to happen, for that is impatience. Real patience is an openness, a willingness to be present for whatever is. It is not a goal-oriented expectation that only creates more tension, grief, and restlessness."[9] Even if the only quality you can refine is your patience, the gains can be tremendous. Quiet, steady perseverance results in the attainment of goals, much as taking one step after another brings you to the top of a mountain. Personal growth is an ongoing, lifelong process, and those with disastrous (or even suboptimal) childhoods can grow past them to rewarding and happy adulthood, *if* they so choose.

Other pertinent concepts for self-awareness development are objectivity (particularly about prejudices), honing your senses, recognizing and developing intuition, and caring about people without letting your concern drain your emotional reserves. Let's consider these things one at a time.

Objectivity

Certain professions demand a high degree of objectivity. Journalism is one example; good journalists strive not to interject personal feelings into their reporting. Emergency medical workers, too, must be able to view their work objectively in order to deliver fair and equal treatment to all patients. Although human nature prevents constant and complete objectivity, we need to strive for as much of it as we can muster.[10]

Objectivity is important because it helps a person bypass naturally subjective inclinations. It is only natural to feel some disgust when encountering something grotesque. A skid row alcoholic who hasn't showered in weeks (maybe months) is not pleasant. You might feel subjectively that the "bum" obviously doesn't care about himself, so why should you? Everyone finds at least one bodily fluid disagreeable, even disgusting. For some, it is blood (such people do not last long without developing a good coping mechanism!); for others, feces; for still others, vomit. But handling these and other unusual substances is part of the job. Having some objectivity improves the chances of a properly thorough physical exam.

---

[9] Stephen Levine, *Who Dies? An Investigation of Conscious Living and Conscious Dying* (New York: Anchor Press/Doubleday, 1982), 210.

[10] Kate Dernocoeur, "Prejudice: Spoiling The Melting Pot Brew," in *The Best of JEMS: Timeless Essays from the First 15 Years* (St. Louis: Mosby Lifeline, 1996).

Objectivity helps you remember that your views are not shared by everyone. Someone with classic heart attack symptoms isn't necessarily "crazy" for refusing to go to the hospital. People have reasons they consider perfectly valid for making such decisions. We need to respect those opinions.

To improve objectivity, learn to observe your actions from a detached point of view. Learn to witness what you say and do in order to assess how your interpersonal style influences the situation. Are you abrasive? Do you let personal feelings interfere with professional duty? When a patient reacts negatively to your style and gets abusive, you can usually avoid a confrontation by remaining objective and employing sound communication techniques to defuse the situation.

Figure 2.3

One technique to assess interpersonal interactions is to envision the scene from a "detached observer" point of view, as if you are looking down from above. This generates a more global feel for the situation.

Self-observation is possible by employing a mental trick that lets you observe yourself from an independent point of view (Fig. 2.3). It's as if you develop, in your mind's eye, a detached observer that can perch outside your mind (perhaps hovering above you) and watch what is happening from that separate angle. With such a clear and wide-angle view, your observer can "see" and "hear" beyond what you would normally notice. You can thereby perceive how others are reacting to what you say and do.

This simple self-assessment strategy works well in any situation, in EMS and in daily life. The different perspective and detached nature of it allows for an honest degree of objectivity. If you notice you feel angry or frustrated on a scene, look at the situation with your "detached observer." You might realize, for example, that because you had your head down while trying to get the IV, no one heard you ask for the stretcher. Instead of harboring anger at the first responders, you've encountered a chance to improve your streetsense for next time!

Five-Sensing

Most people depend almost entirely on their eyesight to perceive the world. They have far less ability to use the sense of hearing. The senses of touch, smell, and taste are nearly forgotten. Such people are visual prisoners.

It can be fun to regain strength in all the senses. All you need is curiosity and the willingness to try. Five-sensing is as much a game as it is a builder of good self-awareness. It is done by consciously experiencing the moment with each of your senses, one at a time. Sometimes it helps to close your eyes to access the other senses because of the dominance of vision. Tell yourself in words the things you are sensing: "I see a park, blue sky, trees, birds, an ant; I hear cars, laughter, wind in the tree above me, a bird; I taste toothpaste; I feel the breeze (it's too warm) and the stickiness of the ambulance seat; I smell freshly mowed grass and . . . what is that? . . . a barbecue! Yum!"

During a five-sensing exercise, your goal is to reach increasingly subtle levels of awareness. Measure in your mind's eye such things as distance, depth, volume, and relative size. It's easy to hear an unmufflered motorcycle going by—but can you also discern the fly buzzing against the back window? It's easy to feel hot on a still, midsummer day, but can you also feel the faint stir of air caused by that passing motorcycle? Maybe there are two radios being played nearby. How near is each one? Did you hear an even more subtle sound—that of a cricket near the apple tree (which has a wonderful scent)? Just how far away *is* that cricket? Would you guess ten feet, or twenty? It is fun to acknowledge consciously the various layers of (pleasant!) stimuli around us. Train your senses, and they will put you in tune with the world around you in a very satisfying way.

Trained senses will also be good allies on the streets as you respond to emergency calls. One paramedic student learned an excellent lesson in five-sensing when he was climbing the third flight of stairs to an apartment with the paramedic attendant. "What kind of problem are we about to encounter?" the paramedic asked as they approached the top. The student didn't know, so the paramedic encouraged him to listen. He wasn't able to distinguish the sounds on the scene well enough to discern what the paramedic had heard: the sound of a bag-mask device being used.

"We have at least a respiratory arrest going on in there," said the paramedic, as they reached the top of the stairs. Five-sensing gave them an extra moment to gear up for a critical call. They were able to react more calmly and quickly because of it.

Intuition

You arrive at a highway accident. Vehicular damage is relatively minor. The driver of the pickup is sitting on the grass by the roadside and claims to feel shaken up, but that's all. Your partner tells you the truck's steering wheel and windshield are intact. The patient's mentation is normal, and unaffected, he claims, by drugs or alcohol. But something tells you . . . a little voice inside your brain is shouting a warning only you can hear. . . .

The patient has a small, suturable laceration on his arm and very vague, diffuse abdominal discomfort. You load him into the ambulance. On the way to the hospital, he still claims to feel fine and doesn't look bad. His vital signs are within normal limits and have remained unchanged in the last twenty minutes. Nonetheless, you start a volume-replacement IV. You can't prove it yet, but you know something is wrong with this patient. Proof soon comes when his blood pressure suddenly drops and his pulse quickens because of a bleeding spleen.

Gut feelings, some call it. "Little voices," "my angel who watches out for me,"—no matter how you express it, intuition is another form of personal awareness. Like a resting violin in an orchestra resonates with the sounds generated by the rest of the instruments, intuition reso-

nates within you to reflect your surroundings. People who ignore intuition are often the ones who later say, "I knew better. I just didn't pay
any attention to my better judgment." They call it by a different name,
but they are nonetheless referring to their intuition.

Intuition is an invaluable tool. It can help shield you (and your
patients) from many hazards. When you respond to a shooting, you
tend to arrive with an extra measure of caution. But where is that caution on the "man down," or "unknown," or other nondescript calls—
especially at 4:00 a.m.? Sometimes you can sense that a scene is rotten
even as you arrive; other scenes "feel" safe. What is it that generates
these feelings? It's largely a matter of intuition.

Developing awareness about intuition essentially requires a mind
that is open to the concept. Just wanting it does not mean it will happen right away; intuition depends on experience. But most people who
have a few hundred emergency calls to their credit agree that there have
been times that their intuition guided them well—or would have, had
they heeded it.

Use intuition as a "sixth sense" and it will help take care of you. But
there is one precaution: Don't use it to the exclusion of the rest of your
self-awareness skills! It is just an adjunct to help you do a good job.

Rational—Not Detached—Concern

Some people get into EMS and do not realize the huge amount of
personal energy they put into it until they are "suddenly" emotionally
exhausted. They have depleted their psyches of an essential tool: the
ability to care. As described by Renee C. Fox, detached concern is when
"the empathetic [practitioner] is sufficiently detached or objective in his
attitude toward the patient to exercise sound medical judgment and keep
his equanimity, yet he also has enough concern for the patient to give
him sensitive, understanding care."[11] Detached concern is not a matter
of not caring. It is a matter of being aware that you should not try to
carry the weight of the world's troubles on your shoulders.

It's difficult to see as much tragedy as we do in EMS without armoring
ourselves with a veneer. Some distancing is natural, but according to
cancer surgeon Bernie Siegel, most people go too far. In the name of
"detached concern," patients are too often left to grapple with major

---

[11] Harold I. Lief and Renee C. Fox, "Training for 'Detached Concern' in Medical Students," in *The
Psychological Basis of Medical Practice*, ed. Harold I. Lief, Victor Lief, and Nina Lief (New York:
Harper & Row, Publishers, Inc., 1963).

life events alone. Helpers cannot truly give because their veneer is too thick. "Too often," says Siegel, "the pressure squeezes out our native compassion. The so-called detached concern we're taught is an absurdity. Instead, we need to be taught a rational concern, which allows the expression of feelings without impairing the ability to make decisions."[12] The goal should be to care about your patients, and at the same time, preserve your personal energy. Balancing your helping capabilities with the ability to give your patients the support they need is a sign of a professional approach toward patient care. This is important, because when people in the human services stop caring, everyone suffers—especially patients who find themselves at the hands of gruff and abrupt helpers during moments when they most need true compassion.

Self-Defense Training

"Don't trouble trouble 'til trouble troubles you."

—Chinese fortune cookie

Part of knowing yourself is knowing how to stay out of trouble. Picking fights is obviously inappropriate, even at times when you feel tempted to settle things with an obnoxious person. (Sadly, such things do happen.) As a professional, you must be aware of your reactions to the prehospital environment. When events threaten the loss of self-control, acknowledge the feelings—but *never* defuse them by abusing patients. No matter how bad it gets (and it can get pretty bad), there is no excuse for maltreating the people we are there to help.

On the other hand, some patients (and their friends) view prehospital personnel as a reasonable focus for their aggression. This unfortunate fact is not confined to the "mean streets" of urban EMS. No matter where we practice, or whether we are paid or volunteer, we cope with people in every degree and type of emotional upheaval. Physical intervention with patients occasionally becomes necessary. It helps to know a few "moves," a few holds, and a few ways to get free of holds. Self-defense skills occasionally come in handy!

Knowing how much physical force is enough (but not too much) is a subtle talent. Certain self-defense techniques are especially applicable to EMS because they are subtle as well as effective. Given the choice

---

[12] Bernie S. Siegel, *Love, Medicine and Miracles* (New York: Harper & Row, Publishers, Inc., 1986), 14.

between a dramatic-looking move or one that does the job subtly, the latter better serves the concepts of communication, safety, and control. For example, pinching the meaty tissue of the hand at the base of the thumb is painful enough to gain the cooperation of patients being "guided" to the ambulance, and is invisible compared to twisting a patient's arm behind his back.

One example of subtle self-defense can be used when approaching a "man down" who is lying on his stomach, trying to sleep. Some people might mindlessly bend over the patient for the "shake and shout" routine. Yet it is not possible to discern whether this person is holding a weapon ready to ward off attackers, not knowing you are there to check on his well-being. By keeping your weight over your feet, with one slightly ahead of the other, you are prepared to push back quickly if necessary. At the same time, poise your knee near (not on) the patient's neck. Have your partner keep a hand or toe over the exposed arm. It all looks casual to bystanders, but it lends control over patients who come up too quickly and aggressively.

The best defense is one that prevents physical conflict, especially where others with poorer communication skills, less self-awareness, and no self-control would have come to blows. To have a personal goal of defusing potential physical conflict is the mark of a true EMS professional. And it certainly beats nursing a boxer's fracture and facing an assault charge brought by a disgruntled patient (see also page 239).

Whether or not to invest time learning specific self-defense techniques is up to the individual. A black belt in a martial art is not essential to streetsense. Many people start a martial art, such as judo, karate, or aikido to enhance their prehospital safety, and end up sticking with it because it is fun, and good exercise. The by-products of martial arts training are the mental discipline, sense of patience, and self-awareness that can help a person avoid having to use the self-defense techniques.

Until that mental maturity comes, though, there is a pitfall in focusing too much concentration on learning self-defense. The technical imperative—the desire to try out those skills—might rise up. It requires presence of mind and self control to avoid doing something just for the sake of trying it. Curiosity about your ability is natural. But let superior interpersonal communications be your first line of defense. Let your mind work to find the right words to control a situation rather than letting your body find the right punch. Physical intervention should always be a last resort.

Summary

Self-knowledge is a big part of self-control. If you know you cannot deal with the way a situation is unfolding, know enough to adjust your response or hand the call over to your partner, if you can.

Acknowledging emotions is particularly important in retaining a positive mental outlook, especially in the tumultuous world of EMS. Although it is sometimes necessary to delay your reactions until after the call is done, don't try to put a lid on your emotions forever. When the time is right, react! Cry, laugh, do whatever you need to (within reason!) and disengage the charge of pent-up emotions. It's important.

Personal growth and self-understanding constitute a dynamic, never-ending process. It's never possible to know yourself completely. And that's part of the beauty of staying in touch with yourself. By making the effort to know who you are and why you respond to things the way you do, the effectiveness of your prehospital care will continually expand. The best EMTs and paramedics either bring personal understanding to the business, or they develop it.

Understanding Others

> Whenever two people meet, there are really six people present. There is each as he sees himself, each as the other sees him, and each as he really is."
>
> —William James

Chapter Overview

Understanding other people is the essence of EMS because medical care is a people business. When seeking to understand people, the EMT and paramedic must avoid the hazard of stereotyping. Although some generalizations can help you develop an understanding of others, view each patient as an individual.

Streetwise EMTs and paramedics have the talent to "read" people, and are good at anticipating various emotions and behaviors. They understand the need to decide on an approach, and they know the approaches to try for the best effect. They know the value of flexibility and can take on certain roles in order to interact efficiently with other people. This includes working with coworkers and other emergency service providers as well as patients and bystanders.

Having respect for others and allowing for their dignity is important. Studying and trying to empathize with the emotions, motivations, and concerns of all the people you meet in prehospital care is satisfying—even energizing. It's a challenge and can make your work in EMS much more meaningful.

Once there was a new paramedic who was impressively intelligent. He could recite every detail about cardiology, pharmacology, physiology, and anything else related to emergency medicine. He wanted to be a doctor. Everyone knew the man would have no problems with the intellectual demands of medical school. What a brain! But when asked to translate book knowledge to human beings, this paramedic failed. To him, every PVC meant lidocaine; "dyspnea" meant "oxygen." Yet some patients with PVCs were unaffected by them, and some people were dyspneic due to hyperventilation. He didn't recognize that these people didn't match the criteria for pharmacological intervention. The paramedic may have had a fine brain, but he had no mind for human beings. He was a "people mechanic"; if a part wears out, fix or replace it. He just didn't understand people.

Such a gap in an EMT or a paramedic's abilities can interfere with street work, because the obvious foundation of prehospital emergency medical care is people. It is essential to understand them.

First, prehospital workers from even the quietest systems will see more emergency situations than the average citizen. We "do" emergency medicine like most people do housework; with experience, much of it becomes as mechanical as scrubbing bathrooms and vacuuming. The psychosocial aspects of EMS become increasingly fascinating because people are what give us variety. To encounter total strangers and be able to understand them well enough within seconds to handle the crisis, large or small, is no minor skill!

It requires practice to develop the flexibility to be able to accommodate the different needs of each individual. It is true that many prehospital workers have gotten by for years without believing that human interfacing is important. On the other hand, old fashioned "ambulance drivers" (who had no tools except reassurance and a fast vehicle) can relate how well patients would respond when someone attended to their emotional needs. These old-timers had a knack for knowing what to say and how to say it, that stemmed from years of having little more for the patient than an understanding heart.

With the influx of modern technology, some of these old-fashioned techniques have lost importance. Reassurance and interpersonal understanding are potent tools in our care-giving toolbox. One thing is certain: It is unreasonable to expect people who need help to accommodate *your* approach. Let's explore some ways to understand other people.

"Reading" People

To learn to read people, make it a habit to observe them consciously. Prehospital workers are stimulus vacuums, constantly taking in information. We are part detective, sniffing out the pertinent details of a scene and its people. "Reading" people is a fun part of the job and is a major streetsense skill.

Your purpose in learning to read people is to develop the ability to predict what individuals are likely to do, how they are likely to react to the circumstances at hand, and how they will respond to you. This requires curiosity! Make it a personal challenge to discover the best ways to blend with the other personalities on each scene. This will allow the interactions to go smoothly and effectively.

The patient, of course, is of primary concern. But don't let tunnel vision interrupt your global view of the scene. There are other people, such as bystanders, to assess and interview about the events surrounding the call. Scenes with multiple patients will make information gathering and coordination even tougher. Your detective work will be all the more difficult—and important.

There are various reasons to assess other people: safety, effective communication, and control. First decide whether they pose any danger to you or your coworkers. Decide this by studying nonverbal clues, both obvious and subtle (Fig. 3.1) Look at the:

- **Body.** How do they greet your approach? Watch for this even while driving up. Is the person you are observing apparently glad for your arrival, or not? Body posture, stance, and activity can indicate anxiety, withdrawal, panic, calm, assurance, belligerence, bravado, and more.

- **Face.** Observe whether the person's facial expression contradicts the physical message. Someone trying to make it look like a broken leg is nothing might unintentionally show pain, anxiety, or some other emotion on his face. Seeing this gives you an interactive toehold that, when used well, will provide an entry to that person's mind. You can assist his efforts to save face in front of his friends, yet pleasantly surprise him with your insight by quietly acknowledging the underlying emotions. If the patient seems frightened, you can quietly say something like: "You're probably not used to all this excitement, huh? It may seem a little frightening to see your leg bent like that, but we'll be as gentle as possible." Mutually recognizing true emotions provides the chance to deal with them together. You have gained an ally who wants to let you do your job well, rather than an adversary who wants to "stay tough."

- **Eyes.** Finally, read the eyes. Eyes are packed with information about what is going on at the other end of the optic nerve, in the brain.

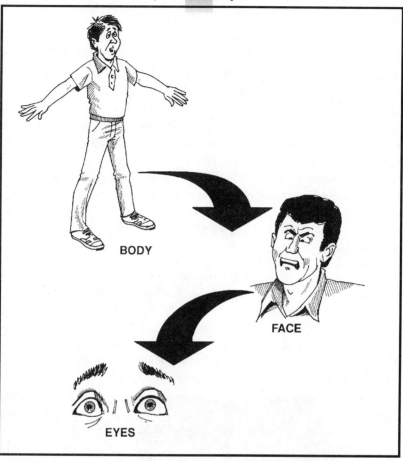

BODY

FACE

EYES

Figure 3.1

You can discern increasingly subtle (and sometimes contradictory) things about people by observing overall body language, then the facial expression, and finally, the messages sent by the eyes.

The truest emotions are held in the eyes. Notice the information, and use it to your benefit. Eyes can express relief, exhaustion, pain, anxiety, anger, happiness, maliciousness, sadness, fear, and every other emotion—even when people are trying to mask those feelings. For example, how would you react to a man who emerges from his house holding a bloody butcher knife? With that information alone, you ought to use utmost caution. But if you see that his bodily stance is nonthreatening, that his face is full of concern, and that his eyes are calm, you have gained information which can be used effectively. As it turns out, he has taken the knife from his suicidal wife (who is not badly hurt).

When you assess people, remember that the more carefully you "read" them, the more complete your knowledge of them will be. Sometimes your assessment of stance, for example, tells you that the person is aggressive—but your assessment of the facial expression and eyes tells you that the bodily pose is bravado. Handled appropriately, you can build a framework of trust and cooperation. Had you decided to act on the more obvious aggressive signals, things might have turned out very differently. Similarly, had the man with the butcher knife been misread, a benign situation could easily have been misunderstood and handled poorly.

Kinds of Minds

It does not take long, in prehospital care, to realize that there are lots of different kinds of minds out there. It takes years for people to realize, as they grow up, that other people have different values, lifestyles, and living circumstances. Many live their entire lives within a narrow social niche. They never have the chance to discover how other people live and think. If nothing else, EMS certainly provides hands-on experience with the full range of the human condition!

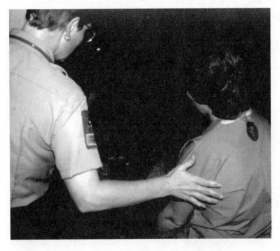

The more we tune into the minds we meet, the better we can understand the ways other people live and perceive their world (Fig. 3.2). There are all types: aggressive, helpless, provocative, beseeching, explosive, sweet, good-natured, ill-willed, cynical, helpful, defiant, angry, apologetic, "normal," "abnormal," happy, sad, judgmental, harsh, belligerent, meek. They are affected by alcohol, both illegal and prescription drugs, pain, anxiety, fear, grief, and frustration. They each have personal needs for physical health, mental stimula-

Figure 3.2

Take time, when possible, to talk with people to better understand and appreciate them as unique individuals.

tion, fun, recreation, relationships, financial support, spiritual fulfillment, and careers. The EMS provider meets all sorts of people in all kinds of circumstances. Every encounter is individual, of course, but there are some generalizations which can help assess the ways that your emergency care can be delivered efficiently and safely.

One of the most difficult attitudes to handle is denial. It is very difficult to understand (or help) someone who denies wanting, needing, or asking for EMS assistance. The conflict is even more difficult if a serious medical problem such as chest pain exists. It is not pleasant to be caught between the anguish of a concerned family and the patient's "stubbornness."

Another difficulty we face is the diversity that is inherent in cultural differences. Cultural factors have to be recognized when choosing an approach to take with others. When you encounter people of a typically polite culture, you may find a high degree of cooperation by matching that politeness. When you encounter people of a highly emotional culture, you need instead to find an approach that will control the chaos and calm the scene.

Cultural differences among patient populations add interesting "spice" to prehospital care. It has been noted that EMS systems find it difficult to recruit nonwhite EMTs and paramedics. Personnel rosters at most EMS services do not reflect the ethnic mix of the people served.[1] Learning how to interact effectively with people with different ethnic backgrounds becomes relevant to streetsense. View it as a challenge to study and appreciate the distinctions between people. By doing so, you can develop a really diverse, flexible, and more capable prehospital style.

Part Actor

Another aspect of reading others is understanding their need for you to adopt an interpersonal style to suit their situation. In addition to being part detective, the adept EMS provider is also part actor. Once you discern the best way to work with someone, you must be able to play the part. Develop a repertoire of interpersonal approaches, and the effectiveness of your interpersonal communication will blossom.

Improvisation means having the ability to take the scenario you're given, and use various communication strategies effectively. There's no precise script, but you know the general idea of the "play." Despite the

---

[1] Kate Dernocoeur, "Where Have All The Paramedics Gone?" *JEMS*, 13 (April 1988).

fact that every EMS student does scenario drills in school, real-life EMS is impossible to truly duplicate, because every situation is unique. We must be masters at reacting on the spur of the moment. The better you can rapidly interpret the world and the people in it, the better you will be able to provide the solutions each scene demands.

The capability for effective interpersonal communication is best when you maintain a flexible, interactive style. A rigid style does not work well. The same relaxed flexibility plays an important role in effective interaction with coworkers, people from other emergency agencies, radio personnel, on-scene physicians, and anyone else the situation tosses at you. That means being a different person for different people, even at the same emergency scene. Acting these roles doesn't compromise your integrity as a person or as a prehospital worker. It simply helps you get the job done effectively.

The Effects of Crisis on People

After handling a lot of calls, many EMTs and paramedics find that the focus of their enthusiasm shifts. The initial challenge (such as getting a call at all) becomes routine. The search is on for more "dramatic" calls, exciting calls, calls that bring back the thrill of achievement.

Although crisis becomes familiar to us, it cannot be overstated that it is *not* familiar to most people in the general public. Maintaining sensitivity to others, no matter their cause for complaint or its relative degree of seriousness, is essential. To the uninitiated, a finger laceration is very scary. Some people do faint at the sight of blood. When someone has a reason to call, they are asking for help. It's your job to provide that help, without prejudice for the quality of the complaint. An emergency exists in the "eyes of the beholder." What seems a crisis to you may not to someone else—such as the mechanic who can magically get your car running or the seamstress who can fix a torn jacket in no time. We are medical emergency experts. A situation that we perceive as minor is nonetheless more than those who called can handle. Something perceived as an emergency by a lay person is often, unfortunately, scoffed at (sometimes openly) by the very people who should be the most sensitive to those perceptions.

Emergency medical patients (and their friends) probably do not normally behave the way we find them. Human beings who are perfectly nice under regular circumstances can be quite changed by a crisis. No one can maintain self-control at all times, and when people encounter situations beyond their ability to cope, they call for help. By doing so, they are acknowledging the overwhelming nature of the event. Just as a child often turns to an adult for help with child-size struggles, patients sometimes cope by resorting to behavioral regression.[2] The importance of remaining tolerant, understanding, and nonjudgmental about the specific reactions people have is obvious (unless they threaten to do harm).

Everyone responds differently to a crisis, so be prepared for anything. There was once a team of paramedics who worked a cardiac arrest on a man who collapsed at the kitchen table. While they worked, his wife did the dishes at the sink behind them. It seemed bizarre at the time, but in retrospect, they realized that her mechanism for coping with crisis was to do something familiar and mechanical. Even in small communities where you are likely to know many of your patients already, you must be prepared for anything. Just because you have known Bessie Anderson all your life does not mean that you know how she will respond to medical emergencies in general, or to *this* emergency in particular.

Many people postpone their reactions to a crisis. It is not uncommon to be called to help a sick person at the airport and discover that the person is on the way home from a funeral. Grief reactions are often delayed until after the funeral, when people finally allow themselves the chance to react.

One way to help people cope with a crisis is to make them feel like they are not just a cog in the emergency process; they *are* the emergency! Different EMS systems run things differently, of course, but from the patient's perspective, an emergency situation feels much more manageable when there is one "point person" interacting with them at a time. While the use of first responders has greatly reduced response times, once the primary caregivers arrive, the transfer of care should be handled so that the patient does not feel like a ping-pong ball. When the paramedics arrive, introduce the patient, give a brief report, and step back. Let them begin to build their own rapport. Similarly, transfers of care to the transporting ambulance crew or to the emergency department should be as dignified and individualized as possible.

---

[2] Michael Weissberg, *Dangerous Secrets: Maladaptive Responses to Stress* (New York: W.W. Norton & Company, Inc., 1983), 29.

Stereotyping People

Stereotyping is an insidious trap that can cause endless problems in emergency medical care. Don't do it! Although it is tempting, perhaps, after too many uninteresting calls to a particular neighborhood, to regard everyone in that area as a bum, it is wrong (not to mention dangerous) to stereotype any person, group of people, or area of town. Train yourself to enter every scene, no matter the location, with a nonjudgmental attitude.

For example, one typically stereotyped group is children. Many people in EMS feel the least comfortable when helping children. It is not unusual to enter a scene, see your pediatric patient, and think, "Oh no!" One likely reason for this is that many EMS workers have had little experience working with children—or they have experience with children (perhaps as parents) and empathize too closely with the situation. Not only that, but situations where children are involved almost always involve highly emotional parents or care givers, which adds another dimension to the on-scene interpersonal challenge. Also, children are highly intuitive. They know when people are unsure and afraid. Children reflect their world. They don't understand that they are the very source of your discomfort! One thing is certain: No one likes to see children in a situation of injury or poor health. It is a challenge to try to understand patients such as infants and toddlers who cannot express their hurts and worries. At such times, it is especially vital to use your senses, much as veterinarians use theirs.

> The most important thing to remember is not to stereotype any person, place, or thing.

But the most important thing to remember is not to stereotype any person, place, or thing. Approach all people as individuals and you will often find them quite delightful—even during a crisis. Disciplining yourself this way will help you avoid a lot of hassles.

Emotions In Others

In addition to maintaining an awareness of your own emotions, as discussed in chapter 2, you must be aware of the emotions of others on an emergency scene. In particular, there is a lot of anger, fear, anxiety, and embarrassment among the people we meet. Unfortunately, since ours is a profession of upset and tragedy, the "happy" emotions are notably absent, except in childbirth situations where the child was wanted by the parents, or when people greet your arrival with sincere relief. By anticipating unpleasant emotions and understanding their nature and genesis, we can be more tolerant of the people expressing them.

Anger

We encounter a *lot* of anger in the streets. People have a right, in a sense, to be angry. Their lives have been disrupted and tossed into chaos, often because of someone else. For example, it can be infuriating for your vehicle to be hit by someone else who ran through a stop sign.

Some people are chronically angry. This negative approach to life leads to frequent altercations. They are, therefore, also acutely angry when we arrive to help. Sometimes that anger, originally directed at another source, is turned against us. There is a clear safety issue here, but it is nonetheless often possible to defuse the high pitch of emotions through using appropriate communication techniques.

One way to defuse anger is to acknowledge a person's right to it, and then to appeal to that person to calm down so you can help. Refuse to "take the bait" when an angry person tries to provoke a fight. As a professional, you should be above that sort of behavior.

Anxiety

Being unexpectedly tossed into a disruptive situation makes people anxious. Anxiety is an unpleasant emotion that arises when someone senses an impending danger or frustration that is vaguely defined. It happens when personal security is threatened. Obviously, anxiety is therefore one of the most common emotional undercurrents found in emergency patients. It may not be blatant when combined with other responses, such as fear, anger, frustration, and grief, but it's usually present to some degree. People are anxious about dying, losing control, "the unknown," or getting stuck with a needle. They are anxious about when (or whether) they might be coming home again, or whether the dog will be fed while they are gone.

Relatives and bystanders are often just as anxious. In fact, even if they don't know the patient, witnesses of a medical emergency are reminded of human frailty and vulnerability, which is enough to arouse at least a little anxiety in most people.

Anxiety may manifest in a variety of ways. Some people become belligerent, and attack the problem. Others withdraw and try to hide, at least psychologically. Others try to deny that anything is bothering them. This is as true of the prehospital team as it is of the people you are trying to help.

The reasons for anxiety may be subtle. One young Mexican teen who had been hit by a car and needed hospitalization was extremely anxious and did not want to be transported. No one could focus on the basis of her feelings until the hospital chaplain discovered that her main concern was that as an illegal alien, she was much more anxious about the possibility of being deported.

Fear

Fear is another very common emotional undercurrent in EMS. It helps to empathize with it, even when it is interfering with your medical care, because resisting an emotion—especially fear—often just escalates it. If you resist in any way—psychologically or physically—you become a threat to those in fear. A frightened person, just like a frightened rattlesnake, might quickly strike at and hurt you. Instead, a willingness to work with fearful people can help you get below the surface and assist in more positive ways.

> A frightened person, just like a frightened rattlesnake, might quickly strike at and hurt you.

The main distinction between fear and anxiety is that fear arises in the presence of a clearly palpable, often immediately present danger.[3] A good example of providing reassurance against a real fear occurred after a young man named Richard had been trying to pry something overhead with a crowbar. The tool had slipped and caused a gruesome two-inch deep, one-inch wide depressed fracture in his forehead. Despite the morbidity of the wound, he was alert and oriented. When a patient cannot inspect his own wound, the only "mirror" is in how others react—and he had seen the panic in the faces of his relatives.

On the way to the hospital, Richard was inordinately restless. Despite persistent efforts, the paramedic could not touch the right emotional nerve to help calm him down. Finally, the reason for his agitation occurred to her. She took a risk: "Richard, are you afraid you're going to die from this?" she asked. He admitted so, and they discussed the likelihood that despite the nasty-looking wound, he probably was not

---

[3] Nathan K. Rickles, ed. *Management of Anxiety for the General Practitioner* (Springfield, Ill.: Charles C Thomas, 1963), 4.

going to die. Although it is essential to guard against giving false reassurance, the reassurance in this case was honest and appropriate. The patient's relief was dramatic and immediate.

Embarrassment

Another emotion that is common among many people calling for emergency help is embarrassment. Most people hate having a fuss made over them and dislike being in the spotlight. Even on the telephone, these people are mostly concerned about asking that the ambulance *not* use the siren. They are embarrassed that they might disturb the neighbors. Once you arrive, they keep apologizing for "bothering" you. The kicker is that often these people have allowed their embarrassment to interfere with a timely call for help, so they are often quite sick by the time EMS helpers arrive. This has been known to generate frustration and contempt, just when a more empathetic approach is needed. "How could you have been so stupid to wait?" the insensitive helper may think— while his or her body language says it aloud.

The terms "shame," "self-conscious," and "confusion" are part of the definition of embarrassment. We are such a control-oriented society that people are upset (embarrassed) when they have to relinquish control. Consider the feelings of someone who loses continence, especially for the first time. It is embarrassing! And hurtful. The more professional and kind you can be, the less awful such events will be for your patients.

Pain

Too many EMS workers assume that the only way to fix pain is to administer an analgesic. Modern prehospital care has made us quick with the aspirin, the nitrous oxide, and the morphine. But physical pain can be reduced or even eliminated by employing some very basic techniques. First, of course, comes basic care, such as competent splinting and bandaging in combination with gentle, considerate handling. But along with physical care comes good, old-fashioned reassurance. Just knowing that someone is honestly concerned helps the patient cope.

The response people have to pain can be looked at through an analogy. One way is to visualize standing in knee-deep ocean water with a series of two-foot waves coming in. Some people try to stand square to the waves and stop or block them. The waves just crash into these human bowling pins—and win. Others stand sideways and, as each wave approaches, lean into it with the near foot and rock back onto the shoreside foot as the wave rolls by. This is a much more accepting and integrating approach to surf—and to handling pain as well.

In many cases, a person in pain escalates that pain through muscular tightening and rapid, labored breathing. Interestingly, most people are not even aware of this. You can encourage such patients to take slower, steadier breaths, and to untense muscle groups one by one. Explain the process. Have them breathe with you, slowly. Be sure to use specifics, not the unhelpful command of "just relax!" Tell patients this is a good way to help minimize the pain.

To acknowledge the emotions of your patients (and those of relatives and bystanders) is to help in a way many people overlook.

To provide such genuine help to a person—even when the injury is "minor"—you have learned something valuable about understanding others.

Nonphysical pain goes back to understanding the distress of crisis. When your mind tells you something hurts, it hurts—even when there is little physical reason for the pain. An example of how good interpersonal understanding and empathy can relieve nonphysical pain comes from comparing the following situations:

The assistant instructor of a wilderness-oriented first aid course went out to the woods to play the role of "victim" in each weekend's mock rescue. In two subsequent training sessions, the value of reassurance was aptly and vividly demonstrated. On the first weekend, the rescue took place on a beautiful, warm, sunny autumn day. But the rescuers haphazardly passed the instructor's emotional needs off to each other. The result was a very real sensation of emotional neglect. The next weekend was miserably cold and rainy. The instructor was "trapped" with a fractured femur under a fallen tree on a steep, muddy slope, and was actually somewhat hypothermic by the time the rescuers arrived. But the student who posted himself at her head and talked her through the extrication was an artist at interpersonal warmth. Despite the rigorous working conditions, the end result was dramatically positive.

To acknowledge the emotions of your patients (and those of relatives and bystanders) is to help in a way many people overlook. People feel better when they know it is acceptable to react to a situation, but they often don't understand this until you give them "permission." The benefit to you is that people who feel relatively comfortable about what is happening are much easier and safer to work with.

Patients Who Decline (Or Are Refused) Transport

EMS enjoys a positive reputation in most communities. Most citizens like knowing that, if something terrible happens, emergency medical services will respond. However, it takes little time in the field to realize that many individual calls do not result in transport. Either the patient refuses it or the EMS providers deny transport, each for a variety of reasons. No transport may occur, depending on the EMS system, in 25–70 percent of EMS responses. However, non-transport of patients is also the reason for 50–90 percent of litigation directed toward EMS![4] It is important to understand why a patient, once contacted, is being left behind. Is transport truly unnecessary? Other reasons, such as power-tripping on the part of the EMS provider, or failing to act on behalf of the patient, in spite of the negative interactions that can erupt due to intense emotions, may come back to haunt you.

Relatives and Bystanders

The desire to demonstrate an understanding of people is what separates excellent prehospital workers from those who, despite excellent technological and medical capability, are less interpersonally skilled. Events at a prehospital scene can go well or not, depending on whether you develop a good working relationship with the people you are there to help.

This includes relatives and bystanders. These "significant others" play a very important role. For one thing, they can provide valuable input. When you respond to them and listen well, you gain information and also reduce their anxieties. The benefit: a more trusting, cooperative scene. When you ignore them, you not only risk getting an incomplete story, you also might cause needless aggression (Fig. 3.3).

Why are bystanders such a legendary issue for prehospital workers? In part, it's a sense that these people are in our way and have no business being there. We are only grudgingly more tolerant of relatives; relatives have *some* business being there, but are often viewed as even more pestering and interfering.

Because bystanders and relatives are a fact of life on the streets, it helps to consider some of their motives. Through this increased awareness, you can develop a more professional and tolerant attitude. Any

---

[4] Brian S. Zachariah, et al, "Follow-up and Outcome of Patients Who Decline or Are Denied Transport by EMS," *Prehospital and Disaster Medicine* 7:4 (October–December 1992), 359.

Figure 3.3

Although most bystanders do not threaten or interfere with prehospital care, others require emotional support or other intervention for safety purposes. Always watch your bystanders.

time you can turn a liability into an asset—in EMS or in life generally— you stand to gain. As is often the case, you can start this discovery process by considering your own, pre-EMS past. You probably always watched emergency vehicles running "hot" for as long as possible, and wondered about their destination. You probably always slowed down at accidents, curious whether anyone was hurt. You may have been fascinated by reports of mass casualty on the news, and felt some relief that it was not your tragedy. You felt a real surge of adrenalin the first time you actually witnessed an emergency, and it felt a little exciting. Once you got to help, you got a sense of importance by being part of a newsworthy event. It gave you a story to tell your family and friends, and that gave you a sense of being special.[5] None of this means you are snooping, or nosy, or eccentric, or a repulsive person. It simply means you are not indifferent about your world or apathetic about what happens to your fellow humans.

---

[5] Marie Nordberg, "The Bystander Mindset: Where EMS Goes, Crowds Follow," *Emergency Medical Services*, 17 (January/February 1988), 31–35.

All the words used above describe bystanders as well: curious, fascinated, relieved ("it wasn't me"), excited, feeling important for being part of history in the making. Such responses from anyone participating in an unusual event are normal!

View bystander relations as a challenge, not a war. Bystanders and relatives who are treated with fairness and compassion will almost always give you space to do your job. What it takes is recognition of their presence, a quick communication of your expectations, reassurance about your ability to help (beginning with a professional demeanor), and providing them with a sense that *this* emergency is important. If someone else from the EMS team is available, that person can interface with the family. Even if you are very busy with a critical patient, there is usually time to look bystanders quickly in the eye, explain that you realize they are concerned, and tell them you will explain things to them when the patient does not need your complete attention.

Because of the tremendous variety of encounters we have with strangers in crises (including the bystanders who are also upset), it is easy to generalize. But it is unhelpful to treat *all* groups of bystanders the same way. Acknowledge the individuality of each scene and *all* its players.

Respect and Dignity

Understanding other people during their crises is a lifelong project. As you work at it, keep in mind that there are two things that every human being will appreciate:

- Respect from others
- Personal dignity

The flurry of activity at an emergency scene can strip a person of these things astonishingly fast.

Understanding other people depends on attitudes that are as nonjudgmental as possible. Although it is often difficult to feel much respect or bestow much dignity on some of the people we meet, especially those who do not seem to care about themselves, it still matters to try. It is sometimes a challenge not to let judgmental or other blundering statements slip out. But making disparaging remarks when lugging an obese patient from his third floor walk-up apartment is inappropriate. Consider how the patient and the people who like him would feel to hear you say such things. Making wisecracks is a common method for blowing off stress in EMS. We all do it. Just don't do it in public.

Why care more for a patient than he does for himself? Because as a professional, you have made the commitment to provide the service of emergency care to everyone who calls for help, regardless of actual medical need and regardless of the circumstances in which they are found. When anyone in EMS starts believing that people can be categorized according to their condition, our mission is at risk and everyone stands to suffer. We are here to make things better (we hope), not worse.

Respect for the Dead

Much has been written, in the past few years, of the near-death experience, which is when people who are successfully resuscitated can accurately describe what those caring for them said and did as if they were really there.[6] Whether or not you believe these reports, it is important to be respectful around dead or dying people. One case where this did not happen was when a man was in cardiac arrest on a city street. In their efforts to monitor the femoral pulse, the prehospital workers exposed—and left exposed—the man's genitals to a large crowd. To cover him with a blanket would have taken but a moment. This is the kind of detail that often does not receive attention, but which someone with streetsense should attend to.

A sense of respect is just as important when a person is declared dead at the hospital. Those first few minutes when CPR has been stopped and people busy themselves with paperwork and cleaning up are hard. It is easy to employ some gallows humor to help snap the intensity of loss after a resuscitation effort. But be considerate, of both the dead person and your coworkers, about the form that humor takes. Just think how you might feel, even in death, to have this happen to you.

If your system allows practice of invasive maneuvers and intubation on newly dead corpses, be careful to handle the body with respect. If you cannot get the tube, manage your frustration with professional demeanor. It will take only one immature response witnessed by the wrong person to deny future EMS workers this valuable training opportunity.

---

[6] Raymond A. Moody, Jr., *Life After Life* (New York: Bantam Books, 1975).

Essential Elements of Compassion

Compassion and empathy are hallmarks of the caring professions. It has often been assumed that a person "just knows" how to be compassionate. But knowing how to be compassionate is a skill that can be learned, given the tools. Expressing compassion is an invaluable part of understanding others.

The opposite of compassion may be detachment. Many people in EMS armor themselves with interpersonal detachment—a strategy which can be helpful, to a degree. But it can also interfere with honestly participating in the care of others. Many people forget that detachment is a tool, not a way of life. Making the choice to be appropriately compassionate to others involves taking the risk of dropping the detachment armor. Done right, it can lead to very rewarding sense of interpersonal understanding.

To build compassion is a multi-step process:[7]

1. Tune into your physical self.
2. Feel the emotions present in the moment.
3. Be able to name those emotions.
4. Tolerate what you feel. Hold the experience honestly.
5. Tune in to the other person.
6. Empathize. Feel the other person's emotions.
7. Tolerate their discomfort.
8. Communicate your capacity to hold their pain.
9. Communicate your desire to relieve their suffering.

There is a blend of self-understanding and understanding of others that has to occur in order to develop your compassion. This helps underscore the importance of the first two chapters. It requires knowing how to be empathetic. "People who are empathetic are more attuned to the subtle social signals that indicate what others need or want."[8] No, EMS providers cannot get too emotionally involved with the tragedies they are present to handle, or else they'd be no help at all. Yet there is a tendency in EMS providers to become so steeled against being hurt that they forget the skills and benefits of remembering how to have feelings.

The skill of compassion is used by EMS providers far more often than splinting, CPR, or many other medical skills. And—contrary to popular opinion—this skill can be learned![9] Once you can name your

---

[7] Mike Taigman, "Get A Life", at *EMS Today,* Albuquerque, NM, March 1996.
[8] Daniel Goleman, Ph.D, *Emotional Intelligence* (New York: Bantam Books, 1995).
[9] Mike Taigman, "Can Empathy and Compassion Be Taught?" *JEMS,* July, 1996.

own emotions, you can truly tune in to the other person. When you can see the worth in honestly tolerating the discomforts of others, your caregiving can deepen to a compassionate level. And once you can communicate effectively, it all blends into the vision of an EMS provider you'd like to have care for someone you love.

Understanding Coworkers

Because of the shared interest in EMS, the common assumption is that we automatically understand coworkers. Nothing, of course, could be further from the truth. Despite the tight bond of EMS, we are a diverse group of individuals. People in EMS tend to be rugged individualists with assorted interests and backgrounds.

The bond among coworkers in EMS is especially tight. We depend on each other for personal safety. We rely on each other for teamwork. A team spirit evolves whether you meet just twice a month as volunteers for a few hours or you spend ten 24-hour shifts a month with each other. As part of a profession with unusual demands, you are part of an unusual social group.

One requirement for being in EMS is to "fit in." In situations where a group of people share a long-term station assignment, the arrival of new recruits and station reassignments threaten the bond. This may result in hazing the newcomer, to discover how well this person will fit in and how far he or she can be pushed. Regardless of how stable the group is, many hours are spent waiting for calls. Waiting is stressful, and sometimes it leads to interesting station mischief. Such antics are a natural part of group bonding. It is tribal and has serious intention despite being presented in lighthearted terms. The group has to feel confident that those who belong do, in fact, fit in—especially when their lives depend on each other. Volunteer groups also engage in hazing.

Each group has its own traditions and rules. In the past, new squad members had to be able to keep up with the others in consuming liquid refreshments after training meetings. More ideally, newcomers are tested for interpersonal skills and medical knowledge.

When everyone gets along and has similar attitudes about the important things—what TV shows to watch and when to eat—life in EMS is fun. But it doesn't always work out that way. When a person does not fit the particular mold of a group, peer pressure often builds until that person is forced to leave. Unfortunately, not fitting the overall "culture" of the local EMS squad—volunteer or paid—has been an insurmountable barrier to some would-be EMTs. In fact, getting along with coworkers can sometimes seem the hardest part of the job. This is particularly true in services with high turnover. Getting to know co-workers is an investment of time and effort. If they keep leaving after just a few months, the sense of "team" can be left in tatters. If you never seem to have the same partner two weeks in a row, it takes a long time to feel you know the other people in your EMS service well enough to trust them with your life.

Developing an understanding of coworkers involves discovering how your personal "chemistry" fits theirs. For this reason, it is not fair to rely on the reputation another person has acquired. You never know what hidden agendas or personal mismatches other people may have when they try to tell you what someone else is like. Make your own decisions about how you regard others.

Seniority in the group is another factor that dictates the understanding that develops between coworkers. Pecking order is real. For optimal interaction and understanding, mutual respect by both the old-timer and the young upstart goes a long way toward overall team cohesiveness.

It is important to recognize that everyone has off-days. No one functions up to par at all times. When a partner's performance is lack-luster, it is vital to be willing to back him up. This not only reinforces teamwork, it also serves as a safety net. If you show this consideration of your partner, your partner will hopefully reciprocate when you need it. Whether or not you agree with each other's judgment calls, whether your partner is "green" and a pain to deal with, whether you feel like it or not, part of the job is to back each other up and present a team image to the public.

Obviously, there is no room in EMS for physical conflict with co-workers. But it happens. One of the most chilling, lonely experiences on the streets is to work with a partner who refuses to back you up.

Beyond the immediate circle of your EMS agency is the rest of the health care team. It helps to spend time getting to know the concerns, roles, and personalities of those people as well. One of the biggest difficulties with this, at least in areas with lots of "players," is that you might know a person's face well—but not his or her name! It does not take long to become familiar with the faces at the emergency depart-ment and among the various first responders. Now, if everyone would please wear name tags that are easy to read from a "social" distance—about three to four feet. Think about it: By the time you feel comfort-able interacting on a more personal level, you are often too embarrassed to ask another person's name! If everyone were to put their first names and title on a larger name tag, much of the interpersonal awkwardness would end.

Everyone on the EMS team has the same final goal: good patient care. When the team is strengthened by good relations and mutual understanding, that goal is not so hard to attain.

The Impact of EMS on Family

The impact of EMS on *your* significant others is worth consideration. Imagine what it is like for them to see you swept up by what can only be described as a passion? In training, you live, breathe, and sleep EMS. You talk about events and body parts that most people shudder to think about. You devote many hours to work, if you are paid—often 24 or 48 hours at a stretch. You sleep away from home, and when you *do* sleep at home, your pager or tone alert joins you in the bedroom. Your friendships might begin to revolve around others in EMS because they are the only ones who can really understand. Former friends and pastimes may be gradually forgotten. Even your annual vacation is spent at an EMS conference!

It is wonderful to love what you do. The precaution is not to immerse yourself to the point that there is no one there when you come up for air. Be sensitive about the effect of your EMS involvement on family and friends. Talk to them about it. Share the good and let them help you grieve over the bad. No, they cannot understand with the vividness of having been there, but they *can* help to some extent, *if* you let them. Show them the equipment, and draw them in, if they are interested. Respect the wishes of those who do not wish to be drawn in. For them, make a deliberate effort to share time on unrelated pursuits.

Some relationships—notably those where everyone is immersed in EMS—have been strengthened by the bond. Others have split up, and blame it on EMS. The blame probably lies with a host of factors. After all, these are tough times for *any* relationship. But EMS does contain an unusual number of things that can place a significant relationship at risk. What you can do is develop acute awareness of these risks and then manage them. Three methods to try are:[10]

- *Commit to the relationship.* Confirm and reconfirm it whenever traveling the path together becomes too hard.
- *Communicate with each other.* This goes beyond logistics such as what's for dinner and who is going to pick up a child. It means

---

[10]John Becknell, "Marriage and The EMS Experience," *JEMS*, 13 (June 1988), 30–33.

taking time to communicate about personally meaningful things, such as goals, desires, fears, etc.

- *Quantity time.* "There is no shortcut to a happy relationship." Quality time—as important as it is—is not enough. That's difficult news in our fast-paced world, but it's the honest truth. Quantity time matters, too.

Summary

Whoever you are striving to understand in life, try placing yourself in that person's shoes. What is the perspective? What is the view of the world? Have you ever been a patient—or worse yet, a family member— in an emergency? It is very enlightening to be dumped into the position of "just" family. It is certainly more easy to appreciate the concerns and needs of family members at prehospital scenes after being on that side of the fence yourself.

Is it really possible to understand, not to mention respect, people who are provocative, conniving, or deliberately abusive? What about the people affected by mind-altering substances? What about all those people we meet who do not appreciate our expertise and commitment? The ones who, knowingly, call you for really trivial complaints? Or the ones you know by name who call at 3:00 a.m.? What about the interfacility transfers, which many people deride as not being "real" calls? What about the "scum bums"? Isn't it time that such derogatory terms were eliminated from our collective vocabulary?

The point is not whether or not you like the less exciting or rewarding people who are also part of EMS. Learning to work with them anyway is simply streetsense. If you do not understand patients, bystanders, and other health care providers well enough to find some small way to appreciate them, you will not like the work. By making the effort to understand their concerns and viewpoints—whether or not you agree—you acquire some benefits that cannot be bought.

Understanding others is a challenge. It is difficult. No one can honestly expect to work effectively with everyone they meet. But by making the effort to develop as broad an interpersonal capability as possible and by continuing to learn from the experiences of working so often with strangers, your prehospital care will be greatly improved, no matter how long you've been in the field or how long you stay.

Effective Interpersonal Communication

> "Be careful of the words you choose
> Make them short and sweet.
> You never know from day to day
> Which ones you'll have to eat!"

Chapter Overview

Perhaps the most important skill a prehospital worker can have is the ability to communicate effectively. Other people—particularly patients—may not communicate well. But we need to. And we need to individualize our communication efforts. A method that worked well on one person may not on the next.

There are certain specific communication techniques that anyone can learn. They all address the human component in simple ways. They include making a good initial impression, effective introductions, eye contact, touching, correct positioning, and non-verbal communication. All serve to build trust and (ultimately) make our job easier to do.

Being a good listener is also important. People who think someone else is really listening feel acknowledged. This builds rapport. Listening well is not usually a strong skill in most people. Good interviewing is also important, and is a great challenge for prehospital personnel due to frequently suboptimal circumstances. Reassurance is another essential tool of the prehospital craft. Patients and bystanders require care for both their physical and their emotional needs.

This chapter also presents a variety of problem areas in interpersonal communication. Such things as noise, interference, inappropriate expectations, and certain personal factors can confuse and complicate even the most well-intentioned effort. By knowing about them, you can eliminate or overcome most of these problems.

Interpersonal communication is something that everyone does, but few people do it effectively. It is a highly complex process that few people do well without specific training. Honing your communication skills will enhance streetsense, for these skills improve access to the minds and emotions of others. A patient who senses that you honestly care will feel more trusting, and may therefore tell you things you might otherwise not have heard. With effective communication, the ability to assist the physical and psychological needs of people will increase. The combination of physical care and of "touching others' minds" through good communication leads to more thorough prehospital care. For example, imagine how vulnerable and embarrassed a person being undressed in public might feel. Say you're caring for an elderly woman in the presence of others (often a group of strangers). The experience can be transformed if you look her in the eyes and explain reassuringly that it is very important to listen to her breath sounds and apply the electrodes. An emotional nightmare can then be transformed into an experience where she feels genuinely cared for.

Good communication is also essential to prehospital safety. For example, psych patients often "demand" (verbally or not) understanding and respect for interpersonal space. A safety-based strategy is to stay well away from such patients, take the time to build rapport, then request permission to come feel a pulse. The experience is less threatening to the patient, thus less hazardous to you.

Good communication is also vital to scene control. When chaos and confusion are managed with effective communication, the message to others on the scene is that someone is, in fact, in charge.

Interpersonal communication in EMS is the link between the problem, whatever it is, and its solution. To reiterate the theme of the last two chapters, the key to effective communication is good self-awareness and a sound understanding of lots of different people. We need to be aware that channels of communication extend from ourselves to:

- Our partners
- Other coworkers from our own organization (for example, when more than one ambulance is needed, or when several members of a volunteer organization show up to help)
- People on the scene from other emergency agencies (police, fire, first responders, or if you are the first responders, your advanced life support backup)
- Relatives and friends of the patient, each with legitimate needs and concerns of their own

- Other bystanders (who can be a help, or a hindrance)
- And not least, the patient

The job is compounded, of course, when multiple patients swell the numbers of people involved, until your communication challenge reaches impressive proportions.

Communication Approaches

Most people feel their ability to communicate is adequate. After all, they can talk to people and get an answer. Isn't that "communication?" They use methods developed experientially. They get the job done. Well, that can be like handling a disaster with wheelbarrows—everyone eventually gets to the hospital. That job gets done, too. But it certainly wasn't done as well as it could have been!

Because you know you cannot expect other people to communicate effectively, you must learn to listen critically to them, to assess their actions as well as their words, and to sift the reality of what is happening from the mire of pretense. These are challenging tasks. Not every situation can be resolved. Patients sometimes don't want to talk, or deny having a problem, or are overwhelmed by anxiety or fear. Sometimes you don't speak their language. Sometimes they clearly don't want you there. It is tempting to react unprofessionally to the negativity we so often witness. It is also easy to focus on the obvious physical problem—for instance, slit wrists—without addressing the more difficult issue of why it happened. Suicidal gestures are a desperate form of communication.

Effective communication requires patience, and a positive attitude. If you rush your patients' answers, don't listen, or behave rudely or inappropriately when they do not communicate well, nothing is gained. With patience, you might discover something unexpected. A person with slit wrists may finally begin to speak about the spouse abuse or incest at the root of the problem.

Effective communication requires patience, and a positive attitude

While arriving at a prehospital scene, the alert EMS provider is watchful for the innumerable hints about how to approach each patient. You should be incorporating this data at the same time that you are assessing on-scene safety and control. When encountering someone you have never met, the interpersonal slate should be clear. As soon as you begin interacting (even nonverbally), the relationship is established and will continually build upon what has transpired. You cannot begin again. Thus a good prehospital technique is to "start easy and get tough." That is, you can ease into the relationship neutrally during those initial moments, while deciding the best approach to use. Then, if necessary, you can slide up the scale from gentle interaction to increasingly firm or tough interpersonal approaches until the communication between you and your patient is most effective. A key point is to be careful when deciding how forceful to be. Once you have overstepped your bounds and become too tough, it can be difficult to soften your approach again, since it's hard to "start over."

When approaching other people, it helps to be able to distinguish some of the ways they perceive their helpers. Sometimes it helps the patient cope with the situation if you act a certain role. In chapter 3, the concept of being part actor was presented. Another analogy is to regard yourself as part chameleon. A chameleon is a small lizard that can change the color of its skin to match the colors around it. This allows it to blend well with its environment. The better you can blend with a scene, the safer and smoother it will be.

Part of this blending has to do with the role-playing discussed in the last chapter. Taking different roles sometimes involves being something you are not. For example, you may need to be parental to someone older than you because they respond to crisis by regressing. Others need a different approach because they get depressive. Still others get aggressive, demanding yet another role from you. It seems odd, but acting different roles works! Knowing which to employ on each call is partially a matter of experimentation, both with your own acting abilities and with your ability to rapidly assess others' needs. Experience is an excellent teacher. A short, general list of some ways you might interact with patients is:

- **As a parent.** They want to be told how to behave and what to do, the way their parents once told them. One uninjured man in his twenties, so the story goes, was so inordinately upset and out of control as a result of his auto accident that the EMT finally had to take a parental role and tell him to, "Just sit down and be quiet!" The patient burst into tears and said, "But I've never had an accident before. I don't know how I should behave!"

- **As a teacher.** You are a source of information. Many people want an explanation for everything that is happening. Otherwise, they do not cooperate well. With your help, the experience is less frightening and confusing to them, and easier for you.

- **As a son or daughter.** This is especially true with elderly people. Acting as a surrogate child is often the only way to get someone to do what is right.
- **As a friend.** Some people need to feel that your help is as good as having a friend by their side.
- **As a spouse.** Sometimes patients need more than a friend. They need a more intimate, yet peer-like style. Husbands and wives (or people playing similar roles) can often get their spouses to do things that no one else can—such as go to the hospital.
- **As an authority figure.** Sometimes patients will respond only to a very tough demeanor. For a prehospital worker who is unused to being "the tough guy," this can be a particularly difficult role to play, but sometimes it's the only method that works. Make it a believable part of your repertoire.
- **As a pleader.** Sometimes, patients feel more in control if you let them feel they are doing you the favor of going to the hospital.
- **As a strictly business, professional person.** Sometimes, you can just be yourself! It works for some patients to simply do your job without making a big fuss.

Playing these roles requires the willingness to be flexible. Some prehospital workers are not flexible and demand that their patients (and coworkers) deal only with an unyielding style. This attitude interferes with the goal of creating a cooperative and effective working environment. You need to be able to employ different stances, postures, word choices, and tones of voice for your various roles. Also, sometimes it becomes necessary to switch roles on a scene (be a chameleon). Sometimes your first approach was not effective, and you find you need to try something different. Or perhaps something about the scene changes. For example, perhaps your patient is a frightened battered wife. Your likely role will be gentle, calm, and soothing. Then the angry husband reappears and you have to change quickly to a more authoritarian, in-command role. When you return your attention to the patient, you must revert to the gentle mode. The need for flexibility is obvious. If, after dealing with the husband, your "tough" presence lingers, the patient may become frightened and defensive. Your earlier rapport will be ruined. Your demeanor must also adjust when dealing with co-professionals on the scene or at the hospital.

Is it wrong to be something you are not? Not when you understand clearly who you are, so that your own identity is not lost in the process.

Your purposes for being like a chameleon are worthy. Another analogy is to see good prehospital care as if it is an ongoing improvisational theater called "the streets." The scene is your stage, and everyone there has a role. You, as patient attendant, are the director; your partner is the stage manager. Lighting and props set the stage, and the scene noise is the "orchestra." Helpers are stage hands. The family and bystanders are the audience (including critics!). The hardest role belongs to the patient, for he is the star of the show, yet has not had a chance to read the script, much less learn his lines.[1] Professional actors go from role to role over the years and do not forget who they actually are. They also learn to give a good performance over and over during the run of each play, and understand the relevance of playing to a friendly crowd. This freshness of approach can benefit us in the streets. It helps when patients are led to believe theirs is the most important emergency of all. Flexibility and choosing the best approach each time is the challenge—and the thrill.

First Impressions

The physical appearance of arriving rescuers makes an important impression on the people there. First impressions are based almost entirely on nonverbal communication. They influence subsequent interactions with people and are difficult to overcome when they are negative. Your uniform is the symbol of your EMS affiliation, and looking good will have important implications that go beyond the immediate call. It is to the benefit of everyone in the system for each individual to look as clean and professional as possible. Even if you are the best paramedic in your system, your appearance still matters.

> A sloppy appearance says, nonverbally, that you do not take good care of yourself. It makes patients wonder how well you'll take care of them.

Of course, it is difficult to stay clean when you have to mess with ambulance engines or try to provide medical assistance in "the mud, the blood, and the beer" of the streets. Every EMS insider knows that! But the public does not. A sloppy appearance says, nonverbally, that you do not take good care of yourself. It makes patients wonder how well you'll take care of them. If the shirt's tails are out and it is wrinkled,

---

[1] Arthur R. Ciancutti, *The View From The Gurney Up: Dealing With People in Crisis and Emergency* (Lancaster, Pa.: Technomic Publishing Co., Inc., 1984).

smelly, and stained (particularly blood-stained), the public will be reluctant to extend much, if any, confidence. Inevitably, calls come in the middle of eating a hamburger with a big slab of onion on it, or when you are scrubbing the ambulance's bloody walls. But I know that when my mother was picked up, the paramedics had to be free of body odor, bad breath, and dirty fingernails. Otherwise, they would never have won her trust. She noticed these things, and so will a lot of people like her.

It is also important that people with long hair keep it out of the way. A bun rather than a ponytail maintains not only a neater appearance, but is also safer. The hair is then out of reach of both people and dangerous machinery. Also, be careful about wearing fragrances. Perfume or after-shave just do not make it on the streets—not in our sort of street work, anyway! It may smell nice to you but not to your nauseated patients.

Presence

Beyond personal hygiene and physical neatness is "presence." This is another subtle, immediate communication. Presence, according to the *Random House Dictionary*, is "the ability to project a sense of ease, poise, or self-assurance, especially the quality or manner of a person's bearing before an audience." Your demeanor says a great deal to the people in the prehospital environment. Coming onto the scene in a calm, organized, polite manner demonstrates a sense of confidence about yourself and your ability to help. This is automatically reassuring. Your rapport has begun to build even before you have said a word. Even when you don't *feel* confident, projecting a presence that "says" you are is very helpful to first impressions.

Introducing Yourself

Once you arrive at the patient's side (assuming that he is conscious), introduce yourself. Put yourself in the patient's shoes; how would you feel if a troupe of strangers came in and started touching and poking you and wiring you to a bunch of machines? The experience would be much more tolerable if you at least knew someone's name. The subtle, but extremely positive effect is that people will respond to you more positively once you have become a human being with a name, than if you simply barge in and take over anonymously.

Overdoing the introductions, though, can be confusing. It's not a tea party! If all the rescuers introduce themselves, they remain a bewildering pack of people, except that now they all have names. Limit introductions to those who are interacting directly with the patient. Those who are interacting with bystanders or relatives should provide introductions to those people.

Make introductions bilateral. Find out how to address the patient. An effective way is to say, "Hi, my name's _____ , and I'm a paramedic. What's your name?" By offering not only your name but your title as well, you help the patient understand your role in this experience. Note that members of the public often do not understand abbreviations. State the entire title. "I'm an Emergency Medical Technician" means more to the uninitiated than "I'm an EMT." Similarly, don't assume people can get the information off your patches. Think about it: Most patches are worn on the sleeves. They are useless as cues to people you are facing straight on.

> . . . people will respond to you more positively once you have become a human being with a name, than if you simply barge in and take over anonymously.

Be conscious about whether or not to use the other person's first name. Medical culture has a bad habit of addressing people by first names. This is often inappropriate, particularly with elderly people. It demonstrates respect (and thus builds rapport) to address people formally, at least in the beginning.

There are two ways to determine the acceptable way to address each patient. In most cases it is apparent, by observation and intuition, that either a first-name or a last-name basis is appropriate. The best cue is to note the way they introduce themselves. However, when you ask a patient her name, if she says, "Emma Jones," you still don't know which she would prefer. In this case, do not hesitate to ask outright: "And how would you like me to address you?" This gives the patient the option to say, "Oh, just call me Emma," or "Everyone calls me Mrs. Jones." When in doubt, it never hurts to be formal. It's much more respectful to call a 65-year-old man "Mr. Tyler" than "Tim."

The difficult part about names, of course, is that every time you try to use a last name, you get hit with a multisyllabic tongue twister! This is a time to ask the patient's permission to call him by something you can pronounce. Even by making that small effort, you demonstrate a helpful sense of consideration.

Remembering Names

Learning to remember names is not so much an inborn talent as a learned skill. Most people remember names long enough for them to fly out the other ear. Once you decide to concentrate on this important detail, though, it gets easier. The best tip is to employ all three learning systems at once, auditory, visual, and kinesthetic:

- Say the name three times in the first minute, out loud.
- Visualize the name in your mind's eye. Imagine a blank sheet of paper posted in your mind, primed to fill in with the patient's answers to questions about medical history. At the top of the "page" put the patient's name in imaginary capitalized, boldfaced letters (Fig. 4.1).

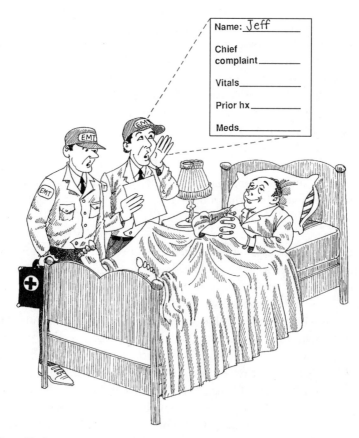

Name: Jeff

Chief complaint_____

Vitals_____

Prior hx_____

Meds_____

Figure 4.1

Visualizing your patient's name in your head in addition to saying it out loud right away is a good technique for remembering names.

- Feel the act of "writing" the patient's name on that imaginary blank page. Some people write the name on their paperwork. This is less effective than the mental imagery because it interrupts the flow of gaining rapport at too early a stage.

Introduction time is also a good chance to modulate your voice appropriately. Pay attention to your volume. Speak up if the person is hard of hearing or difficult to control. Speak quietly and in low tones if the situation indicates the need. Check the pitch; some people are pitch-deaf, and people with high voices are hard for them to hear. Also, check the rate. Be especially aware that people in crisis have difficulty taking in information at a normal rate. They are too overwhelmed. More will be accomplished faster, believe it or not, by slowing down. Speak slowly and distinctly. As always, address patients as individuals.

Positioning for First Impressions

The topic of positioning is relevant to all three realms of streetsense: communication, safety, and control. The first priority, of course, is personal safety. Quick on its heels, though, must come an awareness of the impact of positioning on effective communication. Three elements to consider are distance, vertical relationship, and frontal positioning.

An early consideration involves your distance from the patient. Develop a finely honed awareness of interpersonal space. One way that humans protect themselves is by maintaining a certain physical distance from other humans. In general, how far we distance ourselves from others depends on the situation at hand and how comfortable we are with the people around us. There is also a distinct cultural component in the concept of interpersonal space. Generally (in America), intimate space is within 18 inches of our bodies, personal space is 18 inches to 4 feet, social distance is 4 to 12 feet, and public distance is 12 feet or more (Fig. 4.2).[2] People of other cultures may greatly shorten or lengthen these parameters.

When plunging into a stranger's life to take care of business, remember that some people are extremely protective of their "space." They may get agitated, nervous, or even belligerent as you approach, especially if they are intoxicated or psychologically disturbed. "People mark a boundary by a variety of behaviors that include backing up to maintain a fixed interpersonal distance, staring or glaring at the intruder, or

---

[2] Stewart L. Tubbs and Sylvia Moss, *Human Communication: An Interpersonal Perspective* (New York: Random House, Inc., 1974), 145.

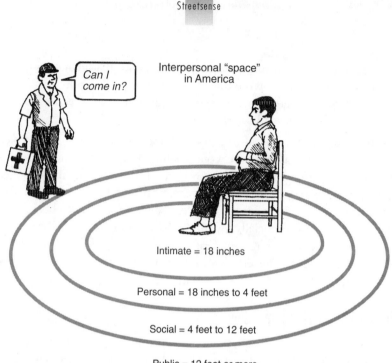

Can I come in?

Interpersonal "space" in America

Intimate = 18 inches

Personal = 18 inches to 4 feet

Social = 4 feet to 12 feet

Public = 12 feet or more

Figure 4.2

Zones of interpersonal space vary from culture to culture. In America they tend to be as shown.

verbally admonishing him."[3] What is troubling to the other person could well be your violation of his or her sense of space. If there is a chance you're causing the problem, step out to the next zone of interpersonal space and see what happens. Often, the person will visibly settle down. Then take time to build a rapport before trying to re-enter that space—if the circumstances of the emergency permit.

Vertical relationship has to do with your eye level in relation to the eye level of the person you're speaking with. What's appropriate depends on your assessment of the best role to play. Do you want your eye level above the patient's eyes? This is one way to denote authority and control. Would it be better to be at the same eye level as the patient? This will denote neutrality or equality. Or would it be best to position yourself with your eye level below that of the patient? This imparts some control to the patient. Your choices usually will range from decid-

---

[3] Norman Ashcraft and Albert E. Scheflen, *People Space: The Making and Breaking of Human Boundaries* (New York: Anchor Press/Doubleday, 1976), 48.

ing whether to stand up, sit, kneel, or squat. For example, if a patient needs a "confidante" approach, you would probably choose to sit beside her rather than tower over her, to build congruency in your interpersonal approach. Although concurrent medical care such as starting an IV while you talk may sometimes dictate your position, there is potent nonverbal communication in how you position yourself.

Finally, think about frontal positioning. There are times to face a patient squarely from the front, and there are times to position yourself to the side with your body turned. In a situation that calls for a tough approach, a front-on wide-stanced position looks solid and thus imparts nonverbal toughness. By standing slightly sideways, you "soften" your presence and give the patient a better sense of control.

People may also respond well when you verbalize that you understand their threatened feelings. You can say, "I know you don't want me to get too close to you and that's okay, except that I can't take care of you from over here." By taking the time to build some trust and rapport, you are likely to have better results than if you simply barge right in.

A versatile prehospital worker can employ all the factors about positioning to optimal advantage. Knowing how to do this requires experimentation and experience, but awareness of the components at least provides some methods to try.

Classic Components of Effective Communication

All of the preceding statements rely on your ability to use four essential tools of effective interaction:

- The ability to listen
- Eye contact
- The ability to touch
- Good nonverbal communication

Each of these is important to any interaction, but they matter especially in our quest to get people to do things they do not want to do. (Who ever *wants* to go to the hospital?) They are a big benefit during encounters with strangers—which is what EMS is all about.

Effective Listening

Listening is a vital skill in effective communication. You've done it all your life, but have you done it well? Hearing is to listening what having a brain is to having a mind. Without listening, you can hear what people say and yet miss the meaning of their words. If you listen just for facts and details, you may miss the true intention or underlying emotions of what the speaker is saying. Listening well is complex, and very difficult! Listening is a six-part process and if any piece is missing, miscommunication can readily occur:

1. Hear: the sounds travel to you (a physical process).
2. Attend: shift to become the listener and select the stimuli you want.
3. Understand: interpret what has been said by decoding and assigning meaning.
4. Retain: put the message into memory (selectively, of course!).
5. Evaluate: decide how you want to judge the message after weighing all the evidence.
6. Respond: provide feedback, verbally and non-verbally.

Three common errors in listening include:

- Not paying attention to what is being said
- Paying too much attention to the words without accurately interpreting the overall message
- Not providing verbal and nonverbal cues that you are paying attention to the speaker

It is easy, especially when a medical situation is critical, to ask a question and then be in such a hurry to ask the next question that you never really hear the answer. If you ask a question, stop and listen to the person you have addressed. Wait for an answer. Be patient. During a crisis, many people become overwhelmed. They need extra time to process your questions—just when you may feel there's little time to spare! (This is especially true of elderly people, and children.) When an answer is given, pay attention to it. Otherwise, in the long run, your sense of urgency may actually cost you on-scene time.

Listening includes noticing not only words, but also vocal tone, volume, underlying emotion, as well as nonverbal messages broadcast by the body. If the patient is saying, "I'm okay, really—I'm fine," but the words sound distressed, and she's crying and looks frightened; the overall message, of course, is that she's not "fine."

Why is it that some prehospital workers seem to get a complete and accurate patient history in no time, when so many others never seem to get it right? Part of the answer rests with how they encourage the speaker by sending cues that they are, indeed, listening. EMS requires that we often do two or three things at a time, which can make the speaker feel ignored. As you bend over to start the IV, take a moment to get eye contact and say, "Go ahead, I am listening—but I also have to look at your arm for a minute." Encourage speakers with head nods or "uh huh," or "go on." Follow-up questions that use words that reflect you were listening are also helpful, such as, "When you said you've been upset, what do you think causes that?"

If you are unsure of a message, repeat your perception and see if the message sent was the same message received. Say something like: "Let me see if I have this straight. Are you telling me . . ." This helps confirm the accuracy of your listening.

In addition to listening carefully to the patient, and relatives or bystanders, it is just as vital to listen to the other people on the prehospital team. When you are right in the middle of things, it can be easy to miss details that are obvious to someone else who is standing back. Be capable of hearing that person's input about what you seem to be missing! Otherwise, you can lose valuable information—all because you were not listening.

If you want to be a good listener, avoid internal commentary or arguing, focusing on irrelevancies, labeling, and listening selectively. Listen wholeheartedly, attentively, and fully. Frame your response after the other person finishes the thought. Above all, never finish others' statements for them!

Eye Contact

Eye contact is one of our most powerful tools because the eyes are the windows to the soul. Eye contact can reassure, express gentleness and hope, glower, overpower, command, demand, request, delve, threaten,

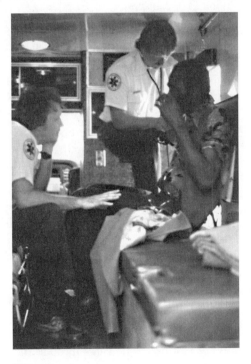

Figure 4.3

Notice the paramedic's excellent use of positioning, eye contact, and defusing hand gesture, while the other paramedic stays to the side. This patient was agitated, but easily calmed through such methods.

even challenge—all without words. The messages are subtle, but they tend to express true underlying feelings. By learning to "read" others' eyes and to make statements with your own, your streetsense will be greatly strengthened.

Eye contact works two ways. As we look into the eyes of another person, we can receive messages—but our eyes also send messages to the person. For many people, using eye contact is disconcerting and uncomfortable. This is because it is tremendously personal, powerful, and honest. Eyes hide very little.

Establishing eye contact is easy; simply look into another person's eyes. But doing it well takes practice and an awareness of the effect of your efforts. There are degrees and depths of looking at people. You would not look at a medical patient whom you have just met with the softness of a gaze into your lover's eyes. The range of expression is vast, and developing a good repertoire requires both curiosity and the willingness to experiment. A good way to begin learning this skill is to look at the bridge of another person's nose, right between the eyes, at first. Once you are more accustomed to looking in that general direction, look into the other person's eyes for a few seconds at a time until your comfort level rises. Eventually, you will find that you have acquired a new interpersonal skill!

Be aware of the interference caused by sunglasses. They should *never* be worn when interacting with a patient. It is disconcerting to talk to someone whose eyes are guarded, particularly by mirror-type sunglasses. Masked eyes make people wonder what you have to hide. Wear sunglasses to the scene, for driving, and after the call—but take them off during contact with patients or bystanders.

Compassionate Touch

Another potent communication tool is the skill of compassionate touch. (Fig. 4.4). The value of this skill is easy to see when comparing the interpersonal results of those who use it to those who do not. Patients relax visibly when in the care of a person who has the ability to "tell" another that he or she cares through the use of touch. Compassion will be transmitted even if you are wearing gloves. Touching communicates caring to your patient, and even to bystanders (especially relatives). It is reassuring. When a person's plans are pushed out of kilter because of a medical emergency, perspective can be regenerated by a caring soul who takes the time to touch. Whether you squeeze a shoulder, hold a hand, brush away a tear, or give a hug, this sort of touching communicates your concern for the human being experiencing the death, disease, or disfigurement you were called to help handle. Done right, compassionate touch can make a significant difference to the patient's emotional response to the situation.

Figure 4.4

Touching for compassion (not just medical care) is a potent interpersonal communications tool. (Photo courtesy of JEMS Publishing Company.)

There are two sorts of touching in EMS: the type of touching you do when performing a head-to-toe physical exam, and compassionate touch. Although ours is not generally a touching society, EMS providers have routine permission to enter strangers' "intimate space" and touch them all over for medical evaluation. Touching is a necessary element of the job. However, to many EMS providers it seems very risky to demonstrate compassion through touch. They wonder whether touching with the intention of transmitting emotional support might be misunderstood. This is a legitimate concern. It takes time to learn to pick up on the appropriate degree and style of touching that will work for different individuals. Be aware that misreading a person's need for personal space is one reason that touching can occasionally backfire. You have to be careful about reaching right out and grabbing people, whether you are doing it to reassure them or even to do a regular physical exam. It requires judgment to know which patients will respond positively to which sort of compassionate touch.

Developing that judgment requires a learning curve. As with remembering to use the methods for remembering names, compassionate touching is a skill many people have to learn. It can be difficult to do, especially at first. Even conducting a thorough hands-on physical exam is embarrassing and awkward for most beginners. But the skill will improve with experience. Watch other people, too. Note how overzealous touching can be aggravating to the patient, while none at all can leave a patient feeling miserable. Watch how many patients who are overwhelmed by fear and pain can be easily controlled and reassured by well-timed, well-delivered, compassionate touch.

Take the time to learn to touch in a natural, genuine manner. As you practice and improve your touching ability, consider your own feelings. Is there a sense of genuine concern flowing through your hands to the patient? Or does it feel unnatural and contrived? Don't worry; many people feel uncomfortable touching other people at first. Give it time. At least you are trying. Keep in mind that compassionate touch is a *learned* skill, one that can be improved with effort. Don't vow never to try it again if it doesn't work well right away.

Nonverbal Communication

There are two sides to nonverbal communication, just as there are with the other components of good communication. You can gain a lot of insight about patients by observing their nonverbal clues, and they can do the same about you. People can read things about you and your thoughts by observing the tone and volume of your voice, your facial expression, your body position and tension, your skin moisture, even the thickness of your lips. Without saying a word on a scene, you can "tell" people that you are capable, interested, and in control; you can also broadcast disgust, fear, or panic. If you are fumbling and sweating and your eyes are too wide, you will never impart an impression of control and reassurance simply by saying: "Now everybody just stay calm!" Your actions have already betrayed your words.

Keep in mind, though, that nonverbal behavior does not stand alone. It is *one* component of communication. It serves to "reinforce, replace, or contradict" what's been said in words.[4] A prehospital worker who is standing, hands on hips, with an arrogant facial expression will have a difficult time convincing any patient that he is concerned.

Learning to assess others' nonverbal behavior helps us interpret their subtle messages. One important element is to notice whether the verbal and the nonverbal messages are congruent. If the husband of an assaulted woman says, "Oh yes, I love her very much. She's a wonderful wife" but is clenching his jaw, with tight shoulders, hands in fists, and using a sarcastic tone of voice, which do you believe? To perceive a lack of congruency is to have an opportunity to steer the discussion toward the real truth.

Recognizing and accurately interpreting nonverbal behavior is, like so much of streetsense, a matter of awareness combined with experience. You must be capable of looking at the total picture, not simply its individual components. Take, for example, the assault victim who won't cry until she feels completely safe. Certain clues in her nonverbal behavior will be shouting out that she would like to cry, but her sense of dignity or need to retain control prevents it. If it is appropriate, you can respond to the signals—the ones she may not even know she's sending—and say, "You know, it's okay to cry." You have just told her that you are aware of her need. If this helps her feel safe enough to cry, you've helped in an important way. If she cannot cry yet, at least you've given her the option for when she feels ready.

Nonverbal communication is complex. Your own combines constantly with that of others. Sometimes the messages are confusing; sometimes they are misread or misunderstood. Nonverbal behavior can be intentional, such as when a paramedic shows disgust with a chronic ambulance abuser. Or it can be unintentional, such as when the same person, exhausted from twenty calls in 10 hours, slumps into a chair while discussing options with a patient. Should the patient misinterpret the posture and say, "If you don't care about me, then just leave!" the aware prehospital worker can explain the mixed message and hopefully salvage the interaction.

Even the EMS uniform is a nonverbal statement. How a person wears a uniform can signal pride—or not. Part of a uniform are the patches. Patches are popular items in EMS. It takes a lot of effort to become a

---

[4] Tubbs and Moss, *Human Communication*, 162.

first-aider, or certified in CPR, or an instructor, or nationally registered, or to become an EMT or a paramedic. The practice of sewing every patch on an available spot on the uniform is debatable. What is the nonverbal message when you can't see the rescuer for his patches?

Other Techniques For Effective Communication

Choices

When possible, give people as many choices as possible. This works especially well with children. Patients who resist transport are often just acting on a perception that they have lost control. Maybe they *have* lost control of the big picture, but this does not mean you cannot give them part of the situation to handle. Something as simple as offering the choice of walking versus riding on the cot, or letting them choose which bath-robe to take along makes a big difference. As minor as such choices may appear, the technique makes it easier for you to assert yourself when it does become necessary to do things about which they have less choice, such as starting an IV.

Choices give people a chance to come to their own (guided) conclusions about what to do. Instead of telling Mr. Jones that he has to go to the hospital, you can phrase the same information to include an illusion of choice: "Well, your leg certainly does look broken. Which hospital do you prefer?" Feeling like he has a choice in the matter helps the patient feel more in control. You can explain the problem in simple terms and indicate your advice without making you seem bossy.

Handling Delusions

Handling delusions and hallucinations presents another communications challenge. Everyone who stays in EMS long enough has bizarre stories to tell. It is interesting, certainly, to meet the King of Bavaria, or a prominent Indian guru's right-hand man, a woman who moved all the furniture out of her house (including a very heavy sofa) solely with the help of God, someone being hotly pursued by the CIA, and other similar, interesting characters.

The time that we spend with such profoundly affected people is so limited that there is no chance of making much of a therapeutic impact. It is also inappropriate to yield to the temptation to ridicule, subtly or overtly, people who are out of control in this way. They deserve respect and dignity along with the rest of the human race.

A good prehospital approach is to let the patient carry on with the delusions as long there are no safety hazards. You should neither fan nor try to extinguish the psychic fire. If your patient is upset by the bugs crawling on the ambulance wall, first check to be sure they really do not exist (some ambulances are cleaner than others!), then tell your patient something like: "I understand that you believe there are bugs, but please be assured that I don't see any, and I'm going to be careful not to let anything hurt you."

Verbalizing

One good communications trick is to verbalize often. There are several components to thorough verbalization:

- Explain what is happening.
- Describe what needs to be done.
- Explain how you plan to accomplish the tasks involved.
- Tell why your actions are important. The "why" is especially important.

Consider nasotracheal intubation. It may seem silly to verbalize what you're doing, and why, to an unconscious person, but it makes sense for two reasons. First, of the senses, hearing is said to be the last to fade away and the first to return. You never know whether an unconscious person can hear you. If she can, verbalization at the earliest possible moment can be a real benefit. Can you imagine waking up to all the chaos of rescue efforts after a critical event without having someone talking to you? Second, many of our activities in EMS, especially nasotracheal intubation, look very barbaric to the uninitiated. Verbalizing the benefits of a procedure tends to calm bystanders. Explaining why it is important to do a mean-looking or painful procedure makes you seem less of a sadist. Acknowledging the unusual nature of your interaction makes the whole situation less frightening, and thus more manageable—for everyone.

Verbalizing lets people know that what they feel is legitimate. It helps patients understand that it's safe to react to what's happening (Fig. 4.5). This builds trust and rapport, and helps everyone cope with an upsetting experience. For example, you can verbalize to a child with a broken leg, who is bravely trying not to cry, that it is okay to react. Help that person identify the feelings—fear? pain?—and that it's all right to have feelings about the situation. Who wouldn't? Say something like, "Hurts a lot, huh? It's okay to cry if you feel like it." Any time a feeling, a fear, or a concern of any kind is aired, it opens the channels of communication, and your chances of communicating effectively increase.

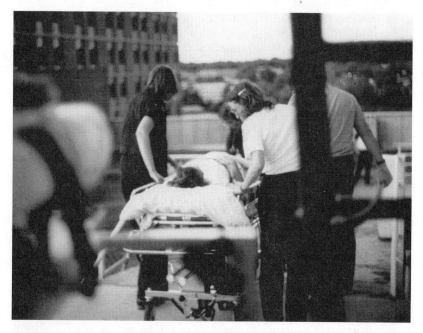

Figure 4.5

The paramedic (in white) is talking with the patient, who has just had her first helicopter ride. The excitement and high-tech feel of an emergency situation is often overwhelming. Encouraging patients to verbalize their feelings is often very helpful.

Reassurance

Reassurance often seems like a nearly lost art, when all the machines, IVs, and other technologies distract us from the person being helped. But a softly spoken word and gentle touch work—like a charm, sometimes. It is a great and powerful skill to have.

It's hard to overdo reassurance. Some prehospital workers would like to believe that there's no reason to "bother" with it, but those are likely to be people who are also uncomfortable with the human component of EMS. If you genuinely care about people, you can sense when their needs cannot be met with more technology.

One story dramatically serves to demonstrate the value of reassurance: A patient had been working on his car when it jumped the blocks and ran over him. He fractured both femurs, broke his back, and badly burned his chest and one arm. He was slightly hypotensive, but conscious and alert.

The paramedic made a specific point to take the time from the many physical challenges of the call to talk to the man frequently. This involved going to his head, gaining eye contact, verbalizing every move to prepare him for transport, and using compassionate touch. Every tool in that paramedic's communication toolbox was used that day, and the sum of the parts was a powerful dose of reassurance. Because of this effort, the man was able to hang on to his self-control, making him exceptionally cooperative throughout a difficult and lengthy extrication.

The only time the paramedic was unable to maintain frequent contact with the patient's emotional status was during the radio report on the way to the hospital. In those two minutes, the patient lost control and started to panic. At the conclusion of the radio report, the paramedic again made contact, by touching, talking, and using eye contact. The man immediately regained control.

Be careful not to offer false reassurance, though. Although we often inadvertently say that "everything'll be all right," it may not be for every patient. What seems a simple broken collar bone maybe a big blow to an athletic child who now faces missing the all-school field day. Any disruption—large or small—interferes with life as that patient had expected it to be. In more serious cases, false reassurance is about as fair as telling a child that an IV "won't hurt a bit."

Much of your reassurance is transmitted nonverbally. Words mean nothing when your actions contradict them. If the case is critical and your limits are being tested, you may inadvertently show the intensity, and your concern. Nonetheless, you can be reassuring and still be honest: "We're doing everything anyone else could do for you right now. I know you're in a lot of pain, but hang in there. We're nearly to the hospital."

Humor

There are times when the right bit of humor can make all the difference in EMS, even on a call. Some people have a knack for it, and some do not. The tricky part is to use humor appropriately. No one should feel the "brunt" of a joke, especially in public. Everyone should see the humor—or don't use it.

The pluses of good humor are that it serves to reduce stress and can help establish rapport. However, done wrong, it can be very offensive. It can be perceived as sarcasm, or as a put-down. Something that's hysterical to one person may anger the next. There are obvious professional image and safety issues to the topic of humor, when it is used publicly.

EMS providers are notably prone to "gallows humor." Some insist it's the only way they stay sane. But there is a proper place for our unique brand of humor. We have to be very careful where and when we choose to use it. More than a few EMS providers have cleared the surrounding tables at restaurants . . . be careful!

Interviewing Techniques

The goal of the prehospital interview is quickly to obtain information pertinent to appropriate prehospital medical care. It is part of the art of EMS to gather a good, thorough history, from both the patient and bystanders.

A good interview usually carries you from the general to the specific. It is like drawing a picture. An artist sketches a framework on the page before putting in the details, and so do you. This is why you always begin with the chief complaint. You need an outline—"I can't breathe"—before you can start to fill in the reasons why.

The interviewing process always varies, so to do it well requires (once again) the hallmark quality of versatility. Lack of versatility is a frustration among many beginning prehospital workers, because to master the art of interviewing requires a breadth of experience that comes with time and effort. When you first start conducting interviews, you rely on lists of questions that are categorized according to the various chief complaints. Every conscientious student of EMS does this. The volume of things to remember is extensive, and it is vital not to leave anything out. For example, it is potentially hazardous (not to mention embarrassing) to interview a patient with shortness of breath and not inquire about associated chest pain or discomfort.

While structure is essential to a good interview, however, the common error is to let these lists of questions and concerns become too engraved in your mind. Consider the perspective of the person being interviewed. The patient does not know about that set of questions in your mind posted under "Things to Ask." If the part about prior health problems is the sixth question on the list but the patient talked about that when answering the third question, rapport is undermined when you ask question number six anyway.

The most important thing is to ask all the appropriate questions. In the beginning, the only way to do this is to rely on learning tools such as those question lists in your mind. But do not let it become a bad habit. The tendency when learning to interview is to fill in the blanks mentally after each question as you run down the list. Your eventual goal is to be able to fill in those blanks as you go along—without forgetting anything—regardless of the order the answers are given. Once you have some confidence in your interviewing, break the list habit and develop flexibility in your lines of questioning. The transition from the list method to the free flowing (but still complete) interview is a challenging process, one that will give pleasure as your abilities blossom.

Word Choices

Choosing the right words can facilitate an interview just as much as choosing the wrong words can wreak havoc. Prehospital workers can often relate more effectively with lay people than other health care workers (including doctors and nurses). But we still have to be careful. The classic story is of the medical intern who asked a patient, "Can you void?"

> Choosing the right words can facilitate an interview just as much as choosing the wrong words can wreak havoc.

The patient said, "Whaddya mean, doc?"

The nurse explained, "We need you to urinate."

The confused patient said, "Huh?"

The paramedic walking by overheard the conversation and said to the patient, "Can you pee?"

The patient said, "Oh—sure!"

Awareness of the word choices you make also helps ensure that you ask questions that are congruent with the patient's perceptions. For example, people in EMS think so often about cardiac problems in terms of "chest pain" that it is easy to forget that some people don't perceive the sensation in their chests as pain at all. If you are dealing with a possible cardiac situation and your patient denies chest pain, try rephrasing the question. You could discover a feeling of discomfort or squeezing or some other unusual sensation. One myocardial infarction patient described her problem as "a soft substernal whisper." Using words the patient clearly understands improves not only communication but also the patient's perception of being able to help with the health care process.

Similarly, be careful of using jargon. Jargon is language peculiar to a particular group. It is relevant to know street names for drugs of abuse so that you recognize a "sweetie" (Preludin, a stimulant/anorexiant) for what it is. In one humorous case, a new medical resident and a patient were overheard in the emergency department. The woman, an inner-city black, was using typical speech patterns and cultural jargon. They were not communicating at all. She finally said, "I think you a foo' [fool]," to which he replied, "Yes, I am through." It was a classic case of miscommunication. She was speaking "fluent jive" and he was speaking "fluent Kansas," to quote the paramedic telling the story!

Uniformed prehospital providers are wise to avoid using jargon in a misdirected attempt to "connect" with the people they meet. You are set apart by both your uniform and your mission, so trying to fit in through the use of jargon can seem contrived. It sometimes works for some EMS providers who know what they are doing. Just be careful not to adopt jargon that is unnatural to your own interpersonal style. If you do, you will be perceived as a phoney. This will make rapport building even more challenging.

Kinds of Questions

There are various ways to phrase questions. Which kind of question to use depends primarily on the prehospital situation at hand. When you need answers fast, you may opt to ask one sort of question. When things are less critical and you have some time, another sort of question may be better. If the patient cannot breathe, you do not want to ask questions that require a lot of words. However, if you need details, a question that encourages the patient to elaborate may be the one to use. If the patient is reluctant to verbalize much, one sort of interview format may work, but the same format is a disaster when the patient is ready to explain a detailed life story.

> The goal is to develop a sense for which kinds of questions will most efficiently draw out the most accurate information.

The goal is to develop a sense for which kinds of questions will most efficiently draw out the most accurate information. To accomplish this task within the time-pressured framework of EMS is a real challenge, and exhilarating when done well. Experiment with various kinds of questions and remain flexible and patient. Different situations require different approaches. Knowing how to use assorted methods of questioning is good.

Questions during patient interviews are either open or closed. They are essentially opposites. An open question allows for a free-form response. It is the best kind of question to use when there is time and when the person being interviewed can be guided from drifting too far from the point. Examples of open questions are:

- "Tell me what has happened here?" ("I climbed the tree to try to rescue my cat, but went too far out on the branch and it broke. I fell from way up there!")
- "What have you had to eat today?" ("I had eggs, bacon, and toast for breakfast, and a Reuben sandwich with chips and a glass of milk at lunchtime.")
- "What's going on?" ("My chest feels like it's in a vice and I can't breathe.")

Closed questions seek to confirm information with a short answer. Possible answers are limited, and are often simply "yes or no," such as:

- "Can you move your feet?" (Yes or no.)
- "Have you eaten today?" (Yes or no.)
- "Did the pain begin at rest or during exertion?"

There are two kinds of questions that are seldom (if ever) helpful: rhetorical and loaded. A rhetorical question is one that requires no answer. For example, when you say to a person with two broken legs, "We have a problem here, don't we?" you are being rhetorical. A loaded question implies an answer simply by the way it is phrased, such as "You've been depressed, haven't you?" It can sound accusatory and can thus cause problems that, phrased more carefully, could be avoided. "Another binge, huh?" is a loaded question. To an alcoholic, this question may unleash negative feelings. There is a cynical, sarcastic, negative feel to rhetorical and loaded questions. Questions phrased positively work better and will be regarded as the more professional approach. Try something like, "How many days have you been drinking?"

One of the greatest challenges of conducting a patient interview is to gather an accurate picture of the event and of the patient's prior medical history. It is remarkable how a story can change! Not infrequently a prehospital provider will come through the emergency department doors with what seems to be a clear story—only to have the patient tell an entirely different story there. In many cases this is unavoidable; perhaps being away from the scene of the emergency has allowed the patient to calm down. Perhaps seeing a whole new set of faces causes the patient to remember things that he forgot to mention.

However, the cause of an inaccurate history is often poor questioning that led to misleading answers. If you are in too much of a hurry to listen or to ask good, appropriate questions, there is a high risk of missing crucial information. Once a person begins to tunnel-vision into the apparent problem, it is rare to stop, backtrack, reconsider the facts, and fill in the missing pieces.

> **If you are in too much of a hurry to listen or to ask good, appropriate questions, there is a high risk of missing crucial information.**

Give the true story every opportunity to be told. Ask questions in a way that lets the patient respond with the honest answer. Be ready to be led down unexpected pathways. Confirm information with follow-up clarifying questions.

A common trap is to phrase questions in a way that suggests an answer. This is known as a leading question. Patients are usually eager to please their rescuers, and if you say, "Does the chest pain move into your left shoulder?" many will say, "Yes," whether it really does or not. Leave questions as open as possible; when time demands a more rapid interview, choose your words carefully. For example, ask, "Do you feel the discomfort anywhere else?" rather than assuming the patient perceives the pain as "moving" around.

Sometimes the answers you get are the result of timing. EMS personnel are brazen about asking a lot of very personal questions. We need to know intimate details about people quickly. It may seem odd that we can ask strangers about their bowel habits and sexual activity when we would never consider asking our own friends these things! In order to ask personal questions effectively, be aware of your sense of timing. This is largely an intuitive process, but developing it can yield a higher percentage of honest answers.

Poorly timed questions often do not achieve their purposes. If you encounter a woman who, in your view, is overreacting to what appears to be a minor assault, you should be curious. Was she sexually assaulted? But if you ask her this before you have enough rapport, she may not be willing to admit it. You will miss out on vital and pertinent information—all because of poor timing.

The information gathered from people in the prehospital world is often unique. If nothing else, EMS certainly is a good place to witness the variety of the human element! Sometimes you have to work very hard to get the answers to questions; in critical situations, this can be especially frustrating. A willingness to be patient and flexible—once again—is important. The capability to rephrase a question or information several different ways is an admirable skill. When a significant interpersonal problem arises, sometimes it is because you have not built a foundation for effective communication. The result may be that people do not answer you at all, the answers are only partial, or they are completely irrelevant, inaccurate, or ververbalized.[5]

> The capability to rephrase a question or information several different ways is an admirable skill.

It is impossible to overstress the importance of perpetually improving your patient and bystander interview. If you cannot find out exactly what the problem is, you cannot treat it appropriately. The interview—in conjunction with a good physical exam—provides you with essential information for providing your medical care.

Gender-Based Differences in Communication

There are certain general differences in male and female patterns of interacting that are interesting.[6] It has been found that the communication patterns of a three-year-old person more closely parallel those of someone aged 24 of the same gender than they do of another child the same age who is the opposite gender.

The general male pattern is to seek status and independence, to be separate and different from others. People with male patterns tend to relate to the hierarchical pyramid, where the goal is to be "king of the mountain." Conflict helps establish hierarchy. They engage more commonly in speech patterns dubbed "report-talk," in which messages are intended for negotiation or to maintain status. (Note: many women have male-pattern styles!)

The general female pattern is to seek connection and intimacy, to minimize differences and appear equal to others. The intention is to build

---

[5] Tubbs and Moss, *Human Communication*, 189.

[6] The information in this section comes from the book, *You Just Don't Understand: Women and Men in Conversation*, by Deborah Tannen, Ph.D. (New York: William Morrow and Company, Inc., 1990). It is intended as awareness-building information that can help EMS providers understand why communication between the sexes can be such a struggle. This is only a brief primer of her outstanding material, so if it interests you, read the whole book!

consensus and create networks. Conflict is viewed as diminishing the chance for connection. People with a female style commonly engage in speech patterns dubbed "rapport-talk," in which messages are intended to promote togetherness. (Note: many men have female-pattern styles!)

When they are in public, men tend to talk more. It's OK to boast. And when they get to the privacy of home, they are "off-stage" where there's no need to impress anyone. They get quiet. When women are in public, they avoid standing out. If anything, they'll be self-deprecating in order to maintain connection with others. Only in private do they feel free to truly express themselves! There are also large gender-based differences that are non-verbal, such as how to engage in eye contact, and where to position yourself for conversation. It's fascinating information which has many implications to effective interpersonal communication in EMS, and off-duty as well.

Problems in Communication

There are certain problems in communication which threaten even the most well-intentioned efforts. Some are self-generated, and others are a function of the prehospital environment. Two rescuer-generated problems in interpersonal communications that are worthy of constant attention are bad moods and lack of energy. Both of these can be detrimental to effective communication with strangers. A willing attitude is essential for success. If your patient senses that you are genuinely interested in helping, half of your communications challenge has been met.

Mood is a big factor in interpersonal communication. Sometimes it seems that you cannot cope with another mediocre chief complaint, or yet another interfacility transfer. Maybe you just handled your first pediatric death and this joker's had foot pain for two weeks. Yet the public does not understand the demands of our work. That "joker" doesn't know, or care, what kind of day you've had. We are human, yes, but we must also try not to let our moods affect the way we handle calls. Shelve the personal problem and take each new call with a clean emotional slate. A steady, levelheaded approach is a characteristic of some of the most successful prehospital workers.

It is also important to monitor your energy levels continuously. EMS is exhausting work, particularly for people who work 24-hour shifts (or more!). It's understandable to feel impatient with a chief complaint of "WADAO" ("weak and dizzy all over") at 3:00 a.m. when you feel the same way! Nonetheless, it's the hallmark of a professional when a person can work past feelings of exhaustion in order to remain capable of communicating effectively. Best yet, eat nourishing foods, rest well on days off, and use other self-care methods discussed in chapter 12.

There are other problems in communication that are avoidable, once you are aware of them. They include:

- Assumptions
- Noise
- Clogged filters
- Hysteria
- Unrealistic expectations

Assumptions

Assumptions are downright hazardous—and people make them all the time. The word "assume" breaks down to show what it really means: If you ASSUME something, it is likely to make an ASS out of U and ME! If you assume a patient is "just drunk" and you do not do a complete physical exam, you may miss an important finding (Fig. 4.6). Believe it or not, one crew once missed a fractured femur that way.

Many people who are shot accidentally assumed that the gun was unloaded. You may think that you have the full story, when in fact, half of it has been left out because you have not given your patient a chance to fully explain. If you assume that Elsie's epigastric pain is another heart attack because she's already had two, make sure that it isn't her preemergent ulcer trying to cope with a breakfast of pizza and hot sauce.

A person who is prone to making assumptions can strive to interrupt this bad habit by using some of the self-awareness techniques mentioned in chapter 2. By noticing when you make assumptions, you can sometimes backtrack to clarify your intentions. One paramedic assumed the patient with severe chest pain would want to go to the hospital. The pale, diaphoretic man with the IV, monitor, and oxygen adamantly refused. Had the paramedic indicated the need for transport earlier than the moment the stretcher was positioned by the man's bed, there may have been a chance to build the case. As it turned out, they reluctantly had to leave him behind, against their wishes and advice—all because of a bad assumption.

Several times a day we would get "smoke scares" from nervous residents that saw barbecue, fog, or whatever. The major problem was pinpointing the smoke without driving all over the district, so a greater than average burden was placed on the dispatcher to get directions, landmarks, etc. My infamous call went something like this:

Dispatcher: 1644. Fire Department Emergency.

Caller: Yes, I see some smoke.

Dispatcher: Yes ma'am, can I have your address?

Caller: 13 Bobolink Rd.

Dispatcher: OK, and you see smoke.

Caller: Yes

Dispatcher: Can you tell me what direction it's coming from?

Caller: What?

Dispatcher: The smoke, what direction is it coming from?

Caller: I don't know.

Dispatcher: Can you see out your front window from the phone?

Caller: Yes.

Dispatcher: OK, looking out the window, which way does the sun rise? In front of you, in back, to the left or right?...

Caller: It rises in front of me.

Dispatcher: OK, that's east. OK, looking in that direction, which direction is the smoke coming from?

Caller: What?

Dispatcher: Looking out the window, which way is the smoke coming from, left, right, or what?

Caller: Well, it's coming from the right.

Dispatcher: OK, that's south. Can you give me a landmark?

Caller: What?

Dispatcher: Well, is the smoke near a PG&E tower or water tank or something?

(Pause.)

Caller: Mister, the smoke is coming out of my closet!

Dispatcher: Oh! We'll be right there!

Figure 4.6

This transcript demonstrates well the problem with making assumptions. (W.H. Lamm, "Dispatching in Emergencies," *Western Fire Journal*, January 1980.)

Noise

This persistent problem comes with the territory in EMS. It is distracting to us and does not help the people who are unaccustomed to crisis cope any better. Eliminating noise is an early consideration for both scene control and effective communications. Ask someone to turn off the TV or radio, to close the ambulance door, or to help you get the patient quickly to a more suitable environment (for example, off the highway and into the ambulance). Unless the patient is trapped, it is nearly always possible to find or create quieter conditions.

Clogged Filters

At a certain point, everyone reaches a limit, when the barrage of stimulation from a situation can no longer be filtered out. The result: an overwhelmed person. It's like an overloaded circuit. The person cannot function effectively until the problem is adjusted and the circuit reset. Seek a less chaotic or overwhelming site to work with these people. Do this either by moving or by stopping the source(s) of stimulation. Bystanders can also be overwhelmed, especially when they are just watching and feel unable to help. If you are interviewing an overwhelmed bystander, it often works to guide the person out of sight of the crisis.

Hysteria

Hysteria is when the emotional outbursts that are a normal part of EMS become uncontrollable. There's no room on an emergency medical scene for it. No one can work effectively. If the patient is the one who is hysterical, delivery of care is delayed until the extreme emotional response is handled. If bystanders are hysterical, they must be removed from the scene to wind down, perhaps with help from spare, savvy EMS providers.

Hysteria is especially common in hyperventilating people. They are convinced they cannot breathe, yet that sensation is caused by the excessive respiratory rate. One way to break the vicious cycle is to explain that there is no magic that can fix the problem. Only the patient's own self-control can slow down the respiratory rate. When educated (diplomatically) that you cannot "just fix it!" people regain control surprisingly well.

It helps to realize that hysteria is a form of regression. The nature of crisis implies a loss of control. People out of control want (need) someone else to help them cope, just as a temper tantrum is an extreme way for children to force others to pay attention and help with a difficult time. You must have the tolerance and patience to recognize the message underlying the hysteria, without letting the frustrating delivery of that message affect your professional approach.

There are several primary interpersonal strategies to break through the haze of hysteria. They are eye contact, touching, a combination of firmness and compassion, and a consistent, compassionate tone of voice.

Whether the hysterical people are bystanders or patients, it has to be made clear that you cannot really do anything for the cause of the hysteria—the crisis—until they settle down.

One effective technique to use on hysteria is called "repetitive persistence." There are four components:

1. Use positive phrasing (e.g. "Once you settle down we can take care of your child. . . .")
2. Use the person's name.
3. Use a neutral tone of voice.
4. Repeat the same sentence over and over using the *same* tone of voice. For example, say, "Mrs. Jones, I can help you once you are calmer." Eventually, the immovable object meets the irresistible force and something has to give.

Avoid negative and punitive-sounding messages such as, "Don't scream," or "Just relax!" or, "Acting this way is only hurting your friend." Be sure that your voice is firm but helpful and does not emote disdain or frustration. Eventually, people yield and you can proceed. Although this technique was described for Emergency Medical Dispatchers to use in telephone interrogation, it is applicable to field care as well.[7]

Occasionally, people are completely out of control and it is impossible to restore order in a reasonable amount of time. Police may be needed to clear the scene of such disruptive people. Maintaining a positive working relationship with law enforcement in the community is an obvious benefit for the teamwork needed at such a time.

Unrealistic Expectations

Unrealistic expectations on the parts of both rescuers and the public can interfere with effective communication. On the part of rescuers, unrealistic expectations cause problems such as:

- Thinking your patients know how to behave in an emergency. Remember that most people do not encounter emergencies every day. They called you because they couldn't cope, so do not expect them to.
- When the rescuer tells everyone, "Now everyone just relax!" Emergencies—even "minor" ones—are not relaxing. Many people cannot control themselves when they have an adrenalin rush, and even those who can control themselves usually take awhile to calm down.

---

[7] Jeff J. Clawson and Kate Boyd Dernocoeur, *Principles of Emergency Medical Dispatch* (Englewood Cliffs, NJ: The Brady Company, 1987), 37-40.

Telling people to relax just does not work. Acknowledge their anxiety, yes—but don't ask them to relax.

Unrealistic expectations on the part of patients or bystanders can be a problem as well. It's not uncommon to encounter people who shout in a panic at you, saying, "Stop wasting your time! Hurry up! Just go to the hospital!" The public is still learning that modern prehospital care is beyond the days of "You call, we'll haul." Certain TV shows have given the lay public the idea that emergencies always have a happy ending. While the boost to our morale has been nice, keep in mind that unrealistic expectations may erupt if things do not go "happily."

Summary

Poor interpersonal communication is a major cause of many of the problems that occur between people. Maybe the questions were not thorough enough, were inappropriately phrased, or were poorly timed. Maybe distractions prevented good listening. Maybe the patient was uncooperative. Whatever happened, you obtained incomplete information, and there was a negative impact on your subsequent decisions.

Alternatively, effective communication can be downright exhilarating. When a patient outcome is directly impacted by strategies that you use when communicating, you deserve to notice and feel proud! Effective communication is a huge challenge, and an area where each of us has a life-long learning opportunity. The techniques described in this chapter are intended as a starting point.

Occasionally, the nicer touches of communication must, by necessity, give way to the priorities of rapid emergency medicine. Reassuring the patient's family must be delayed while you concentrate on lifesaving efforts. Sometimes communication between coworkers will get strained in the intensity of a high-powered scene. Despite our best intentions, it is impossible to communicate effectively all the time.

Practice effective communication whenever the opportunity arises (even off duty!). Even if you're not in charge of a scene, you can practice effective communication. "Helpers" are often the ones who interview bystanders or relatives, and who care for those with minor injuries at multi-casualty scenes. A willingness to strive for excellence is all that's necessary. You cannot expect yourself to like everyone you meet. But you do have to be willing to communicate the best you can with everyone—patients, bystanders, and other members of the health care team—you meet in the line of duty. Sometimes your efforts to communicate well will be thwarted. But keep trying. Watch the communicational strengths and weaknesses of others, and decide how you would do it differently or better.

In the end, there is no easy recipe for success. The goal, ultimately, is to build a toolbox filled with ways to reach out, not only to sick and injured bodies, but also to scared and frustrated minds.

Death and Dying

"Death is a horizon, and a horizon is nothing save the limit of our sight."

—Unknown

Chapter Overview

Death and dying are not easy concepts for many people to ponder. The process of dying is shrouded in mystery by society's traditional attitudes of denial and abhorrence. Involvement in EMS does not exempt a person from the difficulties of grappling with this certainty of life. In our helping role, we find that people look to EMS providers for support and guidance at the time of a death. We need to attend to our own feelings about this process so we can provide that help as genuinely as possible.

Although some discussion about death and dying usually occurs in training programs, the constraints of time may result in superficial treatment of the topic. Also, students tend to deal with the issue from an abstract point of view. When you finally encounter real dead or dying people, you may have only fragile protection from some real precipices of emotion. Learning as much as possible about death and dying is like getting a vaccine shot. It will prevent you from having a more difficult experience with it than you would have had otherwise.

EMS providers encounter sudden death the most often, so it is emphasized here. There are special sections on the particularly difficult situations of suicide and sudden infant death syndrome. However, because death research has been focused mostly on anticipated death, parts of this chapter have drawn on that body of work as well.

Grief and mourning are obviously closely related to the topic of death and dying. Suppressing painful feelings is harmful to this vital process. How you handle survivors, particularly the way you talk with them and what you say, can have a large impact on the way they feel grief and how they mourn. This challenging task, done sensitively, can be very rewarding when you know that you have helped.

The reasons that a healthy grief process is so important are included in this chapter. This will enable you to explain grieving to survivors. And it will be important in your own life at some time as well.

Two paramedics once took a psychology class on death and dying at the local university. They were astonished at the reactions of their classmates, who were very reluctant to discuss the topic even though the course was elective. The paramedics rediscovered how difficult it is for lay people to face death and dying issues. At the same time, they realized how familiar death had become to them.

How we, the rescuers, feel about death and dying affects the people we are trying to help. Death affects us whether we like it or not, and whether or not we knew the person. Most people change in the presence of a dead body, because it is an unusual experience (even though it happens about 144,900 times a day, worldwide[1]). They are unsure how they *should* act. Armed with forethought and good information, our response to death can become more natural.

In many households, death as a topic of conversation is still taboo. It is an awkward and distasteful topic to contemplate. It evokes painful feelings, especially in those who have had a loss. No one likes to be reminded of human mortality, especially one's own. But ignoring death won't make it go away! Fortunately, the nature of the taboo is changing. Ever since Elisabeth Kubler-Ross brought death "out of the closet" in the late 1960s (about the same time that modern EMS got off the ground), much has been done to make the topic less fearsome and intimidating. There is an increasing willingness to acknowledge and understand this reality of life.

Of the health care team, EMS providers are the ones who encounter dead people with the tragic vividness of the prehospital setting. It is difficult to see a grossly mutilated body, a suicide by hanging, or a drowned child. Our role requires that we delay our emotions while we

---

[1] *1996 Universal Alamanac*, 356.

do what we can to save lives, attend to other injured people, or help a relative grapple with the shock of sudden death. But eventually, we also need to attend to our own wounded psyches.

First, on a practical level, we need to decide what, exactly, death is. This has been redefined since the era when the absence of a pulse and respirations meant both biological and clinical death. Now, there is a clear separation between clinical death (when heartbeat and respirations stop) and biological death (when brain death ensues, generally believed to be between 4 and 10 minutes). Prehospital resuscitation has played a large role in this redefinition. Now, researchers even question the 4 to 10 minute time frame. Central nervous system tissue may be viable, given certain conditions, for much longer. Other tissues, such as muscle and skin, can survive for up to six hours after total circulatory interruption.[2]

There are strange cases popping up in the literature every day, though, that are keeping people in the health sciences on their toes when it comes to defining death. What about the situations in which a brain-dead woman is kept on a life-support system for weeks or months until her child can be delivered via cesarean section? What about keeping the vital functions going in brain-dead people long enough to salvage transplant organs? What *is* death? Here is one person's attitude: "Death does not occur in a moment. It is a gradual process that continues for some time after instrumentation is unable to measure its presence. In reality it is not that death has occurred in that moment but that life is no longer accessible to instrumentation and gradation."[3]

Traditionally, medical science has viewed death as its nemesis. The purpose of medical science, after all, is to make people well. Death has been the enemy. People spend enormous amounts of money and effort to cure illness. When a person dies, the medical team is left with a sense of failure.

It wasn't easy to open the doors of the death taboo. When renowned death and dying researcher Elisabeth Kubler-Ross began her work in 1968, and was trying to find out who was dying on the wards, other health professionals actually spit at her in the halls of the hospitals because they thought her work was morbid and disgusting. The prevailing "wisdom" at that time was that patients should not know they were dying, that talking about death was inappropriate and detrimental. She persisted, and found out who the terminal patients were. When she talked to them, only

---

[2] Marvin L. Birnbaum, "Brain Resuscitation," *JEMS*, (October 1984), 72–77.
[3] Levine, *Who Dies?*, 269

one of the 200 dying people she contacted refused to talk about the seriousness of their illness.[4] What she found, and what has been reaffirmed continually, is that dying people are curious about what is happening to them and want to discuss their feelings. In addition, the relatives and friends of those who are dying want information as well.

Kubler-Ross proved that the majority of dying patients wanted information about the dying process. Yet it took years for the majority of doctors to favor giving it. Now, health care providers are much more willing to help their patients grapple with their death processes. Now, classes on death and dying are common.

There is a strong element of fear surrounding the topic of death. Three of the strongest fears expressed are the fear of dying, fear of what will happen, and fear of ceasing to be.[5] Other fears commonly expressed include loss of control, pain, being alone, and interruption of goals.

> Awareness of the finality of life can generate a broadened appreciation for both living and dying. Acknowledging that our lives are limited gives value to the time we have.

An alternative attitude that people can develop is to acquire a positive personal philosophy toward death. Awareness of the finality of life can generate a broadened appreciation for both living and dying. Acknowledging that our lives are limited gives value to the time we have. Having a view of death that does not include fear, says Kubler-Ross, lets you live more fully and well. She views this as a vital, inherent part of the growth of life.[6]

Medical Roles

Let's consider the proper medical role for situations where a death has occurred. The obvious priority is to resuscitate if there is any indication for it. But in some cases, there is no question that a death has occurred. Resuscitation is not needed. Your duties should then shift to care of the survivors.

The circumstances surrounding scenes where death has occurred are not always crystal clear, and if wrongfully interpreted can lead to legal and

---

[4] Elisabeth Kubler-Ross, *On Death and Dying* (New York: MacMillan Publishing Co., Inc., 1969), 257.
[5] James B. McCarthy, *Death and Anxiety: The Loss of the Self* (New York: Gardner Press, Inc., 1980), 9.
[6] "The Plowboy Interview: Elisabeth Kubler-Ross on Living, Dying . . . and Beyond," *Plowboy Magazine* (May/June 1983), 17.

professional problems. Two worst-case scenarios demonstrate the extremes:

- A woman was found outdoors, apparently dead. She was left for the police investigators. A few hours later, a police officer noticed that she was breathing, and another hypothermia victim subsequently was saved. Tragically, stories about people found to be alive after being presumed dead are not so rare in the EMS literature. This is obviously something to be guarded against very carefully.

- In the same EMS system, the medical advisor was understandably cautious about subsequent field death pronouncements. Telemetry EKGs on all apparently dead people were required. Several years after the hypothermia case, a paramedic called in a DOA on a person who had been hit by a train. The nurse requested an EKG. The paramedic asked: "When I put on the electrodes, do you have a preference which piece of the body I should use?"

There is no doubt of death in many other cases where patients are neither decapitated nor decomposing. By the rules, a person once had to be in an extreme state like that if field personnel were to be allowed to make a determination of death, but not anymore. And no longer are "heroic measures" always desired. They can be futile and expensive—and expense, these days, has become a real issue. Therefore, EMS systems increasingly allow EMS providers to make field pronouncements. Radio confirmation with a physician is an important legal backup. One example of a humanistic deviation from strict medical protocol happened when a paramedic team encountered a young man who they had known from his frequent emergency department visits. As they walked into the house, they found that he was finally ending his lengthy battle with a debilitating, wasting disease—but he still had a very slow pulse and agonal respirations. What to do? Start CPR? One chest compression would have shattered his fragile ribcage. For what? Everyone understood that he was dying. The decision was to support the family, and let him die. With the consent of the base physician, the paramedics and first responders stood by until the patient was asystolic. The case was unusual, but everyone agreed it was one of the most moving and dignified scenes they had ever witnessed.

The decision to "spare the heroics" should be rare, and done with extreme caution. You do not really know if the family is not just after the life insurance money! To establish death in any but the most blatantly obvious situations is a hazard, not only to the human lives involved, but also to our moral and legal framework. In every situation where there is any question at all, it is far better to face the consequences of your actions than those of your inactions.

Do Not Resuscitate (DNR) Orders

There are times when the decision whether or not to resuscitate is cloudy. Living wills and DNR orders—available for years to physicians—have long been used in controlled settings where the issues could be dispassionately addressed with patients, their families, and medical providers. EMS personnel, however, have frequently been trapped between the patient's wishes and the legal system.

Fortunately, legislation is increasingly providing the clarity that EMS providers have long needed. A legal framework is emerging that will protect EMS providers from the consequences of misguided or unintentional interference with a patient's wishes regarding the right to die. More than half the states now have legislation regarding the "nonhospital Do-Not-Resuscitate" orders needed to address the unique circumstances of the prehospital setting (Fig. 5.1). Montana was among the first to pass such legislation. In that state, a patient who is declared terminally ill by his physician, or who has a valid DNR order, can obtain Comfort One identification. To withhold resuscitation, all the EMS providers need is to see a Comfort One identification form, bracelet, or card plus patient identification. They may also take a direct order not to resuscitate from a physician, in person or by telephone.[7]

STATES ALLOWING NON-HOSPITAL DNR (AS OF DECEMBER 1995)

Alaska	Montana
Arizona	New Mexico
Arkansas	New York
California	Pennsylvania
Colorado	Rhode Island
Connecticut	South Carolina
Florida	Tennessee
Georgia	Texas
Hawaii	Utah
Idaho	Virginia
Illinois	Washington
Kansas	West Virginia
Kentucky	Wyoming
Maryland	

[Source: Choice in Dying, Education Program Department, 200 Varick St., NYC, NY 10014]

Figure 5.1

This list of states allowing non-hospital DNR is growing every year.

---

[7] *EMS Insider*, Carlsbad, California: JEMS Communications, Inc., (May/June 1991), 2. (A good resource for this topic: Choice In Dying, Inc. [formerly Concern for Dying and Society For the Right To Die], at 212-366-5540 in New York.)

"A non-hospital DNR order is a relatively new type of advance directive . . . designed for people whose ill health gives them little chance of benefiting from CPR."[8] Responding EMS personnel are not caught in the on-scene bind caused by living wills or medical powers of attorney, neither of which is recognized in an emergency. A non-hospital DNR must be filled out by a physician according to the rules of each state. Be familiar with the forms!

The time to grapple with vague DNR orders is not during the throes of a medical emergency. With the social emphasis changing from "Resuscitate at all costs!" to something less absolute, EMS providers must be careful to know and understand their local protocols and clinical standards.

Grief and Mourning

Grief (the feelings of distress or sadness over a loss) and mourning (the process of displaying and, ultimately, dissipating grief) are integral to the death and dying topic. Part of the reason that discussing death has been so taboo is that many people are uncomfortable with their feelings about death and their reactions to it.

Just as death becomes more understandable through education, so do the dynamics of grief and mourning. A healthy grief process allows someone to resolve a significant loss and continue a normal life. Grief reactions in the aftermath of sudden, unexpected loss are more pronounced,[9] because grief tends to be more difficult when there has been no chance to say goodbye. Also, grief reactions in parents are predictably more profound than in widows and widowers.[10]

The way people react to the news of a death is influenced culturally. People of some cultures are extroverted about their reactions. They scream, tear their hair, throw things, and let go of self-control. People in other cultures are expected to show no emotion, to maintain self-control, and not to cry. Most people fall somewhere between these extremes.

When people hear that someone they love has died, they experience a short-lived but terribly intense response dubbed the "grief spike." "This is a paralyzing, totally incapacitating surge of grief that is exactly comparable to the incapacitating pain of an acute eye or testicle blow

---

[8] Correspondence from Choice in Dying, Education Program Department, April 1996.

[9] T. Lundin, "Morbidity Following Sudden and Unexpected Bereavement," *British Journal of Psychiatry*, 144 (January 1984), 84–88.

[10] T. Lundin, "Longterm Outcome of Bereavement," *British Journal of Psychiatry*, 145 (October 1984), 424–428.

in that the whole world shrinks down to that acute pain."[11] The grief spike lasts only five to fifteen minutes. It can be blunted (although not prevented) by providing the survivors with intermittent and incremental preparation for bad news through a process called "Acute Grief Preparation" (discussed later in this chapter).

The grief spike is the first of four relatively predictable stages of mourning. The second stage lasts four to six weeks. The survivor will experience intense grief, which is manifested by a feeling of complete emptiness and longing for the dead person.[12] The length and intensity of this period depends on numerous interpersonal factors. Obviously, the closer the relationship (parent, child, spouse, sibling, partner), the greater the sense of loss. Unresolved issues in the relationship may intensify the distress. Conversely, the intensity of the loss might be eased if the dying person is able to reassure the family that, for example, "I have no regrets," and "I'm not afraid to die."

During this second period of the grief process, feelings of anger or guilt may also be prevalent. These particular responses may occur for many reasons, but let's consider two examples:

- **Anger.** Elisabeth Kubler-Ross describes five stages of loss, of which one is anger. When the patient dies while angry, survivors may carry some bitter final memories. Maybe there was an argument, or the dying person lashed out at loved ones, who might then feel resentful or intolerant of being the brunt of that anger. The self-recrimination among the survivors is painful, and they are left to resolve significant emotional upset.

- **Guilt.** In one memorable case, the paramedics were called to a man in cardiac arrest, who they worked on and transported. As they were preparing to leave, the wife, with a guilt-ridden expression, told the paramedic, "We had a fight, and he went upstairs to lie down." In addition to the grief of sudden death, this woman faced the guilt of wondering whether the fight could have precipitated his death, ending their lengthy marriage in a tragic way.

The third stage of mourning comes when the intense second stage fades slowly into a phase dominated by a sense of loneliness. This generally lasts about six months. It finally blends into the fourth and

---

[11] Peter Rosen and Benjamin Honigman, "Life and Death," in *Emergency Medicine: Concepts and Clinical Practice,* ed. Peter Rosen (St. Louis, Mo.: The C.V. Mosby Company, 1983), 18.
[12] Mattie Collins, *Communication in Health Care: The Human Connection in the Life Cycle,* 2nd ed. (St. Louis, Mo.: The C.V. Mosby Company, 1983).

final stage of mourning, which is a period of recovery. The survivor begins, at last, to view the loss more objectively and to rediscover an interest in living.

After the loss of an important relationship, it is *entirely normal* for mourning to take a year or more, even for mentally and emotionally well-adjusted people. When talking with survivors, it can be very helpful to verbalize that it is completely normal for the process of resolving such a big loss to take a year or so. Tell them not to expect to feel "just fine" when life resumes its normal patterns soon after the funeral, and not to let others try to impose that frame of mind on them, either.

Pathological Grief

Most disruptive of the ways to mourn is the "pathological grief process." It can interfere with a person's life terribly. Pathological grief is when a person cannot stop grieving and lets it become a way of life. It can also mean grieving to such an extent that it causes physical complaints or disorders. EMS providers who are called for one chief complaint may identify an element of grief that is causing or worsening the original complaint. Something may cue you during history gathering to inquire whether your patient is grieving a loss. If this is so, then make a point of mentioning it during hand-off at the hospital. Some bereavement counseling might help.

Talking To Survivors

The way people react to the news that a death has occurred is unpredictable. Sometimes, the responses are unnerving! The EMS mission is to save lives. When a life is lost, though, we have to break the news and help survivors through those first difficult minutes.

Some people believe it is not the role of the EMS provider to break the news of a death with the on-scene family. This viewpoint is unrealistic. What are we to do when, for example, we emerge from a bedroom where someone has died during the night? We were called because something was obviously wrong. We arrive, carry lots of equipment into the room and emerge, bags in hand, a few minutes later. Our inaction reveals us. The image of death, no matter how peaceful, has had an impact. Our expressions reveal us. And there, in the sitting room, is the family. Or, worse yet, a single, elderly person is anxiously awaiting news. Perhaps this survivor has known the dead person for decades. Are we to walk out the door? Are we to mumble something vague, then leave? No. If ours is indeed a helping profession, the people sitting there are the ones who now need our help. It is helpful to survivors to talk with them.

How to break the news? As always, acknowledge the individuality of each situation. Put all your skills for reading other people to work, assessing quickly how they are likely to react. This is the time for the most sensitive and effective communication. Remember that this person or group is about to receive some very difficult news.

Before you start talking, be sure that you are speaking to the appropriate people. In most cases, this is not difficult. You can ask an open-ended question such as, "Who do we have here? Are you all family?" The spokesperson for the group will usually then say something like, "Yes, I'm his wife, and these are our children." This cues you where to focus your attention.

If the group awaiting news is large, consider the appropriateness of a general announcement. In one situation, the group seemed capable of handling the news, but the ensuing hysteria proved that analysis wrong! Sometimes it works better to identify family leaders, take them aside, tell them the news, and then let them handle the announcement to the rest of the group in their own way.

When preparing to talk with survivors, try to be in a position where your eyes are level with those of the person you are primarily addressing. This might mean sitting on a nearby stool or chair, or squatting. To stand or lean over a person is intimidating in any situation. This is a good technique for other cases, but not here. Face the person directly, use compassionate touch if it is appropriate, and employ eye contact. The eyes can often express more compassion than words. Look from one person to another, if it is a group, but keep the eye contact open.

Never simply walk out the door of the home where a death has occurred, for fear of what to say. There are important things to say to survivors.

Downcast eyes signal to them that they should not reach out to you or to each other, and the result can be that they withdraw into their individual grief. This is not a healthy way to initiate mourning.

Never simply walk out the door of the home where a death has occurred, for fear of what to say. There are important things to say to survivors. Do not be reluctant to use the words "dead" and "died." "We find that euphemisms for death such as 'didn't make it,' 'passed away,' and 'gone home' serve only to confuse people and increase the likelihood of misunderstanding and denial."[13] It is also helpful for survivors to hear that there is nothing *anyone* can do to help the dead person. They may wonder whether something more could have been done at the hospital; assure them this is not the case. Tell them that you are now concerned with their well-being and that you are available in case anyone else needs medical help.

It also helps many people to have a brief explanation of what to expect regarding logistics. Most people do not know what to do with dead bodies. In this respect, it is important to find out what your local rules are so that your information will be accurate. Prehospital workers in many systems cannot stay at the scene of a death indefinitely. Clearly, if your expertise is needed elsewhere, the priority is to go. If you have to leave, though, encourage the family to call back anytime. If the survivor is alone, try to stay until a friend, relative, or representative of the clergy arrives. Many people are comforted by the presence of these people, and it's helpful if you can make the call. Occasionally there is no one to call. Still, make the effort to find someone—maybe a neighbor—to come, or wait until the police arrive. The point is not to leave someone who has just received a death notification utterly alone.

Unfortunately, in EMS systems where only the coroner can pronounce a death, prehospital workers are stuck in an awkward situation. The patient is dead—that is clear—but the EMTs cannot say so. In this case, you may be forced to explain that there is nothing you can do to help the patient and that the coroner has been notified. The family is forced to draw its own conclusions. This is less optimal, but your supportive presence will be appreciated nonetheless.

Talking to Survivors Who Are Also Injured

A different situation exists when your survivor is also a victim, such as from a multiple-injury auto accident or other violent incident. In these cases survivors are often obsessed with knowing the condition of the dead person. At such times, the news of death is probably inappropriate. It's a matter of timing. The survivor has injuries. You may already be challenged with the physical demands of prehospital care. You may be a long way from the hospital. Control of your patient must be the priority. To tell someone in this situation that the other person has died

---

[13] Rosen and Honigman, "Life and Death," 18.

could unravel the last shred of self-control—not to mention your patient's desire to survive. In such instances, it may be more beneficial to side-step the issue. Tell these patients that you are concerned only with them and that news will be provided when it is feasible.

Talking with Children in Death Situations

Scenes that include surviving children can be difficult. How children view death is clearly a developmental process. One of the first to study this, Maria Nagy, found that young children (ages 3 to 5) tend to have a very impermanent concept of death and tend to be most concerned with their feeling of separation, without understanding that it will be permanent. Children from five to nine years old tend to personify death as something like a "bogeyman." They do not develop an adult view of death until they are between nine and 12 years of age.[14] Figure 5.2 shows a more thorough and up-to-date synopsis of how children view death.

In their own grief, adults sometimes leave the child(ren) to grapple with their confusion alone. In one terrible in-hospital situation, four young adults were hysterical with the shock of a sudden loss. They were violently throwing keys, purses, and books, and knocking over chairs in a small "quiet" room. In the midst of the fray was a very confused and frightened 4-year-old with eyes as wide as they would go. In that case, the best approach was to pick up the child, hold him securely, and talk to him quietly while the others vented their emotions. Eventually, they were able to calm down and regain self-control.

When a child confronts death, it is almost invariably in the company of adults who are having to cope with their own sense of loss. You can help by taking special care to talk to children personally. Depending on the age of a child, appropriately express comfort and stability. For many, this means holding the child, or at least letting the child have "safe harbor" in your lap. For others, it may mean respecting their sense of interpersonal space while making eye contact and telling them you care. Explain to children that the adults are very sad, and that it is all right to be frightened or confused by the commotion.

> If you are compassionate and concerned, you can have a positive influence on the survivor's initial reactions . . .

---

[14] Maria Nagy, "The Child's Theories Concerning Death," *Journal of Genetic Psychology,* 73 (1948), 3–27.

DEVELOPMENTAL NEEDS & EXPECTATIONS OF CHILDREN REGARDING DEATH

Infancy	Any separation from the nurturer affects an infant. Distress at suffering a loss is visible, but the infant is usually easily soothed.
Up to 5/6	Death is believed to be a temporary state. Death might be viewed as punishment of the child due to an emerging understanding of "consequences" generally. The child has magical thinking powers to fantasize the return or healing of another. A child might believe he or she could catch the same illness and die. There may be a strong need to talk a lot about illness and death, in an effort to master the concept.
Up to 8/9	Children this age may prefer to hide or disguise their feelings out of concern about "looking babyish." An understanding that death is real is emerging, but they still fight to feel invincible, and may take the view that those who die are too slow, weak, or stupid. There is a strong fantasy life in an effort to make everything the way it was. Denial seems to be the most helpful coping skill.
Up to 11/12	A true understanding of the irreversibility of death begins. May seek information as to the details and specifics of the situation, and may need repeated, explicit explanations. A child's hard-won sense of independence becomes fragile, and when it is threatened, a common response is anger—toward the ill/deceased, the self, or other survivors.
Up to 17/18	The child's preference might be to retreat to the safety of childhood, yet society expects him or her to act as an adult (while struggling with the coping skills of a child). The responsibility of assuming different roles in the family may be incongruent with the awkward and demanding developmental processes faced by teens normally. Feelings may be suppressed in order to "fit in"—leaving the teen feeling isolated and vulnerable.

[Courtesy of Lisa C. Zmich, MSW, CSW, Patient Care Social Worker, Hospice of Grand Rapids, Michigan, personal correspondence, 1996]

Figure 5.2

Uncontrolled scenes can have a lifelong negative impact on the way a child deals with death. If you demonstrate some steadiness and control, you may instead have a positive influence on a child's subsequent attitudes toward death.

How well you help others receive the news of death is pivotal to how they handle their grief. Your personal style has a lot to do with your effectiveness in this situation. If you are compassionate and concerned, you can have a positive influence on the survivors' initial reactions, and start them out with a strong foundation of support at a difficult time. If you are really uncomfortable, though, you can make them feel uncomfortable and ill at ease. One way to combat this is to be honest. Say something like, "This is a situation that is always hard for me, and I understand it is a hard time for you, too, but . . ." This will make them feel less defensive about your reactions. Strive to remain as supportive as possible.

Acute Grief Preparation

Another way to help survivors cope is to prepare them for bad news while working on a life-threatened patient. Whether your patient ultimately dies or not, the family deserves to have some advance warning of the potential for loss.

Acute grief preparation requires talking with survivors at regular intervals—every five or ten minutes, or whenever you can feasibly break away from the technological demands of the call. It entails giving them clues, which are progressively more clear, that there is a chance the patient may die. Sometimes, an extra member of the EMS agency can sit with the family to provide support. However, it is best for someone central to the resuscitation effort to handle the acute grief preparation because he or she will be the best informed about the patient's progress.

In these situations, be aware of the tremendous power of denial. It is astounding that people can watch a full-blown resuscitation without realizing that death is probable. One woman watched as CPR was performed on her husband for two and a half hours on an airplane. One and a half hours into the effort, she asked if he was still talking. There is no reason (or time) to confront the denial head on. Don't say, for example, "you cannot deny what is going on here." Yes, they can! Denial can be a healthy filtering response that humans use during overwhelming situations. As the medical professional, recognize the denial and try to offer reality in bite-size pieces to the people involved. This gives them the opportunity to make their own (hopefully more appropriate) conclusions.

Things you can say might include a progression of statements such as the following:

- "Your husband's heart has stopped. We're trying to get it going again, but in the meantime, we're keeping his blood circulating."
- "You deserve to know that his condition is critical. We're doing everything possible to help him."
- "His heart still is not beating on its own, but we have everything here to try that they would have at the emergency department. It is a critical situation, but we're going to keep trying."

- "I know this is very hard for you. Hang in there, and we'll keep you informed of any progress. So far, there's been no change. His heart is not beating on its own. We're still working at it."

By interjecting "progress reports" at regular intervals, you give the family the chance to prepare for bad news. The result of grief preparation is that when the news *does* arrive, survivors have had thirty or forty minutes of clues that can soften the blow. At least you can feel good about helping the family begin its grieving in a stronger way.

When It's Someone You Know

A difficult blending of roles occurs when, as a prehospital worker, you respond to a call and discover that the patient is someone you know. It is especially jolting when that person has died. This is a relatively common experience for EMS workers in communities where most people in the area know one another.

When you are called to a familiar address, do not expect people there to behave in familiar ways. Many will. But others may react with astonishing departures from "normal"! Be flexible. Be ready to give the survivors permission to react in whatever way they need.

On scenes involving someone you know, you have a dual role: as a rescuer, and as a family member or friend. How people handle themselves in such situations depends, as always, on the individual and the situation. A sudden death comes without warning, of course; it is less shocking when you knew that the person had been battling a terminal condition.

No matter how the scene unfolds, it is important to keep in touch with your own feelings. Some people feel compelled to deliver hands-on care, so they will know their loved one received the best possible chance. One nurse, for example, went with the ambulance to an auto accident, and ended up doing CPR for forty-five minutes on her own daughter. If the role of rescuer becomes overwhelming, however, you must be able to back off and let someone else handle the call. Maintaining objectivity is the most important principle. Know that your efforts to help are, in fact, helpful.

In the aftermath of the death of someone you know, especially in the first few weeks, you may be asked to be something you are not. That is, others will look to you, the EMS provider, to be a "pillar of strength." They mistakenly believe that you know all about death and dying; you see it all the time. They think it cannot be as hard on you.

They rely on you for strength. You might, therefore, fall into the trap of feeling that you must not express your own grief. You may mistakenly perceive that it kills your image, and is a sign of weakness. Such pressures, inadvertent though they may be, are inappropriate. Disallow them. We are all human. We all need to express our emotions. Let yourself grieve properly.

There is one important logistical note regarding scenes where everyone knows everyone else. Many people in such communities listen to radio scanners. An ambulance run is big news. Consider who might be hearing radio transmissions from the field. Even though everyone knows to whose address you have responded, avoid using names on the air. This will avoid both violating the patient's right to confidentiality, and creating an upsetting way for an eavesdropping loved one to receive bad news.

Sudden Death

Sudden death is common in the prehospital arena. There are approximately 500,000 deaths annually due to coronary disease, a majority of which are sudden deaths. About two-thirds of deaths from heart attack occur before the victim reaches the hospital."[15] That is about 1.5 sudden, out-of-hospital deaths per minute—and those are just heart attack figures. Sudden death has many other causes: suicide, accidental trauma, other cardiovascular collapse, assaults and other aggressions. In fact, trauma—by definition a sudden event—is the leading killer of people under the age of forty.

Sudden death is difficult because it is so terribly abrupt. No one is ready. It often seems a quirk of fate. One minute a person is fine, the next, dead. Someone walking next to a building dies when a section of the stone facade falls. A drunk driver misjudges the intersection. Lightning strikes. Sudden death leaves survivors feeling robbed of the chance to say goodbye.

Two forms of sudden death, suicide and sudden infant death syndrome, pose such discomfort that they will be addressed specifically.

---

[15] American Heart Association, *Guidelines for Cardiopulmonary Resuscitation and Emergency Cardiac Care: Recommendations of the 1992 National Conference*, reprinted from *Journal of the American Medical Association*, 268:16 (October 28, 1992), 2174.

Suicide

Suicide is a particularly difficult form of death for many people to handle, both personally and professionally. The taking of one's own life is abhorrent. Every year, about 32,000 people in the United States kill themselves. It is the fourth leading cause of death among children 10 to 14 years old, and the second leading cause of death for those in late adolescence and early adulthood. For every completed suicide, there are 50–120 attempted suicides among adolescents.[16] Among the general U.S. population, it is the ninth cause of death overall.[17] Suicide rates in all the highest risk groups are growing.

Although two-thirds of suicidal attempts or gestures are made by women, males are successful twice as often. This is because males tend to use more definitive methods, such as guns, hanging, and jumping from height. Successful suicide reaches peak numbers in males after the age of 45, and after the age of 55 in females. "The elderly attempt suicide less often than younger people, but are successful more frequently, accounting for 25 percent of the suicides although the elderly make up only 10 percent of the total population."[18]

People are particularly susceptible to suicide during holidays because many people feel miserable during these supposedly "happy" times. Another springboard for suicide comes with sensational suicides that are given front page newspaper and major broadcast coverage, especially for more than a day. It is not unusual for a rash of similar suicides to happen over the next few days or weeks. It is also increasingly believed that many single-car, high-speed fatalities are suicide, as are other "accidental" deaths. Among victims of domestic violence, one in ten attempts suicide, and of them, half try more than once.[19] The greatest potential for risk of suicide is found in patients who:

- Have developed a specific plan
- Have concurrent alcohol or drug abuse
- Are socially isolated
- Have low levels of hopefulness[20]

---

[16] Kurt J. Isselbacher, et al, *Harrison's Principles of Internal Medicine*, 13th ed. (New York: McGraw-Hill, 1994), 2405.

[17] H.L.P. Resnick, "Suicide," in *Comprehensive Textbook of Psychiatry/III*, 3rd ed., ed. H.I. Kaplan, A.M. Freedman, and B.J. Sadock (Baltimore: Williams and Wilkins, 1980), 2085.

[18] Resnick, "Suicide."

[19] Robert B. Taylor ed., *Fundamentals of Family Medicine* (New York: Springer, 1996), 130.

[20] Isselbacher, 2405.

There are many persistent myths about suicide. It is untrue, for instance, that suicidal tendencies are inherited and that a person who talks about doing it will not really do it. All persons who make suicidal gestures of any kind must be taken seriously. These people need intervention.

In general, the more concrete plans and methods a person has, the greater the danger that a suicide will occur. When patients say "Yes" when you ask, "Are you thinking of suicide?" ask how they intend to do it. It is a myth that referring to the possibility of suicide plants the idea. If they name a specific method, such as "My father has a gun, I'll use that," or "I've been saving my pills," the suicide potential is greater than in someone whose methods remain vague. A suicidal person who does a sudden emotional and behavioral turnabout and appears to be miraculously "well" is at very high risk. Often, this means that the person has decided to go ahead and commit suicide. Making the decision removes a lot of the conflict, thus the suddenly peaceful demeanor.

A difficult situation for EMS providers arises when the patient did not call you, but your agency has somehow learned of the patient's suicidal intentions. You have been dispatched to a person who does not know you are coming and who probably is not interested in seeing you. This scenario often occurs because the patient calls a friend or therapist at the last moment. The patient's friend calls 9-1-1, and there you are, with a hostile patient.

Your job is to convince a person who has chosen to die to get crisis intervention, now that official sources are aware of the problem. In some states, attempting suicide is against the law and the legal basis for transporting people against their wishes is clear. In other states, there is no law against suicide. Fortunately, there is usually recourse to the "mental health hold." If you can have a mental health hold placed, you can meet your goal of transporting the patient to a medical facility.

When a suicide results in nonresuscitatable death, the role of the EMS provider must change. First, preserve the scene for police investigation, if appropriate. Second, since there is no medical intervention to be done, turn your attention to the survivors. There is little difference between talking with survivors of a suicide and talking with survivors of other kinds of out-of-hospital death, except that suicide is particularly shocking and upsetting. Family reactions can be even more difficult than usual to predict. One family that had appeared to be in control went absolutely berserk at the news that the patient was dead. In another case, when a young man killed himself with carbon monoxide, the scene was gruesomely revealed to his mother when she came home and pushed the automatic garage door opener. Her reaction upon viewing her son after the resuscitation effort had ended was to say simply, and in a forgiving manner: "I'm so sorry you felt you had to do this." Then there were the elderly parents of a man who hung himself; the paramedic took them into a private room, away from the large crowd of friends and neighbors. Told that their son was dead, they sat very still, weeping for a minute, and then the mother sighed and said, "Yes, well, our other son did the same thing five months ago."

Sudden Infant Death Syndrome

SIDS is another tragic form of death. It is the leading cause of death for post-neonatal infants. The incidence of SIDS is 2 to 3 per 1,000 live births, peaking at age 2–3 months.[21] Almost all SIDS situations occur before six months of age. The first health professionals to help are almost always those in the prehospital emergency response, since SIDS nearly always happens unexpectedly, at home, to an otherwise healthy infant.

SIDS is *not* a condition that can be definitively identified in the prehospital setting. SIDS is a diagnosis of exclusion, after investigators consider (among others) airway obstruction, unrecognized congenital causes, and child abuse. Be careful not to assume the cause of death; leave that for the medical examiners.

SIDS poses a strain in three ways: It is emotionally difficult; the challenges of advanced life support on infants are daunting; and parents and bystanders are typically extremely distraught, often hysterical. The situation is undoubtedly one of the least favorite among prehospital workers. Most EMS services transport the child, no matter how it died. Transport reassures everyone that everything possible was done to save the child, and gets the family into the controlled environment of the hospital where there is access to appropriate emotional support. According to one SIDS expert, a major complaint among parents (in the aftermath) is that they are left behind. If you have an infant in cardiac arrest, do everything possible to transport a caregiver in the ambulance cab. Being left behind is devastating to a parent.

In addition to parents, keep in mind that an *entire* family is affected, including siblings.

A baby may have been in the care of day care center, a sibling, or babysitter when the death occurred. These caregivers will also have

---

[21] Taylor, *Fundamentals of Family Medicine*, 99.

intense emotions. Parents may initially respond by blaming the caregiver. Be ready to intervene and assist *everyone* with their initial responses.

The most inevitable response to presumed SIDS is guilt. Parents wonder what they did wrong that their healthy baby died. In fact, they did nothing wrong. Try to plant that idea in the early stages of their grief. In most states there are now SIDS hotlines and counseling and educational programs, which are usually listed under "Sudden Infant Death Syndrome" in the telephone book.[22] It has helped many families to have been able to talk with other people who have had the same experience.

As for your own reactions to this tough situation, you were far too busy during the call to consider your own emotions. For professional reasons, your responses were shelved. But when the call is over, review and decompress the situation. Work through any upset feelings. This is much healthier than denying and suppressing them.

Anticipated Death

Most death and dying research has been focused on people with a long-term terminal illness where there is time to prepare. Although EMS providers encounter anticipated death less often than sudden death, much of the information is pertinent and relevant; the information may also help someday if you have to deal with an anticipated death in your private life.

Elisabeth Kubler-Ross's classic study identified the five predictable stages of dying: denial, anger, bargaining, depression, and finally, acceptance.[23] These stages have since been identified as part of working through any loss. Each, except for acceptance, is self-explanatory. "Acceptance" may range from resignation about the process to a feeling of true resolution with it. Although, in her initial research, it appeared that people followed this progression in order, this is not always the case. "People with any kind of loss go through these stages—all in an hour, day, week, jumping back and forth and sometimes never getting beyond one or two or three—or none!"[24]

How long a person grapples with each stage is completely individual. It depends on personal viewpoints, cultural or familial teachings, and support. Not everyone has enough time to work through every

---

[22] For more information, contact the National Headquarters of Sudden Infant Death Syndrome Alliance, a private, non-profit organization, at 1-800-221-SIDS (7437) in Maryland.

[23] Elisabeth Kubler-Ross, *On Death and Dying*, 38–137.

[24] Carolyn Jaffe, R.N. (20-plus year veteran at Hospice of Metro Denver, Colorado), private correspondence, Summer 1988.

stage before dying. This may lead to the consequences during mourning that have already been discussed.

When a person sustains a sudden, lethal condition, such as a heart attack or critical trauma, and knows that death is likely within a few days, one has to wonder whether an accelerated version of the Kubler-Ross stages occurs. At least there is more of a chance to prepare for death than there is when a person dies in moments or minutes. Survivors have at least a little time to brace for loss and to say goodbye.

There are various ways to interact with a person who is dying. Two researchers, Glaser and Strauss, developed an interesting interpersonal model about the way people respond to an impending death, that depends on the interpersonal dynamics of a group. When a person is dying, the surrounding people share that process in one of four ways: closed, suspicion awareness, mutual pretense, and open. "Closed awareness" of impending death is when no one in the group, including the dying person, acknowledges that death is imminent. "Suspicion awareness" is when everyone suspects that the others might know what's happening, but still no one talks about it. "Mutual pretense awareness" is when everyone knows what is happening, but pretends not to know. None of these levels of awareness provides a forum for sharing thoughts or saying farewell. "Open awareness" is the only interpersonal approach that allows those involved a chance to verbalize their feelings and perceptions of what is occurring.[25]

Why do social groups handle death so differently? There are long-standing societal and cultural perceptions of how one "should" cope. Part of the increased understanding of death and dying has evolved because of the hospice movement, which had its modern beginnings in England in 1967. The philosophy of the hospice has been to help provide a dignified and caring environment for people with life-threatening illnesses. Patients

> By treating death as a natural process which can be made less devastating with education, compassion, and support from experienced helpers, the morbidity of death has been diminished for many people.

are often cared for at home, among familiar sights, smells, and sounds, although inpatient hospice programs are also available. Volunteers and health professionals assist families in caring for the dying person, and also

---

[25] Barney G. Glaser and Anselm L. Strauss, "Awareness Contexts and Social Interaction," *American Sociological Review*, 29 (1964), 669–673.

provide predeath bereavement counseling. Follow-up programs also help the family and friends after the death, and through the mourning process.

The hospice movement has been instrumental in returning the fact of death to a more natural environment than the impersonality of institutions. Even in-patient hospice programs have had a profound effect on the attitudes people have toward this major life event. By treating death as a natural process which can be made less devastating with education, compassion, and support from experienced helpers, the morbidity of death has been diminished for many people.

Behavior Around the Dead

Being in the presence of a dead person is not the easiest task, no matter how experienced you are. But many might agree that, among EMS providers, the perceptions and ability to cope are different from other people because death is more familiar. From this familiarity stems occasional inappropriate behavior among prehospital personnel. It is not intentional, but it is nonetheless irreverent and disrespectful. For example, sometimes while one member of the crew talks to the family, the other member of the crew is outside chatting with the first responders. Maybe someone cracks a joke to break the tension—without realizing their laughter can be seen from inside the house, and misunderstood. In another case, the paramedic was explaining something about the call to curious first responders in a voice that could be heard through the door of the room where the family was gathered, and in terms that seemed disrespectful. Be careful what you say and do on the scene of a death.[26]

It is equally as important to be aware of behavior around dead people in the emergency department. In some hospitals, prehospital workers are allowed to practice certain techniques (such as intubation) on cadavers. Although gallows humor is a known defense against the disquieting thoughts of our own mortality, it is poor form to make disparaging remarks about someone who is dead.

---

[26] See also the section on "Respect and Dignity", chapter 3, page 49.

Summary

Familiarity is the advantage that prehospital workers have over most people when faced with death or dying. But anyone who believes after awhile that "nothing affects me" is deceiving himself. We cannot expect to see death as much as we do, and not be affected by it.

Some deaths affect us more than others. When we encounter a particularly memorable death, whatever the reason or cause, we can—and need to—grieve. Mourning in a healthy, constructive way is important, especially when you knew the patient.

Your concept of death is developed through introspection and soul searching. You do not need to let aggregate losses overwhelm you. Every person has to look for a balance between remaining sensitive and retaining the ability to cope.

Perhaps because of all the unpredictability in life, EMS workers are given one of the greatest lessons any person can receive. That is, we can learn to appreciate the value of each moment that we are alive and well. We know how easily people can be snuffed like the flame on a candle. This can help us appreciate and nurture significant relationships and heighten our genuine appreciation of each new day. It lets us keep in tune with life even as we strive for the goals of tomorrow.

Special Populations, Special Challenges

How far you go in life depends on your being tender with the young, compassionate with the aged,
sympathetic with the striving, and tolerant of the weak and strong.
Because someday in your life you will have been all of these.

—George Washington Carver

Chapter Overview

There is a perception among prehospital workers that certain
kinds of calls pose greater challenges than others. These often occur when dealing with patients from special populations. These
calls tend to be difficult in their own way because of:

- *Emotional reasons.* For many, the most emotion-rousing patient
  is a child. Other emotion-laden calls are often those that involve
  physically or mentally handicapped people.
- *Practical reasons.* These occur when we encounter individuals
  with unusual religious or social backgrounds. Their concerns,
  fears, and methods for coping sometimes oppose or contradict
  the traditional systems we tend to represent. As such, the response to a crisis can be misinterpreted by the prehospital worker,
  resulting in unnecessary confusion for everyone.
- *Logistical reasons.* Some people use ambulance services inappropriately, often for selfish, manipulative reasons. They pretend
  to have problems which in fact they do not have. Others stall their
  departures from the scene to the point of exasperation. Another
  type of logistical challenge can occur sometimes during our
  efforts to assist the elderly.

By increasing your understanding of some of the beliefs and
underlying concerns of these populations, you can reduce frustration and enhance your care-giving capabilities at the same time.

As always, the objective is to maximize all-around field performance. Handling these special challenges smoothly and appropriately is both valid and admirable.

Each emergency call has unique challenges. But some are especially challenging: you can sense these kinds of calls even as you arrive. They have certain attributes that complicate the goals of basic prehospital care. Such calls demand special sensitivity to the diversity among people. By making the extra effort with people who present special challenges, you make the situation easier for both yourself and the patient. This benefits everyone.

Cultural Differences

The melting pot of America has attracted a diverse and (at times) seemingly incompatible array of cultures. The media deluge us with reports of hate crimes and other clashes between groups. However, many people actually have very little cross-cultural interaction in their lives. They live, often by choice, within narrow cultural, religious, and socioeconomic bands. Prehospital care transcends every boundary. We have a rare opportunity to meet people from all backgrounds and social conditions, on their own turf, and in many different circumstances (Fig. 6.1). Prehospital workers in even the most homogeneous communities have a unique chance to witness the differences between people. The potential to develop our capability for human understanding is tremendous.

Since 1820, more than 50 million people have come to America from all over the world.[1] Those in the more recent immigrant waves are often regarded in much the same way as is the new guy at the ambulance company: The arrival is a threat ("Is he going to interfere with my status?"). This person has no seniority. ("Hey, this new kid on the block has a few things to prove!")

The social position of new immigrants is the most tenuous. When these people encounter the additional crisis of a medical emergency, you can be a source of either kindness and understanding—or terror and confusion. The choice is yours.

---

[1] Hana Umlauf Lane, ed., *The World Almanac and Book of Facts, 1983* (New York: Newspaper Enterprise Association, Inc., 1983), 592.

The important thing to remember is not to generalize about people of different backgrounds. Better to acknowledge the variety. People *are* different. It's just that they are not different in the same way, simply by virtue of cultural background or any other demographic factor. So never try to "make" individuals fit your preconceived notions. Someone else may have a response to a crisis that is not what the members of your family would choose. This does *not* mean the response is wrong.

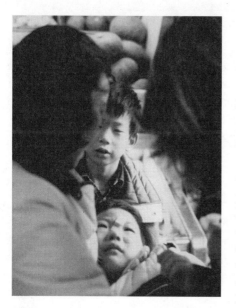

Figure 6.1

Working with people who are culturally different is a tremendous learning opportunity.

Yet the "different is wrong" concept is pervasive. This is a poisonous social attitude. It inhibits tolerance and creates chasms between cultures that sometimes seem impossible to cross. If nothing else, your sense of professionalism should stimulate you not to label another's approach to life as wrong, at least when you are wearing your emergency service uniform.

Folk Medicine

One common source of the "different is wrong" attitude stems from a misunderstanding of folk medicine. For example, Southeast Asians have a folklore medical treatment called "coin rubbing." When a person has a fever or other medical complaint, such as a sore throat, medicinal oils are rubbed into the skin with a coin or other solid object, hard enough to raise a welt. The belief is that this draws out the illness. However, because of a lack of cross-cultural understanding, charges of child abuse have been brought against people because sick children have had welts on their necks, backs, and arms. In fact, the elders were simply treating the child according to their own medical folklore.

If the mother of a Chicano child says that the child has "susto" (fright), or "mal ojo" (evil eye), you have again encountered folk beliefs. Prehospital workers in different places will encounter folk beliefs and practices common to the populations in their area, so it is helpful to try to learn what to expect.

Folk medicine is not necessarily ethnically based. One "street remedy" believed to awaken overdosed narcotics users is to inject them with table salt mixed in water. While there is no medical basis for doing this potentially harmful maneuver, users will try to insist that it is a valid "remedy."

Use of Interpreters

One of the most difficult aspects of handling people from different cultures is the language barrier. The first priority when this comes up is to try to find an on-scene interpreter. This way, it may be possible to get at least the essential information. Recognize that the information may not be accurate, and will almost certainly be incomplete.

There are some predictable problems in using interpreters, even when their English is fluent. Some tips for avoiding problems include:

- Make sure that you phrase your questions very carefully so they are clear to the interpreter. Something is always lost in translation, but when your helper is not fluent and is also confronted with questions of a medical nature, your success rate could nosedive. Effective interpersonal communication is difficult enough when patients speak English; the quicksand of translation via a third party is obvious!

- Interpreters are often children. Many are learning English at school, and children tend to acquire new languages quickly. However, it is unfair to expect a child interpreter to understand very much. A young child might not even know, yet, about things like menstruation and birth processes. Keep the concepts and vocabulary at an appropriate level. Would an 8-year-old understand the phrase "shortness of breath"? Or would "trouble breathing" be a better choice of words? Similarly, consider saying, for example, "feel like throwing up" instead of "nauseated."

- Recognize that much of the information you receive may not be reliable, for a couple of reasons. There may be an unintentional misinterpretation of your question. For example, if you ask, "When is the child due?" and the interpreter says, "Now," you haven't really determined whether today is the due date or whether the mother simply knows that the child is about to arrive, prematurely or not. Or, in other cases the family may be fearful of trouble and will try to answer the way they think you want, instead of telling the truth.

For example, if you see an old fracture, yet the interpreter tells you it just happened, it may be that the family thinks they did something wrong. Consider how you ask questions from their point of view. How you say, "When did this happen?" may sound accusatory and generate unfounded fear. Any time answers sound unreliable, try rephrasing the questions: "What time did this happen?" may garner a more appropriate answer.

- Account for potential cultural differences of perception. If you inquire about pain, but your patient is particularly stoical, you may never know that he has a sensation of discomfort ("like an elephant on my chest") unless you are careful in phrasing your questions.
- Ask one question at a time. Time and again, poor medical histories have been gathered (and not always with the excuse of a language barrier) because the interviewer was rushed and unclear. If you ask the interpreter to ask, "Does the discomfort go anywhere and has it ever happened before?" the "Yes" answer could mean one, the other, or both—but you can't be sure which until you ask again. Instead of finishing faster, you will actually have a net loss of time.
- Address both the interpreter and the patient. It is easy to miss including all concerned parties. Even though you're not speaking directly with the patient, the conversation is about him or her. The patient is still very interested in the proceedings! The goal is to find out answers to your questions and to generate a care plan based on those answers. Use nonverbal encouragement, such as head nodding and gentle eye contact to draw both people into the "conspiracy of success." The more everyone concerned accepts these goals, the more likely you are to succeed.
- Recognize the emotional component of the situation. All the "emergency emotions"—fear, anxiety, embarrassment, and more—are as prevalent as ever. In addition, many non-English-speaking people are wary of American authority—and, whether or not you like it, your uniform may represent a threatening authority. One way to minimize strong emotions is to use caring facial expressions and reassuring body language.
- Above all, have patience. Even in cases where you want to dive into doing things, don't rush. If you do, you will lose efficiency because you may intimidate or rattle your interpreter, who must remain calm to do a good job. Providing lifesaving care is an obvious priority, but otherwise, put yourself in the interpreter's shoes; if you had a rudimentary knowledge of another language, how well

would you do when the pressure was on? Don't forget that your interpreter is probably not used to emergencies, and is probably quite anxious.

Identity

People from all over the world live in America. Even though they may be second or third generation or more, cultural uniqueness persists. The difficulty of spoken languages aside, there are differences in the styles and approaches that people have toward life. While you should note ethnic background to develop a spectrum of approaches to patients, it is important to avoid stereotyping patients. For example, within the wave of Southeast Asian immigrants, there have been people from different countries, such as Laos, Cambodia, Vietnam, China, and also different tribes, such as the Hmong mountain tribe. Be careful not to misidentify people. Either use a broad regional term (such as "Southeast Asian") or ask patients specifically where they came from. Even those who speak almost no English know what you mean when you say in a questioning tone of voice, "Where are you from? Laos? Vietnam?" The sense of identity people carry from their homelands may be one of their only possessions. Don't take that away from them too.

Learning to understand and interact with a variety of people is one of the most enjoyable aspects of prehospital care. Some are vibrant and easily excitable; others are languid or sluggish. Some are stoical; others easily become hysterical. Some cooperate easily; others do not.

Religious Differences

A person's religious convictions do not generally interrupt our efforts to provide emergency medical care. Although many people we help may be praying to their various gods while we work, they can separate their beliefs and prayers from the medical tasks at hand. At most, you may have to work around someone touching your patient's hand or foot while they pray, or you may have to delay departure to give a priest a chance to give last rites.

Occasionally, however, religion interferes with prehospital efforts. Certain religions dictate the extent to which medical care can be given. Although people practicing these religions tend not to call for emergency help, confusion may arise when someone has a medical problem in public and well-meaning bystanders do not know the person's religious convictions. In this section, the religious tenets of Christian Scientists and Jehovah's Witnesses are explained so that you can have a basic understanding of their beliefs.

Jehovah's Witnesses

The conflict Jehovah's Witnesses have with medical care has to do with receiving blood or blood components. The basis for this aspect of the faith stems from the Biblical passage Leviticus 17:10, which says: "Whatsoever man . . . eateth any manner of blood; I will . . . cut him off from among his people"; and from Acts 15:20: "Abstain from . . . things strangled, and from blood." Thus Jehovah's Witnesses cannot receive blood through the mouth, nose, or intravenously.

Jehovah's Witnesses can have both colloids and crystalloids for volume replacement. According to Milton Henschel, a spokesman for the Watch Tower Bible and Tract Society (the governing body for Jehovah's Witnesses), a Witness would rather risk "temporary death rather than accept a blood transfusion and incur God's disapproval."[2] "Temporary death" refers to the Witness belief in resurrection for those who obey the laws of God.

Generally, Jehovah's Witnesses can and do seek medical care other than receiving blood or its components. Even surgery is possible, including organ transplants, since the Bible does not specifically disallow them. But no blood can be used for transfusion, not even a Jehovah's Witness' own predeposited blood. Once removed from a body, blood cannot be used, regardless of its original source. One study done of 542 surgeries on Jehovah's Witnesses (362 requiring cardiopulmonary bypass) showed that only 15 died of blood loss or anemia. The conclusion was that these patients enjoy an acceptably low risk of death.[3]

Christian Scientists

The views of Christian Scientists are more complex, and prehospital efforts are definitely affected by their religious tenets. Christian Scientists believe that certain things are real and that certain other things are not real, even if they seem apparent. Health, as part of spiritual reality, is real and is therefore eternal. "Disease and illness are aspects of false-

---

[2] Milton G. Henschel, "Who Are Jehovah's Witnesses?" in *Religions in America*, ed. Leo Rosten (New York: Simon and Schuster, 1963), 101.
[3] David Ott and Denton Cooley, "Cardiovascular Surgery in Jehovah's Witnesses," *JAMA*, 238 (September 19, 1977), 1256–1258.

hood—delusions of the human mind which can be destroyed by the prayer of spiritual understanding."[4] Therefore, the power of prayer is what lifts a Christian Scientist to the reality of health from the mortal illusion of disease. "When ill, the Scientist treats himself by dwelling upon the thought that illness has no divine source or origin, that God does not create nor include it, and that it is therefore spiritually powerless and factually unreal."[5]

Christian Scientists also employ the prayer skills of people called "practitioners." These are people approved by the Mother Church in Boston who can pray for the benefit of others, whether or not they are geographically nearby. Interestingly, Christian Scientists do use medical doctors for childbirth; "the Christian Scientist does not presume to do what he is neither trained nor licensed to do."[6] Some also seek help from the medical establishment for treatment of fractures.

Even this simplified explanation of the beliefs of Christian Scientists demonstrates how medical intervention by EMS providers can clash with the beliefs of Christian Scientists. It is not easy to be prevented from providing what we consider to be lifesaving care for people who reject it due to religious convictions. However, there are times to respect the beliefs of others despite the conviction that our skills are needed. The Christian Scientist view of death is that it is not final. In fact, in speaking of death to a Christian Scientist, it is valid and proper to use the term "passed on," since death (like illness) is a mortal illusion. The individual continues to live, on one side of the grave or another, until such time that death occurs in the spiritual sense.

Children

It's not an easy time to be a child. Pediatric trauma is at an all-time high in the U.S., with 16 million emergency department visits in 1994 resulting in 600,000 hospitalizations and 22,000 deaths (more than all medical cases combined). Most of these (10,010) were motor vehicle related, but 5,030 were homicides and 2,580 were suicides. Drowning accounted for 1,900 pediatric deaths, and 1,600 were due to fires or burns.[7] In addition, chil-

---

[4] Leo Rosten, ed. *Religions in America* (New York: Simon and Schuster, 1963), 40.
[5] Richard Thomas Barton, *Religious Doctrine and Medical Practice* (Springfield, Ill.: Charles C Thomas, Publishers, 1958), 83.
[6] Rosten, *Religions in America,* 44.
[7] Michael Stoiko, MD, DeVos Children's Hospital, Grand Rapids, Michigan, lecture on "Pediatric Trauma in the 90's, 1995.

dren are increasingly exposed to illicit and recreational drugs, AIDS, date rape, child abuse, and other violence. Even young children are increasingly prone to violence. One nurse shared the story of two kindergartners who were fighting over a doll. One went home and got a butcher knife, returned to her friend's house and stabbed her. And EMS personnel are often the first to contact a child in a medical emergency.

Working with children is often viewed as the most challenging job in emergency medical care. The emotional toll alone is tremendous.

Working with children is often viewed as the most challenging job in emergency medical care. The emotional toll alone is tremendous. Most people feel extra-concerned when they discover that a call involves a child. Being the one who others look to, to have the answers in an emergency is pressure-filled. Children aren't "supposed" to be hurt or terribly sick. It feels unfair. People younger than us aren't "supposed" to have health problems. Working with children is indeed a special challenge.

One of the major causes of anxiety when working with children is their size. It is common to witness the "China doll syndrome"[8] among helpers who have handled few infants or children (Fig. 6.2). They are miniature people, yes, but children are not china dolls! They do not break as easily as it seems they should. There was one 3-month-old who survived a fall from a third-story window to a porch, then off the porch to

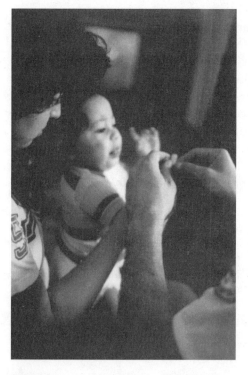

Figure 6.2

Children can be delightful—or very difficult—to work with. The more genuinely comfortable you feel with children, the more they will instinctively trust you.

---

[8] Term coined by Jim Dernocoeur, Paramedic, PA-C.

the ground without injury. So do not be too uneasy about holding children, of any age. Support infants' heads to prevent them from flopping back, but otherwise there is no "correct" way to hold children, just as there is no single way of doing anything else in EMS. When it is appropriate and feasible, let a child stay in the familiar arms of a known caregiver, such as a parent. If you need to use the stretcher, it can help to keep a familiar face and voice within the child's view (presuming your helper is calm enough to be an asset!).

A major concern, of course, is that we know children can mask life-threatening problems for a long time; a 20-month-old child who had been run over in the driveway looked and seemed just fine for the first hour. In fact, the child had massive internal injuries and a fractured femur. Once her physiological condition reached a certain point, her vital signs nosedived and caught a number of people in the emergency department by surprise.

Lack of experience is a source of much rescuer anxiety when they handle children. Many people have had little (if any) previous experience with infants, toddlers, preschoolers, or even elementary-school-aged children. Conversely, experience with children is also a source of much rescuer anxiety. Once you have your own children, being part of the illness, disfigurement, or death of any child becomes tremendously painful. Encountering a child who is close in age to their own has rendered many otherwise competent prehospital workers useless.

Each stage of growth has its quirks. It can be intimidating not to know how to most effectively approach a particular child. A child's view of medicine may be negative, if that child relates medicine to receiving shots. Children do not necessarily differentiate our medical intervention from the kind they get at the doctor's office. They are often overwhelmed by the fanfare of an emergency response. Remember, their caregivers sensed a loss of control when they called for help. Children usually pick up on those strong, panicky responses. Add to this our classical self-image as helpers. It does not feel good to be perceived as the bad guy, which is exactly the way children sometimes view us.

> **Taking the time to be with children under normal circumstances is one good way to bolster your self-confidence for the times you encounter a child in crisis.**

The important thing to learn is to dissipate your own tension. It's like working with animals. They k*now* when a human does not like them or feels afraid! Therefore, one of the best things you can do is learn to feel more comfortable around kids. Taking the time to be with children under normal circumstances is one good way to bolster your self-confidence for the times you encounter a child in crisis. Practice being around children of different ages. Find out how they view their world. It also helps to interview adults who work with children. Let them teach you the tricks they have learned.

Physical Exam

A complete physical exam is as necessary to pediatric patients as it is for anyone else. That is not always easy when the focus of your efforts is squirming, struggling, and screaming. Not every child is that way, of course. Many children are extremely cooperative (especially when your communication is effective). The response you will have to efforts to touch the child is somewhat age-dependent. One good tip is not to automatically do the exam from head to toe. Sometimes it's better to start at the toes and go to the nose. Other times, it works best to check everything else before zeroing in on the site that most concerns you. A general breakdown about what children will tolerate at a certain age is:

- *Infant.* Infants usually tolerate just about anything as long as you keep them warm. You can often undress and place them on the stretcher or another soft surface. It helps to start the exam at the feet and do the head last.
- *6 to 18 months.* At some point during this phase (at about 7 to 8 months of age), children may have some separation anxiety. They begin to discriminate their regular caregivers from everyone else. They may not like being isolated on the stretcher, so leave them in a caregiver's arms, when possible. Take the time to play a little. Let the child touch your stethoscope (but not with it in your ears!). Clothing removal is not usually a problem. Do not start the exam at the head.
- *18 to 24 months.* Children of this age may not like being touched or having clothing removed. They may be easily frightened and will often cry easily. Even the parents often have difficulty comforting a child of this age!
- *2 to 4 years old.* It can be particularly helpful, if a child is reluctant, to ask someone familiar to demonstrate tasks to the child. For ex-

ample, have the parent hold or play with your stethoscope for a minute while you talk, so that the child can see it is "okay." Many children are fearful. Good strategies include moving slowly, talking gently, explaining everything, letting them explore, and being honest.

- **4 to 5 years old.** This is a generally delightful age. Children are cooperative, and it's easy to "enlist" their help in undressing and doing the exam. Let them listen to their own hearts with the stethoscope. As long as you are gentle and honest, they respond willingly to your efforts and are curious about what you are doing. The major fear among children this age is mutilation or bodily harm. A child may also feel some responsibility for what has happened, and may be feeling guilty, even if the situation is not his fault.
- **5 to 12 years old.** Children in this age group are old enough to be somewhat familiar with some basic medical procedures. Therefore, start with tasks, such as taking a pulse and blood pressure, that are familiar. Work them into being confident that you will not hurt them. For school-age children, the main fear is loss of control. Ask questions to engage them, and when you answer their questions, be sure not to "talk down" to them. Don't hide the fact that something is wrong. The more matter-of-fact and informative you can be, the better. If a child is a "screamer," keep a steady tone of voice and talk through the screaming. Unfortunately, there may be times you have to proceed with tasks despite a child's fear. If one person can remain calm and talk to the screaming child, sometimes the other can work around the hysteria.[9] These children may appear to be brave, but may really be wishing to be held close and safe.
- **Adolescents.** Teens are very concerned about their bodies, and about loss of independence. It helps to reassure frequently that they are normal in development. You can do a regular head-to-toe exam, although some sources suggest saving the genital region for last. The more matter of fact you can be about everything, the better. One unfortunate 14-year-old was sliding down a shingled roof when a nail went through his pants and up the shaft of his penis along the natural line of the urethra. Obviously it required physical examination, but the paramedic helped the youngster cope with his extreme embarrassment (and pain) with a nonjudgmental and forthright—yet appropriately sympathetic—approach. Anytime you encounter adolescents, use the interaction as a chance to educate them

---

[9] See the section on "repetitive persistence," in chapter 4, p. 88.

in some small way about their bodies, such as where to find a pulse and what a normal rate is, if you have time. Ask for their opinions and try to involve them in decision making when possible.

When working with children, introductions are vital—and use the touchstone of a child's name often. Be careful not to clam up and work silently. Even if your own anxieties and the pressures of the medical requirements of the call are taxing your limits, verbalize! Tell the child everything: what you are looking at ("Now let's look at this arm . . .") and why it's important (". . . so we can be sure it's okay, too."). Explain the equipment. If there is time, let the child see how the equipment works. Above all, explain what you intend to do, even to very young children ("Alexander, I am going to make your leg hurt less by making it so that it can't move in this splint. To get it there, I need to move the leg some. It might hurt some, but after that, it should be a lot better than it is now. Okay?"). Use straightforward language with a calm and gentle tone of voice. Use lots of kind eye contact, and compassionate touch. Keep in mind that even if the child cannot understand you (you think), your tone of voice is reassuring and your words and actions *will* be meaningful to the family and bystanders.

Ask for feedback frequently, wait for an answer, and acknowledge that answer. A child who trusts you will often verbalize his or her fears (such as: "I'm in trouble," "My parents are gonna kill me," "Will I ever walk again?" "Everyone was laughing at me," and so on). You may have a tremendous opportunity to help a child cope with the emotional trauma if you keep open the lines of communication.

Be aware that children, especially younger ones, are very literal. Word choices are important.

Be aware that children, especially younger ones, are very literal. Word choices are important. Don't "take" pulses, blood pressures, or temperatures. "Measure" them. A BP cuff doesn't "squeeze." It "hugs." Medication might seem easier to a child when he expects it to feel "warm" instead of "burning." Think about what you say!

Most of all, children appreciate honesty and the feeling that they can trust you. When something will hurt or will be at all uncomfortable, tell them. If you are fair about the hard parts, you will find greater overall cooperation because the child knows that you won't spring any unexpected, nasty surprises. Being gentle is an obvious corollary. It inspires a lot of self-confidence to discover that, indeed, you can develop a child's trust.

Crying

One thing that children tend to do is cry. Children do not usually cry quietly. They bellow! It makes us feel that we must be doing a bad job when a child starts to cry, even if intellectually we recognize that the child's response is not personal.

Crying is not sign of failure. People (not just children) cry for many reasons, including fear, pain, anxiety, frustration—all of which have everything to do with a crisis. It has nothing to do with whether or not you are doing a good job. When you tell a child that something will hurt, expect tears—but know that the crying would have surely been worse if you had not warned him or if you said a procedure wouldn't hurt at all.

When a child cries, try to prevent anyone, including parents, from saying, "Don't cry!" No one can simply shut off the tears because of an order to do so. In fact, being told to stop crying usually increases the tears, because the child now may think he is being naughty for crying. Acknowledge the reason for the tears—whether it is fear, anxiety, pain, or whatever—and encourage the child to regain control when ready. One good way to say it is: "Go ahead and cry until you do not want to cry any more."

Advanced Procedures

The last major difficulty with working on children is anxiety about doing advanced procedures. It is often harder to start an IV on a child. This evokes an inappropriate "cut-and-run" reflex in us, which then precipitates a rebound anxiety: You worry that the child's care would really have been better if you could have started that IV. In coping with this anxiety, realize that although children are not small adults, they are still human. The skills for aiding a child are the same as those for an adult; what is lacking is the confidence in your ability to deliver those skills. The cut-and-run reflex could also be legally hazardous. Isn't it inequitable that an adult can get extensive prehospital cardiac care when a child may not?

Take time during your training to practice so that you have a high level of confidence. Intubate and start IVs on as many children (or manikins) as you can until you are certain that you can provide for a child's needs. This will greatly reduce your anxieties about working on pediatric cases.

A few tips on how to be more successful when starting IVs on small children may be helpful:

- Recognize that when an IV is indicated for a child, the situation is generally serious. There will be a heightened sense of urgency. Still, move efficiently without rushing. If you'll be starting an intraosseous line, verbalize what the brutal-looking process is for, and why you're doing it, for the sake of on-lookers.

- Make yourself wait a minute or so after applying the constricting band before starting to search for possible IV sites, so you may have better success. It is common to see someone apply the constricting band, and then immediately start searching (usually vainly) for something to poke. Give the veins a chance to fill up. If possible, ask someone to obtain a warm washcloth and put it over the site; this will help raise the vein as well.

- Immobilize a young child's extremity before poking; that way, your efforts won't be thwarted by an ill-timed squirm.

- In a medical situation, consider the external jugular vein. It often stands out better on a small child than arm or leg veins. This idea does not apply to trauma, of course, since the technique involves turning the head.

- Give yourself the best chance of success by using familiar equipment. If you are not adept with butterfly IVs, don't use them. Use a small-gauge needle of the type you are accustomed to using. Most of all, be confident. If you can start IVs on the thready, tortuous veins of an elderly person (which you no doubt can), you can start them on children!

- Since small children have no broad, flat surfaces for anchoring IVs, loop the IV line around the toe or thumb, and then tape it across the sole of the foot or the palm of the hand. If you have started an IV in the scalp, you can use the ear for looping and anchoring the IV line.

- Pediatric IVs are often more positional than IVs in adults. They require close monitoring. If you are confident that the line is good, do not yank it out too quickly if it stops running.

Parents

Understanding children also involves understanding their parents and other caregivers. The difficulty of pediatric calls is compounded by the presence or impending arrival of a parent or caregiver. Most are dealing with a peak degree of anxiety and other emotions. With effective communication strategies, you can often defuse their reactions. This has an obvious impact on scene control. In fact, one child abuse and neglect researcher has recommended worrying only when parents are *not* a little overwhelmed by their child's emergency.[10]

The difficulty of pediatric calls is compounded by the presence or impending arrival of a parent or caregiver.

Focusing specifically on pediatric emergency care has been a relatively recent innovation in EMS. Many training programs now emphasize the special nature of pediatric care. Research on prevention and improved treatment has been implemented. Resources are increasingly available. Caring for children is special in many ways, and the EMS provider is wise to be well educated about this important topic.[11]

Gangs

One special population which has swept across America in recent years are youth gangs. It's a burgeoning problem throughout society, although not a new one. The members of the Boston Tea Party in 1773 were, by definition, a gang. In the context intended in this section, a gang is a group of people who come together with the purpose of committing illegal acts or to do harm of some sort.

The scope of the problem is huge. In Los Angeles, by 1995, there were 950 gang groups with approximately 100,000 members. Chicago has more than 135 known gangs. The trend trickles into mid-size and smaller cities, too. And the degree of violence by gangs is reaching terrible proportions, much of it random. Drive-by shootings and initiation killings happen more frequently than anyone could wish—and EMS personnel are often the first to arrive.

Gang members are mostly between the ages of 11 and 19. Through the use of turf (an area of control), "colors" (common identifiers, such as apparel), shared traits, and a hierarchy of status, gangs lure youngsters in through intimidation or the appearance of being exciting and

---

[10] Kate Dernocoeur, "Maltreatment of Children, Part 2: Understanding The Problem," *JEMS*, 8 (1983), 44.

[11] For more information, contact the National EMSC Resource Alliance at 310-328-0720 (California). (EMSC stands for "EMS for Children.") This non-profit group has compiled an EMSC catalogue filled with a variety of pediatric products and resources.

glamorous. It's a place where a person can belong, be noticed and accepted, and have a sense of clear social structure—feelings which are absent in the family situations of many of today's youths. The gang often becomes the member's surrogate family. Gang life can be very rewarding emotionally, physically, and financially. Members tend to be extremely "street-smart" and proud of their gang affiliation.

Weapons are a big part of gang life. Gang experts are fond of saying that these are kid-size mentalities trying to take on adult-size problems with adult-size tools. Power is regarded as strength, and firearm power is common. Weapons tend to be carried by those perceived as least threatening—the youngest members and the females (who are called "mules" when carrying the male's weapons for him).

Drug-running is a common gang activity. It is very lucrative, especially in a world where a child may come from a low socioeconomic niche or from a minority group where hopes for a promising future may be limited. The EMS provider may have to contend with drug-related problems as well.

There are three basic sorts of gangs. First are organized corporate gangs, such as Mafia-type gangs. Membership is based on your worth to the organization. Second are territorial-type gangs, in which a gang claims a specific turf. (This turf may be geographic, or it may be in relation to drugs, prostitution, or other illegal activities.) Third are scavenger groups, which tend to be the source of the more petty, senseless, and spontaneous crimes. Members in the third type of gang have little in common besides impulsive behavior and the need to belong.[12] They are typically outcasts from other gangs, and control minor turf that no one else wants. This is the sort of gang that engages in "wilding" (random acts of senseless violence).[13]

There is a target-shaped power structure in gangs. Around the edge are the fringe members, often referred to as "wannabes" or "pawns." These are usually younger children, willing to do practically anything to prove themselves to other members of the gang. They may be used in the most visible roles, such as lookouts, because they are considered expendable. Although frequently hassled or arrested by law enforcement officers, "wannabes" are usually young enough to avoid conviction.

---

[12] David Maatman, "Gangs, Violence and Kids" presentation, *Stayin' Alive* seminar, Grand Rapids, Michigan, March 1996.
[13] Denis Meade, personal correspondence, April 1996.

The next ring of the target consists of "associates." These members are committed to the gang. These people may have lengthy criminal records. Associates are arguably the most dangerous of gang members, especially to EMS providers, because they will do whatever is necessary to save face with their colleagues. They are smart, and they will go to great lengths to seek revenge if they feel it is warranted.

At the center of the power structure are "hard core" members. These are the select members of the gang. To be accepted to this level, a member may be required to have done a felony to prove total loyalty. This group has made the gang its full-time job.

Gang names and identities shift and develop off-shoot branches. There are abundant signals, such as clothing, hand gestures, graffiti, and more, that provide relevant information to the educated observer. EMS providers should know which gangs are operative locally, and how to identify them. There are complex rules which the EMS provider can inadvertently break. Being constantly aware of where you are and of the people at the margins of every incident is important. Don't think gang-related crime and violence cannot happen in your community. You would be surprised!

General gang-related do's and don'ts:[14]

DO:
- ✔ Be aware of your surroundings at all times.
- ✔ Know whose area (turf) you are in.
- ✔ Demonstrate respect (without compromising your position).
- ✔ Use gang leaders to manage crowds, when appropriate.
- ✔ Conduct a thorough weapons search. Be careful of mini-booby traps such as fish hooks in seams or razor blades in the belt line.
- ✔ Explain medical procedures to patients (verbalize what and why).
- ✔ Handle personal articles with extreme respect. They are considered an extension of the individual. For example, don't toss a gang member's coat casually to the squad bench.
- ✔ Know when to leave!
- ✔ Use extreme caution when in the presence of gang members anywhere, anytime—even at convenience stores between calls.

DON'T:
- ✔ Approach a scene where multiple gangs are present (without appropriate back-up and cover).

---

[14] Denis M. Meade, "When Colors Kill," *Emergency Medical Services* 21 (January 1992), 20–26, and also by personal correspondence, April 1996.

✔ Assume your presence is "welcome."

✔ Separate the patient from other gang members until you are ready to leave. Be aware that female gang members who stay close may be "mules," who are carrying the male member's weapon(s), and may be under orders to stay near their men.

✔ Treat a suspected gang member in the open. Get in the emergency vehicle and close the doors.

✔ Cut "colors" (gang clothing), especially not in public. This is a sign of disrespect, and you could be marked for retaliation.

✔ Treat a gang member childishly, even if he is still a young child. Treat each gang member with a respectful interpersonal style.

✔ Stay any longer than necessary.

✔ Ignore the crowd or focus only on the patient.

✔ Provoke a gang member. He or she *will* remember you.

Elderly People

Like children, elderly people often pose a special challenge for prehospital workers. One reason may be because many of us have had relatively little personal experience with people in this age group. Also, aging tends to be viewed with trepidation. Yet the numbers of people in the United States aged 85 and up will only increase in the coming years. As of 1994, there were 18,712,000 persons in the United States who were age 65–74 (6.5% of the population), 10,925,000 aged 75–84 (3.3 percent), and 3,522,000 aged 85 or older (0.8 percent).[15] More than ten percent of the United States population compose this special group, and they are major consumers of prehospital health care services (Fig. 6.3).

Elderly people have survived decades on this earth. This fact alone warrants sincere respect. Yet some prehospital workers view old people with disdain. Perhaps that disdain stems from yielding to the temptation to ridicule someone whose mind is no longer acute enough to understand what you are doing. This attitude has overcome more than one person "stuck" with another unwanted interfacility transfer, and is inexcusable. Nursing home transfers are part of the job in EMS. If you think you would rather be out handling "real" calls, consider the idea that a true prehospital professional recognizes that "real" EMS includes providing compassionate, reliable service to everyone, including people in nursing homes.

---

[15] U.S. Bureau of the Census, *Statistical Abstract of the United States 1995* (115th edition), Washington D.C., 1995.

Figure 6.3

Elderly patients can be tremendously interesting, if you take the time to chat when possible. Show an interest in them. Ask what they've enjoyed most about their lives. You may be rewarded with a fascinating life story. Or ask, "What's one thing you could recommend that I do in my life that you wish you'd done differently?" You may receive some insightful advice.

Another source of contempt stems from taking care of people who have no control of their bodily functions. It is unpleasant to slide your arms underneath a person, only to find yourself covered with a wet, squishy surprise. This is still no excuse for either overt or covert patient abuse.

Perhaps EMS providers develop a skewed view of elderly people because of the concentration of experiences with those who are somehow debilitated. Maybe it will be reassuring to know that the majority of elderly people function quite independently, and have good lives. Perhaps, with aging research, lives will be lived better, and longer, than we can even imagine.[16] It's important to gain a positive and respectful way of engaging with our elderly population.

Part of understanding the special needs of the elderly is acknowledging more than ever the individuality of people. A long-lived person has had ample opportunity to become very much an individual! Some elderly people are cranky and obstinate; others are cooperative and

---

[16] Michael Fossel, *Reversing Human Aging* (New York: William Morrow and Company, Inc., 1996)

apologetic for troubling you. Elderly people are often extremely set in their ways. The disruption of routine is a difficult adjustment. Simply acknowledging that fact can help patients identify this as the source of much of their anxiety. Try to allow elderly people as many choices and as much control as possible in decision making.

A difficulty commonly encountered with elderly patients is that many simply cannot hear you. Don't make any assumptions about this, though. It's remarkable how often people automatically raise their voices a few decibels in the presence of an older person. Avoid the embarrassment of having to be told to pipe down because they can hear you fine! During introductions, assess whether the patient seems to understand you. If you are unsure simply from the conversation, don't hesitate to inquire whether the patient can hear you. Volume may not be the only factor. Perhaps your voice is too high-pitched or too soft, or maybe there are too many competing noises. Finally, assess your rate of speech. Older people tend to process information more slowly. The anxiety of an emergency almost certainly worsens this tendency. Slow down. Wait for responses longer than normal. Maybe those responses are forthcoming but have not yet made their way across the patient's mind.

It is relatively common to be called for an elderly person who has fallen. Often, these falls result in injuries that do not seem terrible— until you look at things from an elderly person's point of view. With our relative youth and vigor, the prospect of bouncing back from an isolated fracture may seem easy. But it is not that easy for older bodies. Of all elderly emergency department patients who sustain a fall, 20 to 25 percent are dead within twelve months. Each year, one-third of all people above age 65 and half of people above age 85 sustain at least one fall.[17] When injuries are multiple, survivor statistics show that 50 to 75 percent are unable to return to previous levels of independence.[18]

Elderly people face death as their next major transition or "rite of passage" in the life process. Address their fears if you think it is appropriate. If Mrs. Jones appears to have an uncomplicated disease process, but still needs hospitalization, it will greatly reassure her and her family (especially the grandchildren) to hear that you think she will be coming home again.

---

[17] Teresita M. Hogan, M.D., *Geriatric Emergencies: An EMT Teaching Manual* (Turlock, California: Medic Alert Foundation, 1994), 88–89.
[18] Alice "Twink" Gorgen, "Grandma Mildred Fell," *JEMS*, 13 (July 1988), 61.

Caring for Disabled People

There are strong emotions that can arise when encountering people with mental and physical disabilities. Prehospital workers usually enjoy robust physical health, and enough mental capability to complete EMS education programs. Many people seldom encounter physically disabled or mentally-challenged people. It can be disconcerting. (It can also be problematic to know the proper way to refer to people with unusual life challenges in terms considered currently proper. Knowing the right words is difficult, because it changes from time to time and place to place! EMS providers should at least know the difference between disabilities and handicaps. The terms are often used synonymously. However, there is a distinction: "Whereas a 'disability' is a physical, mental, or psychological impairment, a 'handicap' is an environmental barrier to the independence of disabled people."[19])

Again, though, there is no room for ridicule or belittling. The best approach, as always, is patience and understanding. We, who are so quick to act and react by virtue of our job, must slow down and blend with people whose lives tend to go along differently. For example, one patient's sole means of communicating was an alphabet board. He could point to letters and spell out his message, but the process was agonizing. It was tortuous just to watch him move his hand. Yet his condition was not life-threatening. He deserved the chance to express himself.

Do not be surprised if disabled patients are sometimes somewhat defensive. Until you gain rapport, they may be unsure you'll be able to work within the framework of their abilities. In one case, a driver with cerebral palsy was at fault in an auto accident. Near tears, but wanting desperately to maintain her dignity by not crying, she visibly shrank from the paramedics as they approached her vehicle as if to say, "I can handle this situation." The attending paramedic realized that she needed some time to regain her composure. Through using appropriate interpersonal space, calm reassurance and patience, the paramedic soon earned the patient's trust, and an interaction that started poorly had a fresh start, with better success.

If the exact nature of a person's disability is unclear, do not hesitate to ask. "What is the nature of your disability?" is much more effective than "Why is your body like that?" or "What's wrong with you?" Some

---

[19] Marilyn Schwartz, *Guidelines for Bias-Free Writing* (Indianapolis: Indiana University Press, 1995). Although written for writers, this source could help the EMS provider choose appropriate words when caring for special populations.

patients will have a disease process or disability that you do not understand; if the mechanics of the call allow it, inquire about it. Explain that, as an emergency responder, your specialty is not chronic disease. Learn something about it. You never know when you will have another similar patient.

Persons living with sensory impairments pose a surmountable logistical challenge. There are various approaches to try. Hearing-impaired patients who cannot read lips and do not have someone to interpret sign language may be able to write notes. This can be slow and painstaking when you are trying to communicate in a hurry, but it may be the only solution. If it is night, and the patient can read lips, be sure that the lips of the speaker are lit up, and that no one is effectively blinding the patient by shining a flashlight on his or her face. Speak normally, and do not over-enunciate.

Visually-handicapped patients who are otherwise able might require certain unique support. When walking with a blind person, do not grab that person's arm in an attempt to lead. Instead, offer your arm for that person to hold. This imparts an important sense of control. Be aware that many people inadvertently raise the volume of their voices in the presence of a blind person. Speak normally. One thing that can dispel anxiety in blind people is to verbalize everything that is happening, especially before you touch them. One 8-year-old who had lacerated his eyelid on a chain-link fence was essentially "blinded" by the treatment of covering both eyes. Naturally the child was anxious, but because the paramedic explained virtually every move, the boy stayed calm and cooperated fully.

In the end, there is really nothing so different about disabled people except that our perceptions interfere with our intentions. Basically, every human being has the same baseline needs, fears, and frustrations. By talking with people in a straightforward fashion, and by treating them with respect and dignity, everyone benefits.

"Fakers" And "Stallers"

Another group of particularly difficult patients are the ones who make us feel that we are being manipulated and abused. Let's look at them separately.

People Who Fake

Is it even possible to say that people fake their illnesses and injuries? The very thought can generate moral and legal troubles for the EMS worker. But the fact is, some people clearly abuse the system by calling for help they do not need. There are people who enjoy the attention that surrounds the excitement of lights and sirens, who have done things like walk out to the middle of the street, lie down, and claim to be paralyzed. Most EMS systems have a few such folks; we usually get to know them by name, and if we approach them on the scene with, "What's the matter today, Bill Smith?" they know the charade is up. It is a frustrating game, but it's part of the ambulance business.

The infuriating thing is that driving through the streets with lights and sirens is hazardous, both to us and to the well-being of the people we pass. Thus, people who fake their problems are not a joke, and the understandable tendency is to want to teach them a lesson. The need for self-restraint is obvious, if for medicolegal considerations alone. The most obvious precaution against labeling anyone a "faker," of course, is that you could be wrong. Anyone can have emergency medical needs. Just because you have been to Jack Sprat's house a million times and the chief complaint has always turned out to be nothing does not mean that this time won't be different. Just because such people are crying, "Wolf!" doesn't mean that we won't end up in court for not rendering appropriate care the one time it was needed.

> The most obvious precaution against labeling anyone a "faker," of course, is that you could be wrong.

In addition to people who abuse the system maliciously, there are some who could be viewed as fakers who actually are not. For example, is this woman faking? She is about 28 years old, lying curled on her side on her kitchen floor. The household is in an uproar. Children are crying, first responders are standing by awkwardly, and several angry adults are being held apart by police officers.

The paramedic checks to be sure that on-scene hazards have been eliminated, then kneels cautiously next to the patient, noting no obvious external trauma. Her eyelids are fluttering as she tries to appear unconscious and still see what's going on. The paramedic conducts the secondary survey and finds nothing, yet she is still "unconscious." So the paramedic leans down very close to her ear, and quietly says, "Look,

I know you can hear me, because I can tell you are awake and listening. Are you hurt?" She quietly mumbles that she is not. The paramedic says: "If all you want is to get out of this place, we can arrange that, but the best way to do it is to just stand up and walk out with us, okay?" As if miraculously healed, in the eyes of her family and friends, this is exactly what the patient does.

The moral of this story is that people sometimes "fake" their conditions for very good reasons. She had been receiving a beating, and the only escape she could devise was to "faint." Others, often women, have had to create similar self-styled "emergencies" as escape maneuvers from the true underlying problem.

When you think people might be faking the chief complaint, consider whether a secondary cause for the call for help could exist. If you can isolate that cause through good communications and a professional demeanor, everyone benefits. Tempers need not run hot because you think your services have been unjustly summoned. It may be frustrating personally, but understanding some of the alternative reasons people call for help can help you better defuse your own feelings.

Stallers

Here is another frustrating situation: Some people dawdle when preparing for the trip to the hospital. This, of course, happens only when you are due to get off in a half hour, or in the middle of the night!

Fortunately, most people do not consciously intend to delay their departure to the hospital. A certain amount of patience is appropriate for people who want to be sure that household affairs are in order. Accommodating reasonable requests is part of the job. It does not hurt to take the time to collect a few items that the patient wants to take along if the situation is not critical. This may include retrieving false teeth and eyeglasses, checking the stove and other electrical appliances, hiding money or other valuables, and getting a wallet or purse from another room. If you really cannot delay, you can still be kind about it. Consider which statement you'd rather hear if you were the patient:

> **Accommodating reasonable requests is part of the job. It does not hurt to take the time to collect a few items that the patient wants to take along if the situation is not critical.**

- "We really need to be going, but I'm sure they can make you very comfortable at the hospital. Maybe a friend or relative can gather your personal items and bring them to you later."
- "You don't need all that. We don't have time to waste."

Do you really know better than the patient what things to take? Your haste can also be interpreted in a frightened person's mind to mean that you consider him a waste of your time.

The problem of stalling arises when your patient keeps finding things to do before leaving. Such people erode your willingness to be patient and helpful. Coping with the exasperation might be easier if you consider your patient's underlying anxiety. For many people, leaving home means leaving their cocoon of security. Of course, in critical incidents, such behavior is unacceptable, and your patient often has to be whisked away. But when the patient is awake and resistant to departure, the frustration can build rapidly. The more you push to get going, the more the patient digs in his or her heels, and soon you have a real impasse.

For example, one elderly woman with an acute hypertensive crisis and epistaxis was a classic staller. It was 2:30 a.m., and she had called her grandson for help. He had called the paramedics. Because she hadn't called them herself, she resisted professional medical attention from the start. When told of the need for evaluation at the hospital, she did not specifically refuse to go, but suddenly she found innumerable ways to delay her departure. As soon as one obstacle was cleared, she would create another.

Learning to cope with people who stall highlights the need for flexibility in approaching people. Had the paramedics used a mono-approach to this patient, she would have completely refused transport and the family would have witnessed a display of battling wills. Instead, the paramedics used a constellation of approaches. At first, they were polite and cooperative. Then they tried setting limits: "We'll do this, and then we really have to go." She agreed—and then found another reason not to leave. The family was encouraged to intervene; that didn't work. The paramedics pleaded with her in order to give her a sense of control. They tried being authoritative, but she started to get feisty, so they backed away from that approach. Then the paramedics specifically addressed her anxiety and tried to get her to verbalize what,

> Often, a patient who stalls is simply afraid—of the hospital, of dying, of not coming home.

exactly, was causing the delay. Often, a patient who stalls is simply afraid—of the hospital, of dying, of not coming home. If you can address these fundamental fears directly, the patient often becomes cooperative at last.

The paramedics were on the verge of the last resort of strong-arming the patient onto the stretcher when one remembered a last-resort technique. They got on each side of her, each held an elbow, guided her to the stretcher and showed her where to sit. She did! All the while, the paramedic verbally agreed to everything the woman asked. They got her to lie down, and buckled her in. The patient continued to ask that various tasks be attended to all the way to the ambulance—but they got her there!

Prejudice

Prejudice is an unfortunate reality among humans. It cannot be tolerated in prehospital care. No prejudice in EMS, you say? What about caring for cops and kids? Don't we try harder for them? This is not bad—but serves to demonstrate that there is a gradient of care. The concept turns morally sour only when someone is treated *below* the minimum standard of care because they belong to a less favored population. Like it or not, prejudice is an inescapable aspect of life.

One reason that prejudice occurs is fear, especially of the unknown and of differences between people. Why else would people cross the street when they saw an honors student who was also an athletic star approaching? Because they were white and he was black. Why else would many EMS personnel speak so contemptuously of "lousy drunks"? Because in the hierarchy of life, skid row is about the bottom of the heap (Fig. 6.4).

> EMS demands that we rise above the prejudices that urge us, sometimes, to be unkind to other people.

People are our business. We certainly do not see them at their best, so our views are skewed by disproportionate contact with people who are sick and in pain. To deny that you have prejudices is wrong; to admit them, define them, and then leave them at home when providing prehospital care is what matters. EMS demands that we rise above the prejudices that urge us, sometimes, to be unkind to other people.

When you walk into a home that is unlike your own, it is not unusual to consider the differences to be wrong. But it is not wrong; it is only *different*. Just because you may have learned that it is important to seek early medical intervention for a health problem does not mean, for example, that a Mexican-American is wrong for trying to live up to the "macho" edict of his culture; in that culture (like many), illness is a moral weakness. Also his employer may not offer sickness benefits. No work, no pay. Such pressures compel many people not to yield to illness until late in its course. What is considered normal to people of some cultures might be regarded as incomprehensible to others. Some people are uncomfortable if they do not have their large, extended family surrounding them in times of illness; others prefer to be left alone during a crisis. Trying to work within the (reasonable) parameters of patients' cultural needs and belief systems helps gain the trust and cooperation of the people you are trying to help.

Figure 6.4

Homeless or skid-row people are often the objects of needless and cruel derision. Understand your prejudices—and do *not* act upon them.

Unfortunately, EMS is obviously a two-way street. Others may respond unfairly to *your* cultural background, ethnic background, race, or sex. We are as subject to the prejudices of our patients as they are to ours—except that, by virtue of our position, we cannot act on our prejudices while they remain free to voice their opinions. It may seem unfair, but part of professionalism is understanding and accepting this inequity.

So prejudice is an inescapable aspect of our lives. As prehospital workers, we must pay attention to it, come to terms with it, and be as quick and willing to treat the town drunk as we are the town mayor.[20]

Summary

In many cases, what causes a call to seem more difficult than others is the perception of its "value." It is human nature to be more excited by a dramatic, highly visible, lifesaving scene. But prehospital care is much more broadly defined than many EMTs and paramedics wish. We do not simply give technical care. We spearhead the emergency medical care team, and our intervention sets the tone for the remainder of a patient's experience.

When faced with the types of calls that tempt you to roll your eyes and—at least inwardly—feel unjustly used, or frustrated, or disgusted, consider the implications of your reaction. Most prehospital work is routine and noncritical. Most patients are people who need help but do not stretch our mental or technical capabilities. It is necessary to cope with mundane situations. This becomes much more tolerable when we decide to treat everyone without judging the quality of their needs. Fix what you can, but don't fight the things you cannot change. Leave your prejudices at home, and be patient and tolerant of the special challenges of the job. If you do, the job will be a lot more fun.

---

[20] Kate Dernocoeur, "Prejudice: Spoiling The Melting Pot Brew," in *The Best of JEMS: Timeless Essays from the First 15 Years* (St. Louis: Mosby Lifeline, 1996), 77.

Service Orientation & 7
The Nature of Routine

"How poor are they that have no patience . . ."

—Shakespeare, *Othello*

Chapter Overview

When children dream about doing something "exciting" with their lives they often think of EMS. They are fed on the TV shows that pack a year's worth of EMS excitement into 30 minutes (with two commercial breaks)—and it all comes out happy in the end, too. How different is the reality of EMS, as anyone knows after just a short time on the streets! Just as with any other pursuit, we have to handle a lot of routine things in EMS. It becomes necessary to adjust our expectations—but how? A fresh view of the nature of routine may be helpful.

Additionally relevant is a clear understanding of the concepts surrounding service orientation. A person can choose to work from a range of attitudes regarding service orientation. The ability to provide medical care to all callers with sincerely good service requires a clear discerning of the needs of others along with honest self-understanding. Closely tied with good service is the concept of conflict resolution. Strong skills in this area are especially relevant in the world of EMS.

EMS has some tremendously exciting moments! It is important not to lose sight of that. Saving lives, easing pain, going into unusual and sometimes dangerous places to perform a rescue, meeting all sorts of people at very vulnerable moments in their lives *is* exciting.

And that isn't all there is.

The "juiciest" moments in EMS are like a powerful cooking spice. You only need a little bit to appreciate the flavor. Too much will spoil the recipe. We'd all love more of the peak moments—and they aren't going to happen very often. Therefore, the professional EMS provider is wiser to devise a plan for living graciously with the fact that EMS can be downright tedious sometimes.

Some of the routine aspects of EMS are:

- Checking equipment
- Washing the emergency vehicle
- Handling interfacility transfers
- Waiting
- Paperwork
- Trainings and other meetings

Already, for some, the yawns begin and the eyeballs begin to roll. "Isn't this the stuff you just 'put up' with in order to get to the good parts?" some may ask. People in EMS don't sign up because they are drawn to the routine tasks. "Rescuer mentality" is a term that describes the insatiable appetite people in the rescue business have for excitement. One tongue-in-cheek definition of EMS: "It's hours of boredom punctuated by moments of sheer terror!" How are you going to use those "hours of boredom"?

> There is no rule that anyone has to enjoy the mundane parts of the job, but it is helpful to make a truce with the situation.

Routine tasks and the tedium they represent are part of the job for everyone in EMS. There are choices about how to view them. Why fight the fact that the rig needs to be cleaned? Why complain about the paperwork? Why gripe about the interfacility transfer you've been assigned? There is no rule that anyone has to enjoy the mundane parts of the job, but it is helpful to make a truce with the situation. People who stay in EMS for any length of time learn to tolerate the less-exciting routines.

In-Between Time

EMS providers are not alone in their quest for exciting moments. Athletes train many hours for the few minutes of their sports performances. Actors and actresses practice their lines and rehearse their roles for weeks before opening night. In medicine, you endure thousands of hours of schooling before you're allowed to care for patients. A climber takes thousands of steps before the one that lands on top of the mountain. It doesn't make sense to honor only those few moments in the chain of events when you reach the peak.

George Leonard, in his book, *Mastery*, expresses a concept called "in-between time:"

> Our preoccupation with goals, results, and the quick fix has separated us from our own experiences. To put it more starkly, it has robbed us of countless hours of the time of our lives. We awaken in the morning and hurry to get dressed. (Getting dressed doesn't count.) We hurry to eat breakfast so that we can leave for work. (Getting to work doesn't count.) Maybe work will be interesting and satisfying and we won't have to simply endure it. . . .
>
> In any case, there are all of those chores that most of us can't avoid: cleaning, straightening, raking leaves, shopping for groceries, driving the children to various activities, preparing food, washing dishes, washing the car, commuting, performing the routine, repetitive aspects of our jobs. This is the "in-between time," the stuff we have to take care of before getting on to the things that count. But if you stop to think about it, most of life is "in-between." When goal orientation comes to dominate our thoughts, little that seems to really count, is left. During the usual nonplayoff year, the actual playing time for a National Football League team is sixteen hours. For the players, does this mean that the other 8,744 hours of the year are "in between"? Does all time take its significance only in terms of the product, the bottom line? And if winning, as the saying goes, is the *only* thing, does that mean that even the climactic hours achieve their worth merely through victory?
>
> There's another way of thinking about it. Zen practice is ostensibly organized around periods of sitting in meditation and chanting. Yet every Zen master will tell you that building a stone wall or washing dishes is essentially no different from formal meditation. The quality of a Zen student's practice is defined just as much by how he or she sweeps the courtyard as how he or she sits in meditation. Could we apply this way of thinking to less esoteric situations? Could all of us reclaim the lost hours of our lives by making everything—the commonplace along with the extraordinary—a part of our practice?[1]

---

[1] George Leonard, *Mastery: The Keys to Success and Long-Term Fulfillment* (New York: Penguin Books, 1991), 141–142. [Used with permission]

For some reason, in the EMS culture, in-between time has come to be that period of time between "real" calls. What is a "real" call to you? Is it a call that stretches your capabilities, that gets the adrenaline flowing? Such calls are a ridiculous minority of the total number of calls handled each day by prehospital care providers. Maybe ten percent of 9-1-1 calls are critical, and of those, maybe one percent is life-threatening to the patient.

> An EMS provider who makes it a point to see each patient contact as "real" has a much higher percentage of satisfaction.

What about the other ninety percent? Do they not count? Now add in the thousands of interfacility transfers handled daily by EMS providers. How do you suppose it feels to a patient to be in the "you don't count" category? An EMS provider who makes it a point to see each patient contact as "real" has a much higher percentage of satisfaction.

What about other typical EMS activities? While you wait for *any* call involving a patient (emergency or not!), you may be asked to handle equipment deliveries, errands for the front office, building inspections, or meal pick-ups for the dispatchers. Are these contributions to the workings of your organization merely "in-between" time? A person with true team spirit sees the value even of these tasks.

The lesson of in-between time is that EMS providers who want to master the practice of prehospital care must learn to write exceptional reports, shine their vehicles, use waiting time effectively, bring a learning attitude to class, and more. Every part of the whole deserves attention. The clear-sighted rescuer who strives for well-rounded excellence in the craft of EMS is admirable. Why not let that person be you?

Coping with Waiting

There is a spectrum of waiting that extends from one end (doing nothing at all), past the common, everyday tasks already mentioned, to the other end, which is handling exciting 9-1-1 emergencies. Certain personality traits common to emergency personnel include being action-oriented and easily-bored, with a high need for immediate gratification.[2] In addition, many EMS providers are relentlessly in the public eye, especially in systems using dynamic dispersal of emergency vehicles. There may be few places to duck out of sight, to get "off-stage." You,

---

[2] Jeff Mitchell and Grady Bray, *Emergency Services Stress* (Englewood Cliffs, NJ: Prentice-Hall, 1990), 21.

your patches, and your vehicle—and all the behavior you display while in them—represent your EMS organization constantly. How you wait may have an important impact both on your own view of the job and on the view others have of you.

Whatever it is that EMS providers are asked to do, many of them will see it negatively. If the system is quiet, there are comments about how dead it is. If there is a stack of transfers to run, there are comments about wanting something "real" to do. If a spate of 9-1-1 calls come in, there are even remarks about being overloaded. Without an altered perspective on waiting, it's a no-win situation!

The answer to the dilemma of how to view all this is to become conscious of the choices. Boredom is a frame of mind. Tedium is just an attitude. "One person's junk is another person's treasure." The waiting in EMS, the parts some see as "in-between time," will never go away. Those who stay involved eventually are able to come to terms with the total picture. The best see every part of the world of EMS as a chance to grow and develop in many valuable and often unpredictable ways.

With the advent of managed health care, people in the emergency services are increasingly recognized as potential providers of primary, out-of-hospital care. Within a few years, it is likely that EMS will provide many non-emergency medical services. On-site ear checks, immunizations, minor suturing and other medically routine tasks may begin to consume more and more of the EMS provider's time. The evolution of health care in the late twentieth century will likely include a diminishing focus on emergencies. How a person resolves the incongruency of being an "emergency" provider in a world of routine is the key to surviving in this still-rewarding line of work. However, EMS providers who insist on focusing only on "real" calls will likely feel increasingly frustrated. What is a "real" call? Perhaps it would be best for everyone concerned (not least, the patient!) to choose the attitude that *every task assignment has value*. That way, there is no waiting. Every moment is part of the job.

Pride and Professionalism

It requires a hefty amount of personal pride to get into EMS. To feel capable of learning the material and then to go out there and practice it requires intelligence, drive, and a level of confidence that many other people lack. Once in a while, we make life and death decisions. On less crucial calls, we are asked to help others, based on our judgment,

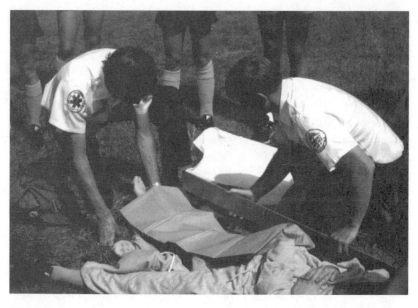

Figure 7.1

These paramedics are a different kind of "team" than the one they are currently assisting. Through appropriate actions and interpersonal communication, they are demonstrating good teamwork and pride in their EMS affiliation.

with big decisions. Our approach to people must be professional yet flexible. It is hard work physically, mentally, and emotionally.

Over time, many people seem to have forgotten how proud they were to wear their first uniform in the service of others. They slip into bad habits, or simply slip away. Turnover in EMS is appallingly high. But those who stick around find the value of being proud of their work, and of being consistently professional. They know they provide good care, yet they remain pragmatic about the realities: they'll never get rich, they may get killed, they might lose more battles with tragedy and death than they win. None of this diminishes the fire for excellence. Such role models have a drive for excellence that is based on parameters within their control. They continually hone their medical knowledge. They don't let seemingly trivial calls generate disdain. They retain appropriate respect for the streets.

Pride and professionalism should matter to each EMS provider (Fig. 7.1). In companies and agencies where these values are held in particular esteem, few people get away with inappropriate behavior because of peer-driven excellence. If you are rude to someone, your partner will be the first to speak up. If your medicine is shaky, your peers will pressure you to tune up—and they'll probably be more than happy to help. They are proud of their *team*. They will ensure that the team remains worthy of pride—or you will be out their door. When a group of people share similar good values and the knowledge of right and wrong, how lucky are the patients and everyone else the team contacts in the course of a day! Peer-driven excellence qualities can be developed and nurtured. It does not just happen; it is the result of people with the vision and the drive to make good things happen. It is the result of pride and professionalism.

Service Orientation

Modern EMS, as a 30-plus year old concept, has matured tremendously. Although people providing emergency care have enjoyed increasingly positive public opinion, this continues to be a time for caution. In the early days, there were some unflattering stereotypes and enough public distrust in some places that EMS workers were branded as rowdy, renegade cowboys in fast vehicles. Then came the honeymoon, as the casts of *Emergency!* and *Rescue 9-1-1* endeared EMS to the general public. Who would not love us? Johnny and Roy saved people far more often than not, did not get too dirty, never had a cynical or nasty tone of voice, and they were handsome to boot. William Shatner always has a happy story to share. But as people encountered off-screen ambulance personnel, many felt deceived and wronged. The miracles so common on TV do not happen nearly as often on the street. Every time an EMS representative flips the bird at passing motorists, looks disheveled and smells dirty, threatens or uses undue force on patients or bystanders, or expects favors from fast-food joints, the image of EMS is further tarnished. Sadly, *all* of these things go on more than anyone would like to believe. In fact, the pendulum has swung again; the public increasingly wonders about the motivations and abilities of ambulance personnel.

A shift from an image of saving lives to something more all-encompassing is happening.[3] Times have changed. The public is not necessarily satisfied merely with having an ambulance crew show up. They want *good service* from start to finish. This demand for proper attention is not unique to EMS. The general public has realized that it wants more than

---

[3] Erik Gaull, "Toward A New View of EMS," *Academic Emergency Medicine* [prepublication copy, publication pending], Spring 1996.

a quick burger, a fast roll of stamps, or next-day telephone hookups. All of us want fast-food servers to smile and ask, "Is there anything else I can get for you today?" We want hassle-free post office experiences and telephone operators who thank *us* for calling. So it is in emergency medical services. The word "service" may be the final third of our name, but it should always be at the forefront of your mind. It's the last word, and the bottom line. It means making a bigger interpersonal effort. It requires more energy. But the payoffs are worth it:

- People are more likely to understand what you need to do when you use superior interpersonal communication skills, and will be more cooperative.
- People are also more likely to cooperate when you demonstrate maturity and patience. This is, among other things, a safety issue.
- You are less likely to be caught off guard in hazardous situations through appropriate threat assessment and conflict resolution. This generates a less over-reactive and more rational response.
- Satisfied "customers" are less likely to dial their lawyers and might even write thank-you notes once in awhile.

Because we cannot pick and choose our clientele, we need to be ready for anything. Of course, we frequently manipulate the prehospital environment. It is part of the job. Naturally, there are many things beyond our control—that is part of the thrill of the streets! But there is danger in the power we wield. Poor understanding of our mandate can (and does) lead to inhumane and inappropriate treatment of other people. Therefore, our actions must always be justifiable, not just medicolegally, but from a moral and ethical point of view. EMS service must be in-fused with the desire to do the right things, even when doing them right is harder.

Medical care is tightly interwoven with appropriate service orienta-tion. Understanding others, including their emotions and perceptions, is as important as understanding their diseases and injuries. Investing time to generate positive first impressions, to build trust and rapport, and to help others understand you and your mission *matters*. This is just as true of routine transfers as of high-drama emergencies. None of it is just "fluff." From a global point of view, it is essential.

Customer Service

Being nice to all people in all situations is a challenge, but it is an obvious part of the job. This is what is known as "customer service." Although our responsibilities are far greater than in most other service industries, we must maintain interpersonal standards that keep the community pleased with our *total* approach to patient care—or risk unsavory results. For example, in 1984, an incident in Dallas, Texas involving interpersonal antagonism between a caller and the call screening nurse resulted in a disaster.[4] The caller's mother died, and the situation received sustained national attention. Because of one person's poor customer service, field personnel in that city bore the brunt of the public's outrage. Physical assaults against EMTs and paramedics skyrocketed. Citizens felt less like protecting their "protectors," because of the widespread perception that the EMS system had failed its mandate.

Who is a "customer"? Ever since the term "customer service" became a buzzword in the 1980s, there has been an uneasy feeling among many EMS providers about using the term "customer" for medical patients. Indeed, EMS providers will always enjoy a unique relationship with patients, and this is as it should be. But who says patients are the only people EMS providers serve? You provide customer service to many other people (while preserving the uniqueness of the medic/patient relationship):

- Within your own organization, you serve the others by being a reliable, knowledgeable, and compatible teammate.
- If your agency does interfacility transfers, you provide customer service to the medical professionals on both ends of a job. Interfacility transfers have always been among the least favorite of routine tasks. One reason is because of a tradition of poor customer service. There are long-held biases, both by facility staffs (such as nursing homes) and by EMS crews. Some nursing home staffs see the "ambulance drivers" as nothing more than horizontal taxi drivers. The EMS providers react negatively to the lack of respect they receive from the nursing home staff. The patient's needs often get lost in between. With attention to customer service (by both sides!), these attitudes can shift over time. You can do this by receiving and giving professional reports, interacting civilly, and being prompt. It's a matter of professionally meeting the needs of the customer—in this case, the nursing home staff.

---

[4] For a complete manuscript, see Jeff J. Clawson and Kate Dernocoeur, *Principles of Emergency Medical Dispatch*, 2nd edition (Salt Lake City: MPC, Inc., 1996 [release pending].)

- There are often several emergency agencies responding on emergency calls. Yet bad relations and interagency arrogance has caused many problems over the years. Improvements in this area stem from attending unrelentingly to the concepts of good customer service. Meet others' needs. Treat others as you would wish to be treated. The advantage of shifting to a more professional and respectable interaction will lead to smoother and more enjoyable subsequent calls. The nondiscerning public also will no longer have to witness confusing interagency squabbles!

- There is an element of customer relations at play each time you deliver a patient to the emergency department, in terms of your relationship with other medical personnel. It is important to be on good terms with your organization's in-hospital "customers" (the nurses, doctors, and staff). Mutual respect will serve everyone when there is a disaster in your town.

On a larger scale, EMS providers are in the service of the entire community. Just being present in the public eye leaves an intangible perception of safety and security. It travels with us as we go on 9-1-1 calls, handle transfers, and pick up lunch for the office staff. All actions that will encourage members of the public to trust us to do the job kindly, appropriately, and on time will bolster our image in the community. Alternatively, any action that can be construed as inappropriate, rude, or overbearing erodes the public's trust. Smart EMS agencies work constantly to keep their local image gleaming.

Although many people believe that being able to "get along" with everyone is an attribute of personality, the greater truth is that it is a learned skill. There are techniques and strategies that every prehospital professional can use. Many are described and recommended throughout this book. But the willingness to make the effort must come first. The attribute of patience, the ability to listen, the skills of verbal reassurance and compassionate touch, and leadership all are important. None happen easily. And each is part of customer service.

Manners

Each time you are identified as a member of the EMS community, have your "customer service" hat on. You will leave an impression. It may as well be positive and reassuring. Then that person will spread the good news about "those wonderful local EMS providers!" You may not even be on duty. You may not even be in uniform. But, whether or not it's fair, you are held to a higher standard and your behavior speaks for all EMS personnel.

Manners are a basic tool for getting along. They indicate that you feel another person is worthy of your respect. They are the tangible— or at least audible—evidence that you appreciate another person's presence and actions. Yet, to see the way many people interact, manners seem to be a dying art form. Taking our cues from politicians, the media, the legal system, and even from those in our own homes, we are collectively more rude and nasty than was once deemed proper.

So what? Among other things, absence of good manners "is a nastiness the country can ill afford, because it amounts to a kind of social deafness," according to philosopher Martin Marty.[5]

Good manners can carry the EMS provider through some very tough and tense times. If used when a first responder helps out, they can build a sense of teamwork that money won't buy. When meeting strangers in crisis, they can generate immediate rapport and trust, especially among people who may be starved for the display of respect that good manners represent. Many people appreciate attention to this detail. To give it a business spin, "Manners are the new status accessory, pricier than a Rolex, more portable than a Day-timer, and shinier than hand-made shoes. Polished graces can get you where you're going faster than a speeding BMW."[6] In the name of professionalism, the use of "please," "thank you," "pardon me," and other phrases are simply good technique. The actions that stand behind a consciousness of good manners are even better.

How To Be A Team Player

Another valued attribute among EMS providers is knowing how to be a team player. Being a team player matters because EMS is a team sport. Patients do not survive solely due to the efforts of one or two people; they survive because of the *system.* Systems rely on strong individual components the way a wheel relies on each spoke. At minimum, you must be a good teammate for your partner; each of you relies on the other for medical and safety backup. The importance of a team approach is even more obvious when the discussion turns to mass casualty inci-

---

[5] "The American Uncivil Wars," *U.S. News and World Report,* April 22, 1996, 66–72.
[6] Ibid.

dents and mutual-aid responses. (Could lack of a team approach be one reason that so many mass casualty incidents run poorly?)

By its nature, EMS is a loose-jointed venture. Our world is split by many clearly defined boundaries. There are allegiances to this or that hospital. Individual organizations (and in some places, individual stations within those organizations) are in competition with one another. The primary industry magazines have uniquely loyal audiences with relatively little crossover. Only a few people read two or more of them. Crews that work for the same agency may only know one another in passing. Lucky are the EMS services that enjoy good, genuine, company-wide camaraderie. This tends to happen more often in smaller communities. EMS services there are more likely to be blessed with a cohesive and united bond.

Unhappily, team building is not a priority in most EMS services. For one thing, industry turnover prevents a sense of teamwork because it's hard to get to know each player. Individuals may have to be around a long time before others will trust that it is worth investing the time and effort to regard them as true teammates. In some places, team building is actively discouraged by administrators who misunderstand the need. It's even more unusual to see anyone reach out to colleagues from other agencies. A certain amount of crossover may occur at continuing education classes—but we still tend to sit with people who wear our uniform. Some organizations structure ambulance assignments so that even simple two-person partnerships are discouraged. We may even be barred from trying to build teamwork: For example, in one western town, EMTs are not allowed in the emergency department even when multi-patient situations overwhelm the staff.

Interagency, interterritorial relations beg for improvements in teamwork. For example, a paramedic once volunteered to spend time at the first-aid booth at a state agricultural fair. Upon arriving, one of the other volunteers, an EMT, found out that she was employed at the busiest EMS service in the region. "Oh, you're one of those snotty City Hospital paramedics," he said with a sneer. He did not even know her name—but was already prejudiced because of her EMS affiliation. In the discussion that ensued, the EMT realized the harm of his attitude, not only in interpersonal relations but in interagency relations as well (Fig. 7.2). Any time you judge another person in your EMS system solely by their title or agency affiliation, you will injure your credibility and your chances for area-wide teamwork.

How to achieve improved teamwork? Start with top-to-bottom commitment. A gung-ho administrator can come in and mandate improved relations with the other emergency agencies, but it will never work until field personnel are also committed to the idea. And vice versa: Field personnel who understand the wisdom of improving interpersonal and interagency relations will have an uphill battle without managerial support. Plan for team building to take time, whether it is inside or outside your organization. One EMS agency spent five years working to establish a consistent and sincere habit of good teamwork with the first responders. There were rough times, but day by day things improved. It *can* be done.

For the individual, becoming a team player involves being willing to yield at times. Too many "chiefs" on an emergency scene are both common and disastrous. Even when someone else takes an approach that is different from the one you would choose, that's okay, if it will not affect patient care negatively. Psychological studies have shown that we are a particularly independent and control-oriented group—*all* of us. We are a bad mix for ourselves! Be ready to lead, when necessary, but also be willing and able to follow. Give suggestions, as well as praise and positive feedback (Fig. 7.3). Wear a name tag with letters large enough to be seen at a social distance—at least four feet—so that others can

Figure 7.2

Good interagency cooperation is particularly reassuring in the "tough" parts of town. It comes from nurturing good relations at all times, not just at emergency situations.

get to know you by name. Learn *their* names! When problems arise, be careful to deal with others in the proper forum. Getting into a brawl with the extrication folks at the scene is downright stupid—but it has

Figure 7.3

Always be mindful that the dispatcher is also a member of the team. Stop by the communications center when possible, and put faces to the voices. Mutual respect is born of such efforts.

happened. A better approach would be to wait until after the call to file a report. In all, the goal is to be polite and professional in your dealings with every colleague in EMS, from your partner on up.

Despite constant lip service about the need for teamwork, EMS does not generally encourage a *true* team approach to patient care. Emergency medical services face a rotten historical precedent. There are petty (and not so petty) rivalries, hometown pride ("us versus them"), and other barriers erected through time and space. But the precedents need to be shattered. Any efforts to generate a genuine team in your hometown— from first responders to in-hospital personnel—can have only one effect: improved patient care. That should be our universal goal.

The Basics of Conflict Resolution

"It's time we honored the battles that were never fought."

—Ralph Weymouth, US Navy Vice Admiral

EMS providers have ample opportunity, thanks to the situations that arise, to become true masters at the art of conflict resolution. An adeptness in the skills of conflict resolution is a true service to others. These skills and strategies apply to patient care situations, to coworker relations, and even to your own home life.

Every step you take moves you toward a resolution of your conflict with gravity. Most well-adjusted people prefer to minimize the pain in their lives and seek the more pleasurable end of a pain-pleasure spectrum.[7] Because conflict may be viewed as painful, many spend a lot of energy avoiding it. However, there are times when a healthy engagement in a debate is beneficial to everyone concerned, or when a mutually-agreeable solution to a conflict leaves everyone feeling like a winner. A very important principle is that conflict is neither good nor bad. It just *is*.

Conflicts arise for innumerable reasons. Typical causes are personality differences, problems in interpersonal communication, differences in objectives (why a person is doing something), and differences in method (how things are being done). Unresolved cultural, gender, racial, or religious differences may also contribute to conflict. The topic of diversity among people is an important piece in conflict resolution.

Whatever the cause, there are conflict-handling styles that depend partly on how assertive a person is, and also how much cooperativeness is involved. These styles are:

- *Accommodating.* Low on the assertiveness scale, and high on cooperativeness. An accommodating person values the relationship more than the outcome of the issue.
- *Competing.* High on assertiveness, and low on cooperativeness. Conflicts are regarded as win/lose, and winning is more important than the relationship.
- *Collaborating.* High on both assertiveness and cooperativeness. Exchange is open, and high value is placed on both the outcome and the relationship.
- *Avoiding.* Low on both assertiveness and cooperativeness. Silence is golden, and avoiding disagreement is the goal.
- *Compromising.* Moderate on both assertiveness and cooperativeness. Rather than seek gain, one seeks to protect against loss. Bargaining is a primary tool used to split the differences.[8]

Once again, the concepts of understanding yourself and understanding others comes into play. Can you readily identify conflict and why it is happening? Some conflicts are very subtle! What is your typical conflict-handling style? What are the needs of the other person? If the two

---

[7] Tony Robbins, *Unlimited Power* (New York: Ballantine Books, 1986).
[8] Judith R. Gordon, *A Diagnostic Approach to Organizational Behavior,* 3rd ed. (Needham Heights, Mass.: Allyn and Bacon, 1991), 483.

styles are incongruent, can you, for professional purposes, adopt a different style in order to handle the situation?

Much of conflict resolution also meshes with the importance of excellent interpersonal communication skills. What you think you are saying may not be what others are hearing. Conflict may be due to misinterpretations of your body language. For example, if you are leaning against a door frame at 3:00 a.m., other rescuers will recognize this as exhaustion—but the family may interpret it as not caring.

Conflict often involves a high pitch of emotion. When anger rises up in you or in others, ask yourself what its *sources* are. Anger is a defense against feelings of guilt, hurt, loss, anxiety, fear, and of being bad, wrong, or unworthy.[9] No wonder there is so much anger at both routine and emergency EMS situations! (Fig. 7.4)

Take each conflict as it comes. Notice the other people involved. Decide whether it would be best to separate them, or go to a private place and help a person "save face." Notice when a situation may involve discrimination or prejudice, either your own or that of another person. Differences are often threatening, causing conflict to flare. Managing diversity effectively is part of conflict resolution, especially in EMS, since we interact with all sorts of people. Find a way to respect, appreciate, and accept others. Building rapport builds trust in others, even in people who are very different from ourselves. "Trust is to constructive relationships what oxygen is to breathing. When it is limited, relationships are harder; when absent, they die."[10] You don't

STRATEGIES FOR MEDIATING CONFLICT

Begin by taking a deep breath.

Then:

1. State your own feelings clearly, without being accusatory. Begin with "I feel..." instead of "You always..."
2. Never interrupt or finish another person's sentences.
3. Concentrate on what is being said to you, rather than on your response.
4. Maintain eye contact.
5. Ask questions to clarify what the other person is saying.
6. Repeat the other person's ideas as you understand them.
7. Never put anyone down.

[Source: *Teaching Tolerance* magazine, Fall 1992, 49.]

Figure 7.4

---

[9] "Conflict Management Skills for Women," (Mission, Kansas: SkillPath Seminars, 1993), 12.
[10] Del Nykamp, "Respecting, Appreciating, and Managing Diversity," lecture in Grand Rapids, Michigan, March 1996.

have to like others to work effectively with them; you just have to be committed to finding win-win solutions.

Learning to manage conflict in a healthy and effective way can be a life-long pursuit. Those in EMS who take on the challenge will grow in their own lives at the same time they are serving the public in an honorable manner.

The Pursuit of Quality

The concepts of quality improvement and quality assurance have long-since entered the EMS consciousness. Part of the difficulty in managing and supervising field personnel lies with the basic structure of field care. Another lies in the way personnel are recruited and selected.

Supervising and managing EMS personnel is an unusual challenge. Most people in the workforce share common work space and time with their colleagues. A sense of communal purpose is relatively easy to create and maintain. People in everyday businesses have a better chance to appreciate a sense of "company" than when personnel are scattered across both the map (in small groups) and the day (24 hours, seven days a week). Effective managers and supervisors connect frequently with personnel, even if it means traveling to distant stations or showing up at odd hours.

Assuring high-quality care involves more than holding a hammer over the heads of field personnel. Yet many companies employ negative management principles. At such places, the only time one sees a supervisor is when there is trouble. Healthier companies, on the other hand, like to catch people "doing it right."[11] Good feedback, proper coaching, and effective reprimanding give field personnel much more incentive to do a good job. The impact on EMS providers—and the health of their organizations—is obvious.

In the end, *true* quality cannot be legislated or mandated. It comes from within. A vital element in quality organizations is dedication to stringent pre-employment screening. This brings in people with the right attitudes and values that indicate an applicant is dedicated to the highest principles of service orientation, medical care, and team-work. It's much more than straight medical knowledge—although that obviously matters, too. There must be a willingness to clean equipment properly,

---

[11] Kenneth Blanchard and Spencer Johnson, *The One-Minute Manager* (New York: Berkley Books, 1982), 39.

be kind, patient, and compassionate to every patient, be a team player, represent the company in a mature manner, and practice a healthful life-style. Once-prevalent attitudes (including blatant patient abuse—mental and physical—and "we're only here to save lives")[12] no longer have a place in EMS.

Because prehospital workers are relatively autonomous, finding the right people to staff ambulances matters. It requires maturity to do the right thing because it is right, not because someone is watching you. A clear-cut pre-employment screening process backed up by enlightened management and supervision minimizes the company's risk of sending individuals unable to live up to a tremendous responsibility into the community.

Each individual in an EMS organization must believe that the company philosophy includes "permission" to have the courage to believe in excellence as a goal. Change is hard. People who have worked in *any* job dislike new eras. But the reality of EMS in the last decade of the twentieth century is that archaic attitudes and approaches to patient care are no longer acceptable.

The part about EMS that is *never* the same is the "people part." Doing any medical care—even routine procedures—is made different by each person's response to it. Your mood can influence the situation from one patient to the next. There are unlimited nuances to service orientation. A person who decides to be conscious to the process can't help but be endlessly fascinated. Every conflict, large or small, internal or external, becomes fodder for self-improvement. Everyday routines seem less tedious when you choose to take on a positive attitude. It's a matter of seeing the individual way that you affect different people. Learn from the hard situations, honor those that are tragic—and always remember to celebrate the ones that leave you feeling good!

Summary

Provide good service to all people—hungry dispatchers, frazzled office staff, nursing home supervisors, ED personnel, your partner, and, yes, the general public. Meet your patients—each of them—with an open heart and a willingness to serve them well. Engage in conflict resolution with the intention of creating as many win-win results as possible. Push yourself to the highest standards of care possible. Each of these is a hallmark of excellence. Choose this route, and EMS will serve *you* well.

---

[12] Thom Dick, "People Care: Are We Missing Something?" in *The Best of JEMS: Timeless Essays from the First 15 Years* (Carlsbad, California: *JEMS* Communications, 1996), 62.

Prior to Arrival **8**

Chapter Overview

Prior to arriving at medical care settings, prehospital workers must attend to a number of tasks which are also part of the job. Certain things, such as checking equipment, are (or should be) daily routine. Other tasks may not seem vital, but doing them demonstrates your interest in doing a thorough job. This quality mindedness helps generate a reputation for professionalism, whether you are paid or volunteer. Developing an interest in every component of prehospital care broadens and strengthens your overall capability. Much of it consists of attending to the "little" things. It is wise never to forget that there's always something more to do to prepare for both emergent and nonemergent patient care.

There are a variety of activities related to the following three phases of emergency care:

- Waiting
- En route
- Arriving at the scene

How you use the time available in these phases may be rewarding or not, depending on your motivation.

Waiting Time

The philosophical edges of this topic were discussed in the previous chapter. But there are logistical edges as well. Whether your noncall time is closely or loosely structured, it really boils down to waiting. Sometimes lay people point to emergency crews sitting at the station and comment about how they would love such an "easy" job. Little do they know!

Chapter 7 encourages a new approach to waiting time. Still, some people need to think about the impact of waiting. Waiting for calls is more difficult than it sounds. There are two extremes. One is that your mental conditioning will wilt and you will end up unable to accomplish anything. You can't even get out of your chair to get the map and stare at it, or to get your notes for review. You get caught up in the stress of boredom, which, silly as it sounds, is exhausting. The other is that you so continually recharge your anticipation and personal readiness that you wear yourself out. You need to have a balanced undercurrent of readiness for response at any time that does not drain you.

Both paid and volunteer EMS providers are subject to the same in-between-calls tasks and activities that are part of all prehospital care. How you use noncall time depends on various factors. Sometimes, the most you can do is "veg"! On the other hand, if you push yourself, there is always something more productive to do. For example, at some point everyone has to direct some attention and effort to tasks such as checking and fixing equipment, cleaning the vehicle or the station, cooking a meal, washing ambulance linens, studying maps of the community, and reading medical journals and other continuing education materials.

Equipment

One universal task is checking equipment. It is embarrassing to discover at a scene that something you need is not there or is not working. It is also a potential legal liability. A comprehensive checklist of equipment to be found on the emergency vehicle should be properly filled out at the start of each shift change. Agencies without a checklist are missing an opportunity to close a potential legal gap, and those that do have lists, but do not assure their use, are being even more cavalier and irresponsible.

Checking equipment is (or should be) one of the first things you do each shift. It is not enough to accept the word of off-going colleagues that "everything's fine." The only way to be confident of that fact is by checking the equipment yourself. It is not enough just to poke your head into the patient compartment and see that everything is there. A thorough equipment check takes time. Is the monitor adequately charged? Is the suction working? Is the EKG paste tube clogged? Are all the medications in the drug box? Did anyone retrieve the traction splint from St. Mary's Hospital? Visual inspection does not answer these questions. Do a hands-on "hello" to each piece of equipment. This is repetitious, true, but the self-discipline and patience required for this simple task are both attributes that will often come in handy on the streets (and in life). It's a good place to practice them.

In a perfect world, there would always be enough time to check out the ambulance thoroughly. Unfortunately, there are times when you walk in for a shift and the off-going crew greets you with unmasked relief: "Great! You're here! *You* have a call to . . ." and off you go. On the way, then, at least check the jump kit, drug box, suction, oxygen, and monitor. There's no time on a fast-breaking scene to troubleshoot problems with these items.

If there is a piece of equipment you do not know how to use, which is not uncommon when riding along or just joining a new company, practice working with it until you feel comfortable. Sadly, many people who have not wanted to seem incapable have bluffed—or tried to bluff—knowing how to do something important. Once, a new employee did not realize that the suction tips did not seal unless the hole on the handle was sealed with a finger; they were not that way where she had worked before. Obviously, her equipment check had been superficial. Such actions risk the well-being of patients. They also display a disturbingly irresponsible attitude.

If a piece of equipment is broken and needs repair, note it. Better yet—fix it. People in EMS have notoriously creative mending abilities. For example, once there were two paramedics en route to an emergency call when a tailpipe dropped and started dragging. In a few seconds, they had that tailpipe jury-rigged back in place. Their motto: "If it can't be fixed with an ET tube stylet and white tape, it can't be fixed!"

In addition to medical equipment, be sure also about the road-worthiness of the vehicle. Although some may joke that they missed their "Mechanics Module" in training, it is true that prehospital workers need a basic understanding of vehicle maintenance. Ambulances work harder than other vehicles, so it is important to check all vital components regularly. This includes brake fluid, oil, transmission fluid, windshield cleaner fluid, and tire pressure (Fig. 8.1). Take the time to become familiar with auto mechanics. As the saying goes, stupid questions are easier to deal with than stupid mistakes. That is what one paramedic discovered after spending half an hour getting a quart of oil down "that teeny little pipe"—the dipstick hole!

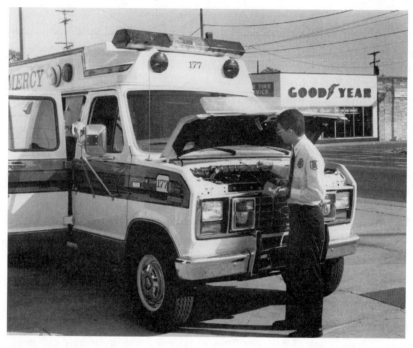

Figure 8.1

If you do not inspect and maintain your vehicle, how can you entrust it with your life?

Know Your Territory

Precall preparation also involves studying your territory. Learning the streets and roads of the community is a major part of prehospital care. If you can't find 'em, you can't help 'em.

Many people place little (if any) emphasis on this critical detail. But have you ever wandered through the maze of a modern housing development in the dark while your partner desperately tries to read a well-thumbed, minuscule map with an inadequate map light? It is especially disconcerting when you are in relatively unfamiliar territory because you are backing up an unavailable crew.

A good way to practice route finding is to stare at the ambulance maps. Any EMS service worth its salt has a large map of the district on a convenient wall. Learn street names, their rotations, how they intersect, the main through-streets. Then ride around in your car or on your bicycle in your off time until the general lay of the land is familiar. As you gain experience, you can increase your territorial awareness by learning the side streets and shortcuts. It is an obvious advantage to have lived where you are working. But even a person's hometown may be less familiar than you can imagine. People have routines in everyday life that keep them to the same few streets—but not in "other" parts of town. No matter how well you already know a place, you can accelerate and reinforce your knowledge about it by giving some special attention to map study in the empty time between calls.

The time *not* to practice route finding is during emergency calls. Prudence alone would dictate that choosing a tried-and-true route is smarter than trying one that will "probably" be quicker. Similarly, there is a difference between excellent route-finding and flat-out racing. It is admirable to know your area; it is irresponsible to make squealing tires and burning brake pads a regular part of getting there.

Do not underestimate the importance of knowing your turf. There is a special satisfaction in knowing esoteric routes that land you at an address ahead of someone who has not studied the lay of the land. Patients and their loved ones appreciate it, too!

Weather Awareness

EMS providers work in all kinds of weather. Rain, snow, heat, fog—it all impacts the safety and comfort of EMS operations. Between calls, it may be possible to minimize the impact of weather extremes by paying attention and responding appropriately. If it is hot and humid, take plenty of high-quality nutrition and fluids. If you got soaked in the rain on a previous call, take time to dry out or change clothing. If it is winter, dress appropriately. Layers are best, so it's easy to adjust to changing exposures. If it is foggy, be careful at scenes to maximize your individual visibility and check around yourself carefully, especially when working on roadways.

Consider the impact of weather, too, on the people to whom you will respond. They may be especially irritable and difficult, just because of nasty weather. To prepare for this in advance is to give yourself an improved chance of interacting effectively.

HEAT STRESS INDEX

	RELATIVE HUMIDITY								
	10%	20%	30%	40%	50%	60%	70%	80%	90%
104	98	104	110	120	132				
102	97	101	108	117	125				
100	95	99	105	110	120	132			
98	93	97	101	106	110	125			
96	91	95	98	104	108	120	128		
94	89	93	95	100	105	111	122		
92	87	90	92	96	100	106	115	122	
90	85	88	90	92	96	100	106	114	122
88	82	86	87	89	93	95	100	106	115
86	80	84	85	87	90	92	96	100	109
84	78	81	83	85	86	89	91	95	99
82	77	79	80	81	84	86	89	91	95
80	75	77	78	79	81	83	85	86	89
78	72	75	77	78	79	80	81	83	85
76	70	72	75	76	77	77	77	78	79
74	68	70	73	74	75	75	75	76	77

TEMPERATURE °F (vertical axis label)

NOTE: Add 10° F when protective clothing is worn and add 10°F when in direct sunlight

HUMITURE °F	DANGER CATEGORY	INJURY THREAT
Below 60°	None	Little or no danger under normal circumstances
80°–90°	Caution	Fatigue possible if exposure is prolonged and there is physical activity
90°–105°	Extreme Caution	Heat cramps and heat exhaustion possible if exposure is prolonged and there is physical activity
105°–130°	Danger	Heat cramps or exhaustion likely, heat stroke possible if exposure is prolonged and there is physical activity
Above 130°	Extreme Danger	Heat stroke imminent!

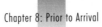

WIND CHILL INDEX

		TEMPERATURE °F												
		45	40	35	30	25	20	15	10	5	0	-5	-10	-15
WIND SPEED (MPH)	5	43	37	32	27	22	16	11	6	0	-5	-10	-15	-21
	10	34	28	22	16	10	3	-3	-9	-15	-22	-27	-34	-40
	15	29	23	16	9	2	-5	-11	-18	-25	-31	-38	-45	-51
	20	26	19	12	4	-3	-10	-17	-24	-31	-39	-46	-53	-60
	25	23	16	8	1	-7	-15	-22	-29	-36	-44	-51	-59	-66
	30	21	13	6	-2	-10	-18	-25	-33	-41	-49	-56	-64	-71
	35	20	12	4	-4	-12	-20	-27	-35	-43	-52	-58	-67	-75
	40	19	11	3	-5	-13	-21	-29	-37	-45	-53	-60	-69	-76
	45	18	10	2	-6	-14	-22	-30	-38	-46	-54	-62	-70	-78

A   B   C

	WIND CHILL TEMPERATURE °F	DANGER
A	Above -25°F	Little danger for properly clothed person
B	-25°F / -75°F	Increasing danger, flesh may freeze
C	Below -75°F	Great danger, flesh may freeze in 30 seconds

Figure 8.2

The outside environment takes its toll. Dress appropriately, and attend to your own nutritional and fluid status, especially in severe weather.

Heat stress and cold exposure are particular concerns, especially when a situation becomes prolonged (Fig. 8.2). EMS providers are just as susceptible to heat stroke and hypothermia as anyone else who sustains an exposure. And although it will not kill you, frostbite is very debilitating. The time to prepare for the weather is before a call.

Some EMS providers may have access to a properly-implemented Emergency Incident Rehabilitation center on prolonged situations. The purpose of Emergency Incident Rehabilitation is "to ensure that the physical and mental condition of members operating at the scene of an emergency or a training exercise does not deteriorate to the point that affects the safety of each member or that jeopardizes the safety and integrity of the operation."[1] Although each person has personal responsibility for his or her own well-being, an Emergency Incident Rehabilitation site provides a place and the equipment to rest, medically monitor (vital signs and general assessment), and prepare to work again. It is recommended that emergency services personnel work no more than 45 minutes between mandatory 10-minute (minimum) rest periods at sustained operations. The rest site should be environmentally comfortable and away from the sights, sounds, and fumes (if any) of the situation. Such programs may be available through your local fire department. If none is pre-planned, maybe you could use some non-call time to help implement it for the benefit of all EMS providers in your area.

Continuing Medical Education

Another area of noncall emergency care activity is continuing medical education (CME). CME may come in the form of formal training, run reviews, clinical time in other medical care settings, reading EMS and other medical journals, reading texts, or going to conferences. However you do it, CME is vital to your continued growth as a prehospital care provider.

There has been a tendency among some practicing EMTs and paramedics to put away the books once they hit the streets. Streetwise people know the folly of this. You cannot remember all you learned in training, especially if you do not use the information often. For example, without reviewing, even people in busy prehospital systems may not see enough challenging cardiology cases to remember the rules for differentiating a widebeat supraventricular tachycardia from ventricular tachycardia. If you don't read, you certainly will not stay ahead of what is new. Medicine is a "living science" that is constantly evolving. Technological and equipment development alone is significant, as is our understanding of various disease and injury processes.

The most important mandate for self-motivated CME is called "professionalism." The desire to be an excellent EMT or paramedic burns inside, where no one else can see it. The mental curiosity to reach out for new ideas and knowledge, even after the tortuous months of training, is a given for top-notch providers.

Yet, resolve for self-study can fall easily by the wayside, the victim of exhaustion, disinterest, or sheer inertia. Try to avoid this! If you can coax yourself and your coworkers to continue the learning process, you

[1] USFA, FA-114: *Emergency Incident Rehabilitation*, July 1991.

will be better off. (So will your patients.) Even if you live in a remote area, you can find plenty of new material to read and discuss in the trade journals and magazines, through joining state and national EMS associations, and by attending regional and/or national EMS conventions. The benefits of attending at least one high-quality EMS conference annually includes the refreshment that comes just from getting away from your ambulance district. Being "let off your leash" gives you time to reflect on your commitment to EMS. Meeting like-minded people is vivid reinforcement that you have colleagues beyond your home territory. Hearing their problems helps put your own in perspective. Seeing the vendor displays is eye-opening. Attending a good EMS conference is exactly the boost many people need to re-light their fire about EMS.

Another effective CME tool is a "Journal Club." With a minimum of time investment, a group of prehospital workers can teach each other. One group formed, and chose a monthly topic. Various people each received a different article to present to the others. Sometimes the topics were related, sometimes not. Each participant received a copy of each article discussed. When centered around a social occasion, with refreshments and casual clothes, a journal club can be a great success on several levels.

Too frequently, individuals neglect their CME. Do not rely on the training institutions, regulatory agencies, ambulance managers, or medical control committees to do it for you! Each of these entities may be a resource, but CME is not their responsibility. It is yours. There are obvious medicolegal reasons for keeping up with national standards (see chapter 13). The more important principle is to make your medicine, and that of your colleagues, as "cutting edge" as possible. It's good for patient care—and it also attracts high-quality applicants for job openings. The whole team is strengthened.

Other Precall Concerns

Non-call time provides an excellent opportunity to nurture professional relationships with people who respond with your organization to emergencies or who receive patients at the hospital. This may mean stopping by the police station to share the outcome of a particular case, informally chatting with the first responders, or helping out in the emergency department. You get to know the names that go with the faces—and they get to know you. Assuming that you conduct yourself respectably and professionally, the effort results in earning respect from your colleagues and peers. The cohesiveness that emerges over time clearly enhances the effectiveness of your emergency care.

When you work at developing relationships with other personnel, remember that there is a flip side. If you are offensive or in any way unprofessional in developing these relationships, you can find yourself combating a bad reputation. It takes a concerted effort and the proof of time to shake off a reputation for being cocky, sloppy, too buddy-buddy, or perhaps worst, untrustworthy.

Regardless of how professional you are, whenever you are a new-comer to a system, expect to endure a certain amount of "hazing" while the established members of the group test to see how well you will mesh. Many times, this has little or nothing to do with your medical knowledge and ability; the important thing to the group is that you fit in. Unfortunately, there's no handy recipe for fitting in because every group has its own personality and needs beyond emergency medical care. Fitting in depends on your own personality and objectives, and those of the group. Mostly, it takes time—and those hours between calls give you the chance to show that you can get along.

Call Nature

At last! A call comes in! Any up-to-date dispatch center provides re-sponders with a report of what seems to be the matter—the chief com-plaint. This is an excellent example of system integration. To ask prehospital workers to walk onto a scene—particularly an emergency scene—with little or no idea of what to expect is to invite eventual disaster.

The more precisely the Emergency Medical Dispatcher (EMD) elic-its the call nature, the better (Fig. 8.3). The premier model for gaining quick, appropriate, thorough information is the medical priority dispatch model. Properly trained EMDs use a time-tested system of computer-based algorithms (formerly flip-chart cue cards). Properly-implemented EMD systems have had a major impact on timely and appropriate emer-gency response in the past two decades. The advantage is that there is no such thing as a generic emergency response due to a lack of infor-mation; they send the *necessary* response based on a brief, concise series of questions.

Figure 8.3

Your dispatchers are your link to information and safety. Respect them.

In addition, EMDs nowadays typically assist callers with "post-dispatch instructions." These range from cautioning bystanders to do nothing at all, to basic first aid (such as direct pressure for bleeding), to CPR. Properly implemented emergency medical dispatch systems have a profound impact on medicolegal comfort levels, patient outcomes, and not least, rescuer safety.[2]

In addition to the obvious safety issue, EMS also provides responding crews with a chance to prepare medically. Going on a call for "trouble breathing" and you have not used Alupent in a year? There is time to review dosage and delivery. On the way to a possible pediatric cardiac arrest? You and your partner can agree on certain tasks ahead of time.

Keep in mind, though, that hearing the dispatcher's perception of the call nature is a double-edged sword. It can benefit *and* hinder the way you handle the actual situation. View the call nature as a general guideline only, and there is more chance you'll remain open-minded enough to be able to react appropriately to what you find on arrival. The actual situation may not fit into a preconceived notion. For example,

---

[2] Jeff J. Clawson and Kate Dernocoeur, *Principles of Emergency Medical Dispatch*, 2nd ed. (Salt Lake City: MPC, Inc., 1996) [release pending].

two paramedics were dispatched on an electrocution. They arrived to find a teenage boy with a gunshot wound to the abdomen. It took a few moments for the paramedics to readjust to the actual problem at hand because they had been "expecting" something else. As it turned out, the boy and his friend had been afraid to admit on the telephone that an accidental shooting had occurred.

In another situation, the paramedics were sent on "a rollover" on the elevated portion of a nearby highway. As they went up the on-ramp, they looked over to the highway to make visual contact with the accident. They were taken aback to see not a rollover, but a 60-car pile-up. Obviously, their problem-solving priorities required immediate adjustment!

By heeding the dispatcher's perception of call nature, you can gain a ballpark idea of what to anticipate. Ask yourself questions. At minimum, is it medical or trauma? If it's trauma, is there a chance the scene is criminal or violent? (Always keep in mind that *any* scene can involve violence, but predictability is higher on some than others!) In general, things are not always what they seem. Vehicle crashes do happen because of underlying medical causes. Scenes that "should" entail some violence, in fact, do not. Listen for the call nature—and be careful not to assume it will be accurate until you arrive. The tendency to tunnel vision is prevalent enough without being sucked into the whirlpool of a mistaken notion before you ever get to the scene.

En Route

There's still much to do before arriving on the scene. People brand new to emergency medicine inevitably feel a strong surge of adrenalin the first few-dozen times the alert tones sound. This is predictable because you are encountering the unknown, armed with untested knowledge and unproven abilities. And no one fantasizes mundane calls. Like everyone, you imagine horrible scenes, full of people with life-threatening conditions.

The inevitable adrenalin rush can be alleviated with a few slow, deep breaths and concentration on the three most important elements of field care, the "1-2-3's of EMS":

1. Personal safety
2. Appropriate medical care
3. Superior interpersonal communication

It will help focus your excitement to silently repeat the words "1-2-3's, 1-2-3's, 1-2-3's . . ." This works well because thinking about the meaning behind them while en route keeps you focused on the correct priorities when you arrive at the scene. (In bygone years, the universal basics of EMS were said to be the ABCs. The mantra of responders new to the game was "ABCs . . . ABCs . . . ABCs . . ." No longer! Safety has—finally—taken its rightful place as the highest priority.)

In most EMS systems, a person just getting started will watch other people run calls for a period of time before being given the responsibility for handling them personally. Watching is an excellent chance to observe the styles of care other people have, and lets you make some decisions about which interpersonal techniques work (or don't work) without the pressure of risking personal failure.

Driving

One admirable quality in any EMS provider is knowing the territory "like the back of your hand." And few drivers actually know *everything* about the response area. Thus there are times to refer to road maps. Any time you are unsure of the route, take the time to be certain of where you should be going before putting the vehicle in motion. If you aren't, "heading in that direction" while your partner fumbles through the map books is a sure way to have a net loss of time. It is also ridiculous and quite embarrassing to be running with lights and sirens and to have to make a U-turn!

Both the driver and the driver's partner are responsible for safe arrival at the scene. In addition to helping find the route, the partner can watch the road. Many drivers rely on their partners to "clear" the right-hand intersections. Watching the road is vital to your mutual safety. Also, if an accident happens, it helps if both members of the emergency crew can report what happened. One driver had no such backup after he was hit, because his partner was looking down, trying to scrub blood off his shirt at the time of impact.

Driving safety, a complex topic beyond the scope of this book, is an art unto itself.[3] Much of it, though, depends on the same qualities that are found in a person who has good streetsense. The traits of common sense and good judgment are particularly relevant. Safe driving includes leaving enough room ahead to avoid the panicked drivers who simply jam on the brakes. It means exercising utmost caution at stop-

---

[3] See Bradford J. Childs and Donald J. Ptacnik, *Emergency Ambulance Driving* (Englewood Cliffs, NJ: The Brady Company, 1986).

lights. It means appreciating current road conditions and traveling at appropriate speeds (Fig. 8.4). It means leaving behind the child in you who likes all the fun and excitement of driving fast with lights and a siren, and caring, instead, about why we have been allowed to have these unusual driving privileges.

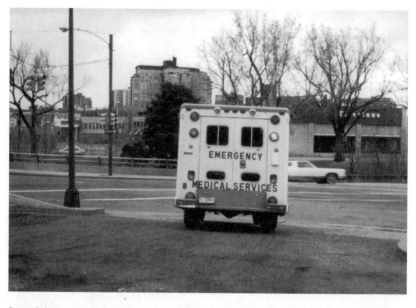

Figure 8.4

Every time you head out on an emergency call, recognize and respect the privilege and power you wield. Go carefully! (Photo courtesy of Jeff Forster.)

Sleepiness and Shift Work

EMS can be exhausting. This is a real hazard. Shift work is a primary culprit. Personnel who are up running calls for too many hours are bound to become dangerously tired. In addition, shifting on-duty hours or rotating shift patterns too frequently has been shown to cause chronic fatigue. This interferes with a person's ability to rest effectively. Altering the body's natural rhythms as little as possible is important.

If you have to work shifts, pay attention to your sleep regimen. This is relevant to your stress management and to maintaining a positive outlook toward your job and the people in it. If you are a day sleeper, try to mimic a nighttime environment by sleeping in a cool, dark, quiet place. Use a "white noise" maker. Turn on the answering machine. Prevent unwanted visitors by posting a "Day Sleeper" sign on the door. Also, figure out your "anchor" time of day—that time which, for you, is the equivalent of others' middle of the night. These are the several hours that you can reliably expect to rest without interruption, even on days off. (It's best not to try to completely revert to a daytime lifestyle on days off.) For example, a night worker may view anchor time from 8 a.m. to noon. On days off, that person might go to bed "early" at 3:00 a.m. and get up at noon, and alter those sleep hours on work days to 8:00 a.m. to 3:00 p.m.[4]

For the best sleep, regardless when you do it, do not eat a heavy meal or exercise right before bed. It also helps to unwind appropriately after a shift. These strategies allow for the most rest-inducing condition prior to sleep.

The exhaustion of EMS can easily lead to sleepiness. People tell of becoming aware they had a call only when they were already at the scene. One driver who had this frightening experience had to inquire where they were in order to know which direction to go when they were ready to transport! Ambulance personnel have died because of sleepiness; one team returning from a transfer in the mountains of Colorado went off the road twenty miles from home at 3:00 a.m. The driver probably fell asleep at the wheel.

Volunteers also face a problem with sleepiness, because calls naturally seem to happen at the most disruptive hours. In addition, many rural services in America face lengthy transport times, particularly when transferring a patient to a distant city. For example, the hours it took to drive 137,000 miles in two years in an ambulance on Pine Ridge Reservation, South Dakota, no doubt involved some sleepy drivers![5] In fact, according to the U.S. Department of Transportation, the risk of having a motor vehicle crash is at least ten times higher between 4:00 a.m. and 6:00 a.m.— and as many as 200,000 traffic crashes per year may be sleep-related.[6]

Rescuers are not immune to human needs, even though there sometimes seems to be no alternative except to carry on when our bodies are screaming for sleep. There are some strategies for attempting to shock yourself into alertness. Open the windows. Gently slap your face or the side of your neck under the ear. Get something to drink. Some people

---

[4] *EMS Safety: Techniques and Applications* FA-144, April 1994, 139.
[5] Kate Dernocoeur, "The Far Limits of Rural EMS: Challenges on Indian Reservations," *JEMS* 13 (April 1988).
[6] Russ McCallion and Jim Fazackerley, "Burning the EMS Candle: EMS Shifts and Worker Fatigue," *JEMS* (October 1991).

find hot works better than cold. Caffeine, of course, can help promote artificial wakefulness (but for good health, avoid making it a habit). Turn on the radio. Sing along. Talk out loud. Stop the vehicle if the nature of the call allows (such as on a long-distance, non-emergency transfer) and stretch for a minute, or walk a few yards down the road. But if you have tried everything and you still cannot stay awake, perhaps the safest thing is to admit that you must get some sleep.

Is this realistic? Yes and no. You cannot just quit driving in the middle of an emergency transfer. Yet there's also a macho element. No one wants to admit being not "strong enough" to stay awake. No one wants to jeopardize a decent job. (If you're pushed that hard, is it really a "decent" job?!) But consider the risks to yourself, your partner, your patient, and your employer's $100,000 rig if you do, in fact, fall asleep at the wrong time.

Preoccupation and Complacency

Another insidious hazard to shake off as you leave the station is preoccupation. Inevitably, emergency calls come in exactly when you wish they wouldn't. It is easy to lose sight of the priorities when the tones go off while you were in the middle of something you regard as important. Your tendency is to linger mentally with whatever you were doing as you head out on the call. Try to avoid this inappropriate, if human, impulse. Shelve every other concern, and focus on the situation at hand when you leave to assist somebody (Fig. 8.5). This is true regardless of the call nature, but applies particularly to emergency calls where safety issues are largest and the need for mental crispness is greatest.

One strategy for achieving such mental clarity is to imagine in your mind's eye a set of compartments similar to the mailboxes at a post office. Each concern of your life—each relationship, the mortgage payment, your mother's upcoming birthday, your league baseball game on Tuesday—has a compartment. Whatever project you were working on when the tones go off is rolled up neatly and put back in its "compartment." This frees your mind to focus on the newest project: the medical call. Avoiding the preoccupation trap is an important safety skill. Without it, for example, you may not see what happened in an accident, or you may miss important environmental and situational clues as you arrive on the scene.

Figure 8.5

Turn your attention to just one project at a time. When an EMS call comes in, put what was "on the table" in its mental slot and focus on the new task—attending to a call for help.

Along the same lines, and for the same reasons, be conscious of complacency. Don't let it creep into your approach to EMS. It's not uncommon, after running a few hundred calls, to presume that you have "been there, done that." The more calls you handle, the easier it is to begin to believe that calls tend to run smoothly and nonviolently—which they usually do! Complacency makes you a prime target. Stay poised for the unusual. Extensive experience is admirable, but even more so when the masks of preoccupation and complacency do not become part of your prehospital style.

Pulling Up to the Scene

There is a distinct advantage in acquiring as much information as possible during your arrival. Many important details about the scene and the people who are there can be gathered even before you get out of the ambulance. The considerations are endless. Look for places of vulnerability and sources of refuge. You and your partner should trade observations and devise a mutual plan. For example, if you are the attendant and you see that the green car is most badly damaged and still has someone inside, tell your partner you will check that person first if she will check the people who all seem to be up and walking.

Arrive discreetly. There is an advantage to shutting off the emergency lights and siren one or two blocks away, when possible. EMS is not a carnival. Roaring up to the address like a screaming light show can be hazardous. It inevitably attracts a crowd, and crowds are not always fun to have around. Be aware, of course, that once your emergency lights and siren are off, you are no longer in "authorized" emergency mode. Drive accordingly, for those last few hundred yards. Obey the rules of the road, especially if you will be crossing any intersections. The last intersection prior to arrival is a frequent source of accidents because the attention of the responding crew has often jumped ahead. Let completion of your driving task be as important as juggling clipboards, reaching for jackets, and using the radio. Try to do these tasks without the cab lights on, for the purposes demonstrated in Figure 8.6. There is no sense making an easy target of yourselves before you know whether the scene is safe.

One site where it is advisable to leave on emergency lights is at road accidents at night or in bad weather. This is for your protection. If visibility is good, you can reduce the drain on the ambulance's electrical system by turning off the less visible emergency lights. The siren can almost always be turned off well before you arrive at a roadside scene. That way, you do not interrupt (and deafen) people already on the scene.

Another reason to shut off your emergency lights and siren prior to arriving on the scene is for the benefit of patients and their families. Many callers request that no lights or sirens be used. They do not want to disturb the neighborhood. They do not like to have their troubles broadcasted. But if the situation sounds potentially critical, facilitate your arrival with lights and siren to within a few blocks. That way, you accommodate both your mission of safe haste and their desire for privacy. The result is a more cooperative encounter. Families who know you will respect their wishes are more likely to call back if they need you again.

Figure 8.6

(Top) Pulling onto a scene with cab lights on gives someone who wants to do harm an easy target. (Bottom) See how much protection a darkened cab offers? Use a penlight to write down arrival times.

Minimizing the dramatics of your own arrival also prevents you from subtly altering the scene. You have the chance to assess it before everyone realizes you are arriving. This results in a more accurate impression of it. What do you see? Is there a crowd? Chaos? Hysteria? Do the people seem to welcome your arrival, or are they hostile? Is there police cover? If not, do you want to call them before getting out? Is the scene suspiciously dark and quiet?

Park the ambulance in a way that minimizes the risk to yourself by playing on the expectations of others. True, most emergencies will not threaten your safety, but you cannot know which ones do until you get closer. Give yourself an advantage. Consider driving *past* the address to which you are responding, so you can eyeball three sides of the house. Never back into the driveway (as is shown in some misinformed media shots!). Doing that gives people *lots* of time to cause harm, if that is their intention. Better to walk a few more feet than to fall into an ugly trap. Such seemingly minor tactics can save your life.

Tombstone Courage

Sometimes, for some reason, people in EMS make the choice to attempt foolhardy heroics in a gamble against injury or death. This is a personal decision, but one which usually crosses the line of prudent decision making. The term "tombstone courage" was coined for such actions by police, but it has obvious applications in EMS as well. An example of tombstone courage would be when someone enters a hazardous scene without appropriate backup.[7] You are asking for trouble.

Sometimes there is no backup available. Maybe you are twenty miles from town and the undersheriff fell back to sleep after the telephone notification. He's on the way now, but you and your partner are being pressured by bystanders to enter a notoriously violent household. In another scenario, maybe EMS and local law enforcement personnel have poor working relations. No one on your service ever calls for backup, so you are certainly not going to be the first one to cross that invisible line of pride. Or maybe you decide to ignore your screaming intuition because the provided call nature was nothing to get excited about.

When a scene feels rotten even as you arrive, you have to decide whether or not you will go in before it is secured by the proper au-

---

[7] Pierce R. Brooks, ". . . *Officer Down, Code Three"* (Schaumberg, Ill.: Motorola Teleprograms, Inc., 1975), 171.

thorities. This is a very personal decision. On one hand, a basic premise of emergency care is that you cannot help others if you are hurt. On the other hand, we have rescuer personalities! We got into prehospital medicine because of a strong underlying desire to help people in distress. When you know someone has been shot and may be dying inside, yet your intuition tells you the hazards are sky-high, you are caught in a dilemma that only you can resolve.

Some paramedics readily admit that they will ignore their own safety in order to save another life; others feel differently, and will not. In the end, you are responsible for your own actions. There is a difference between taking calculated risks and jumping headlong into a situation that could kill you. It is an individual choice, but one that is important to ponder before the moment to decide arrives.

Summary

In a way, actual patient contact is just a small part of EMS. How we spend time prior to arrival and between calls has a great deal to do with how well we ultimately handle people and their concerns.

A major component in preparing to handle calls, day in and day out, is attention to safety for everyone concerned. Maintain safety as a prime consideration in everything you do in prehospital care.

The Scene

"He who can handle the quickest rate of change survives."

—Major John Boyd, USAF fighter pilot

Chapter Overview

One of the most delightful and yet challenging aspects of prehospital care is that patients are on their own turf. Witnessing the actual scene is an advantage EMS providers have over in-hospital providers. It puts events into their natural context.

The approach you use at the scene will depend, as always, on how quickly and accurately you form perceptions of the people and their environment. Remember the 1-2-3's of EMS! You should learn to assimilate the information that can make or break the scene even before you check the patient's ABCs. Attention to these details can make the difference between a call that is well handled and one that is not. How you walk in and greet the people who called, even how you knock on the door, influences the success of each call.

Much of what happens on the scene has to do with control of the other people and choreography of their activities; these components of streetsense are addressed later. This chapter addresses common sense considerations of the physical layout and presentation of the scene, and how to redesign it, if necessary. The intention is to optimize your personal safety and efficiency. It also discusses scene distractions, considerate handling of bystanders and relatives, and strategies to gain on-scene cooperation among the people of various emergency agencies.

Personal safety is the basis of much of your scene assessment. It sometimes seems like all we do is jump at shadows, expecting bad things to happen, but this is not just paranoia. The best EMS providers have trained themselves to pay attention to *everything* that's happening. This is true of ace pilots, or those 5 percent who account for 40 percent of air combat victories. On the other hand, of those pilots who are shot down, four out of five never saw their attacker until it was too late—if at all.[1] Likewise, EMS providers need to be able to acquire and filter a great deal of information, if they are to stay alive and well.

Those who do not acknowledge the possibility of personal injury when approaching strangers during a crisis situation are asking for trouble. Better to decide that a situation is benign after assessing it for hazards than vice versa. For starters, it is difficult to over-emphasize the importance of knowing the call nature. The more precisely you can speculate about the impending encounter, the better. Of course, it is equally as foolhardy to rely on the call nature as a fact. Be ready for surprises. What you find is not always what they said you would find.

Getting Out of the Ambulance

Leaving the ambulance is a time of transition. The ambulance is *your* turf. Outside, the territory belongs to the people you see through the windshield. It is a specific (if psychological and tenuous) boundary.

There are two things to remember about leaving the sanctuary of the ambulance. Before opening your door, make it a habit to check the rear view mirror for traffic coming from behind (Fig. 9.1). It is easy to presume that motorists (who *saw* the ambulance stop) will realize that someone will probably be getting out. But you never know! More than one EMS provider has been injured (or nearly so) by passing motorists. Open the door slowly enough to alert passing traffic that you are emerging. Caution riders in the rear compartment to be careful as well. Better yet, have them exit via the rear doors when parked in the street.

Check your portable radio and pager when leaving the ambulance. If possible, put the page on "vibrate" mode, and turn the radio down as far as possible. It does no good to broadcast your position inadvertently should either tool squawk or squelch at the wrong moment! If a scene seems particularly unnerving, place your hand over the radio speaker to further maintain quiet until you have more information about the scene.

---

[1] Bill Atkinson, "Health Care in America" lecture at *EMS Today*, Albuquerque, NM, March 1996.

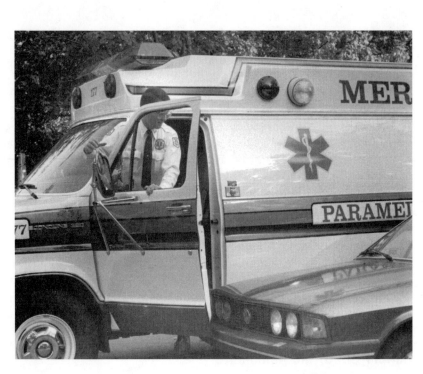

Figure 9.1

Be careful when getting out of the ambulance, especially when your door is opening into traffic.

As you arrive, begin the process of being an "information vacuum." Watch, listen, gather any clues that answer the 1-2-3's of EMS: information about safety precautions to address, medical information, and ways you'll first attempt to communicate with these people. This process begins while still in the ambulance, and will continue throughout the call, even on routine transfers. The peak period of this information gathering, though, is in the initial on-scene moments. It is important to focus solely on your current activities without being preoccupied.

General On-Scene Considerations

Protective Equipment

Emergency scenes can be physically hazardous. Do you have protective equipment? At minimum, EMS providers should have access to: appropriate reflective gear for nighttime; protective masks, gloves, and gowns for both infection control and hazardous materials purposes; protective helmets, and sturdy footwear (preferably steel-toed). In addition, many EMS providers are increasingly choosing to wear body armor. This equipment should be available in the emergency vehicle.

The other half of the equation is that prehospital personnel should *use* protective equipment as needed. For example, reflective gear can be life-saving. Without it, drivers approaching a group of emergency vehicles at night in the rain will *not* see the solitary figure waving at them to slow down 200 yards closer. This is especially true of drivers whose windshields are pitted, or who are drug impaired.

Assessing the need for protective gear takes on a new twist in situations such as cliff rescues or river incidents. If you live in an area with hazards, such as mountains or water or caves, consider learning the additional skills necessary for safe access to these areas and effective extrication of people. If your scenes are often complicated by specialized technology, such as agricultural equipment, make the effort to become thoroughly acquainted with the specialized equipment, and personal protective gear. If access to the patient is beyond your personal training and expertise, plan to wait for others with the right know-how and proper equipment to bring the patient to you. This is frustrating when you know the patient needs medical intervention, but sometimes common sense has to prevail. Don't be reluctant to admit your limits.

Cover and Concealment

Cover is best defined as a place that deflects or stops bullets. This may include crouching behind the engine block of the ambulance (by the wheels, to minimize the risk of ricochet), behind a stout tree or telephone pole, or behind a full trash container or fire hydrant. Concealment is a place that hides you from view, but which will not stop bullets. Examples of places for concealment include an open ambulance door, a wooden fence, darkness (until an arriving vehicle's headlights illuminate you) or dense bushes (Fig. 9.2). As you enter every scene, notice places that you could use quickly for concealment or for cover, depending on your needs. Naturally, in overtly hostile incidents, stay in a safe location out of the way until law enforcement personnel secure the scene.

Figure 9.2

Paramedics held at bay by this child with a toy gun are demonstrating concealment and cover. The paramedic on the left could be completely concealed by the bushes—but a bullet could easily penetrate. The paramedic on the right has chosen good cover; a bullet would be stopped by the trees.

Distractions

Distractions will interfere with your ability to attend to the patient and still be aware of the other details of running an emergency scene. There are two types: physical and mental. Both need to be eliminated to the best extent possible. Even if you are not bothered by distractions, they may prevent others from concentrating on their roles. The patient certainly does not need any more sensory input—the crisis itself is enough.

One obvious physical distraction that is easy to eliminate is the noise generated by electronic media. There may be radios or televisions turned on at the scene. By turning them off, you direct everyone's attention to the task at hand. This is particularly true for TV when your patient was watching the same thing you were before you got the call. If it is a slow, noncritical situation, the helpers could too easily get reabsorbed in the football game, especially if their skills aren't needed. Should their assistance become necessary, it can be difficult to regain their attention!

Some people are very sensitive about who touches their electronic equipment, so it may not be effective for building rapport to march in and snap off the TV or radio without comment. Take a moment to explain why it's important. People will appreciate your consideration, and that will help build trust. If you won't be trans-

> **In order to have appropriate mental focus for the task ahead, shelve all preoccupations when an ambulance call comes in.**

porting, it also helps to leave the scene as you found it. An elderly person who was enjoying a good show appreciates not having to get up to turn the TV back on.

Several mental distractions previously mentioned in regard to effective interpersonal communication may play a role in safety as well. Preoccupation is a classic. In order to have appropriate mental focus for the task ahead, shelve all preoccupations when an ambulance call comes in. Put your five senses—as well as your intuition—on alert to act on your behalf instead of stewing about an unrelated matter. Let your focusing be as intense as a laser beam, undiffused by other concerns.

Another mental distraction is attitude. There is a balance between feeling unsure and timid, and being cocky or overconfident. If you feel inept, others will take advantage and possibly injure you. If you feel invincible, you are denying the unpredictability of the streets. "It" can happen to you, and might—on the very next call. The best and most professional approach is to individualize each call; believe in yourself and your training—but not so much that you miss or ignore important safety cues.

Be careful of clogged sensory filters. Just because we are the "rescuers" does not mean that we cannot feel overwhelmed sometimes. An overwhelmed person stops functioning; clogged filters in your mind are a dangerous distraction. They prevent clear focusing and five-sensing, and encourage disaster. A common coping mechanism—the ability to put our responses to tragedy aside—sometimes breaks down. If you feel this happening, it is vital to step back and regroup—even momentarily—before attempting to carry on. That is, STOP (Stop, Think, Observe, and Plan). If you cannot carry on, then do not hesitate to say so and find a less overwhelming way to help. Remember: Your safety, and that of others, is at stake.

Finally, beware of the distractions that stem from complacency. Say that you have worked with your partner for months, maybe years. You know she is tremendously capable, and it's a low-stress call. Not much for you to do. The cop is a friend of yours. So you start chatting—and before you know it, your partner has things wrapped up and you are out of there. Happens a lot. But there are times when you are not watching, that your partner might need you. When you are not the primary patient attendant, one of your main functions is to protect your partner while he or she focuses on the medical elements of the call. You should be watching the environment for hazards or dangerous people. You should always be ready to assist your partner—and you cannot be mentally prepared to do so when you are complacently hanging out with co-responders (who, by the way, also have a job to do).

Dogs

In general, take the presence of an animal seriously; dogs can be hazardous, especially when they are trained to protect their home. In one case, the paramedics heard the police dispatcher call for routine police cover on an overdose—and four patrol units responded that they would be en route. It sounded more like a shooting than an overdose. The first two police cars arrived at the same time as the puzzled paramedics. One officer explained: "We didn't want you trying to go in there alone. They have two nasty Dobermans at this address." (Now *that* is a good interagency relationship!)

Although many fierce dogs are well-trained and controllable, some are not. In particular, pit bull terriers have acquired a reputation for unmatched ferocity and viciousness. People have been seriously wounded and killed in pit bull terrier attacks. Trained attack dogs and other similar dogs are beyond the scope of these comments and should be handled by trained animal control officers.

In their own way, small dogs can also be particularly unnerving. They are quick, and their teeth are sharp! Often, upon approaching a patient who is sick in bed, you can hear the family pet growling from underneath the bed. Visions of multiple puncture wounds by the valiant ankle-biter have prompted more than one paramedic or EMT to request removal of the threat before doing much beyond the ABCs.

In fact, most dogs are not a problem. Someone may already have the dog well under control, or the dog is outside or in another room. Some dogs are obviously friendly. But you never really know how a pet, that is confused and upset by all the commotion, will respond. Even if the scene is relatively calm, and even if a member of the household assures you that "old Fido won't hurt you," you cannot be sure of that until Fido is being held or has been removed. If nothing else, putting family members onto the task gives them a tangible way to help.

When faced with a threatening animal, according to a postal worker and other voices of experience, do your best not to let your fear show. Animals can sense fear. Act like you are in charge, and speak in a loud, commanding voice. Use language they might respond to, such as "Down!" or "No!" One source suggested using a blanket as a crude form of snare to throw over a small animal when no other recourse exists—say, when that animal is between you and an unconscious owner. One dog that was guarding her dead owner was bribed away with food. Other options for trying to control animals preventing access to patients may not seem kind—but sometimes such measures are necessary. These include a blast from a CO^2 extinguisher, a high-candlelight flashlight beam in the animal's eyes, or a stream of water from a fire hose.[2] Note that *all* of these tactics are meant solely to stun or unbalance an angry animal momentarily. They buy time for your escape—that is all.

Never try to "stare down" a dog; it will be interpreted as a challenge and an invitation to attack. Never turn your back on a threatening animal; this also encourages attack. Face the dog, and put whatever is available (such as your medical kit) between you and it. If you think attack is inevitable, protect your face and throat and try to let a less vital body part take the hit.

Whatever the animal life distraction, you need to decide how threatened you and your colleagues feel. For example, pet snakes are best kept in their cages. Hog pens are to be avoided, since hogs can be very vicious. Rapid extrication is probably in order!

Relatives and Bystanders

Imagine what it must feel like to:

- Encounter a sudden medical emergency, particularly in your own home, when the patient is a member of your family.
- Proceed with the steps for handling the emergency. People hear "Call 9-1-1" but seldom think they will ever really have to do it.
- Wait the interminable minutes for help to arrive.

---

[2] Mike Taigman and Bruce Adams, "Street Survival" seminar, Chicago, May 1988.

- Watch the first helpers arrive and start working. Then, often, watch more and more help arrive in waves. Sometimes EMS has the appearance (and gracefulness) of a herd of elephants. In our zeal to get in on the action, we can seem formidable, particularly to people who did not want to create a lot of fuss to begin with. If you sense that your patient or his family has just become more concerned about the accumulating masses in the house than the medical problem at hand, a few kind words may relieve that anxiety. Say something like, "If you are wondering why all these people are here, it's because sometimes we need every hand to do the job. It's really important for each of us to be here." As soon as you determine that you do not need all the help, unclutter the scene by releasing some of the people to get back to whatever they were doing.

Upon entering another person's home, it is a small but important gesture to show care not to track in the mud and dirt that sticks to the heavy-soled boots and shoes we typically wear. If you make a mess, at least apologize. That leaves the family with a much more positive impression than if you say nothing. The public relations potential (assuming there is time for such niceties) cannot be overstated.

When people misinterpret our medical care, we become targets for aggression

As the call progresses, it helps to explain what is happening. We act on informed consent, but many EMS providers perform procedures without much explanation about "what" or "why." Recall the strategy of "verbalization" from Chapter 4! When people misinterpret our medical care, we become targets for aggression; more than one prehospital worker was assaulted in the early days of CPR by bystanders who misunderstood. For example, consider how barbaric it seems to insert a nasotracheal tube. It eases the concerns of bystanders to hear you say, "Joan, in case you can hear me, I'm putting a tube through your nose into your lungs to help you breathe." Although you never know when an unconscious patient will react to what you are doing, at least this explains the importance of the procedure to everyone else.

When possible, reassure the patient and family about the progress being made. Without making predictions about eventual outcome, which is inadvisable, you can be informative. Instead of saying someone will be "fine," it is more reassuring for bystanders to hear something specific, such as, "The medication seems to have helped your father's heartbeat. That's very good."

If you can take a relative or bystander along in the ambulance, tell that person to prepare to leave early enough to get to the ambulance without causing a delay in departure. In particular, elderly people and those with small children may need advance warning. A spare helper can get the person settled (usually in the cab) and buckled in.

If relatives or concerned bystanders are intending to drive themselves to the hospital, take time to be sure that they understand not to try to keep up with the ambulance. Explain that if they see the lights and siren turn on en route (even when you are sure you will not use them), they should continue to obey traffic laws and drive carefully. If, in your judgment, someone is too upset to drive, see what alternative arrangements can be made. Perhaps a calmer neighbor can drive or the police can provide transport. Emergencies can be very intense for people, and by troubleshooting this kind of detail you may prevent the additional tragedy of an accident.

When possible, remember that the family has to come home when the hospital visit is over. If you have created havoc by moving furniture and throwing trash from drug containers and IV equipment on the floor, have someone clean up while the patient is being moved to the ambulance. (*Tip:* Carry a garbage bag in the drug box, and make a habit of putting the trash in the bag as the call proceeds. This way, you will not lose equipment as easily either.) In one middle-of-the-night case, it was easily predictable that a very elderly woman would be returning home alone, a widow, after a 60-year marriage. Without some forethought by the EMS personnel, she would have found a heavy easy chair on her bed, and her bedroom floor littered with the paper and plastic debris of the resuscitation effort. Imagining her standing in the bedroom doorway in the now-quiet house made it well worth having an extra helper do some quick cleanup.

On-Scene Physicians

On-scene medical doctors are a special breed of bystander (or relative). They can be a blessing or a curse to prehospital workers. A scene can be enhanced greatly by the presence of a cooperative, nonthreatened, emergency-knowledgeable physician. It can be destroyed by poor or inappropriate intervention by a doctor.

Increasingly, medical doctors recognize the capabilities and expertise of EMS providers. Most yield willingly to that expertise if the local services have earned a good reputation. Most jurisdictions by now have local policies for handling this sensitive situation, but a positive outcome still requires a great deal of tact and diplomacy on the part of the prehospital worker.

The problems that arise tend to occur for two reasons. The first is when the physician fails to recognize or admit personal limits. Many doctors do not understand the unique nature of the prehospital environment and are not adept at handling the logistics of out-of-hospital medical emergencies. They assume they should know everything an EMT or paramedic knows. It is unfair to expect someone whose interests are in endocrinology, urology, other specialties, or even general practice, to know about emergency medicine simply because of the title "M.D."—but it happens. Many doctors themselves are swept up by the myth that they have to know everything about medicine. The fact is, people who "should" know better lose their cool when they are outside their own familiar territory.

In one late-evening, worst-case scenario, the paramedics arrived to find a surgical resident trying to orally intubate a woman with major head injuries who had been in a severe vehicle accident. The doctor, who had been drinking, refused to yield to the paramedics and spent 12 minutes on his eventually unsuccessful efforts. They were only six blocks from the trauma center. The patient died.

> Once "burned" by a bad experience or two, we become wary and negative when someone at scene says, "I'm a doctor!" However, it is inappropriate to brush that person aside indiscriminately.

The second cause of problems with on-scene doctors is the prehospital workers' reflex that all on-scene doctors are a problem. Once "burned" by a bad experience or two, we become wary and negative when someone at scene says, "I'm a doctor!" However, it is inappropriate to brush that person aside indiscriminately. Failure to individualize each encounter may lead to unnecessary problems with patient care, and later, administrative scrutiny. There are numerous stories involving reportedly calm, competent, sober, emergency-trained doctors who have been summarily dismissed from the scene (or threatened with arrest) without even the courtesy of a credentials check. This is unprofessional on the part of the prehospital worker. Take the time to find out if, in fact, your on-scene physician could be an asset to your patient's care.

To prevent inappropriate medical "control" by on-scene doctors, some EMS systems have developed delay-tactic policies. This is particu-

larly important when the on-scene doctor demands inappropriate intervention. One common tactic is to have the doctor confer on the radio
with the physician at the emergency department. Some systems will allow
on-scene doctors control of patients if they are willing to assume complete responsibility for a patient's care, including accompanying the
patient to the hospital.

No matter how your system deals with well-meaning but interfering
doctors, the important component is obviously the patient. If the doctor
jeopardizes proper delivery of prehospital care, you have a difficult task
at hand. The intensity of the scene demands quick, decisive action, not
the interference that stems from an obviously too-excited person who
greets you with the words, "I'm a doctor!" Professionalism dictates that
the encounter be viewed as part of the complexion of the call, and
handling of the disruption as a part of the job. *Your* job. The more calm
and communicative you can remain, the more others will back you up
later should the doctor file a complaint. If necessary, however, use
whatever contingencies your system has for removing troublesome
bystanders (including doctors) from the scene. This may include having
that person arrested. Preferably, your patience, interpersonal style, and
tact can prevent this. It is always better to resolve problems like these
diplomatically.

On a happier note, there is a distinct satisfaction derived from
encountering a doctor who remains calm, lets you do your duties appropriately, and cooperates fully. In one case, the paramedics knew their
helper had emergency savvy by the way he was holding the head and
neck of an unconscious girl who had been thrown from a car. But they
had no idea he was a doctor until after the nasal intubation, when he
said to the paramedic, "Nice tube!"

The principles underlying this discussion are obviously pertinent to
on-scene nurses, P.A.'s, off-duty paramedics, EMTs, even first-aiders. The
only difference is the traditional supremacy of the medical doctor. When
dealing with other health professionals, as well, appropriate patient care
is the priority, while you deal with the would-be helper in the most
positive manner possible.

There is also food for thought about the way you approach an
emergency scene when off-duty. Consider how you like capable on-scene
help to notify you of their presence, and deliver your message accordingly. For example, one first-aider helped by showing his first-aid card
to the paramedic as she walked by. He said "I'm right here if you can
use me." He then stepped back to the edge of the crowd. He was sub-

sequently put to good use, because the calm style he had already displayed spoke for his dependability.

Running

As you make your way from the ambulance to the patient, avoid running. Running at an emergency scene is always inappropriate unless you are evading an attack. Your own pulse elevates and you lose both effectiveness and clarity. Some streetwise EMS responders judge the professionalism and general competency of other crews by the way they emerge from their vehicle and move around the scene. If they run, watch out! They are excited, their adrenalin is pumping, they are anxious, and they cannot think clearly.

Instead of running, walk purposefully. Demonstrate genuine interest in reaching the patient with a gait that "says" you are concerned, but which helps you avoid releasing a lot of adrenalin. If it does become necessary to get somewhere more quickly than walking will accomplish (for example, when you have to go back to the rig for equipment), do an easy jog. This will get you there expeditiously without elevating your heart rate or your level of excitement.

Indoor Scenes

Approaching a Building

There is an ever-growing set of information to gather even as you pull up and get out of the ambulance. You can gain more time to make observations by taking an unpredictable route to the door. Instead of walking up the sidewalk to the walkway to the door, cut across the grass. Stay near bushes for cover. And don't walk right next to your partner. Spread out. This creates two targets instead of one. Walk through gates separately. It is a subtle technique, but doing the unexpected confuses those watching you and buys time while they wonder about your approach.

It may seem silly to employ these safety tips, but for your own safety, try to keep people off balance until you can assess the situation. This is only prudent. In particular, tailor your approach to the door when something seems suspicious—when it is too quiet or dark, or when no one is there to greet you. It has happened that EMS personnel have been confused for law enforcement officials, and people involved in criminal activity often want those people out of the way.

Figure 9.3

(Left) Holding a flashlight to the side may seem an insignificant detail, until ... (right) someone uses the beam for a target. If the marksman is a good shot, you're more likely to be injured holding it this way.

If you are using a flashlight to approach the scene, hold the flashlight out to the side rather than in front of you (Fig. 9.3a). The flashlight beam is an easy target.

There are many times that your approach cannot be manipulated, which increases your vulnerability. Perhaps the only route to the patient is up a narrow staircase (Fig. 9.4a and 9.4b), or it requires traversing a central pathway ringed by darkened, silent windows in a notoriously bad part of town. At such times, shake off residual preoccupations and tune in all your senses.

Have a secondary plan worked out with your partner (fight? or flight?) should things go awry. Of course, every scene is different, and in some cases your choice is obvious. For example, one crew had been called to a posh part of town at 3:00 a.m. on "chest pain." They were going up the stairs to the door when a large handgun abruptly appeared at the top, accompanied by an angry voice! The gun handler took two potshots, forcing the medics to flee (fortunately to safety). (This is an example of why it helps to heed the call nature with a measure of skepticism!) Self-preservation in the form of flight is about the only time running on a scene is acceptable. Another lesson from this case: one paramedic went one way at the bottom of the stairs, outside, and the other went the other way, into an enclosed space. Fortunately the gun handler didn't follow them down the stairs! There were some anxious moments before the crew was reunited. Try to stay together.

Figure 9.4

(Left) When ascending stairs, be alert and use any opportunity to scout ahead. Walk separately and stay near the walls. People standing on the landing above have an easy target, made only easier, (right), if you're chatting with your partner and not paying attention.

In most cases when scenes bust loose, there is a buildup of tension that gives you time to react. It helps to have a code word with your partner that means, "Something's wrong; let's get out of here!" It may be that you call your partner by a different name. It may be that you say, "I think we need the blue stretcher, let's go get it." It also helps to know whether your partner's natural inclination is to stand ground or back down (verbally or physically). Sadly, some EMS provider egos do not believe in defusing scenes; such people do not consider fleeing an option except when under fire. This is unfortunate, since there is enough authority-figure confusion on the streets. It is important to retain a "good guy" image for EMS, or our collective safety will certainly be compromised. An EMS professional stuck with such a partner is forced to wrestle with conflicting ethics. The patient care ethic is to minimize or avoid conflict. The EMS ethic is that you always back up your partner, a difficult position at times, especially when your partner has more seniority and behaves in a manner that you have difficulty supporting. This requires maturity and tact. There is no easy solution, because each partnership and situation is unique. Hopefully, as the standards of professionalism in prehospital care continue to be set, fewer people will confuse their roles on the streets.

Knocking on Doors

Another source of potential harm is through doors. In one case where the paramedics fortunately already knew not to stand in front of a door, their knock was met by a chest-level shotgun blast. Inside, they found an angry, elderly woman who thought they had been the neighborhood hoodlums who had been harassing her for days. Another crew had a steel-tipped arrow zing through the door past them.

Make a habit of standing to the side when knocking on *every* door (Fig. 9.5a). Avoid standing in front of windows, and try to stand separately from your partner. If you knock from the side regardless of call nature or the neighborhood, you can easily eliminate one prehospital hazard as part of your normal, regular routine.

There are good and bad reasons to stand on the hinge-side or the door handle-side. Standing on the hinge side lets you see past whoever opens the door to begin assessing the interior. It also puts you easily in that person's line of fire, should that be the intention. (Minimize exposure by flattening yourself against the wall instead of standing square to the opening.) Standing on the door handle-side reverses these considerations. Sometimes, it's a matter of how the doors are arranged, especially in combination with screen doors.

In some places, people have caught on to the technique of standing to the side when knocking, because police also employ this maneuver (Fig. 9.5b). Some draw the figure of a human body on the inside wall just about where someone standing to the side while knocking would be positioned—and then shoot at that target. As unusual as it is for shots to be fired through the door at all, this is still more unusual. Use the stand-aside strategy anyway!

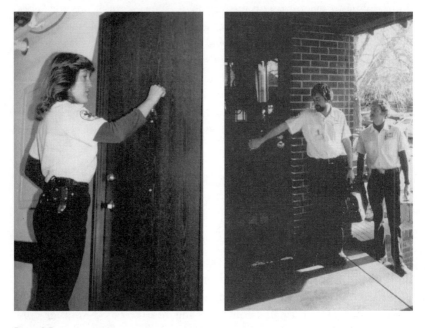

Figure 9.5

(Left) Never knock while standing directly in front of the door. It jeopardizes safety unnecessarily. (Right) Make a habit of standing to the side every time you're knocking on someone's door.

Stairways, Hallways and Doorways

These places leave EMS providers in particularly vulnerable positions. Try to get out or away from them as soon as possible, especially when your intuition is waving a red flag. Ask someone familiar with the building to lead you to the patient, if possible. Do not let someone at the front of the house say, "Yeah, she's back there," and point you to find your own way into what could be a trap. Being trapped in a hall or on stairs between two strangers is something to avoid.

When using stairs, keep quiet, and be observant for sights and sounds of potential trouble. Look ahead, and check overhead when there is an open landing above. One member of the crew should walk against one wall, the other on the other side of the stairs. Check around corners before walking around, and stay a couple of steps apart when on the stairs themselves. The same precautions apply to hallways. Walk along the sides, on opposite sides, and keep talking and radio noise to a minimum. Watch for doors to open along the way. Usually, there is no problem, but routinely employing these strategies may give you a survival edge if a problem erupts.

Get clear of doorways as soon as possible. When standing in a doorway, you are at a focal point that is visible from anywhere in the room. If someone means harm, you are in what is known as the "Fatal Funnel"[3]—the worst place! (Fig. 9.6) Upon entering, scan the entire range of the room, from one side to the other, even if the "action" is concentrated in only one part of the room.

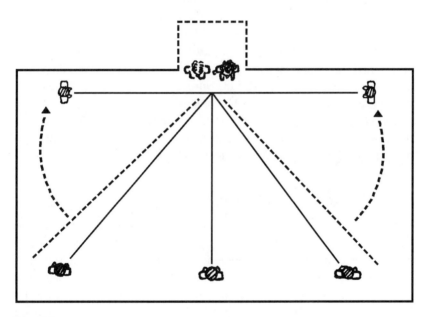

Figure 9.6

As you enter a room, you are dangerously placed at a focal point easily seen from any angle inside the room. This graphic depicts the wide angle from which an attack could come. Quickly move away from the door while scanning the *entire* room.

[3] Ronald J. Adams, TM McTernan, and Charles Remsberg, *Street Survival: Tactics for Armed Encounters* (Northbrook, Ill.: Calibre Press, 1980), 61. [Used with permission]

The Way Out

Another of the golden rules for personal safety indoors is never to let the patient get between you and the way out. Learn to notice alternatives; the door is not the only way out. Should you end up backed into a corner, you may find that you have to scoot under the dining table. Whatever provides a workable escape route! Know your options. The best is to stay where you cannot get cornered. (Obviously, it helps to maintain physical fitness and agility to retain these options for self-preservation.)

One paramedic team nearly got into big trouble because they broke this rule. They went into a residence and encountered a psych patient being held down by his two brothers. (He was later found to be on PCP.) One paramedic tried to control the patient by holding him with a full-nelson, while the other got on the phone to call for help.[4] In the process of applying the wrestling hold, the paramedic got backed into the kitchen corner. The brothers regarded his actions as too-aggressive, and started advancing menacingly. The paramedics were woefully poorly positioned and outnumbered, but fortunately extricated themselves on fleet feet, leaving the brothers to contend with the psych patient until police cover arrived. (A complicating factor of that situation was that the paramedics had never worked together before, so they had not had the time to develop an effective team style.)

Creating a Workable Environment

Sometimes we are forced to work in awkward, cramped, poorly lit, and other inadequate environments (Fig. 9.7). It is an extreme challenge to provide optimal prehospital emergency care in an unworkable setting—for example, when a patient is trapped by tons of material or is in a crunched vehicle a hundred feet off the road and requires significant stabilization prior to being moved. That's the nature—and drama—of prehospital care. Many of these unworkable conditions also occur indoors.

While entering each scene, notice whether the environment needs adjusting. You have three choices:

- Adjust the environment.
- Move the patient.
- Least desirable, adapt to the existing conditions and do the best you can.

---

[4] This case occurred in the days before portable radios were available at that agency. Portable radios are an obvious lifeline, and should nowadays be routine equipment.

The first choice is to adjust the environment. This is often a good solution. Probably the most common thing is to adjust the light. Asking a bartender to turn up the lights (and turn off the music), will improve a bar scene dramatically. Look for overhead lights or lamps in homes.[5] However, there may not be a good source of light. This is why it is vital to carry a powerful and dependable flashlight at all times. You never know when or where better light will be needed—and there are not always lamps and electric sockets available.

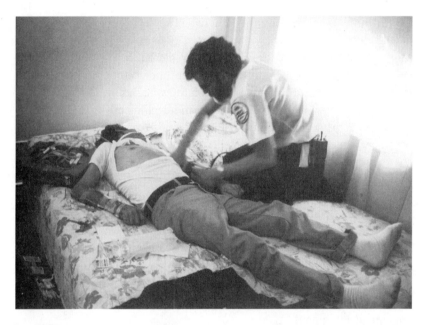

Figure 9.7

This patient was found lying on this bed in *status epilepticus*. The bed was virtually the largest uncluttered space in the house to work. Despite poor bedsprings, the paramedics managed to intubate and start an IV. If there's another option, use it!

Also consider moving furniture. Verbalize your needs and why they are important by saying, "Can you move these items to make room for us to work?" This is a good activity for relatives who may be as anxious about protecting the coffee table as they are about the patient. Putting them to work gives them a positive distraction while concurrently improving your work setting.

---

[5] NOTE: Some self-made "home protection systems" include a shotgun shell placed in the socket of a lamp. Check lamps before turning them on! (Source: Mike Taigman and Bruce Adams, "Street Survival" seminar, Chicago, 1988.)

The second choice is to move the patient. For example, your patient is in cardiac arrest. The room is cramped and unworkable. But as you entered, you were watching the scene for spatial alternatives as well as for safety concerns. You noticed that the nearby living room has plenty of room to accommodate the people (and equipment) needed to do the job. Taking the few seconds to go where you can do the job *right* means more effective CPR and advanced life support. Once monitors, medical kits, and other equipment are open and in use, the option of moving is effectively eliminated. Moving the patient at the outset is a good decision.

In some cases, moving the patient only a few feet or inches makes all the difference. If the cardiac-arrested person is against a wall, pull him out a few feet so that people can work from both sides. Or maybe the head is against the wall, preventing proper positioning for intubation. If you think to pull him away from the wall before setting out your equipment, you will get the job done more efficiently.

Finally, the least desirable alternative is to adapt to conditions as they are. Sometimes you just have to do the job where you find it. Take, for example, the 400-pound woman in cardiac arrest who became wedged between her bed and dresser when she fell. The room was too small to move the furniture, and the corner to the hallway was too tight to extricate a person her size quickly enough. So the crew went to work, doing CPR from odd angles, crawling across the bed to change CPR positions, and trying to start the IV on her arm as it lay partially under the bed. Accounts of conditions under which we have worked make some of our best war stories—but few are much fun at the time.

Equipment Placement

It may seem trivial, but where you set down your equipment at the scene has an impact. Some people never think about positioning their equipment logically, but it is possible that their scenes are also less efficient. If you are working a critical call, you do not have time to be tripping over the crash kits and suction unit. It is frustrating not to be able to see the monitor. Lost moments accumulate while you stretch and strain to use your badly-positioned equipment, and you are not as calm and collected as you might be if you had put it in a better spot. (Good places are by or between the patient's legs, or at an angle near the patient's shoulder; the point is not to interfere with movement around the patient, positioning for CPR, or establishment of airway control and subsequent artificial respiration.) Try to notice placement of other equipment before it is set down as well. If there is a particular spot you would prefer, it is easier to have it put there at the outset. Moving some equipment once it is unlatched and unfolded is not always convenient or easy!

When you are the patient care person, carry the main crash kit yourself, even though it may be tempting to let a rider grab it after a few calls on a hot summer day. By carrying this item, you control where it lands at the scene. You can get at it efficiently without disrupting rapport-building or the flow of care. Do not allow yourself to fall into the complacency trap of not taking any equipment into the scene. Yes, after a few hundred calls, everyone "knows" that the preponderance of "emergencies" do not require much—but you never know. Many otherwise good EMTs and paramedics have become so casual about their work that they do not even carry the minimum essentials. This is both unprofessional and terribly cavalier. In more than a few cases, personnel have been surprised empty-handed with fast-breaking, critical cases. Even when your patient is outside and you can see as you arrive that it is not a complicated or critical situation, take your kit. You will at least need your blood pressure cuff. And don't forget that your kit can serve as a shield against angry animals, patients who kick, and other hazards.

Outdoor Scenes

Many of the same principles apply to outdoor scenes. In addition, though, there are safety considerations related to:

- Outdoor environment
- Roadway operations
- Approaching a stopped vehicle
- Seeking cover or concealment
- Events with large crowds

The Outdoor Environment

One of the nicest things about EMS is that you are not confined to the same old office. No way! You have the sometimes-debatable "opportunity" to be everywhere—and anywhere! At any time, you may have to scramble down an embankment, climb a tree or ladder, wade through snow drifts or swamps, go in the water or into a cave. Heat and cold stress, mentioned in the previous chapter, are just the starting point regarding personal safety outdoors. Being ready for any weather is prudent. You might be toned out on a warm spring morning, only to find yourself in the dark, hours later, struggling through a blizzard on a transfer, as happened to one crew. Pay attention to your fluids and other nutrition, and always have access to layers of varied clothing.

The outdoor environment poses other risks as well. On some scenes, you may work outdoors under the scrutiny of the people looking down from the surrounding buildings. Maybe it's best to move to the relative privacy of the ambulance quickly! Maybe you'll be called to the city park. One crew responded to the park late at night on a shooting, and while caring for the patient, got shot themselves—with streams of high-pressured sprinkler water! There may be overhanging debris, as was tragically pointed out in the fatal head injury to a nurse at the Oklahoma City bomb site in 1995. Wear protective gear, especially in the unpredictable outdoor realm. And obviously, when scenes require specialized rescue and equipment, wait for the experts.

Roadway Operations

The subject of roadway operations is dense enough to fill its own book. The basic principles include parking properly, being conscious of moving traffic, and attending to inherent hazards at motor vehicle crash sites. There are also important interagency relations issues that arise at roadways, as these tend to be cross-jurisdictional events.

When parking, considerations of safety must prevail. Look for on-site hazards such as downed wires or fuel spills, and then choose where to pull in. Park uphill and downwind of sites with ground or air contamination. Sometimes the best site for parking is at the front end of the crash site, sometimes it's in the rear, depending on traffic, road conditions, and whether there's a curve or hill nearby. Are there other emergency vehicles with lights on already at the scene providing warning to other motorists? Which end of the accident are they covering? A 50- to 100-foot buffer zone is advisable, in case of fire or explosion. Avoid parking across lanes of moving traffic; crossings will be needlessly dangerous. Wherever you park, setting the emergency brake will minimize movement should the vehicle be struck.

Before getting out, be sure to put on your protective gear with the most reflective tape or trim. It is remarkable how "looky-lou" drivers forget to use caution when passing an accident! And they are most likely to not notice something as relatively small as you are, especially at night.

At accident scenes, be particularly wary of unreleased supplemental restraint systems (SRSs, or airbags) and hydraulic bumpers. Airbags may not deploy if the crash does not have enough front-end force. Although rare, inadvertent deployment is a risk, and could cause serious injury should they deploy while you are helping a passenger. Avoid working in the path of undeployed airbags, or disconnect the vehicle battery.[6]

Hydraulic bumpers that have been compressed may release unexpectedly during rescue operations. The striking power, should the mounting bracket fracture during impact, is great enough in unusual circumstances to send parts of the bumper as far as 300 feet! However, anyone in contact with a bumper that unexpectedly releases even to its normal position could be seriously injured.[7]

Stopped Vehicles

Some roadway operations do not involve crashes. One man sat for eight hours awaiting help for a diabetic emergency, unable to move to summon help. Another woman had gone food shopping, and heard a loud "bang" from the back seat as she prepared to drive home. Something hit her neck. She reached back and felt something soft, and held it there. She thought she'd been shot, and that her brain was oozing from her skull. She sat very still. Another shopper who had casually noticed her on her way into the store, saw that she had not moved when she came out. "Are you okay?" she asked. The frightened woman eventually found, to her chagrin, that her pop-open rolls had exploded, and that she had been hit by the wad of dough!

Other roadside scenes are more of a problem. If called on an "unconscious party" slumped behind the wheel of a vehicle, you must approach with caution. Park the ambulance on an escape angle, with the wheels pointing into the roadway. Announce that you are EMS on the PA system, and see if there's any response. To approach the vehicle, do not walk to the other car in a way that your body is backlit by the ambulance headlights. Pause by the trunk, look for suspicious circumstances, and again at the B-column just behind the driver's seat. Do not lean into the car or pass the B-column until you are sure the patient means no harm. Ask conscious people to turn on the interior lights of the car, and try to get a view of both hands as soon as pos-

---

[6] "Emergency Rescue Guidelines for Air Bag-Equipped Cars," National Highway Traffic Safety Administration brochure (DOT HS 807-579, Rev. August 1990) and Ronald E. Moore, "Passive Restraints and Safety," *Rescue Magazine*, May/June 1989, 42.

[7] Ronald E. Moore, "New Extrication Hazards: Surviving the New Auto Technology," *JEMS*, October 1985, 30.

sible. Usually, people are eager for your help—but you never know if they are playing possum. If the patient's response is violent, good positioning could be life-saving.[8]

Hazardous Materials Incidents

Hazardous materials are a major problem in today's society—and it's only going to get worse. Four *billion* tons of hazardous materials are carried by air, surface, rail and water annually.[9] Basic safety for hazardous materials (haz-mat) incidents is to step back and let the properly-trained personnel tell you how to help! Because EMS providers are often early to arrive, though, the perception that you have to "DO SOMETHING!" overrides appropriate action. Do the unusual: do nothing—unless you have a clearly-defined role within the hazardous materials response team for your area.

If a haz-mat incident occurs in your community, pray it comes *after* your organization has participated in advance planning and preparation. Handling these incidents requires a strong interagency effort, and leaves no room for misunderstandings, assumptions, or on-site squabbles. The keys to success are planning and cooperation.

A haz-mat incident has several "control zones" in the shape of a target. At the center is the "hot zone," (also known as the "exclusion" or "restricted" area). The next zone is the "warm" zone, where properly-trained and equipped people provide decontamination. This is a limited access area, as is the hot zone. Finally, the "cold" zone (or the "clean" or "support care" area) is at the edge. Here is the command post, and where transport lines would form to receive patients as they are passed outward.

The likely roles for EMS providers at a haz-mat situation are:

- Transport decontaminated patients to an emergency facility.
- Assist in the cold zone and provide medical assistance prior to transport.
- Evacuate medical facilities that lie in the area of risk.
- Provide shelter support for evacuees.
- Monitor members of the haz-mat team.

---

[8] *EMS Safety: Techniques and Applications*, 79–82.
[9] Jonathan Borak, Michael Callan, and William Abbott, *Hazardous Materials Exposure* (Englewood Cliffs, NJ: Brady, 1991), p. xi.

- Assist with decontamination in the warm zone (assuming prior training). It is unlikely that EMS providers would be allowed any closer to a haz-mat scene without cross-training in this specialized form of rescue.

If you arrive at a hazardous materials incident in its first minutes, be careful not to drive through any substances related to the spill. Stay upwind and uphill, if possible! Do NOT enter the area, and warn others to stay back as well. After the incident, if you carry decontaminated patients, it will be important to follow clean-up directions carefully and thoroughly.

Safety in Lifting

Lifting heavy, unwieldy amounts of weight in EMS is part of the job. There is the equipment, of course. And then there are the patients. Picking up patients is a process usually shared by the two people who work on the ambulance, although there may sometimes be other helping hands, especially in volunteer services or when first responders are willing to pitch in. At least it is not like prehospital working conditions in some other countries, where the "ambulance driver" works alone and has to depend on untrained, unproven strangers to help do the job!

Knowing how to lift safely is as much a part of prehospital care as knowing how to splint a leg or navigate to the scene. Lifting is safest when there is one leader calling the shots. Think through the lift; identify anything unusual about it, and communicate the plan. The leader should use a pre-arranged lifting signal. Back injury is the greatest source of on-the-job injuries, probably for one of several reasons:

- People do not understand the principles of lifting. They depend on brute force. The more they use their trunk and arms to secure the load close to their center of gravity, and then let their large leg muscle groups do the lifting, the less they risk injury. (Fig. 9.8).
- People do not ask for help. Some patients are simply too heavy. Sometimes it is not possible to get the right position. A classic example is moving a large person out of a crashed automobile while maintaining good spinal immobilization.
- People do not heed the signals of their own bodies. Some days your body simply cannot do the same work it can on other days. This may be due to exhaustion, minor illness, or because you are hypoglycemic from running calls when you have been trying to eat for hours!

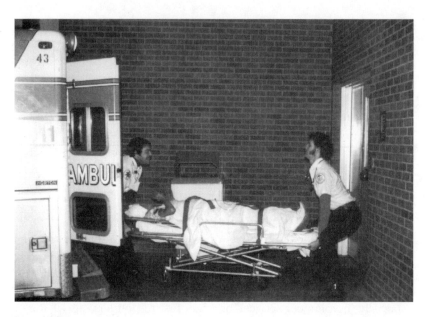

Figure 9.8

You are more likely to be injured on the job lifting than being assaulted. Stay in shape, and know when you should ask for help.

Lifting dynamics begin with a balanced position on firm footing, using a wide base of support. The feet should be set wide (more than shoulder width apart), with one foot ahead of the other. The load should be as close to you as possible, keeping the hands palm up whenever possible. "Lock" in the spine by holding it in a slight extension curve (like the normal lumbar curve). Use the back extensor muscles and stomach muscle to "set" (maintain) the position. Then bend your knees, lower your "butt," and keep your chin up. These actions will allow the spine to stay in proper position, letting the powerful leg muscles take the load and minimizing strain on the fragile spinal discs. (If your knees are bad, don't let them bend more than 90 degrees.) Exhale during a lift, and avoid twisting, even to pick up medical equipment.

Sometimes it is necessary to ask bystanders to assist with lifting. Recognize this as a potential hazard, since it harbors so many unknowns. You do not know if the helper is physically capable of the task; many laypersons are so "swept up" by an emergency that they put their own seemingly insignificant physical limitations aside when asked to help. In addition, you do not know if the lifting group will work as a team.

Offset these concerns by:

1. *Taking the time* to ask bystander volunteers, "Do you have any back problems or other physical limitations?" (Avoid nonspecific questions, such as, "Are you okay to do this?") If they admit they do, thank them and recruit someone else.

2. *Taking the time* for some quick on-the-job training. Explain exactly what to do, and use a counting prompt such as, "Lift on three. Ready? One . . . two . . . three." Explain to your helper(s) that if they need to stop for any reason to speak loudly and clearly, before there's a problem. To insure your instructions are clearly understood, ask if there are any questions and request verbal feedback, "Do you understand?"

Everyone in EMS occasionally encounters a load too big to handle safely with a reasonable effort. Many people have taken unnecessary risks by not asking for help when they needed it. In the face of too large a task, it is a sign of maturity, not weakness, to request help. In a business brimming with hazards, there is no need to let this one end your career unnecessarily. If you have to ask for help to lift often, consider strength training with a weight-lifting coach. The improvements might be enough to save you your career in EMS. If that doesn't work, question whether you are really suited for EMS. No one should begin a job if they are not capable of doing the *entire* job.

On-Scene Interagency Cooperation

People who work with regular partners have the advantage of knowing each others' on-scene style and preferences. Some partnerships reach the point over time that few words are spoken on a scene, yet things run smoothly and efficiently. Most of us, though, have to communicate our needs accurately and—if you want continued good relations with coworkers—in words and tones acknowledging that this is a team effort. Although some scenes demand attention only to the medical needs of the patients, most of the time those valuable "PR" seconds do exist.

The value of taking time for PR is particularly true for interagency relations. If you are a first responder, try to meet the people who will take charge with a brief, professional report as they arrive. If you are arriving, receive that report—no matter how well or poorly done—professionally. Take a moment to thank the first responders and acknowledge their efforts. Never "blow off" someone who has made an effort

to help. This creates unnecessary tension and an uncooperative atmosphere that can escalate (immediately or on subsequent calls) to the
point of jeopardizing the quality of patient care.

Rivalries between various EMS responders persist. We have much
to learn about interagency cooperation. If there is someone at a scene
who you cannot work with, you cannot afford to let that distraction
interfere with patient care. Try to work it out later, when a patient is not
caught in the middle of your differences.

A situation that could have escalated to a real misunderstanding
occurred when one paramedic was greeted at the ambulance door by
a slightly panicked first responder saying, "He's got a bad broken leg!"
The angulated femur fracture of the boy who had been hit by a car was
visible from the ambulance. The paramedic asked if there were distal
pulses in the leg; there were. After that, the paramedic consciously
avoided the trap of tunnel vision by
concentrating first on establishing good
rapport with the boy, and then on the
remainder of the physical exam. It was
disconcerting to the first responders that
the paramedic didn't do something
about the femur right away. While she
was talking to the boy and gaining his confidence, they kept nudging
her, prompting her, "The femur! Look at the femur!"

> First responders are in an odd, in-
> between, often frustrating position.

There were two ways to handle the first responders. First, consider
their position: they are often at prehospital scenes for a long time before the ambulance arrives. Their role is mainly to deliver the critical
lifesaving maneuvers that make first response such an important concept. When a situation does not require their life-saving skills, they can
do little more than reassure the family and wait for the next wave of
rescuers. Theirs is an odd, in-between, often frustrating position.

The paramedic could have ignored the first responders'well-
intentioned prompting, but that would have confused and upset them
more, and made them feel useless. The more positive approach was to
divert her attention from the boy momentarily to quickly explain what
she was doing, and why (verbalization!). She used a positive statement: "I see the leg, but first I need to do a couple of other things.
Could you just make sure that no one touches it for a minute?
Thanks." All the on-lookers (plus the boy) were quickly reassured. Those
few words brought the scene under the paramedic's control. The first

responders appreciated feeling part of the team effort, and the concerned crowd could see that she could handle the situation. It *never* hurts, in prehospital care, to play to a friendly crowd.

Take the Scene Along

It is sometimes easy to forget that the people at the emergency department have not seen what you have seen. Observe pertinent aspects of the scene, and include them in your hand-off report. Emergency department personnel need to know how badly the vehicles were crunched, how far the person fell, and how fast the train was moving. Try to be accurate in your estimates of volume and distance. Exaggeration may add to the drama of the call, but if you develop a reputation for it, they won't believe you when you bring in a truly astounding story.

Estimating heights can be done by guessing how many times you would have to stand on your own head to reach that high; then multiply that number times your height in feet. "The branch was about 2-1/2 times my height, or 11 feet up." If the height involves a building, it is useful to know that each story of a building is generally 10 to 12 feet high. Estimating blood loss is more difficult, especially if it's diluted in another liquid. If a pool of blood is two feet in diameter and a quarter inch deep, it's best to describe it that way than to try to guess what that volume would be in milliliters.

Also describe the environment, especially when the patient's physical presentation might lead to misconceptions. A patient who has been lying in his own excrement for several days is distasteful; mentioning that the home was otherwise immaculate might help create a different impression.

Summary

Your attention to the many small details about each scene will make a big difference in the quality of your work. Some protect your safety. Others, such as creating a workable environment, make the scene work for you instead of against you. There are also ways you can display consideration of others; after all, you are on their turf. Although some prehospital workers may feel that some of the details are too trivial, the people we help often consider many of these "details" to be very important, indeed.

Appropriate medical care is second in priority only to your personal safety. Many strategies and tips in this chapter are dedicated to each. Of course, not everyone on the scene delivers the medical care. Extra personnel can do certain things to make the experience less frightening and more positive for the patient and the family or friends. That we get to see the scene is what makes our particular branch of medicine so unique. Each one carries its unique lessons, if you choose to learn.

In the Ambulance 10

Peter's Law: The unexpected always happens.

—Laurence J. Peter

Chapter Overview

Being in the patient compartment of a moving ambulance is a very high risk proposition. There are ways to make it safer. A moving emergency vehicle is a missile, a traveling capsule of care. The busy people in the back depend on a safe journey.

But the streets do not guarantee safe passage. Accidents happen. It does not require high speeds to cause terrible harm. Develop the habit of hanging on and bracing correctly. In addition to describing those techniques, this chapter will present ways to buckle in patients and equipment safely, and how to restrain people who pose a threat to your safety. It encourages a prospective approach to minimizing other hazards, including hearing loss. It also discusses the driver's role in transport safety.

The accident was minor. The ambulance was traveling at less than 15 miles per hour. But its consequences were devastating for the paramedic in the patient compartment. When the sudden deceleration threw him, he sustained a cervical spinal lesion and was paralyzed from the neck down.

The point of this chapter is to safeguard against such tragedy. You face tremendous hazards every time you climb into the patient compartment. The dangers of being unrestrained in a small room that is traveling at speeds between 5 and 65 (or more) miles per hour are seldom emphasized; to most of us, it is simply another hazardous part of a generally hazardous job. We trust the driver to get to the hospital safely while we are busy working on someone who is sick or injured.

When providing in-transport care, it is normal to move around in the patient compartment. The last thing on your mind, usually, is personal safety. Lights-and-siren runs are one of the greatest times of risk. The chances of having an accident skyrocket whenever a vehicle is traveling in the emergency mode. High speed is not essential for major injury; remember how fast the ambulance was traveling in the accident that paralyzed the paramedic?

People in the patient compartment should change a long-standing habit and use seat belts when the ambulance is moving. Yes, there are times when you need to move around. Even workers who anticipate their needs well cannot have everything available all the time without moving around to get it. For those moments, the concepts of hanging on and bracing described next will serve as temporary strategies. However, it is possible to wear seat belts in the patient compartment much or most of the time. During interfacility transfers, and when there is no medically-based reason to move around the patient compartment, the people in the back should wear their restraint devices. (It is expected, of course, that anyone in the front cab will wear seat belts at all times.) One group of researchers found that ALS personnel in 148 patient encounters felt they needed to be unrestrained to provide patient care only an average of 41 percent of the time. The possibility of being belted existed, in their perception, more than half the time. Even in cardiac arrest, they found seat belts could be used up to 18 percent of the time.[1] For the safety of rescuers, it is time for an industry-wide shift in this regard.

Hanging On

There is no room for a false sense of security when the potential "weapon" is a several-ton vehicle. For protection when you have to be out of the seat belt, it is vital to develop a reliable habit of precautionary body positioning. With it, there is a chance of surviving the potential devastation that accompanies the squealing brakes and sickening crunch of an accident.

Let's borrow some of the rules of rock climbing to describe "hanging on" in the ambulance. Good rock climbers always maintain at least three-point contact with the cliff. That is, of four possible contacts—two feet and two hands—only one is in an insecure position at a time. The

---

[1] Cook, Jr., S.A. Meador, et al, "Opportunity for Seat Belt Usage by ALS Providers," *Prehospital and Disaster Medicine*, 6:4 (October–December 1991), 469–484.

other three extremities hold the climber to the cliff, so the climber is reasonably safe from falling. The same principle applies to hanging on in the patient compartment. If for any reason the driver has to decelerate or swerve unexpectedly, maintaining at least three-point contact at all times gives attendant(s) a chance to avoid being thrown.

People in ambulances have one advantage over rock climbers. They can utilize a fifth "anchor," the seat of their pants. Therefore, depending on where you are moving or what you are reaching for, you can enhance your stability with:

- **_Two feet and one hand._** How many times have you stood up just enough to quickly reach something without hanging on with the free hand? It is far safer to grasp something like the stretcher railing or overhead bar when you stand up momentarily to adjust the oxygen, for example, or to grab a 4x4 from the cabinet (Fig. 10.1). Since sudden deceleration is the most likely alteration in momentum, common sense dictates that hanging on with the hand nearest the back of the ambulance is the stronger position (Fig. 10.2).

- **_Two hands and one foot._** It is essential when you have to walk around in the ambulance—even when taking just one step—to hold on with both hands. Walking puts you off balance because your weight shifts as you move. It may be for only a microsecond, but that movement risked at the wrong moment can result in being tossed like a rag doll. Avoid walking arm-over-arm. Instead, hold onto the ceiling bars and slide your hands along without letting them cross. If you are holding equip-

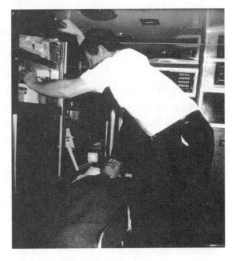

Figure 10.1

If you stand momentarily in a moving ambulance, be sure to hang on with the other hand.

ment when you have to move, either be sure you can hang on adequately while you are holding it, or put it down, or do something creative such as pushing it along the squad bench ahead of you.

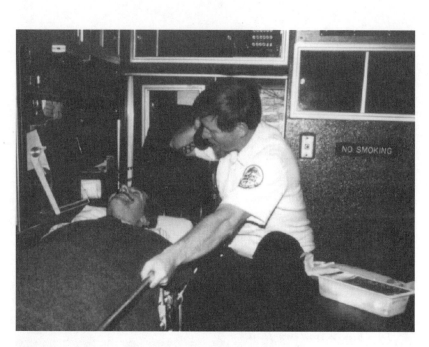

Figure 10.2

Whenever possible, keep your center of gravity low. When hanging on with one hand, try to use the one nearer the back, in case of sudden deceleration.

- ***Two feet and the seat of your pants.*** "Just sitting," is a form of hanging on. If you have to move around, but there is even a brief chance to sit, do so. Lowering your center of gravity whenever possible is an excellent habit. (Remember, if you're able to sit for any length of time, put the seat belt on!)

In all these positions, maintain as wide a base of support as possible. Keeping the feet apart creates a tripod. You are far more easily tossed off balance if the extremities are too close together. Keeping the arms and legs widely separated improves your overall stability, so that you can lean into sudden changes in the ambulance's momentum or direction of travel. Conversely, if you cross your arms or legs, it reduces that base of support. Keep your feet about shoulder-width apart. Keep your arms relaxed, when sitting—yet ready to reach out and hang on at all times.

Bracing Techniques

In addition to hanging on, a greater margin of safety comes with developing the habit of bracing your weight. This means exerting oppositional force against two parts of the ambulance (or equipment), using your feet, knees, hands, a knee and a hip, a knee and a shoulder—whatever works for the position you are in. When seated, hook the back foot under the stretcher bar, or brace against the stretcher wheel. Do NOT use your head to brace yourself against the ceiling. If the ambulance hits a bump at the wrong moment, it could cause a serious neck injury.

Keep a low center of gravity whenever possible. For women, whose hips are the center of gravity, this is easier than for men, whose center of gravity is in their shoulders. Also, you can maintain better balance when standing by keeping your knees bent and flexible, much the way sailors develop "sea legs." Use the principles of shock absorption to the best advantage.

Be creative. There are many available surfaces to brace against. For example, when you take a blood pressure with the patient's arm across your leg as you sit on the squad bench (a time when you might also remember to wear a seat belt), the back foot could hook under the stretcher bar while the front leg braces with gentle oppositional force against the squad bench. It helps to point the forward foot to the front, to allow you to lean into deceleration. You cannot brace yourself as well when your foot is lateral to the direction of travel.

Make bracing a habit, so you never have to think about doing it. The pressure you exert does not have to be excessive; it is there primarily to protect you against the normal bumping, swaying, slowing, and accelerating of the ambulance. In the event of having to hang on "for dear life," being in the habit of bracing will possibly provide the instant you need to hang on tight.

CPR In The Ambulance

The greatest time of risk for in-ambulance rescuers is during the transport of patients in cardiac arrest. When CPR is being done, many other tasks are being done, too, especially in advanced life support ambulances. Doing adequate CPR in a moving ambulance is a challenge. (Just getting to the ambulance with never more than a few seconds' interruption of CPR is a challenge.)

In the ambulance, the person doing CPR is in a risky position, particularly if the trip is not smooth. With body weight directly over the hands, which are on top of each other, the ability to brace adequately is extremely hampered, as is the ability to maintain three-point anchoring. You are left with just two-point contact—the feet. In order to use them to maximum advantage, use a wide-spread, diagonal stance that wedges you in as securely as possible. One foot is back, against the squad bench; the other lower leg is against the stretcher with the foot underneath the stretcher bar. Hopefully, this make-do stance will help you buy time until you can grab more solid support, if needed.

Some people lean into the cabinets with the tops of their heads when they are doing CPR in the ambulance. This is not a good idea! The neck is too weak to withstand the pressures—especially when standing lateral to the direction of travel—that can suddenly occur.

A practical solution for the relative safety of someone doing CPR is to have a seat-belted and anchored helper behind, holding the back of the CPR-person's belt. This has two benefits. A fresh helper is available to take over CPR (which is nice on long rides). And if there is an abrupt change of ambulance momentum, the person doing CPR is less likely to mow down the entire group as he or she goes flying. There are also mechanical pumping devices on the market. These deliver good, consistent CPR without having to compromise a person's safety in a moving ambulance.

Practiced diligently, hanging on and bracing are effective techniques that can make a big difference to your safety. Once they become habits, the protection is there unconsciously. Without them, a person has to rely on luck not to be thrown. No doubt there have been many close calls. The result for others has been catastrophic injury or death.

Securing Equipment

Even if you guard carefully against being thrown, you will be no match against flying debris if equipment is not securely stowed. The devastation in a patient compartment after an ambulance roll-over is incredible. In one case, had the accident happened en route to the hospital with a patient, rather than en route to the scene, the paramedic and patient would have undoubtedly received major injuries. Everyone who witnessed the mess was horrified at what could happen in a bad accident to supposedly "safely" stowed equipment. Debris littered the floor knee-deep. It included IV fluid bags, boxes of IV tubing, board splints, bandaging and gauze pads everywhere, the sharps container, 10-pound sandbags (this was in the "old" days.), the clipboard, the crash kits—and the 40-pound EKG monitor. Imagine all that stuff flying through the air, and then imagine yourself, your helpers, and the patient in there, trying to hang on. The concept of stowing gear safely takes on new importance!

Simply stowing things is not the same as stowing them safely. Stowing things safely is not the same as stowing them safely and having them easily accessible! The cabinets in the ambulance that rolled over were made of plexiglass-type plastic. The EKG monitor-defibrillator was nestled in a specially-designed rack. The squad benches had no fastening system. Everything was stowed—for normal purposes. But for the safety of ambulance crews, equipment must be restrained from ever being dislodged unintentionally. Create an easy-access latch system for cabinets. Put easily-removed straps over and around the monitor and other high-tech equipment. Make easily-undone snaps or latches to keep bench tops closed until someone wants them open.

The same principles apply to keeping the ambulance dashboard clear. It may be convenient to put a book or radio on the dash, but if there is an accident, the people in the driver's compartment may sustain serious injury as these items are launched.

Sharps

Pay particular attention to your sharps box(es). Stowing needles immediately and properly into the correct receptacle is a high priority. It is hard to believe, perhaps, but *years* after AIDS came into our collective consciousness, some EMS providers still stick needles into the squad bench or drop them on the floor. The infection potential (not to mention damage to the vinyl) is obvious. Another habit to change is recapping needles. It is very unwise to insert a sharp, dirty needle into a tiny-diameter hole in a moving ambulance! You are tempting fate and courting disaster. This applies to both clean and dirty needles; one paramedic got a patient's blood on his hands while starting the IV, then inadvertently stuck himself with a clean bicarb needle. In a few short weeks, he was jaundiced with hepatitis B.[2]

Do not "carry" syringes with exposed needles in your teeth. It certainly looks dramatic. But if you get tossed unexpectedly, it is a great

---

[2] Obviously, this is an old story. There was no hepatitis B vaccine yet. He wasn't wearing gloves. *And* they were still using bicarb! But the paramedic to this day faces a much higher risk of both liver cancer and cirrhosis of the liver. Think about it.

way to give yourself an unpleasant (and possibly dangerous) shot. One paramedic who did that spent several hours getting over a big dose of epinephrine.

Keep the sharps container convenient, and use it. Replace it appropriately so that it does not overfill. Make and use a temporary sharps disposal system for the crash kit, to use when not in the ambulance.

When medicating a patient through IV tubing in a moving ambulance, the following tactic can prevent inadvertent needle sticks: Anchor the heels and the free fingers of each hand together while bringing the tubing (in one hand) to the needle (in the other). Both hands move as one unit, allowing you to steadily and safely bring the injection site to the needle regardless of interfering ambulance motion (Fig. 10.3).

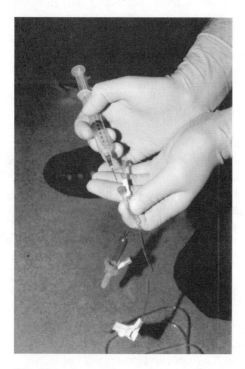

Figure 10.3

When in a moving (bouncing) ambulance, make one unit of your hands. Anchor them together at the wrist and pinkie-side carpals, and then carefully bring the needle to the injection site. Maintain an angle such that if you miss, the needle will stab the air. This minimizes the chances of a needle-stick.

Seat Belts

There are two important reasons to be sure that patients are well secured. First, every patient deserves protection against accident-related injuries. Second, some people are clearly a hazard to themselves and others because of violent, combative behavior; they need to be properly restrained in the patient compartment.

Protecting people from accident-related injury simply means using the seat belts, whether the patient is on the stretcher, the "captain's chair" or the squad bench. Insist on it. Blame it on company policy, blame it on city rules, do what you have to—but put on the seat belt. It doesn't take a crash to cause injury. People can slide off the end of the squad bench during routine stops or turns. Imagine how you would feel if an unbelted patient or family member who was riding along sustained an injury because of not wearing a seat belt.

Sometimes, patients who are well enough to sit up are belligerent and provocative. They focus on the seat belt as a source to cause trouble. They unbuckle it as fast as you can buckle it. This can be frustrating, especially because such people are often influenced by alcohol or other drugs, are playing games with you, and are not interested in your medical care. This is a time to take a deep breath and remain professional. Avoid being drawn into that game. One solution is to turn the seat belt latch upside down and tape the buckle shut. If worse comes to worst and you cannot keep the patient buckled in, document your efforts to protect the patient's safety and how the patient refused to keep the seat belt on.

When a pregnant woman is able (or prefers) to sit, use the captain's chair. Sudden changes in ambulance speed cause lateral forces on persons sitting on the squad bench because they are positioned sideways to the direction of travel. These momentum changes would be much more tolerable for a person seated in the captain's chair. Seat belts are definitely still indicated for pregnant women, with the belt as low on the pelvis as possible. Injuries from a serious accident are likely to be more minimal than if she were catapulted across the compartment. Explain this to women who seem anxious about wearing a seat belt.

All stretcher patients should also be buckled in for safety purposes. The potential liability for failing to secure both the stretcher to the bar and the patient to the stretcher is obvious. A belt past the armpits and across the chest plus one just above the knees is the minimum. Another over the hips is even better. The placement of the chest belt has some implications. Placing the straps under the patient's arms gives a greater sense of freedom, and provides easy access to the arms for measuring blood pressures, starting IVs, etc. It also prevents the straps from sliding up around wriggly patients' necks. Finally, if not medically contraindicated, raise the head of the stretcher slightly. This way, the patient doesn't feel about to slip off the top of the stretcher each time the driver stops the vehicle.

Stretcher belts should be snug, but not uncomfortable. Loose straps allow the patient to wriggle free, and are of little help in an accident. Since some patients dislike being "trapped" by the restraint of seat belts, remember to verbalize why it's so important.

It can be easy to forget to seat belt patients to the stretcher, especially when they climb into the ambulance on their own before lying down. The belts tend to fall down between the stretcher and the cabinets, or you are busy providing medical care and it slips your mind. Since it so seldom occurs, you may not be thinking about how easily your patient can become a projectile. Make seat belting a habit. Then you won't have to think about it.

Helper, Save Thyself

While advice to "buckle up" is practically a cliche, the practice among EMS providers is . . . uneven (at best!). One paramedic never did get into the habit in his 28-year career. Fortunately he only took a few stitches in his rollover accident. Afterward, he *still* did not wear a seat belt.

Interestingly, one study of 102 ambulance accidents between 1983 and 1986 in Tennessee showed shocking noncompliance (greater than 50 percent) with state regulations requiring seat belts. "Of the 48 ambulance drivers that wore restraints, four suffered injuries, the study found. On the other hand, 13 of the 52 unrestrained drivers were injured."[3] This would indicate that your likelihood of injury when not wearing a seat belt is three times greater than when you take the time to buckle up. Doing so in the cab should be routine (Fig. 10.4). Do so as well in the patient compartment when your duties do not require you to move around.

Figure 10.4

Too many people work in ambulances, and still do not use seat belts regularly. Show your good sense, and be a good community role model. Use them!

[3] "Ambulance Drivers Not Buckling Up," *Emergency*, 20 (May 1988), 50.

Restraining Violent Patients

Violent people are a hazard not only to themselves but to the other people in the patient compartment. Whether their violence is based on organic causes (e.g. a serious head injury or a diabetic struggle) or "just" psychotic or behavioral problems, additional restraint during transport is indicated. Before using patient restraint, be sure to know and understand your local jurisdictional rules as written. If these rules are considered inadequate by EMS providers, work through the appropriate channels to amend them properly. When caught between the rules and the needs of a particular scene, protect yourself and others from harm and then document the circumstances carefully.

Restraints should never be applied maliciously or vengefully. Even though it is human to respond angrily when another person lashes out at you, spitting, kicking, hitting and biting, you must not allow good judgment to become clouded. Be dispassionate and professional at all times.

Restraining should be a last-resort measure, after other interpersonal communications strategies have not worked. It is too easy to turn to restraints because you are too tired or don't feel like putting in a big effort, but don't yield to this temptation. Some patients are actually relieved to be restrained, however, because it takes away the need for self-control over their suicidal or aggressive feelings.

If police are handling restraint, note the system used. Metal or plastic handcuffs can impede circulation to the extremities. Position such patients on their sides, and monitor circulation frequently. Beware! If a patient is "hog-tied" with wrists handcuffed, ankles bound, and wrists then attached to ankles, respiration may be difficult for the patient. Do NOT allow such patients to be transported prone; put them on their sides. Two patients transported prone died during ALS transport, apparently due to positional asphyxiation caused by restricted motion of the diaphragm and chest.[4]

Situations calling for patient restraint require careful written documentation. Explain why restraints were applied. An example of reporting why you applied restraints might be: "Patient was striking out and kicking violently without regard for personal injury. Restraint indicated for the protection of self and others."

Use no more than the least restrictive means of restraint necessary. In all but the strongest patients (or those on PCP or otherwise unable

---

[4] Samuel Stratton, Christopher Rogers, and Karen Green, "Sudden death in individuals in hobble restraints during paramedic transport," *Annals of Emergency Medicine*, 25 (May 1995), 710–712.

to feel their own pain), an excellent "soft" method of patient control that is easy and very quick uses the strong three-inch soft gauze bandaging rolls, doubled over. The next-stronger version is easily made by using two rolls of soft gauze bandage. Some EMS providers carry soft restraints; others carry "leathers." The latter are perceived by onlookers as overkill, and you may encounter unnecessary hostility. The gauze bandage rolls, on the other hand, have a medical application and seem more in tune with our mission: patient care.

Gauze bandage rolls are very handy, since they are already in the crash kit for other purposes. Plan to use one per extremity. Do NOT cut them in half. To make a restraint, fold the unrolled bandage in half and fold the looped end over on itself. This makes two large loops, big enough to slip over a hand or leg, even over bulky shoes or boots (Fig. 10.5). Draw the loops tight. There are two theories about the next part of the procedure. Some EMS providers tie off the loops so that they will not occlude blood flow to the hands; others leave the slipknot effect. If the patient struggles, it gets tighter. Then the EMS provider can use it as a bargaining tool: "Now that you are calmer, I can loosen these ties a little—but they'll get real tight again if you struggle. It's up to you how tight they are." Patients appreciate being given a sense of control, even if it is only control over their own discomfort.

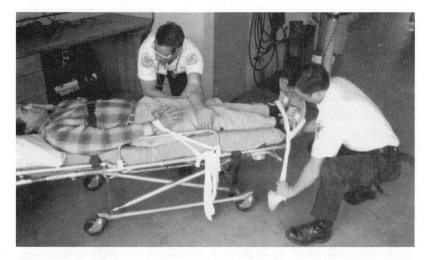

Figure 10.5

Simple gauze bandaging is adequate restraint in most cases. A single loop can be used for both feet. If the ends are tied (out of reach) in a bowtie, it facilitates transfer and reuse of the restraints upon arrival at the receiving facility.

Tie the long ends (out of reach!) in bowtie knots in a secure place on the stretcher. (This facilitates transfer of the patient to a hospital cart, because they are easy to untie.) Secure the feet so that the tie of the restraint cannot slide around the end of the stretcher, which might allow the knees to bend.

Arm and leg restraints used in combination with chest and thigh seat belts results in humane-looking and quite adequate restraint for the majority of cases. Check seat belts to be sure their anchor point on the stretcher is in line with where they are coming up over the patient's body. If they are on an angle, they could slip out of position. Be sure the chest belt is run under the (tied-down) arms and then over the upper part of the chest. This way, the patient should not be able to sit up. (Chest belts placed *over* the arms might displace, allowing some patients to get the belt over their heads, and either strangle or sit up and cause trouble.)

Restrained people who have calmed down should *never* be untied. The rule is: once restrained, always restrained—all the way to the hospital.

When struggling to control a flailing, kicking person, do not hold the ankles. Lean onto the legs just above the knees. Feet can't kick if knees can't bend. Similarly, hold the patient's elbows straight—and let no sensitive part of your anatomy fall within range of the fingers! (Fig. 10.6)

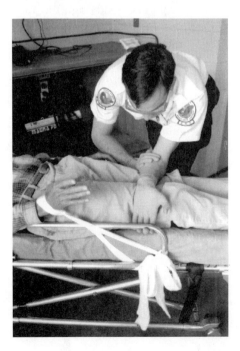

A controversial but quick to apply, and almost foolproof method of restraint has been affectionately dubbed the "scoop sandwich." It should be used only as a last-resort restraint technique for extremely violent people, such as those on PCP with superhuman strength, who are able to break gauze bandage restraints, leather straps, and even police handcuffs.

Figure 10.6

Control kicking by placing weight on the lower thighs just above the knees, as shown. Create a lever-bar with the arm by grasping the stretcher bar on the far side and pressing the elbow down.

It should not be needed otherwise. To apply it, put the patient face down on the stretcher, put the scoop stretcher over him, and buckle the stretcher belts snugly over the scoop. Tie down the arms, one over the head, the other by the patient's side (preferably on the squad bench side, to facilitate taking blood pressures and starting IVs if needed. There may be a potential for positional asphyxiation when using this system. Carefully monitor the patient constantly, and never "crank down" the belts so tightly that respiration is affected. Used correctly, it has been a helpful procedure.

Regardless what restraint system you are going to use, be sure everyone concerned knows that plan, and that it is a "workable" plan. Have enough people—at least three—and get the patient off his feet. Use no more force than is minimally necessary to do the job effectively and safely.

Hearing Protection

Chronic exposure to loud noises endangers the precious sense of hearing. Noise-induced hearing loss is a significant risk in EMS. "One study of personnel in a busy urban system found that exposure just to sirens correlated significantly with hearing loss, accelerating it by 1 to 1-1/2 times the rate expected for age-matched controls."[5] Although this may not be easy to appreciate among the youthful ears so common to EMS, you will thank yourself later for being kind to your aural cilia now. Repeated trauma to the cilia (the most vulnerable being those sensitive to higher frequencies) can cause permanent damage. Hearing impairment is difficult enough without even considering that it could cost you your career.

> Chronic exposure to loud noises endangers the precious sense of hearing. Noise-induced hearing loss is a significant risk in EMS.

It may start, innocently enough, with early warning signals such as complaints that you always say "huh?"; you keep the television at a volume others consider uncomfortably loud (yet it seems perfect to you); or you do not hear high-pitched voices, such as children. Maybe tinnitus (ringing in the ears) starts and becomes increasingly constant. Tinnitus can be such a nuisance that it disturbs a person's ability to sleep.

---

[5] *EMS Safety: Techniques and Applications*, FA-144 (Washington, D.C., FEMA, April 1994), 47.

Avoid having to struggle with learning to lip read or wear a hearing aid. *Prevent* hearing loss! Minimize all exposure to loud noise, both on duty and off. In these modern times, we not only have siren noise, but hydraulic power tools, generators, even loud lawn mowers and chain saws.

Sirens on older EMS vehicles were mounted on top of the ambulance cab. Some years ago, industry practice shifted to placing them on the front grille. This lowered decibel levels in the cab approximately 5 percent. You can add to that good start by closing windows when using lights and siren; open windows raise noise from roof-mounted sirens about 14 decibels, and from grille-mounted sirens about 4 decibels.[6] Shield your ears even more by consistently wearing either earmuffs or earplugs. Earplugs can reduce noise levels from 15 to 26 decibels; earmuffs can reduce them 21 to 28 decibels.[7] Avoid prolonged loud noises off the job as well.

Do not take good hearing for granted. The EMS work environment bombards this important sense with everything from sirens to bypassing traffic noise, to extrication gear and screaming patients. If you are not yet taking appropriate protective measures, do yourself a favor and increase the chances of a lifetime of good hearing by doing so from now on.

The Driver's Role In Safety

The driver has certain responsibilities to the people in the patient compartment during transport. Although it is possible to take tighter corners at faster speeds and whip around traffic obstacles on the way to the scene, the return trip is an entirely different brand of driving. With a patient in the back, the driver is responsible for at least three lives. That number swells with helpers, relatives, multiple patients, and student riders. An ambulance may contain up to six or more people. The driver's responsibility is indeed awesome; to know that another person's life has been changed because of injuries sustained in an accident that happened while you were driving, fault aside, is a thought no one wants to live with.

Even when the patient's condition is critical, there is no good reason to drive fast. This is especially true on curves, at intersections, and in the presence of other road hazards that might require sudden changes in momentum. If the ambulance is moving too fast, the stop-and-go or

---

[6] Glenn Luedtke, "Could You Please Speak Louder?: Coping With Hearing Loss in EMS," *JEMS* 13 (May 1988), 31.

[7] Luedtke, "Could You Please Speak Louder?"

slow-down-and-go routine makes for a lousy and unsafe ride. If the patient is awake, a bad ride no doubt results in unnecessary anxiety.

Patients do not ride in ambulances every day. They are not used to—and don't need—the extra excitement of a nerve-racking ride. Over the years, there must be quite a few patients who were less concerned with their medical problem than surviving the ride to the hospital!

> **Over the years, there must be quite a few patients who were less concerned with their medical problem than surviving the ride to the hospital!**

Drive at appropriate speeds and make the ride as smooth as possible. If you work in an area long enough and enjoy paying attention to detail, it is possible to know every pothole and bump in the road. By having a sense for the timing of a series of stoplights, you can pace your speed to go through them without having to stop. (Always remain alert, of course, to changes in the timing of the lights. Don't depend on them!) Avoid driving in the gutter lanes; they are bumpy at intersections, and cause the vehicle to dip and sway.

One of the most uncomfortable road surfaces is the sort of dirt road that feels like you are driving over an old-fashioned washboard. It is possible to drive dirt roads fairly smoothly with practice. In any suboptimal driving condition, though, the best thing is to travel at an appropriate speed. There is no good excuse to drive "hell bent for leather."

One of the best ways to learn what kind of ride feels good or bad is to strap yourself onto the stretcher and experience it from the patient's perspective. Do this every few months. See how it feels to sway back and forth as you weave through traffic and drive in the gutter lane. Experiment with what it's like with the head of the stretcher all the way down, versus slightly elevated. Try rapid acceleration! Bumps may feel uncomfortable to you—so imagine what they are like for someone with an orthopedic injury. While you lie there, imagine the additional anxieties patients have: "Am I going to die? What is this going to cost? Will my medical needs be painful? What's happening?"

An even greater concern to the driver than a smooth ride for the patient (who is, after all, strapped in) is the quality of the ride for the partner. Prehospital care is hard enough to render without being jostled, bumped, shaken, and tossed. Regardless of how faithfully we hang on and brace, there is always the chance that bad timing could result in injury.

When approaching a road hazard that will cause an unavoidable torque or a bump, the considerate driver can warn those in the back so that they can hang on and brace extra tight. For example, it is handy to know about railroad tracks (especially the kind with a stomach-lifting drop off), as well as tight or poorly banked turns in the road.

Notice the quality of your stops and starts. Are they smooth? It is dangerous and inconsiderate to jam on the brakes, and to "gun it" to accelerate quickly. No matter how critically ill the patient is, smooth speed transitions are important. It requires practice and awareness of the dynamics of motion. In a controlled stop, for example, the brake pedal is released just as the momentum of the vehicle ends; this eliminates the last-moment jostle that occurs in rougher stops.

All in all, the best ride to the hospital is the one the attendant did not notice. That means that the driver did the job well, because the attendant was not distracted from the duties of prehospital care by having to hang on or brace more than usual.

Summary

The key to avoiding tragic circumstances is having a mind for safety. EMS personnel can avert tragedies simply by moving around the patient compartment carefully, driving responsibly, using reasonable judgment, and appreciating the possible consequences of an accident when there is a patient aboard.

It is impossible to avoid every hazard. In fact, the constant presence of hazards is a big part of what makes EMS appealing to rescuers. We love the challenge. To apply the principles of safety is to reduce those hazards to reasonable levels.

Guns, Knives and Other Weapons

"All patients come with a minimum of four weapons: two hands, and two feet."

—Denis Meade

Chapter Overview

This chapter consists of a very basic guide to all sorts of weaponry. For the benefit of people who do not know a great deal about guns, there is a solid body of information about firearms, ammunition, wounding power, and ballistics. This will improve your general awareness, even though it will not change how you treat victims of shooting. Remember: always treat the patient, not the weapon. Nothing can replace quick IVs and extrication, or the surgeon's scalpel!

A more constant threat than guns are the other weapons available to people on the streets. Although most people do not want to hurt us, it is practical to consider the potential for harm. A good habit is to take a "weapons inventory" as you enter each scene. It is important to be aware of what could be used against you. Also, be ready to consider mood—the emotional component of human nature, again!—as a sort of weapon, in the sense that it can be a precipitating factor in aggression. Beyond noting weapons, develop the knack for determining "usage potential." A collection of antique swords may not pose the same threat in the house of an elderly man with chest pain; spiked high-heeled shoes, on the other hand, may warrant attention if the woman wearing them is angry!

Whether or not to disarm a patient or move weapons beyond someone's reach depends on your comfort level and intuition. How do you decide whether it is really necessary? What are the methods for disarming? Most prehospital workers are not police officers, and we need our "good guy" image. There are ways to get the job done without blatantly frisking people. There are also ways to assist law enforcement personnel by preserving the crime scene and its evidence; this, too, is discussed.

It seems strange to have to guard against the very people we are trying to help. Many people who attack may not have any personal gripes with us. They are angry for other reasons and end up venting that anger on EMS providers solely because they are the most convenient source. And most EMS personnel are neither emotionally nor physically prepared to fight. But the streets are tough, and many people out there are hardened in ways that most of us cannot fully appreciate. If nothing else, we often respond to scenes where law enforcement officers have faced down very tough characters. "Resistance is commonplace among today's offenders. About half the people arrested challenge police authority at least verbally. At least 12 percent are violent or aggressive, requiring 'coercive contact.' Today's average [police] officer, however, is smaller, weaker in upper body strength and more middle class-rooted than ever before. Lacking the rough and tumble experience of contact sports or military service, many have never even been *punched* hard, certainly have never been in a fight for their lives. Yet they're expected to subdue people who grew up watching their mothers' friends bite each other's ears off, who were accomplished street fighters by age 6, and who've pumped iron to physical perfection in prison."[1]

Cautious and alert EMS providers can usually defuse a situation, or at least avoid serious injury. The key is your state of mind. Someone with an attitude of "nothing ever happens" is going to miss crucial hints of impending trouble. The habit of professional wariness and alertness should be part of every scene approach. This way, your mental response in fast-breaking situations will be something more effective than blind panic. No matter whether your patient population is rural, suburban, or from the inner city, you never know what strangers in crisis will do.

Weapon Inventory

Weapon inventory begins before you leave the ambulance. Part of your "information-vacuuming" process while getting to the patient should include noticing potentially lethal objects, and where they lie in relation

---

[1] Charles Remsberg, *The Tactical Edge: Surviving High-Risk Patrol* (Northbrook, Ill.: Calibre Press, 1986), 423–425.

to people who might use them. Fortunately, most people out to hurt you are relatively uncreative in their choices of weapons. They tend to think of "real" weapons, such as knives or guns. With more than 200 million firearms in the U.S. (more than 60 million of them handguns)[2] they often don't have far to reach.

Knives

There are literally hundreds of common objects on every scene that could be used to cause harm. The usual alternative to a gun is a "sharp": pocket knives, sheath knives, stilettos, kitchen knives, butcher knives, even meat cleavers. Be careful where you may find them: one way to carry a concealed blade is as part of a stylish belt buckle (Fig. 11.1).

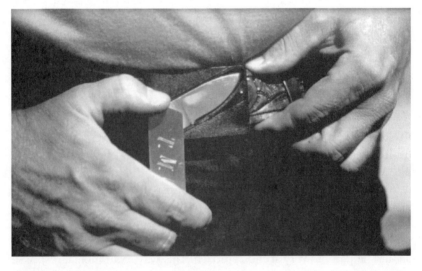

Figure 11.1

Knives, guns and other weapons may be found *anywhere* on a person's body or hidden in clothing. Beware!

Guns

People with guns cause tremendous amounts of grief every year, when they kill 30,000 to 35,000 people and injure between 300,000 and 500,000.[3] EMS providers see it all too regularly. Kinds of guns include:

---

[2] Iris McQueen, "Violence, American Style," *JEMS* 15 (September 1990), 40.
[3] McQueen, "Violence, American Style," 40.

- **Handguns.** Single-shot pistols, revolvers, and automatic pistols are hand-held (Fig. 11.2). Just as the name describes, single-shot pistols have to be reloaded between shots. Pistols with magazines (clips that hold subsequent rounds of ammunition) usually hold between five and sixteen rounds. A revolver has a cylinder with between five and nine chambers to hold bullets. The cylinder may be cocked either by hand or automatically. Actually, the term "automatic" pistol is a misnomer. An automatic weapon fires repeatedly when the trigger is held down. These weapons are more correctly called "semi-automatic," because although they automatically prepare themselves for the next shot when the gun is fired, each shot requires a separate pull on the trigger.
- **Rifles.** These are weapons designed to be fired from the shoulder. They shoot bullets. Rifles may be slide- or pump-action, bolt-action, lever-action, semiautomatic and fully automatic. They may fire a single round of ammunition and then need reloading, or they may have a number of bullets loaded at once.

Figure 11.2

Assorted handguns (l to r); Smith and Wesson Model 29, .44 Magnum; Smith and Wesson Model 10, .38 Special; Smith and Wesson Model 19, .357 Magnum; Colt .45 Automatic; Colt .380; Raven .25 Automatic.

- **Shotguns.** Shotguns are also meant to be fired from the shoulder, although this is not always what happens; some are fired from hip level. They discharge shot (lead pellets that disperse the farther they travel) or a single lead round, called a slug. A shotgun may be single-barreled, double-barreled side-by-side, or double-barreled over-and-under. It may be loaded by slide, pump, or bolt-action. There are semiautomatic shotguns. Sawed-off shotguns have shorter barrels, which reduce the sighting radius and decrease ammunition velocity, but also make them less unwieldy and easier to conceal.

The size of a gun is measured by the internal diameter of the barrel. This is known as "caliber." A .22-caliber gun has a barrel size of 22/100 in. Shotguns are generally measured by "gauge," a system with antiquated roots where gunsmiths measured a weapon's size by the number of lead balls the size of the barrel's diameter it took to equal one pound. A 12-gauge shotgun (the most popular size) has a barrel, or bore, diameter of 0.729 in.

Caliber is a handy thing to report to hospital personnel because it can provide a ballpark idea of the size of the missile. Basically, when referring to bullets (versus shot) the larger the number, the larger the hole. Although you should never add to on-scene time to find out caliber or weapon type, take the information along if it is available. It might help the surgeons anticipate the internal damage.

Mood as a Weapon

Mood can be a very potent weapon. Weapon-like moods that can result in aggressive reactions include anger, resentment, hatred, and frustration. This is a recurring theme in this book because it is so entwined with the theme of streetsense. Be aware of both your own moods and the moods of the people around you. When you are feeling rotten, abused, and irritated, you must separate those feelings from the current emergency medical call. Otherwise, the risk of responding inappropriately to others will increase (Fig. 11.3). When a patient is hostile and aggressive, even level-headed prehospital workers may sometimes be tempted to respond in kind. There have been too many avoidable fights in EMS. If people on both sides are upset, such reactions are, in one sense, an understandable human response. They are, nonetheless, intolerable in EMS professionals.

Other Weapons

Sometimes the choice of a weapon can be a real surprise. Having an empty water heater thrown at you is not something you normally expect, but it has happened. That instance almost caught the paramedics off-guard. Fortunately, they were able to get out without injury.

Different patient populations have different kinds of potential weapons; farms and suburban households contain items that are different from those used in inner-city dwellings. A farmer may be adept with a pitchfork, a suburban housewife with her handbag. Can an executive's pager be threatening? Usually not—but "pagers" (and cigarette lighters, pens, and other pocket devices) that are actually guns or knives are increasingly available. A grab-bag of some of the "weapons" you might see include:

- **Blunt instruments.** Baseball bats, fireplace utensils, sledgehammers, rocks, hammers, pots and pans, bottles (which are increasingly heavy and blunt the fuller they are), and kicking. In fact, kicking has been reported as an increasingly common form of attack in England, where homicide as a result of it once ranked third.[4]

Defusing the "Mood Weapon"

An excellent way to defuse the "mood weapon" is to be willing to back off. A person trying to pick a fight will have a hard time of it when the target (you) refuses to take the bait. For example, one paramedic arrived on a scene to find the patient —a very big, intoxicated, angry man—standing on the sidewalk bleeding from a minor, self-inflicted hand wound. The paramedic got out and began to talk to the patient. Employing the principle of interpersonal space, he stayed about eight feet away and tried to establish rapport from there. When the patient made threatening motions toward the paramedic, he backed off, held up his hands in a conciliatory gesture, and said, "Hey, I'm not here to hassle you. I just want to take a look at your arm." His words and actions had a twofold benefit. They showed a willingness to let the patient decide to be helped. (He never did; he turned out to be one of those rare "gotta wrestle 'em" people but the paramedics waited until police cover was there to help them.) More important, it demonstrated to the sizable housing project crowd that the paramedics were just trying to help, and that the patient brought upon himself the need for restraint. It never hurts to be surrounded by a friendly crowd!

Each situation in EMS demands a customized approach. What works one time may not the next. Handling dangerous moods requires the same versatility that has run as a theme throughout this book. Such flexibility of style can be learned. People who make the effort will appreciate the skills.

In situations where escalated moods affect a group of people, a mob mentality may evolve. Retreat until supplemental personnel arrive.

Figure 11.3

- **Sharp instruments.** Knives, razor blades, knitting needles, scissors, hatchets or axes, nail files, ice picks, pencils or pens, fingernails, spiked

---

[4] J.K. Mason, ed., *The Pathology of Violent Injury* (London: Edward Arnold Ltd., 1978).

high heels. There are spring-loaded knives that look like ballpoint pens. And there are "bolts," which are the short, steel arrows fired from the newest deadly (and completely silent) firearm: a crossbow.

- **Unusual objects.** The influence of TV has resulted in certain dramatic flourishes like the water heater incident. People do pull down bookcases, or heave the entire collection of family china. One patient asked for a match; the reflex answer was that cigarette smoking was not allowed. That was not why he wanted a match anyway. He had wanted to set off a concealed load of dynamite! Less dangerous but ugly nonetheless were the angry couple, both smoking, whose argument escalated to the point that they began using the cigarettes as instruments of burn injuries. Other odd weapons have included crutches and big table lamps. There are neckties and belt buckles that hide mini-revolvers, necklaces that turn into weapons, pop cans that are actually red pepper spray. The range of creativity is astonishing.

- **EMS equipment.** Just as police officers have to be careful not to let their service revolvers be used against them, EMS providers must be cautious with some of their tools. Flashlights can become blunt instruments used against you, as can portable oxygen cylinders. A stethoscope, too, can be used as a strangling device, especially when you consider where many EMS providers carry it (Fig. 11.4). One paramedic described how a very large, intoxicated, angry woman got hold of his stethoscope (the type with a heavy bell), swung it around her head a few times, and flung it at him. Fortunately, he was able to duck what could have been a significant head injury!

- **Pepper spray.** It may be used against you. Or you may have to transport someone who has had it used against them. Pepper spray, available as a direct stream spray, fogger, or foam, contains a formula made primarily of cayenne pepper. It causes instant irritation of the eyes, upper respiratory passages, and skin. Theoretically, it renders attackers helpless with intense pain for about 45 minutes. EMS providers who transport a pepper-sprayed patient may feel some symptoms of exposure, because except for the fogger, the spray aerosolizes the cayenne pepper. Copious flushing, and time, are the best healers. Some EMS providers are now carrying pepper spray for their own self-defense. This is highly controversial. Follow local protocol.[5]

Both finding potential weapons and establishing effective rapport

---

[5] Marie Nordberg, "Assault & Pepper," *Emergency Medical Services* (March 1996), 41–66.

are early priorities. Rather than referring openly to weapons, in regular situations, use your sense of observation. Notice things like rat-tail combs and afro picks sticking out of back pockets, and sheaths on belts. Do they contain knives? Shirt pockets often have a pen or two in them. Bulging front pants pockets may contain a bunch of keys or a pocket knife. Is her hair held up by bobby pins? Does she have long fingernails? Does he have a bulky school-type ring that could add impact to a punch? A purse is a virtual arsenal. Purses contain things like nail files, combs, scissors, keys, and other dangerous objects. Many people also carry chemical sprays or small handguns in their purses. The purse it-

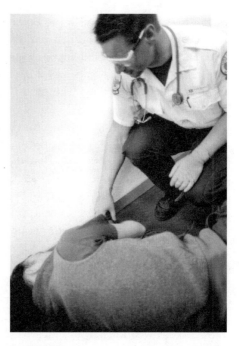

Figure 11.4

Do not let your own equipment be used against you. Although it is most convenient to position the stethoscope around the neck, be aware of the potential harm to you.

self can be swung by its strap to deliver a solid whack.

Sometimes it helps to know the street terms for weapons or a person's intent to use them. One prehospital worker did not respond appropriately to a bystander's threat to get his "Roscoe"—until someone mentioned that, in that city, a Roscoe was a gun.

Usage Potential

In addition to noticing weapons, decide about usage potential. As the saying goes, "Guns don't kill people; people kill people." Behind the weapons are the people wielding them. You naturally tend to respect people of large size and bulk because they seem so powerful. In one case, the patient was a 240-pound man lying on the floor who had "overdosed" and was trying to give the impression of unconsciousness despite his fluttering eyelids and general body tension. His diminutive ex-wife was there; his display was for her "benefit." While the attendant began his exam, intuition in the other paramedic started waving a red flag. Because of the patient's size, the paramedic knew that they would need more help if he tried anything, and started to call for police cover. Before the call for back-up was done, the big man erupted with unbelievable speed and agility. The group barely escaped the house ahead of the wave of his rage.

One reason the paramedic in that case felt uncomfortable was a subtle, but critical observation. The man's muscular tension was incongruous with unconsciousness. His whole body was tense. He was obviously faking. Pay attention to such things, and you might have a moment's warning before someone comes up at you fast. Touch a shoulder or arm (how compassionate it looks!). You will *feel* the movement before you see it—usually with enough time to respond appropriately.

Although large people do tend to be more powerful, size is not everything. One veteran police officer described the most vicious person he had ever encountered as a small, thin, but very street smart woman. She took on three police officers—and nearly won. People who understand how to use their feet, hands, and body weight effectively carry potent weapons at all times!

There is so much potential weaponry on prehospital scenes that it is impossible to notice it all, all of the time. Your index of suspicion is naturally high when you respond to the scene of a violent crime such as a shooting, stabbing, or assault. The given nature of the call reminds you to watch out for yourself and your partner. It is harder to generate a healthy index of suspicion when the call nature is "unknown," perhaps even nonemergent. It is too easy to be sleepy or preoccupied. Unless you get in the habit of monitoring for potential harm (via any source), it is surprisingly easy to miss important clues. One psych patient, who ultimately had to be wrestled down and restrained, had her hands in fists. Not until well into the struggle did the paramedics see the sharp tip of a can opener just barely poking out. They were lucky.

> Intuition plays a major role in assessing whether someone is likely to attack. Although there are stories about out-of-the-blue, unprovoked attacks, usually there is at least a subtle warning that attack is imminent.

Intuition plays a major role in assessing whether someone is likely to attack. Although there are stories about out-of-the-blue, unprovoked attacks, usually there is at least a subtle warning that attack is imminent.

As one police officer said, he worries only when someone stops talking to him. In his experience, he said, people simply do not talk and swing their fists at the same time. In the anecdote about the 240-pound "overdose," had the second paramedic not heeded that wonderful sense of intuition, they may have been unable to escape without harm.

There is a limit to how much you can be distracted from the primary mission of caring for sick and injured people. Fortunately, most people are not out to hurt you. You are free to get on with the job at hand. The point is to avoid being caught off-guard. Stay constantly alert for the possibilities. Never underestimate the potential for harm. EMS providers are trained observers; use this skill along with your basic understanding of other people, and you can avoid a lot of surprises.

Being Grabbed

People sometimes grab hold of their rescuers out of fear, psychological disturbance, organic causes (such as hypoglycemia, hypoxia, or brain-related illnesses), hysteria, or the intent to do harm. Whatever the reason, your safety is jeopardized, and your goal is the same. You need to get free.

There are innumerable ways to react to being grabbed. It is a highly-adrenalinized moment. Maintain a keen mental edge during the event. You need clear presence of mind to respond appropriately. If you are being held hostage with a knife pressed to your throat, you will have different priorities than you will if a frightened victim is clutching your wrists out of blind hysteria.

First, your breathing is likely to become labored and more rapid as your adrenalin surges. Panic and poor breath control go together. Despite your pounding heart, take long, slow, deep breaths—in through the nose, out through the mouth—until you feel yourself settling into the situation. Maintain a survivor mentality. It is natural to have strong feelings when you are directly threatened, but don't just give up. Instead, watch for *reasonable* escape opportunities.

Second, avoid the reflexive urge to pull against the attacker. A push-pull approach unbalances you and escalates his or her determination to hang on. There are hundreds of tactics to use to break holds, depending on the circumstances. Neither this book nor any other can teach them all effectively, because these physical skills need real-life demonstration and practice. However, following are two ways to break arm holds, to whet your appetite to seek proficiency. Practice and expertise with even a couple of self-defense tactics can enhance your confidence.

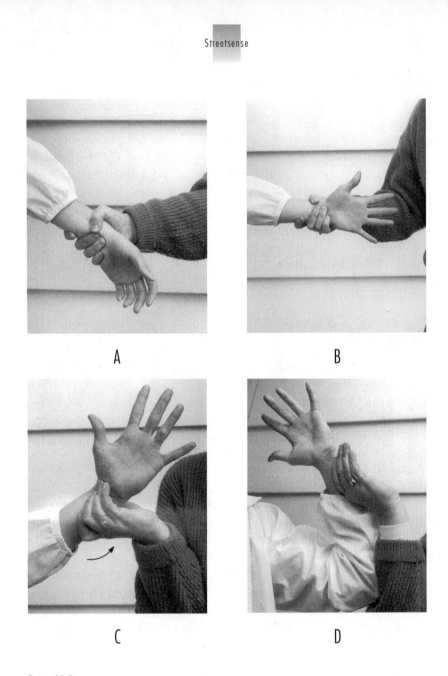

A

B

C

D

Figure 11.5

Look as calm as you can if you are grabbed by the attacker's same-side hand—and then simply scratch your ear! In (a), the rescuer has been grabbed. Instead of pulling backward, she opens the hand wide (b) and extends it toward the attacker. Notice the attacker's elbow beginning to bend. In (c), the rescuer maintains forward extension and begins to draw her hand upward in a broad arc until the attacker's grip begins to weaken. In (d), with a sense of calmness, the rescuer pushes the attacker's arm away with her elbow, brings her hand to her ear, and scratches it.

Scratch Your Ear

When someone facing you grabs a wrist with the same-side arm (left arm to right, and vice versa), open the hand so the fingers are spread wide. Extend your hand *toward* the opponent and swing your arm in a wide arc out and upward without bending the elbow until the grip is broken—then scratch your ear (Fig. 11.5). Keep a calm expression. You are simply taking care of an itch (on your ear)—and also a potential threat. (This can also be done when *both* wrists are being held.)

"Thumbs Down"

Say that someone facing you grabs your wrist with the same arm (left arm to left arm, or vice versa). Make a fist, leaving the thumb up in classic hitchhiker's pose. Bring the thumb up alongside the underside of the opponent's wrist. Extend your arm *toward* the opponent while turning your hand in a "thumbs down!" gesture, letting your thumb make an arc over and close to the other person's arm until the grip breaks.[6]

When done correctly, each technique works on the principles of physics, not brute strength. But neither technique will work if you fail to extend your energy through your arm, outward toward the opponent. As soon as you shrink up and let the elbow bend, you are lost.

When Guns Are Drawn

Cover, Concealment, and Ricochet

It can be eerie to be on a scene where police have drawn their firearms or a confrontation involving firearms is imminent. Although savvy EMS providers enter *every* scene with the thought that violence could erupt, interest in self-preservation really kicks into overdrive when firearms are pulled out. The most important concept for the EMS provider is a clear understanding of cover and concealment. Recall from chapter 9 that "cover" is a hiding place that will stop bullets, such as a tree or fireplug. "Concealment" keeps you from the assailant's view, but will not stop bullets. It may include hiding behind bushes, a plank fence, or

---

[6] Techniques compliments of Sensei Gaku Homma, Kancho, Nippon Kan, Denver, Colorado. The martial art of Aikido, which he has taught for several decades, is particularly adaptable to field medicine in many delightful ways. *Domo arigato, Sensei!*

in the shadows. Notice opportunities for cover and concealment as a part of your information-vacuuming routine.

Ricochet is a misunderstood concept. We are conditioned from too many Western reruns to think of ricocheting bullets as zinging harmlessly into oblivion. However, in real life, ricochet can injure—even kill—people; at least two ambulance personnel have scars to prove it. Indeed, ". . . most handgun bullets and buckshot will skim along from the point of initial impact to where they finally connect with [the] target with a deflection of no more than 1 to 8 inches off the surface (assuming there's not some defect in the surface that interferes with the flight)."[7] Leaping under your ambulance for "cover" is clearly an uninformed decision!

Whenever guns are drawn, you obviously want to make sure the police know you are there, but do not stray into harm's way to do so. Stay well out of the way and let them secure the scene. How many times has an EMT or paramedic been seen walking close behind a police officer with a drawn gun, as if the law enforcement "shield" could protect either of them? Remember, many people want neither the police nor EMS to intrude into their lives. Just because our mission is to help does not mean that their wish is to *be* helped. Basic safety maneuvers for scenes involving firearms include:

- Never use lights and sirens all the way to the scene of a reported shooting. Shut down early, come in quietly, and park down the street. Better yet, park around the corner.
- Keep the cab lights out.
- Keep yourself and the ambulance outside the kill zone, or "that area which an armed suspect in a given location can control with hostile weapons fire.[8] An armed person in, say, an apartment window, commands a wide angle view. Do not cruise into such scenes without pausing to consider what sort of target you are making! Such stealth and attention to detail may prevent injury to you or someone else already on the scene.
- Be aware of the special nature of incidents such as hostage negotiations or terrorist standby operations. Stay well outside the perimeter and obey law enforcement commands to the letter and without discussion.

People in modern society have a very romantic notion of gun fighting. What few TV programs mention, of course, is that real-life shootings

[7] Ronald J. Adams, T.M. McTernan, and Charles Remsberg, *Street Survival: Tactics for Armed Encounters* (Northbrook, Ill.: Calibre Press, 1980), 269.
[8] Adams, *Street Survival*, 49.

are for keeps. A lot of times, the good guys lose. There are innumerable case histories of inadequately trained or complacent law enforcement personnel who have died because of it. Every citizen wants to believe their law enforcement team is the best. Maybe yours is. But beware of tombstone courage in your local cops—and play it safe. Learn all you can about the appropriate responses to situations involving firearms—and then do it right! Put the tactics for survival on your side.

Body Armor

The routine use of body armor (sometimes known inaccurately as bulletproof vests) is on the rise. There are arguments for and against the idea. In one case, a paramedic who was wearing body armor was helping a skid row alcoholic off the sidewalk when he was attacked from behind by someone totally unrelated to the scene. He felt something hit his back, and turned around to discover that someone had tried to stab him. He was glad for his body armor that night! On the other hand, body armor may induce a false sense of security.

Most quality body armor is now made of a synthetic material called Kevlar.® Depending on the weave and number of layers used by the manufacturer, Kevlar® resists penetration by projectiles. A garment with seven layers of Kevlar® is generally regarded as the minimum sufficient to shield you from most bullets; most manufacturers use more. A lighter material under development is a synthetic "spider web cloth" which is reported to be even stronger.

There are some important things to know about body armor. First, it loses its protective capability when it gets wet. Sweat moisture counts. Good-quality products are waterproofed, and some have moisture level indicators. Second, just because a garment is bullet resistant does not mean that you cannot be seriously injured, if not killed, by the blunt trauma of a projectile. A bullet that can put a dent in your body armor of more than 1.73 inches has been found to be probably lethal. A round that hits the back over the spinal column may result in spinal cord injury or paralysis. At the same time, the protection body armor can provide against blunt trauma may be needed more often than in the once-in-a-lifetime shooting. One paramedic told of being in a motor vehicle crash while wearing his body armor. He bent the steering wheel with his chest (despite his 3-point inertia belt) and sustained no thoracoabdominal injury.

Obviously, anyone considering buying body armor is well advised to research the product carefully. Some people regard its use in EMS as overkill; others have had enough close calls that the peace of mind is worth it. Whether or not to wear body armor is a personal decision.

Removing Weapons From Patients

Once you check for weapons and the potential for their use, decide whether any that you find need to be removed from the patient's control. This discussion is not about dramatically disarming someone brandishing a gun or a knife. EMS providers are rarely cross-trained as law enforcement officials. In such a situation, take cover, import the people in law enforcement uniforms, and let them do the job.

Frisking

Frisking is generally viewed as a law enforcement activity. It may be easier to retain our "good guy" image by being subtle in our use of what can easily be construed as police tactics. Our job is to study people and quickly note many details to gain an accurate impression of them and their medical situation. While doing this, though, why not build in the habit of "visual frisking"? No one but you needs to know your routine exam includes an assessment for safety hazards.

Then, during the physical exam, check for concealed weapons. People do not have to know that is what you are doing. During the head-to-toe exam, which is popularly understood as a regular part of our job, you are the only one who needs to know you are touching for more reasons than the obvious ones. People may have guns or other weapons in their belts, under their arms, in their boots or socks, strapped to their calves or forearms, in holsters, behind the head hooked to the neck of an undershirt, in bras or athletic supporters, inside hats, or in their crotches. When working with gangs, watch also for fish-hooks in seams and razor blades in hat brims. Check fanny packs, and hat bands.

Do not assume that a patient who is on a police hold has already been thoroughly frisked. Inquire specifically whether prisoner/patients have been checked properly. Supposedly frisked people in handcuffs may surprise you. Handcuff keys have been found hidden on people, in their waistbands, inside belts, even under Band-Aids.[9] Do another subtle job of frisking when performing the physical exam.

---

[9] Remsberg, *The Tactical Edge*, 261.

Sometimes, people with minor injuries walk to the ambulance before you can conduct a hands-on exam. You can still check for concealed weapons, at least partially, as they climb into the ambulance (Fig. 11.6). Stand behind them, and "help" them up the step by holding them at the waist or under the arms. Both are common hiding places for concealed weapons. At the same time, notice whether the back pockets contain items that could cause harm, such as a rat-tail comb.

Figure 11.6

This paramedic is assisting an elderly man into the ambulance; he is also feeling under the man's coat for weapons. When the man steps inside, he will also look at the man's beltline and back pockets for potential weapons.

If You Find a Weapon

There are several ways to handle finding a weapon. Sometimes it is even acceptable to let a person continue to carry a potential weapon because you judge there is little or no risk it will be used. For example, your female patient with the broken leg happens to carry a handgun in her purse, or your mountain man with a fever "always" keeps a knife on his belt. Lots of people carry knives on their belts. Only a handful intend to use them.

In some situations, make yourself put on a poker face when you find a weapon—and then *look for more weapons*. Take a complete inventory before reacting. If you take away the first weapon you find, the patient may simply reach for the next-available weapon. People increasingly carry more than one weapon, especially those engaged in criminal behavior. One shoot-out victim was thought to have been disarmed at the scene, until the X-ray came back showing a revolver stuck in his belt! In another case, no one noticed until well after the patient arrived at the hospital that a grenade was under the MAST suit. Whenever possible, when it is necessary to disarm a patient, have a police officer to do the job.

If you will be removing the weapon, tell the patient, "I can't let you have this while we're with you, but we'll be sure it's delivered to the Emergency Department." (Don't promise that they will return it—you don't control that act!) Remove the weapon, entrust it to someone appropriate or lock it in the drug box, and carry on. Taking personal items away from people has its risks. Although most people accept the fact that they cannot have an item while they are in the medical system, it is justifiably infuriating for that item to disappear. On the way to the hospital, leave it out of reach, but in sight; sometimes a good place is between the patient's legs. Always document in writing the disposition of confiscated items. Prehospital workers receive enough unfounded claims for "lost" personal property without creating reasons for more.

If you are disarming a known gang member, think of the possible implications of how you do it. It may be perceived negatively if you hand a weapon over to a law enforcement officer, leaving you susceptible to retaliation. "Think of each encounter as an investment for the future," cautions gang expert Denis Meade, of Littleton, Colorado. Try to find a neutral solution.

Will it spur people to be violent if they recognize that you are concerned about potential aggression? You never know—but not usually. This is another time for intuition and appropriate handling of each situation. Sometimes you can honestly explain why you are removing an item; sometimes it is better to make the excuse that your actions are "company policy."

Handling A Gun

Obviously, if someone threatens you with a gun (or other weapon), get to safety and let the police secure the scene. Whenever possible, let the police be responsible for weapons. Improper handling can destroy essential evidence. The only time to touch a weapon at a scene is when you feel it poses a threat and there is no one more qualified to handle it. If the patient is down, dead or dying, and the gun is there, decide if the most prudent action is to put it safely aside. One way to pick up a handgun is by the trigger guard, behind the trigger. This matters especially in terms of evidence preservation (Fig. 11.7). Be careful not to let anything, including your finger, catch the trigger and accidentally discharge the next round of ammunition! Be aware, too, that the balancing of a gun is such that it will rotate when picked up upside down like this. Be ready to control that rotation safely. Another method is to loop a shoelace through the trigger guard. If you must handle the grip, try to touch only the panels (where fingerprints are unlikely).[10] *Never* pick up a gun by sticking anything down the barrel. This can disturb the inside markings that link the weapon to the used bullets. One additional (but vital) precaution is never to point the gun barrel at anything a bullet could injure—such as your partner—should one be discharged accidentally!

Figure 11.7

Prehospital workers seldom handle guns at emergency scenes. When necessary, carefully lift the gun as shown to preserve evidence. Hold the trigger guard *behind* the trigger, and don't point the barrel at anyone.

Guns In Suicide

One report showed that in the United States, a firearm was used by 64.1 percent of the 13,500 males and by 40.6 percent of the 2600 females who committed suicide in one year.[11] It is eerie to enter a suicide scene where a gun was used. The scene is hushed, compared to the loud blast you can

---

[10] Adams, *Street Survival* , 269.
[11] Todd Stanford, "Bulletproof Treatment," *Emergency*, January 1988. [Statistics for the year 1982]

imagine occurring shortly before your arrival, and it is often messy, since many people aim at their heads. The gun is often still there.

One of the first considerations is whether the gun is under control. When possible, let law enforcement personnel secure the scene and handle the gun. People who are desperate enough to shoot themselves and who are still alive may try to prevent you from helping them. If the patient is still a menace in any way, get out and hand the scene over to law enforcement personnel. If you are without backup, and the patient is dead or wounded badly enough to be unable to struggle, carefully put the gun in a safe place.

Keep in mind that there may not always be a gun right there. People don't always die where and when they shoot themselves. In one extraordinary case, a 62-year-old man shot himself under the jaw. The bullet passed upward through the tip of the frontal lobe and through the center of the left frontal lobe, leaving a 1-inch wide exit hole in the skull. A bullet hole and pieces of brain were later found on the ceiling of the garden house where he shot himself. The man subsequently walked at least 165 yards through fresh snow in the garden, and then back to his rooming house. When the landlady answered his ring, he said quite clearly, "I must go to the bathroom," and hung up his coat. It took him hours to die.[12]

If the patient is obviously dead, try not to disrupt evidence for the investigators. Be careful, though: Some wounds that look completely incompatible with life are deceptive. In one case, a patient was found in a bathtub with a grotesque GSW to the head. The gun was dangling from his hand. About an hour later, when the investigators were done, they were preparing to remove the patient. As they reached for the gun, they were surprised by a voice that said, "Don't you dare touch that gun." It was the patient speaking!

> In more than two-thirds of the cases of suicide by GSW, the victim aims for the head, usually at the roof of the mouth or the temple.

In more than two-thirds of the cases of suicide by GSW, the victim aims for the head,[13] usually at the roof of the mouth or the temple. (Unfortunately, those who use a long rifle in the mouth sometimes succeed only in shooting off their faces, causing intense airway challenges and lengthy hospitalization.) In almost all other cases, people aim at the heart. People choosing suicide tend not to aim for the abdo-

---

[12] Douglas J.A. Kerr, "Actions After Being Shot Through The Brain," *Lancet I* (1945), 467.
[13] Brad Selden, et al., "Outcome of Self-Inflicted Gunshot Wounds of the Brain," *Annals of Emergency Medicine* 17 (March 1988).

men or, interestingly, at the eye, and they are usually careful to bare covered skin by pulling the garments aside.[14]

More Firearm Information

The following information about firearm ballistics, wounding power, and kinds of ammunition is intended as background information on a topic too-common to emergency medicine. Shootings are common, and also represent an ultimate test of medical teamwork. One impressive example of handling a shooting well was when a 17-year-old was shot in the neck on the outskirts of Denver. Approximately 28 minutes after his injury, he was in the operating room. Dispatch time to arrival at the scene: seven minutes. On-scene time: four minutes (including intubation). Transport time: nine minutes; ED intervention: eight minutes. A young man who had had 60 percent of his right carotid artery shot away was sitting up and watching a football game 36 hours later.

Spending time asking the details about the type of gun, et cetera, on that call would have been a ludicrous waste of precious moments. But if relevant information is readily available, it may help the hospital personnel to know it.

Ballistics

Matching a particular bullet with a specific crime was first accomplished in London in 1835, when a flawed bullet was matched with its mold. The term "forensic ballistics" was coined when New York established its first department by that name in 1925.[15] Since then, the science of forensic ballistics has become sophisticated to the point that a weapon can be identified by matching the stria, or markings, that are etched by the gunbarrel to pieces of bullet as small as 3 mm^2 (1/8 inch^2).[16]

Ballistics, which is the study of projectiles in motion, has three categories: internal (when the ammunition traverses the gunbarrel), external (when the ammunition is in the air), and terminal (when it hits something). Part of terminal ballistics is "wound" ballistics, or the study

---

[14] Bernard Knight, "Firearm Injuries," in *Forensic Medicine,* Vol.I, ed. C.G. Tedeschi, William G. Eckert, and Luke G. Tedeschi (Philadelphia: W.B. Saunders Company, 1977), 525.

[15] Stanton O. Berg, "The Forensic Ballistics Laboratory," in *Forensic Medicine*, Vol.1, ed. C.G. Tedeschi, William G. Eckert, and Luke G. Tedeschi (Philadelphia: W.B. Saunders Company, 1977), 536.

[16] D.R. Godley and T.K. Smith, "Some Medicolegal Aspects of Gunshot Wounds," *Journal of Trauma*, 17 (November 1977), 868.

of the injuries caused by ammunition. Such variables as the type of gun, mass and velocity of the ammunition, air resistance, distance from the target, unstable in-flight aerodynamics of the ammunition, and the striking velocity, shape, and weight of the bullet influence wound ballistics.

Wounding Potential

Knowing whether the gun was a revolver, a pistol, a rifle, or a shotgun helps determine whether the weapon was of high or low velocity. There are several theories about wounding potential. The theory of kinetic energy is the most popular. Like all the theories about wounding potential, this theory relies on an equation where mass and velocity are the essential components.

Most civilian GSWs are low-velocity injuries, which tend to affect just the tissue touched by the bullet and any fragments it creates. Relatively higher velocity weapons may have an explosive effect on the tissue, resulting in unbelievably huge wounds, or they may pass so cleanly through the body that there is relatively little external damage despite internal devastation of tissue.

The velocity of a bullet is a function of how much force (or pressure) the weapon can accommodate when the gunpowder is ignited. Expanding gases in the barrel are what propel the ammunition; these may cause pressures of up to 40,000 psi in handguns—and more in rifles.[17] Muzzle velocity (how fast the projectile is going as it leaves the end of the gun) depends on such factors as barrel length, internal firearm dimensions, and variations in the ammunition. Ranges of muzzle velocity in handguns are from 635 feet per second (very low velocity) to 2650 feet per second (unusually high for a handgun). Muzzle velocity in rifles ranges from 1460 to 4040 feet per second.[18] This approaches mach 4! A 12-gauge shotgun with a number 6 shot shell has enough velocity to "penetrate a four inch thick telephone book when fired from a distance of twelve feet."[19]

> Muzzle velocity in rifles ranges from 1460 to 4040 feet per second. This approaches mach 4!

---

[17] James Wilson, "Wound Ballistics," *Western Journal of Medicine*, 127 (July 1977), 50.

[18] "Remington Sporting Firearms & Ammunition 1982" (catalogue) (Bridgeport, Conn.: Remington Arms Company, Inc., 1982), 26–30.

[19] James Wilson, "Shotgun Ballistics and Shotgun Injuries," *Western Journal of Medicine*, 129 (August 1978), 152.

Other factors that affect the wounding power of a gun are the mass of the ammunition, distance of the weapon from the target, how efficiently the bullet goes through the air, and whether it gets deformed when it hits intermediate targets (such as ricocheting off the ground) or tissue. Sometimes bullets start tumbling, wobbling, wagging, or even disintegrating as they encounter environmental resistance to flight, which also affects wounding power. To stabilize the flight of ammunition, gunsmiths in the sixteenth century developed "rifling," longitudinal grooving of the inside of the gunbarrel which can impart a spin to the bullet of up to 200,000 rpm.[20] Rifling is usually found in rifles and handguns, but is not a feature of shotguns.

Kinds of Ammunition

Ammunition is propelled by gunpowder, which was developed in the fourteenth century. It was characterized by significant amounts of residue from the black powder until smokeless powder was developed in France in 1885. Ammunition is generally in the form of either bullets or shot.

- **Bullets.** Bullets are usually measured in caliber, although some types developed in other countries are measured by the metric system (Fig. 11.8). For example, a .25 caliber bullet has a 25/100, or 1/4 inch diameter. In each ammunition cartridge is gunpowder, a primer, and the bullet. The primer is ignited and burns very rapidly (0.00001 second), igniting the gunpowder.

  Bullets are made of lead and may be unjacketed, semijacketed, or fully jacketed with high-melting-point metal that helps the bullet retain its shape. Fully jacketed and unjacketed bullets most often remain in a single piece on impact, but semijacketed bullets (either soft or hollow point) can deform up to three times their size if the velocity is high enough. Bullets also come "pre-fragmented," which is a very efficient and deadly version of a hollow or soft point bullet. Some law enforcement agencies use soft- or hollow-point bullets under the rationale that because of impact-based deformity, these bullets are less likely to have enough leftover ballistic energy to exit a criminal's body and injure innocent bystanders. At the other extreme, fully jacketed bullets are high-velocity missiles and have devastating impact. These are actually regarded as more humane by the Geneva Convention because they remain in a single piece.

---

[20] Wilson, "Wound Ballistics," 50.

Figure 11.8

Ammunition comes in all shapes and sizes. A sampling of handguns and rifle ammunition is illustrated.

The weight of a bullet is measured in grains. There are 7000 grains per pound. Weight increases wounding power because it affects the mass of the projectile. Generally, the larger the bullet's caliber, the more it weighs; for example, some caliber sizes of handgun ammunition and their corresponding weights are:[21]

Caliber	Bullet Weight (grains)
.22 rimfire	27–40
.25 automatic	50
.38 special	115–200
.357 magnum	125–158
.44 magnum	180–240
.45 automatic	180–230

- ***Shot Shells.*** The tubing of a shot shell, which is made of paper or plastic, houses a column of plastic, paper, or felt wadding and a cup containing the shot. The tubing is attached to a metal head that contains the powder, primer, and another wad. Shotgun pellets (shot) are measured by a system in which the larger the number, the smaller the

---

[21] Robert Jordan, "Ballistics and Medicolegal Aspects of Gunshot Wounds," (unpublished), 4.

diameter of each ball of shot. Therefore, number 9 shot pellets are 0.08 inch in diameter, number 6 shot pellets are 0.11 inch in diameter, and number 2 shot pellets are 0.15 inch in diameter. Birdshot consists of pellets smaller than those in buckshot, and dove shot is still smaller. You would not have much luck shooting big game with doveshot—and you would obliterate a bird with 00 (pronounced "double-ought") buckshot, each pellet of which is 0.33 inch in diameter!

Because of the different pellet sizes, a variable number of pellets fit into each shot shell. For example, there are 585 pellets per ounce of number 9 shot, 225 pellets per ounce in number 6 shot, and 90 pellets per ounce in number 2 shot. There are 130 pellets per ounce of 00 buckshot, which translates to nine pellets per shell; this does not seem too bad until you consider that each pellet is larger than a .22 caliber bullet![22]

Shot spreads out in a widening pattern at the (very) approximate rate of 1 inch per yard traveled. Its exact aerodynamics depends on the individual weapon and its "choke," which is when the barrel is modified to reduce the rate of the spread of the shot. A shotgun may have no cylinder-bore, which means there is no choke. Alternatively, it may be full-choke or modified-choke. The greater the choke, the smaller the comparative pattern of spread of shot at a given distance. Choke does not significantly affect missile velocity.

- **Rifled Slugs.** Slugs (with rifling to stabilize their aerodynamics) are discharged from a shotgun but consist of a single projectile. The effective wounding power of a slug is derived from its exceptionally high mass; a 12-gauge shotgun slug has a caliber of 0.730 and weighs 295 grams. Slugs were developed mostly for big game hunting, and are obviously lethal.
- **Magnum.** The meaning of this term depends on whether one is discussing bullets or shot shells. With bullets, the cartridge case is reinforced and contains a greater load of powder, which increases velocity. A firearm capable of withstanding the additional pressures of the explosion must be used. In a shotgun, magnum does not necessarily signify greater velocity. Instead, it means that a larger load of shot can be discharged because the shell can hold extra powder and pellets.
- **Blank Cartridges.** "Blanks" may be familiar as the ammunition used at track meets and in theatrical fights. They are called blanks because they contain no projectiles. However, this does not mean that they can do no harm. Fired at point-blank or close-contact range,

---

[22] Jordan, "Ballistics and Medicolegal Aspects of Gunshot Wounds," 6.

enough disruption from the exploding gases alone can be lethal. In one case, "a 14-year-old fired a .32 blank cartridge in contact with the skin of his chest, blowing a hole through the skin, into the costal muscles, pericardium [and] right ventricle." He died.[23]

Constituents of Discharge

When a firearm is discharged, debris is generated in addition to the projectiles. The forensic value of this particulate evidence makes it important for criminal investigators. Be careful to handle the clothing of shooting victims gently. Constituents of discharge include particles of burned, partially burned, and unburned gunpowder, grease from the barrel, and expanding gases. The discharged gases include carbon monoxide, carbon dioxide, nitrogen, hydrogen sulfate, hydrogen, and methane. All of it is very hot.[24]

Residue can be classified by weight. The lightest travels only a short distance and consists of a sooty, smoky deposit. Ash is next, and comes from consumed powder. The partially burned and unburned particles of powder, as well as small fragments of grease and wax lubricants and the bullet itself travel farthest.[25] It is possible for these particles to travel 45 to 60 centimeters or more.[26] Prehospital workers may inadvertently damage evidence; tread carefully at shootings, and watch out for it.

Types of Wounds

Gunshot wounds can look so simple. Sometimes all you see is a small (perhaps slightly blackened) hole. Often, there is no external bleeding. One paramedic, upon seeing a GSW for the first time, recalls thinking: "Is that all there is?" On the other hand, there are gruesome, even nauseating, injuries. High-velocity or close-range shotgun injuries can be explosive, particularly when they hit the skull.

Be careful never to trivialize the possibilities for internal devastation when a gunshot wound looks minor (Fig. 11.9). No matter how healthy the patient seems, any potential penetration of the body, particularly the abdominal or chest cavities, must be considered critical until proven otherwise. A small, simple entrance wound may have a swath

[23] Bernard Knight, "Firearm Injuries," in *Forensic Medicine*, 525.
[24] Knight, "Firearm Injuries," 511.
[25] Berg, "The Forensics Ballistics Laboratory," 563.
[26] Godley and Smith, "Medicolegal Aspects of Gunshot Wounds," 869.

of fragmentation underneath, the result of bullet disintegration, second-ary missiles, and shock waves. The damage depends on whether the weapon was high- or low-velocity, the density of the tissue hit, and whether the attack was contact, close-range, or distant.

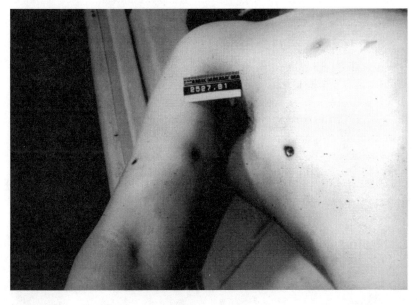

Figure 11.9

Gunshot wounds can look very benign on the outside. This person's GSW went through the arm and into the chest. (Photo courtesy of Stephan D. Cohle, M.D., Blodgett Memorial Medical Center, Grand Rapids, Michigan.)

Gunshot wounds come in all shapes and sizes. With multiple GSWs, it can be difficult to identify accurately how many times a person has been shot. The important thing is to resist the inclination to tunnel vision on the first hole you see. Inspect the patient from head to toe for more holes. They can be difficult to find because they do not always bleed, and they are sometimes obscured by clothing. In one case, the paramedics treated a GSW to the abdomen just fine, but no one saw the insidious hole in the crease of the patient's groin until after he arrived at the emergency department.

Entrance Wounds

It may be difficult to count the number of GSWs a patient has sustained, because it may be hard to distinguish entrance from exit wounds. There are some clues: entrance wounds are generally, but not always, smaller than exit wounds; they might have powder embedded in the surrounding skin ("tattooing") and/or a burn; there may be bullet "wipe" (oil or residual grease on the skin) around the bullet hole.

The appearance of a handgun injury depends on the distance—contact, close range, or long range—from which the gun was fired. Contact wounds (when the gun was pressed against the body) tend to show very little residue. The skin may be torn raggedly by the forces of the expanding gases. A loose contact wound may show some smudging. In contact wounds against a pliable surface such as the abdomen, there is less likelihood of tearing, because the skin had room to stretch. Close-range wounds (from near-contact to 12 or 18 inches) cause the greatest amount of residue. These injuries tend to have a small, circular wound. At near-contact range, there may also be scorching from the high temperatures associated with discharge of a firearm. Residue is not generally seen when the blast came from farther than about 12 to 18 inches.

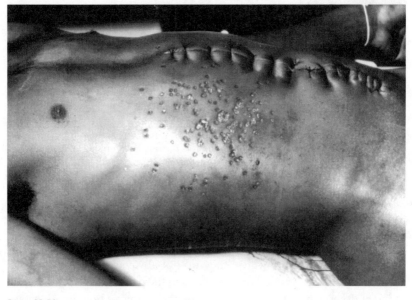

Figure 11.10

Shotgun injuries sustained at some distance will show this "peppered" effect. (Photo, taken post-autopsy, courtesy of Stephan D. Cohle, M.D., Blodgett Memorial Medical Center, Grand Rapids, Michigan.)

Range in shotgun injuries is measured slightly differently than for handguns and rifles. As a general guideline, long range for shotguns is considered greater than seven yards, and usually results in subcutaneous or deep fascia penetration by the shot (Fig. 11.10). Close range is between three and seven yards; the shot penetrates to more vital areas of the body. Less than three yards is considered point-blank, and causes massive tissue destruction, since the shot has had no chance to spread and hits the body as one lethal missile.[27]

Exit Wounds

Exit wounds are usually larger than entrance wounds—sometimes *much* larger. Gaping wounds as large as 10 inches in diameter can occur. The edges of an exit wound may be averted, which means they are turned outward. Note that there may not be an exit wound associated with each entrance wound. There may also be *more* than one exit wound per entrance wound. This happens when secondary missiles (such as particles of disintegrated bullet or bone fragments generated by the blast) exit the body. These secondary missiles often tear the skin raggedly because they tumble unevenly through the tissue.

Exit wounds sometimes look uncharacteristically clean—enough to be mistaken for an entrance wound. This is more likely to happen where the skin is supported by a firm surface, such as a wall behind the victim, or by tight clothing. These things prevent the explosive effect of the emerging bullet from tearing the skin.

Cavitation

The reason high-velocity missiles inflict so much damage is that they affect more than the tissues they penetrate. Because they enter with such force, they transfer energy to the surrounding tissues. Cavitation is the term that describes the shock wave generated by high-velocity (>2000 feet per second) projectiles (Fig. 11.11). The concept of cavitation, originally borrowed from hydrodynamics, was first applied to wound ballistics in 1898. It is "the formation of a vacuum as a result of a solid object moving rapidly through a gas or fluid."[28] As high-velocity projectiles tear through the body, the cavity that forms in its wake releases energy both

---

[27] R.T. Sherman and R.A. Parrish, "Management of Shotgun Injuries: A Review of 152 Cases," *Journal of Trauma*, 3 (1963), 78.
[28] Wilson, "Wound Ballistics," 50.

forward and laterally. That cavity may be thirty to forty times the size of the bullet, and creates huge tissue pressures, as much as 3000 pounds per square inch.[29] "The tissue around the cavity then collapses and pulsates with decreasing amplitude for a few milliseconds, coming to rest with a wide track of destruction of a diameter intermediate between that of the original cavity and that of the projectile."[30] The shock waves generated as tissue ahead of the missile is compressed may move "away from the bullet in all directions at a speed greater than the bullet itself" (at approximately the speed of sound in water, or 4800 feet per second).[31] Associated tissue damage is the obvious result.

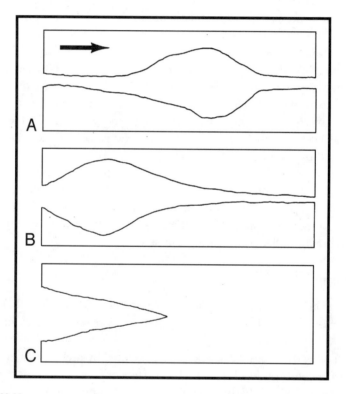

Figure 11.11

Appearance of temporary cavities in gelatin blocks due to (a) full-metal-jacketed rifle bullet, (b) hunting rifle bullet, and (c) shotgun pellet. [From *Gunshot Wounds,* by Vincent J.M. DiMaio (New York: Elsevier Science Publishing Co., Inc., 1985). Reprinted with permission.]

---

[29] John E. Campbell, *Basic Trauma Life Support,* 3rd ed. (Englewood Cliffs, NJ: Brady, 1995), 20.
[30] Knight, "Firearm Injuries," 525.
[31] Ordog, et al, "Wound Ballistics," 1119.

Different body tissues are affected differently by cavitation, depending on their density. Less dense tissue, such as lung, usually sustains a lower degree of cavitation. Especially dense tissues, such as liver or muscle, are more gravely affected. Wobbling and fragmentation of the projectile also increase the damage.

Assisting Crime Scene Investigators

One reason to obtain fundamental knowledge about guns and ballistics is to appreciate the needs of criminal investigators. Medical intervention can obliterate evidence at crime scenes and impede subsequent investigations. Controversy still surrounds the death of President Kennedy, for example, because one of the holes in his neck was used for a tracheostomy.[32] There are some things we can do to make investigators' jobs easier.

First, control the flow of helpers. From a safety viewpoint, the fewer uniforms on any crime scene, such as a shooting, the better. People with guns often do not like the looks of all that authority. Also, it is too easy to destroy evidence. In one case, the EMS service was called to handle a man whom the dispatcher said had had a seizure in a garage. They discovered he had actually been shot in the head—after the six inches of fresh snow outside that might have given investigators some excellent clues had been completely trampled. Be careful never to step on blood, blood stains, spilled body fluids, or splattered material. If you have the foresight, approach the victim by a different route than the victim's assailant used. Then use that same path to and from the victim.[33]

Ballistics experts examine subtle details to determine such things as the direction of bullet entry, and sometimes they can only obtain the necessary information with our help. For example, the shape of the bullet hole can help them determine where the assailant may have been standing, but many of their clues are lost once the patient is moved or removed from the scene. If you can, quickly make a general outline of the patient using adhesive tape from your crash kit. Try to avoid moving furniture or

> Because so much can be gleaned from such minute particles, it is important to be gentle with potential evidence.

---

[32] D.R. Godley and T.K. Smith, "Some Medicolegal Aspects of Gunshot Wounds," *Journal of Trauma*, 17 (November 1977), 868.

[33] Richard C. Vollrath, "Crime Scene Preservation: It's Everybody's Concern," *JEMS* 20 (January 1995), 53–56.

anything else on the scene if it is not vital to medical care.

Because so much can be gleaned from such minute particles, it is important to be gentle with potential evidence. Obviously, save stray pieces of bullet that drop out of the clothes. When cutting away clothing, *never* cut through the bullet hole. When removing clothing, do not shake it or turn it inside out; this can dislodge important gunpowder and bullet fragment evidence. In shotgun injuries, you may see a wad of material. This has been expelled from the shot shell. It is evidence. Don't discard it.

Any trace evidence, such as bullets, bullet particles, and shot shell wads, should not be handled with metallic instruments such as hemostats. These can scratch and alter the evidence. In addition to stria, bullets may have powder indentations or even the weave pattern of the victim's clothing imprinted on them. Place evidence in a plastic container such as a bag or an emesis basin.

> When you encounter possible evidence, and there is no law enforcement to take it, your handling of the evidence could influence its admissibility in court.

Chain of Evidence

When you encounter possible evidence, and there is no law enforcement officer to take it, your handling of the evidence could influence its admissibility in court. These rules governing chain of evidence require that it never move beyond the direct custody of a traceable list of people. It must never be accessible to anyone until you hand it to the proper authority (usually the investigating officer). One realistic way to do this, assuming that the police will arrive at the hospital before you have to leave, is to keep the container of evidence on the ambulance stretcher as you wheel inside, and then within immediate reach at all times until the police take it from you. Always note possible evidence on your documentation, and to whom it was given.

If the victim of a GSW is obviously dead at the scene and you will not resuscitate, try to disturb the scene as little as possible. In one case, the person had been shot at close range by a shotgun, and most of his neck was on the wall behind him. He had been thrown backward onto a bed. His companion had been shot, close range, in the chest. She was obviously dead, too. Their known downtime was greater than 20 minutes. The paramedics were able to leave the scene almost exactly as they found it, since medical intervention was not indicated. All they did was roll the woman onto her back to determine that her injuries were, indeed, lethal, then return her to the position she had been in. The male victim was not moved at all.

Summary

It is unfortunate that we have to acknowledge the existence of weapons and the potential for their use. And what a wide variety of weapons there are! Like it or not, weapons are often a component of emergency scenes. People resent our intrusion, and we increasingly encounter aggression.

Shootings are not a large percentage of most EMS system calls. But when they do occur, they bring special considerations and risks. Therefore, it helps to have a basic working knowledge of guns and ballistics. Even if you are unsure what kind of weapon was used, you can often tell by the wound whether it was low- or high-velocity, and appreciate the probable tissue devastation inside. If nothing else, it helps to know ways to assist criminal investigators.

In truth, prehospital care is not as hostile as this chapter dedicated to weaponry makes it seem. Only a small percentage of emergency medical calls will have such a component. We, who basically just want to have a chance to help fix the world, usually encounter people who genuinely want to be helped. There is little reason to let paranoia interrupt those efforts, as long as a small corner of your mind stays aware of the possibilities. That awareness could someday save your life.

Stress and Wellness 12

Chapter Overview

Emphasis on stress awareness has been intense in recent years, and with good cause. A lot of good EMS providers have quit because of stress. Or worse, they have remained on the job with sour, negative stress-related attitudes. Too much stress is a hazard to everyone, especially in the already chaotic prehospital world. This chapter explains different kinds of stress, including critical incident stress, and what you can do about them.

Wellness is an approach to life that incorporates the handling of stress, but also goes way beyond it. It is important to know how to take care of yourself (and then do so!) in order to maximize the chances of a healthy life. Self care includes knowing how to handle stresses so they do not build into distress. If life reaches distressing levels, then it becomes imperative to be able to recognize and eliminate the sources before they become full-blown burnout. Stress awareness and self care are vital both to wellness and to streetsense, because a person who is consumed by the aftereffects of an unhealthy life may have difficulty helping other people.

About Wellness

Wellness is an attitude. It is a personal commitment that assumes your well-being to be a priority that you are willing to make time for. For some reason, giving care to yourself, if you are typical of people with "rescuer" personalities, is one of the most difficult things to do. This chapter begins with wellness, because making it the top priority matters. Doing so can give you the energy and frame of mind to cope with the rest of the demands of life most effectively.

Wellness is not merely the absence of disease. It is the process of enriching and fulfilling the various elements of your life in a balanced way. It is getting beyond coping with illnesses and into places that expand your scope and horizons. It involves turning attention to the mind, the spirit, and the body. Those who choose the path of wellness will find it to be a lifelong pleasure, and an ever-growing opportunity to discover the riches that are there for the asking.

This short section is just a primer on wellness. It is intended to springboard the reader to the suggested reading list, to the local library—and to a changed attitude on self care. If you decide to seek wellness, rather than avoid illness, your life will be tremendously enhanced.

Mental Wellness

The mental realm includes the intellect and the emotions. Sometimes, when people finish school, they say, "I'm done." They stop active learning. They rely on a passive approach to nurturing the intellect, which is that part of the mind that thinks and understands, which has the capacity to acquire knowledge. Whatever happens to be in the paper or on TV, or what they hear from friends, is the extent of their on-going learning. If you finish school in your late teens or early twenties, it makes the next 60-plus years a desert of intellectual growth!

"Lifelong learners" are people who seek knowledge, just for its own sake. They are curious, and willing to expend the energy to appease that curiosity. You don't need to sign up for expensive classes that require a regular schedule. (Who has a regular schedule in EMS?!) Even reading books or renting non-fiction videos is a start. Interestingly, only a handful of people ever read another non-fiction book after they finish school. Those who read one per year are unusual, and anyone who reads one non-fiction book per month is in a highly select group. If it interests you to be a world-class expert on a topic, just reading 30 minutes per day for five years would allow you the means to master it. One of the nicest things about being an adult learner is that you can choose what to learn; there are no core courses for life, the way there are in many schools and colleges!

> There is something good about having a "beginner's mind." It builds humility. It reminds you that there are still areas of life that you know little or nothing about.

Some people are reluctant to try new things because they are afraid of looking foolish when they are beginners. Yet there is something good about having a "beginner's mind." It builds humility. It reminds you that there are still areas of life that you know little or nothing about. It opens the door to learning so many different things.

Emotional wellness is knowing about all sorts of feelings, how to identify them in yourself and others, and how to function effectively while they are present. For example, some angry people do not even recognize the emotion, and just act on it. This results in fights and injuries that might be avoidable. Once a person can recognize and name strong emotions, it becomes easier to control behavior surrounding it. Note that the feelings are not controlled; the behavior is. No one can "make" a person feel a certain way (in spite of what children often claim!). Feelings just happen, independent of what we might prefer. They are triggered in ways that are unique to each individual. The same scene in a movie might invoke warm, happy feelings in one person, sadness in the next, and guilt in a third. How a person feels depends on life experiences, mood, awareness, and other factors. Learn to identify your emotions, and ways that your interpersonal behavior is affected by them. For example, if you have a hair-trigger temper, try to understand why and then identify ways to alter your behavior. This might help you prevent occurrences you regret later. It all begins with making the commitment to be conscious of your emotions.

Spiritual Wellness

Some people have a regular spiritual practice, such as church, which fulfills their spiritual side. Some used to. Some never have. One paramedic, raised rigidly within the Episcopal church, renounced it as soon as possible and never considered spiritual practice again for decades. Eventually, it dawned on this person that something was missing. After some reflection, the paramedic realized that the spiritual side of life was like a deflated balloon. It was time to turn to the task of filling out that element of life, to reinflate a sense of spirit.

Organized religions are enough for many people. They meet their needs well. But others turn away from organized religion and in doing so, renounce all spiritual practice. Maybe this is because of a bad experience with church dogma. The advantage of separating the two is that the spirit can soar in many directions once it is freed of the bonds of organized religion. It can be felt in nature, in the presence of a dying person, in the wonder of childbirth, in moments of deep love and terrible fear. It may take on a new name for each individual. That's the wonder of the freedom of religious expression that is a cornerstone of the American way of life. As an adult, no one can dictate to you how your spiritual practice should be conducted. If spirit is a side of yourself you haven't visited for some time, turn to it when you are ready. It could be very enriching.

Physical Wellness

People in EMS know too well the ravages of illness and old age. We visit nursing homes and long-term facilities. We intend never to be living there. And then, many of us blithely continue treating their bodies with utter contempt. Without a healthy body, our chances of living robustly into old age diminish with each high-sugar donut, salty corn chip, and couch potato day. We may instead live into old age in bodies that are no fun to be in.

The time to plan for lifelong physical wellness is now. Those who attend to the physical body in a moderate and reasonable style stand the best chance of having a life more free of physical complaints. On immediate terms, even good hand-washing habits may prevent a number of colds and other minor illnesses. For both your current life and the long-term, eating well, maintaining ideal body weight, and staying physically fit will be good investments.

Core elements of physical fitness are:

- Muscular strength
- Cardiovascular fitness (aerobic capacity)
- Flexibility
- Adequate, healthful nutrition

All are equally important! A very strong person with tight hamstrings may jeopardize his back as much as someone who isn't strong. In addition, maintaining ideal body weight matters. Two out of every three Americans is overweight. This places more stress on joints and internal organs, and makes it hard to enjoy a full life. It also increases the risk of back injury.

EMS providers have to consider themselves athletes. It requires physical training—and doing a few heavy lifts (of patients) every day doesn't count. The bursts of cardiovascular activity that come with some EMS situations do not count for cardiovascular exercise. Going from stopped (between calls) to flat-out in just a few seconds exacts a huge toll over time. Those of you who regard physical fitness seriously are well ahead of many of your colleagues.

The way to physical fitness comes one effort at a time. Knowing what to do is the topic of volumes of books. Basically:

TARGET HEART RATE

1. Subtract your age from 220. This is your maximum heart rate (estimated). (For example, let's discover the target heart rate for a 42-year-old whose resting heart rate is 60:
220 − 42 = 178.)

2. Subtract your resting heart rate from your maximum heart rate.
(178 − 60 = 118)

3. Multiply that figure times 0.7.
(118 x 0.7 = 83)

4. Add the figure just calculated to the resting heart rate. This is target heart rate. The benefits of aerobic exercise will be achieved at this rate.
(83 + 60 = 143)

Figure 12.1

To know your target heart rate is to have an objective, measurable means of knowing that your physical fitness program is likely to be effective.

• **To increase aerobic capacity,** it is recommended that you exercise for a minimum of 20–30 minutes at least three times a week, during which you raise your pulse to its target rate (70–80 percent of age-dependent maximum). (Fig. 12.1)

• **To increase strength,** do regular weight-lifting exercises. Learn about proper principles of weight-lifting from a knowledgeable source. Your muscles should be able to exert force (strength), have adequate power (explosive force), and show adequate endurance (ability to sustain a contraction).

• **To increase flexibility,** commit to doing a regular stretching regimen. The purpose is to increase range of motion. There is a difference between "warm-up" types stretches, which tend to be brief. In order to gain flexibility, plan on holding each stretch for sixty seconds. Contrary to common thought, flexibility can be regained—if you work at it correctly and consistently!

As for nutrition, your mother was right. In the early 1990's, a new list of the four basic food groups was approved. They are now grains, legumes, vegetables, and fruits, with meat and dairy products considered "optional."[1] Everything in moderation, including the size of your overall portion, seems the cautious watchword. When possible, delete fat, add fiber, and start learning! There are abundant nutrition fads and miracle diets, each more confusing than the last. If you make the study of nutrition an on-going interest and not an obsession, it is possible to achieve enough balance—and results. Reason can prevail. It is a common cliche in EMS that our four food groups are salt, sugar, fat, and caffeine. Joking aside, though, you can plan ahead and eat well on the streets.[2] Like anything else worth doing, it takes time, energy, and commitment.

Basic Back Safety and Wellness

Back injury is the most likely cause for the end of your career in EMS. Over 80 percent of people in Western society will experience back pain at some time in their lives. This very day, about 10 million of them are in treatment for back pain.

There are two parts to having a good back.[3] First, keep it fit for the work you ask it to do. Second, use proper body mechanics whenever you lift *anything*—not just patients. (See chapter 9 for additional information.) You can minimize the chance of back injury by paying attention to the following:

- Do strengthening exercises. This benefits the "guy wires"—the muscles and other connective tissue—that hold your spine in place the same way wires hold telephone poles up straight. Strengthening your abdominal muscles is as important as your back and leg muscles. Do those sit-ups! Actually: *don't* do sit-ups. An old-fashioned sit up (raising your trunk from a flat position to fully upright) can actually strain the lumbar spine. Those traditional sit-ups use the hip flexor muscles (which attach to the lumbar spine) for more than half the motion. Instead, use exercises that recruit the stomach muscles throughout the entire exercise and that minimize strain on the low back.[4]

---

[1] *Safety: Techniques and Applications* FA-144 (Washington D.C.: FEMA, April 1994), 149–152.
[2] Elysa Markowitz, "Eating On The Run: Finding "Fast Food" That Feeds Your Health," *JEMS* 18 (January 1993), 38–42.
[3] Nancy Manix, MPT, "Oh, My Aching Back," lecture at EMS Expo, in Grand Rapids, Michigan, April 13, 1996, and subsequent correspondence, April 1996.
[4] Nancy Manix, MPT, personal correspondence, April 1996.

- Do flexibility training. For example, flexible hamstring muscles will allow you to get into proper lifting positioning. Shortened ones will interfere. Consider taking up yoga. It takes care of strength, flexibility and your mental wellness.
- Use correct posture—all the time! To stand correctly, your ears should be over your shoulders, shoulders over your hips, hips over your feet. Your pelvic girdle should be parallel to the ground. Slouching (which tilts the pelvis backward) is especially harmful to disc pressures on the back of the disks. A forward tilt of the pelvis is appropriate for "locking in" the back when doing a lift. However, letting the pelvis "hang" chronically in a forward tilt stretches and weakens the stomach muscles. Weak stomach muscles lead to a vulnerable spine. Do those abdominal strengthening exercises! If your pelvis tilts inappropriately, "rock" it to the proper position, notice what the correct position feels like and get in the habit of standing that way. If you have a large belly, see the advice about losing excess weight. And do more abdominal strengthening exercises!
- Get adequate rest. When your spine is non-weight-bearing, the discs can receive nutrition. The discs also receive nutrition during the day, when fluid is pushed through them by way of compression. For optimal disc nutrition, the spine must move well in all planes That is, if you bend forward frequently, but never bend backward, the back areas of the discs will become weak from lack of the nutrition that comes from disc compression. Poor disc nutrition leads to weakening of the fibrous rings around the disk, which increases the chance of herniation or rupture.
- Eat a balanced diet. Here is another reason to eat well! Give your body the fuel it needs to do its job. You wouldn't "gum up" the engine of a motor vehicle by feeding it low-quality gas or oil, would you? Your body is a high-performance machine that relies on you to treat it as such.
- Stop smoking and lose weight if you need to. Each contributes to disk deterioration.
- Use correct body mechanics whenever you lift any object. Avoid reaching for a load. Either move close to it, or bring it as close to your center of gravity as possible. Next, lock in your spine and set your stomach muscles. That means holding the spine in a slight extension curve, using back extensor muscles and stomach muscles to maintain that position. Finally, lower your "butt", bend your knees, keep your chin up, and use your leg muscles—each part is important.

Most back injuries occur because of the cumulative effect of every-day stresses. Your posture, your muscular fitness, your flexibility, your nutrition (or lack of it)—all add up to choices you can make for your own well-being with regard to back wellness. Back injury is the number one career-ending injury for EMS personnel. Don't let it happen to you.

Basics of Infection Control

From a wellness point of view, there is much that EMS providers can do to minimize the risk of infection. There are three factors that must intersect for an infection to occur:

- *The dose* of the infecting organism (the number of live organisms present)
- *The virulence* of the infecting organism (the strength or ability of bacteria or virus to infect)
- *The host resistance* (the ability of the host to resist entry of the infecting organism). Resistance is weakened when the body's natural lines of defense (skin and mucous membranes, for example) are impaired in some way.

The formula for infection, then, looks like this:[5]

$$\text{infection} = \frac{\text{dose} \times \text{virulence}}{\text{resistance of host}}$$

Infection relies on *all three* factors. Have you ever noticed how people who take genuinely good care of themselves are seldom ill? They maintain a strong degree of resistance through healthful living. Conversely, have you ever noticed how some people get sick every time they push themselves too hard without adequate self care? Once the infectious process is clearly understood, you can arm yourself *appropriately* against threats of disease with information about the various communicable diseases. Infection control classes are mandatory for all EMS providers. Keep up to date with that information.

The part *you* can play regarding infection control is to understand your self-care choices:

---

[5] Katherine West, *Infectious Disease Handbook for Emergency Care Personnel* (Philadelphia: J.B. Lippincott Company, 1987), 6.

Personal Hygiene

The greatest favor you can do for yourself to prevent infection is to make thorough hand washing a routine (Fig.12.2). Everyone knows this, yet researchers have found that medical personnel do appropriate hand washing procedures only about 30 percent of the time.[6] And ambulances (with the exception of those in Japan) do not have sinks and soap on board, which undoubtedly causes that statistic to nosedive in the prehospital population. Yet consider our "office." It is the least controlled environment in medicine. Whatever our calls dish out is where we work—in booze halls, industrial plants, slaughterhouses, crack houses, flophouses. We give care in "the mud, the blood, and the beer." Our hands get *dirty!* In fact, one paramedic from a busy inner-city system finds herself washing hands *before* using the toilet.

Figure 12.2

Making hand washing with regular soap a routine is as likely as anything to protect you from infections.

Thorough hand washing includes using an appropriate soap, lathering, and using friction to scrub for at least 15 seconds, rinsing well, and drying with a clean towel. Do not ruin the whole exercise by turning off the faucet with a bare hand; use your towel instead.[7] Plain soap is adequate most of the time, although your EMS agency may use other recommended agents. It also helps to keep some towelettes that do not require water handy to clean your hands when a sink is unavailable. Also, inspect your hands often. "Trivial breaks in the skin, such as dermatitis or chapped hands, have apparently been sufficient to serve as portals of entry of the [HIV] virus on direct exposure to infected blood or body fluids."[8] (By the way, the

---

[6] West, *Infectious Diseases Handbook*, 12.
[7] West, *Infectious Diseases Handbook*, 12.
[8] J.L. Baker, "What Is The Occupational Risk to Emergency Care Providers from the Human Immunodeficiency Virus?" *Annals of Emergency Medicine* 17 (July 1988).

virulence of HIV is downright wimpy, whereas the virulence of hepatitis B is remarkably strong.)

In addition to hand washing, attend to other personal hygiene. If your uniform gets soiled, put on a clean one. Dig the grime out from under your fingernails. Don't pick your nose. Your mother was right! Eating well, getting adequate rest, and exercising all contribute to a healthful body that can resist organisms.

Care With Needles

All the precautions in the world are useless if you get stuck by a needle. Exam gloves cannot prevent illness delivered by needles or other sharp instruments. However, remember that a needle stick—even from a patient with a blood-borne infectious disease—is not necessarily a death sentence. If your resistance is good, trust your body to fight the threat successfully.

At the same time, never assume that nothing will come of a needle stick. Follow local protocols for reporting the event. The time for testing a patient's blood for hepatitis B, syphilis, HIV, and other infectious diseases is while that patient is in the emergency department. It may be difficult or impossible to locate that person again if you get sick. Some of them will even be dead and buried.

Dispose of all needles properly. Easily said, but not so easily made routine. One of the worst things you can do is recap used needles for disposal, yet medical personnel still admit to it. In the field, any effort at routine is even more challenging. IV needles are still jabbed into the vinyl of the squad bench or dropped to the ambulance floor, awaiting removal by the cleanup committee. Sometimes, for example at mass casualty settings or other unusual circumstances, you may be forced to recap a needle for lack of a handy sharps container. The safest recapping procedure for use when no other method of disposal is possible is to put the cap under the sole of your boot with the opening well away from the boot, and carefully insert the needle until it clicks into place.

Immunization

When possible, get vaccinated. If you had rubella, mumps, chickenpox, and other childhood diseases when you were young, you are ahead of the game. Regardless, every EMS agency should have an immunization program that includes vaccinations for the following:

- **Hepatitis B.** This is a one-time series of three shots given in a six-month period. As a clearly identified high-risk group, EMS personnel should consider immunization, and possibly follow-up testing to be sure that antibody levels can insure immunity.
- **Tetanus-diphtheria.** After initial immunization, a booster is required every 10 years. The diphtheria portion of the vaccine was added in 1981 due to increasing incidence of that disease.
- **Mumps.** If you did not have the mumps when you were a child, you *certainly* want to avoid them as an adult, particularly if you are male. The characteristic inflammation of the parotid and other salivary glands may be accompanied in adults by painful testicular or ovarian swelling. This is a one-time injection.
- **German measles (rubella).** This is a devastating disease for fetuses; exposing a pregnant woman to rubella poses grave potential for multiple congenital anomalies in the infant, including mental retardation. Be fair to your pregnant patients and get this one-time injection if you did not have German measles as a child.
- **Flu (influenza).** Yearly inoculations are available, and are based on the two or three most-predicted flu strains for the upcoming "flu season." Over time, an annual flu shot will help you build immunity to a wide range of viruses. It may help minimize the need to take sick days, and will also minimize unnecessary exposure to your patients.[9]
- **Polio.** Because polio has become nearly unheard of since the 1950s, increasing complacency has occurred about getting a polio vaccine. This has resulted in a resurgence of this devastating disease. If you were not immunized (or are unsure about your immunity status), it is not too late. This one does not even require an injection!

In general, vaccination is a gift of modern medicine. Take advantage of it. Although many of these diseases are uncommon and it is hard to believe they could happen to you, why take the chance?

Stress and Its Management

Every aspect of EMS is a source of above-average levels of stress: handling crises, waiting for the next call, dealing with chaos, making rapid life-or-death decisions, dealing with traffic, working shifts. Many people

---

[9] West, *Infectious Diseases Handbook*, 3.

thrive on all this, but it is possible to overdose. To work most effectively, we have to control stress; everyone needs to blow off accumulated loads now and then.

The stresses of EMS—whether you volunteer or do it for pay—include witnessing things that are beyond the normal experience of most people. It is more stressful to witness the body crushed by an elevator, when it is still entrapped, than after it has been gathered into the protection of helping hands and realigned onto a backboard. Some detachment from the stressful reality of the tragedy occurs when the patient is subsequently delivered (hopefully in an improved condition) to a well-lit, emergency department. On-site, "seeing it as it happened" factors often make it harder for us than for in-hospital personnel.

Figure 12.3

Life is often overwhelming! If you feel like you're losing the metaphorical tug of war, find a way to gain control. Use healthy means to regain your balance.

There is always an ebb and flow of accumulated stress in us—compounded, of course, by whatever stressors are occurring in the non-EMS parts of our lives. Some people learn, after plunging into emergency prehospital medical care, that the stress levels are too high for them. They discover they just are not suited for such a load, and quit. Others learn that the *kinds* of stresses unique to EMS suit them poorly. They quit, too, if they are smart. Still others find that they much prefer the stress of EMS to the different—but, in its way, no less stressful—environment of a traditional desk-and-files office. Quitting to eliminate inappropriate stress levels is not a sign of weakness. People should never feel that they have to stick with something that does not suit them, just to "save face." Sometimes things just do not work out the way you thought they would. That's all.

The stressors of EMS are wide-ranging and are not limited to patient care. The exciting challenge of field medicine contains some ugly things on its underbelly which can sorely test personal limits. Can you handle:

- The vomit?
- The unfairness?
- The tone alarm at 3:00 a.m.?
- The abuse thrown at you, the rescuer, by them, the rescued?
- The interminable waiting?
- The death and the dying?
- The administrative insensitivities?
- The long hours and (often) inappropriate pay?
- The demands on you by the ambulance corps—when, after all, you are volunteering your time?

The definition of stress is that it is "the nonspecific response of the body to any demand," according to Hans Selye, a prominent researcher of stress. There are not different types of stress; it is just that the things that stress each of us are invariably different. A certain amount of stress is necessary for survival; without it, we would not be motivated to eat, find shelter and warmth, or provide other essential care for ourselves. It is even stressful to experience pleasant things. It is as stressful to encounter an old friend as it is to encounter an old enemy (unless the enemy tries to bop you on the head!). It is emotionally and physically stressful to restart a dead heart and save a life. It is stressful to deliver a healthy, wanted baby. The joy of the graduating exercises from EMT or paramedic training are as stressful in their good way as are the fears and tensions of your first day on the streets.

There are different sorts of stress:

- Cumulative stress is a long-term event. It may be caused by multiple smaller, unrelated stressors (things which trigger a stress response) joining forces over time to become bigger than they would be alone. It may be caused by the same stressor being experienced repeatedly, such as an inability to get a good night's sleep for many days in a row.

- Critical incident stress is related to a single, overwhelming event of unusual proportions even for someone accustomed to witnessing unusual things. The stress response is accelerated.

Each sort of stress requires attention. A person interested in wellness knows how to effectively handle the effects of stress—and does it. A bad day, a bad week, or even a bad month does not necessarily indicate a problem. Everyone, both male and female, has cycles. Sometimes we are on top on the world, and sometimes we are not. It is not unusual to have a run of bad luck. The low point of a cycle can make it tempting to react negatively. The key is to recognize high stress levels and manage them in a healthy way. The goal is to prevent the problems of too much stress, if possible, or at least minimize them.

Cumulative Stress (Burnout)

Each person has an individual capacity to receive, process, and defuse the various stresses they encounter. Selye calls this "adaptation energy." Some people have the capability to handle more stress than others. Part of understanding ourselves includes the process of learning about our individual limits for coping with stress. When the accumulated pressures of life start to overwhelm your sense of well-being, then the limits of wellness are being approached or exceeded. You are moving along an ever-widening spectrum, past healthy levels of stress to the next level: distress. The word "distress" implies an unwanted state. Your health will begin to break down (Fig. 12.4). Certain signs and symptoms will begin. When distress is not defused by adequate stress management, it can fester, like an infection. Left alone, it will move along the spectrum to the extreme end, to a place vividly referred to as "burnout." The proper term is "cumulative" stress (some say "chronic" stress). This is like when an oil lamp runs out of fuel and flickers out. Some people would like to believe that burnout is a fallacy, but it is not. Burnout is alarmingly common in people in service industries such as social workers, mental health workers, and teachers, as well as EMS providers.

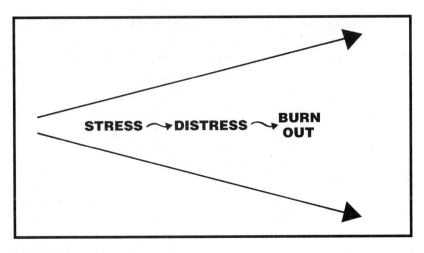

Figure 12.4

The time to address stress is while it's still as far to the left end of the spectrum as possible. Avoid reaching the point of burnout! As soon as symptoms of "distress" occur, take time to diminish the effects through healthy stress reduction measures.

The good news is that burnout is *not* inevitable. Relatively few people reach the inordinate stress levels. Rather than having to overcome the effects of burnout, it is best to avoid it through healthy preventive measures. Whether a person will reach that far end of the spectrum or not depends heavily on education, awareness, and self care.

Each person is susceptible to a unique constellation of signs and symptoms of cumulative stress. The first step is learning to recognize the individual responses to stress that occur in you. Once you know which signs and symptoms to be on the lookout for (see text box), the next step is to monitor for them daily. These signs and symptoms are red flags. As they begin to appear, you have the opportunity to stop a stress response in the early stages. Make the commitment to practice self-care by eliminating or minimizing them as they appear. Don't put it off! That way, you can avoid traversing the spectrum of cumulative stress from bad to worse.

> It is a human trait to seek comfort and avoid pain, especially when there is no perceptible end to that hurt.

Signs and Symptoms of Cumulative Stress

There are several nearly universal signs and symptoms of cumulative stress that occur when a person is past distress and on the way to burnout. It is a human trait to seek comfort and avoid pain, especially when there is no perceptible end to that hurt. When stress has accumulated to a painful degree, there is little that is good to say about the source of all that distress:

- **Negativity** (particularly in a normally positive or even-tempered person). Normally negative people become even more so.
- **Persistent feelings of exhaustion or lack of energy** (both emotionally and physically). People feel as fatigued when they get up in the morning as when they got home from work or went to bed. Nothing seems to help generate a refreshed feeling.
- **Persistent cynicism.** Normally cynical personalities will be more so, while people who are not normally cynical will surprise their coworkers with unexpectedly cutting remarks.
- **Loss of motivation for the job.** How often have people enthusiastically burst into EMS, worked very industriously, and then dwindled away, claiming no longer to care?

There are many other signs and symptoms which tend to arise earlier. These may be physical, cognitive, behavioral or emotional. Some or all might appear in one person, but not in others. People often attribute the signs and symptoms to other causes; for example, a person with physical manifestations of stress may spend a great deal of time and money seeking medical cures without addressing the true underlying problem. It is unnervingly easy to be unaware of what is actually happening. In fact, some people are never aware of what was actually going on until they view the chain of stress-related events in retrospect.

Closely related to the feelings of fatigue and exhaustion are complaints of sleep disorders. In a business inextricably tied to shift work, we have explanations other than too much stress for this! But some people who were burned out have reported, in retrospect, that they had been sleeping 10 and 12 hours a day. Others are plagued by insomnia.

Many people develop cumulative illnesses. They have back-to-back colds, headaches and backaches, or more than their fair share of the flu. Illnesses may be nonspecific, and are primarily nuisance-level problems. Gastrointestinal disturbances are also common, although this may also be related to the EMS habit of eating irregular, interrupted, cold, and often notoriously poorly nutritious meals!

Behaviorally, there may be "short-fuse" reactions. A person becomes increasingly irritable, uncharacteristically impatient, quicker to anger. Scenes that would have gone quite smoothly with a little tolerance and good communication fall apart, and may even become unnecessarily confrontational. A habit of negatively stereotyping people may develop. Even as the nature of the call is heard—for example, "man down"—a burned-out person mutters something like, "oh *#@!, another drunk." Or, the person may cry easily and for no apparent reason.

Many people develop an overwhelming sense of being overburdened. The entire weight of caring for all the sick and injured people in the world seems to be on them. It is more than they can bear. Minor calls feel intrusive and irksome. The result is increasingly defensive behavior. A burned-out EMS provider can make patients feel foolish for being such a waste of time.

Self-preoccupation tends to creep in. People who feel they have given their all to the cause of EMS sit back to see what EMS will give them in return. This is a common response to the accumulation of distress: "This business has been hard on me, so I'm going to take it easy for awhile." Off duty, they may seek temporary relief with alcohol, drugs, cigarettes, or even food. "Drowning sorrows" in any of these ways is misguided stress management that can obviously be very detrimental. Another related behavior is a pattern of gross and blatant disregard for personal safety and the safety of others. The underlying motivations for undue risk taking by burned-out people will vary. Perhaps there is a subconscious desire to push the limits to the point of being fired (rather than having to quit, which means admitting defeat). Or maybe they hope to die a hero's death by going into situations that a more prudent person might not enter. The reckless driving of a person with this attitude is downright dangerous and frightening. They go much too fast, blow through red lights, and recklessly endanger hundreds of lives on every run. This sort of behavioral decompensation is a real nightmare.

High absenteeism is another by-product of burnout. People who are disenchanted with their jobs find myriad excuses for not being there. There is no motivation to get to work, especially when fatigue is making a person feel tired before ever starting the shift. The sense of being overburdened is often directed at administrative and supervisory personnel. "What? They want me to fill out some more paperwork in addition to all my other duties? No way!" gripes the burned-out worker. These people may also begin to handle all situations absolutely by the book, so that when someone does mention that their performance is off, they can point out that they have done nothing specifically wrong.

These people may not sit back passively, though. They sometimes actively strive to block change and progress by lobbying other suscep-tible people in the agency to refuse to implement new procedures or protocols. This is a real frustration for administrators, supervisors, and people in the rank and file who are not feeling burned out. If they are sitting back at work, these people are likely to watch the clock constantly.

People affected by cumulative stress often just want to be left alone. They deny outwardly that anything is the matter. They sometimes try to attribute to the causes of their behavior to problems at home when they are confronted at work and to problems at work when confronted at home. Pathological levels of burnout include feeling suspicious or para-noid toward coworkers. What might help trigger this is that co-workers recognize a prob-lem and are increasingly concerned, but are reluc-tant to speak about it with the burned-out person for fear of having their heads metaphorically chopped off. The person with the symptoms senses their discomfort and so may therefore become increasingly withdrawn and isolated. There may be a spiraling sense of failure as the entire process feeds upon itself. There may be an exterior facade of indifference, but it often masks an internal sense of frustration or guilt for having maltreated other people—patients, coworkers, and family. There may be suicidal gestures—or worse.

> As if all these signs and symptoms are not serious enough, add the next ingredients of cumulative stress reactions: they are pernicious and contagious.

As if all these signs and symptoms are not serious enough, add the next ingredients of cumulative stress reactions: they are pernicious and contagious. EMS administrators must be on guard constantly to avoid significant staff problems by not letting burnout get rooted among the troops in the first place. Like a thorny weed, it requires conscientious prevention, or, once established, aggressive uprooting.

Susceptibility to the Effects of Cumulative Stress

There are both personal and situational factors that contribute to a person's susceptibility to the effects of cumulative stress. There may be internal factors, external factors, or both. Most of the time, the problem is a combination.

There are some specific personality traits that can indicate a candidacy for burnout. These traits may be: a "charismatic, energetic, impatient [person], given to high standards, throwing himself into whatever he does with all his might, expecting it to provide rewards commensurate with the effort spent."[10] Sound like anyone in EMS?

The Right Stuff

Some people simply do not have "the right stuff" to be in EMS. They spend the time and money to get the training, only to find a few months into it that the work does not suit them. To be able to say they "burned out" is one way some people feel they can escape EMS without losing face.

Idealism

Some people enter EMS with extremely high ideals. They quickly learn that reality fails to live up to those ideals. A dose of idealism is not necessarily bad. But when it is a major motivator for becoming involved in EMS, it is often quickly and hurtfully dashed. Certainly it would help if instructors taught students that "EMS is hours of boredom punctuated by moments of sheer terror" on the busy days—and otherwise filled with routine, mundane tasks.

A particularly vulnerable group are people in their late teens or early twenties. This is an especially idealistic age. At this stage in life, people want to devote their time to something that seems particularly significant.[11] The work of emergency medical care, and even interfacility transfers, is so—but often not in the way people first imagine. Our work is *always* significant—it's just that most calls are a huge service to the patient without being much of a challenge to trained providers. A very idealistic person may have been expecting the dramatic call load they saw on television, or may have thought lives could actually be saved more often than they really are. A more realistic outlook from the start could help eliminate this common cause of attrition in EMS.

The amount of cynicism that creeps up when a person's inordinate levels of idealism are flickering out is disheartening. Eventually, many people channel their reformulated view of EMS into a more down-to-earth attitude. Others just disappear.

---

[10] Herbert J. Freudenberger and Geraldine Richelson, *Burnout: The High Cost of Achievement* (New York: Anchor Press/Doubleday, 1980), 103.
[11] Gail Sheehy, *Passages: Predictable Crises of Adult Life,* (New York: E.P. Dutton, Inc., 1976), 28.

Unrealistic Expectations

Unrealistic expectations are closely related to idealism. Again, TV promises highly challenging, intense work which, despite a few hopeless cases, is full of personal achievement. This is a charismatic view, far different from the actual routine. Only about 10 percent of emergency calls demand the use of our most critical medical knowledge. There are long hours of waiting. There is vomit and blood to clean off the floor, walls, and ceiling of the ambulance. There are mechanical failures to fix, and the squad room and kitchen are a chronic mess. Days off are often spent in meetings or continuing medical education. As with anything else, EMS has its drudgery.

Dead-End Perceptions

Some people over time begin to view EMS as a dead-end pursuit. This makes them highly susceptible to burnout. A cynical person can easily boil down field care of the sick and injured into a matter of waiting for calls, arriving, packaging, and depositing a person into the right slot at the right hospital, then going back to waiting. Chest pain? Oxygen, IV, monitor. Neck or back pain? Immobilization. It's a bleak and boring viewpoint. Part of the reason the human component is a major part of streetsense is to avoid this dreary view. Without it, EMS would seem unrelentingly cut and dried.

Age

One last personal component that can lead a person to burnout is the inaccurate perception that EMS is for young people only. Actually, there are an ever-increasing number of middle-age and senior citizens involved in prehospital emergency care.[12] Although the motivation to carry obese people down several flights of stairs may decrease with age for many people, age does not automatically have to be a limiting factor.

Shift Work

Situational factors that contribute to a person's susceptibility for burnout vary. Many situational factors, such as poor pay, have been remedied over the years. Others will never disappear. The most obvious unchanging situational stress factor is the hours. EMS is a 24-hour oc-

---

[12] Kate Dernocoeur, "The Graying of EMS," *JEMS* (August 1991), 67–69.

cupation. Someone is always stuck with the graveyard shift. Volunteers have to answer calls for help at disruptive hours, too. We cannot avoid abnormal and irregular schedules.

Humans are all cyclical, but the disorientation and discomfort caused by rest disturbance will affect some people more than others. To be sure, some people thrive on alternative sleep patterns, even preferring to work at night. Shift work is not a large source of stress for everybody, but one thing is certain: there is no way that shift work will ever be eliminated in EMS!

Underload

"Underload" is another stress-causing situational factor. Although EMS services are increasingly using dynamic deployment of EMS crews, instead of letting them sit in their stations awaiting calls, there is still a lot of waiting. Even EMS providers who stay in a station feel the effects. It is not easy money to sit around and watch TV or pursue leisure-time activities while awaiting a call! The hours soon become long. EMS providers can be sapped of all their get-up-and-go before they know it. The challenge is to maintain enough mental readiness to be able to quickly respond when a call comes in. You can never relax entirely when on duty. For volunteers and people with certain shift structures, that means a 24-hour-a-day pressure.

Pay

The issue of pay continues to be a situational factor. After being spit on and shot at, a person's humanitarian streak can lose its grip when the paycheck does not support even a modest life-style. The dollar compensation for the risk and personal abuse sustained in EMS is often inadequate, not that anyone gets into this business for the money! The fact is, there will never be enough money to pay prehospital workers what they really earn out there. In a sense it is ludicrous to try to assign a dollar value to the job of providing kind service, reducing misery, or even saving lives now and then. It is just that when the going gets tough, the issue of money is an easy target.

Lack of Appreciation

Another form of compensation—a simple word of thanks—is also notoriously absent in EMS. One highly-respected paramedic who has run thousands of emergency medical calls has yet to receive a written note of thanks. Part of the problem is that prehospital helpers are usually long gone by the time patients who might be inclined to say thanks feel better enough to do so. Although we do not really expect people to thank us, it is easy to feel unappreciated when the feedback of gratitude never seems to make its way back to you. Like the issue of low pay, it is another thorn that means little by itself but that adds to the pain of accumulated stress.

Ergonomics

Product developers are finally beginning to engineer tools and furniture with human needs, abilities, and capacities in mind. Ergonomics done well gives us a "user-friendly" world. There's still a long way to go: EMS providers in many systems sit in the ambulance for the entire shift. This is not exactly a cozy office! And many ambulance quarters are still "blessed" with garage sale furniture (old, broken, uncomfortable), broken air conditioning, drafty windows in winter, mice, and bugs. Lighting is notoriously poor for reading, both in ambulances and in quarters. The list of discomforts (and thus stressors) is lengthy.

Exposure to Others Who Are Burned Out

Sitting long enough in the presence of a person who has burned out is like sitting too long in front of a campfire; the heat eventually inspires a reaction. A person can metaphorically catch fire and burn up, too, although the preferable reaction is to get away from the heat. The probability of "burning" depends on the susceptibility of the person to be mesmerized by the fire. The contagious and pernicious quality of burnout must not be ignored.

Administrative Insensitivities

An "us versus them" attitude can be very difficult to shake—on both sides. If field personnel sense a lack of administrative and supervisory support, the company-wide response can be unpleasant. Savvy EMS managers work very hard to maintain relations with field personnel in order to counter this sort of response.

Overcoming Signs and Symptoms of Cumulative Stress

There is much a person can do to minimize or eliminate the effects of cumulative stress and burnout. It's easier the earlier it's noticed, and best of all when a person makes it a habit to handle stress daily. It makes continued involvement in EMS more likely. In fact, people who pay attention to this topic probably make better prehospital workers for doing so.

Problem recognition is the first step. In the case of burnout, a person might be oblivious to it and recognize it only in retrospect. Can a concerned coworker point out burnout to someone who is in trouble? It depends on the relationship between the two people, the degree of burnout, and how the information is offered. Less seriously affected people are more likely to be open to suggestions for help. In many cases, a little push from a concerned friend can appropriately redirect someone who has fallen off track.

Seriously burned-out people can be psychologically fragile. They may be clinically depressed and guilt-laden, despite their negative, cynical veneer. A nonjudgmental, nonpunitive approach, in combination with an action plan, is much healthier than simply demanding that an employee with a poor recent work performance "shape up." In such serious cases, it may be better to refer the person to an Employee Assistance Program. Good EAP programs have trained clinicians to help people with psychological evaluation and treatment (or referral), as well as help for substance abuse problems, which are another common stress-related situation.

It is gratifying to see someone emerge from the long, dark tunnel of extreme levels of cumulative stress. No matter how they overcome the problem, the change is dramatic. They become positive, productive, energetic, helpful, pleasant people again! The change is a big morale booster for everyone, after the weeks and sometimes months of negativity, apathy, or aggression.

There are two general ways to combat burnout:

- Healthy, effective strategies that generate good, long-lasting results
- Palliative remedies that just mask the problem

Palliative Remedies

"Palliative" means relieving or lessening something (in this case, stress) without curing it. A person making "efforts to manage the somatic and subjective components of stress emotions (e.g., anger, anxiety, depression) without changing the actual person-environment relationship"[13] is using palliative remedies that do not get at the root of the problem.

- **Substance abuse.** The classic palliative remedies for distress are increased types of substance abuse. Substance abuse includes alcohol, misuse and abuse of recreational and prescription drugs, caffeine, and nicotine. Compulsive overeating also fits this category; the resulting obesity only compounds the deficit of self-esteem. Interestingly, an increasingly popular substance for anxiety is abuse of Inderal (propranolol) because it creates an impression of calm control.

- **Learned helplessness.** Learned helplessness is an unfortunate response to distress. It numbs personal creativity because people feel unable to initiate creative solutions to problems. They learn not to make independent choices or find independent views of a situation; everything depends on looking to another source for permission to feel or act a certain way. The design of many EMS systems engenders learned helplessness, because development of personal judgment is discouraged. In these systems, workers are strictly the physicians' field arms and legs, and all the orders come over the radio. EMS providers must cope with extreme limitations for delivery of field medicine. When you cannot even start an IV on a cardiac arrest without radio permission, you will soon lose interest in developing your own good judgment. Continuing medical education becomes a drag; why learn anything when you are not allowed to think about what is in front of you on the streets?

- **Ruts.** Some people become obsessive about "plugging away" at the job. There is a perceptible shift from enjoying the work to a grim shoulder-to-the-grindstone attitude. They are in a rut. Their field performance becomes automated and is devoid of the spark it may have had previously.

- **False detachment.** Others build an emotional defense network which results in false detachment from the work. One paramedic earnestly believed that he was never affected by what he did every day. For years, he said, he had not let the various tragedies he witnessed bother him. Yet he could not cite any outlet for the inescapable buildup of stress. The man was an emotional powder keg.

---

[13] Heinz W. Krohne and Lothar Laux, *Achievement, Stress, and Anxiety* (New York: Hemisphere Publishing Corp., 1982), 7.

- **Other excuses.** As the various pressures of the job reach distressful levels, many people begin to come up with excuses to avoid their responsibilities. They are sick and cannot come to work, or to the volunteer squad's monthly meeting. The car broke down. Their grandmother died (for the third time). They claim immunity from cleaning chores because they say they have done more than their share for years. They get out of taking ordinary responsibilities because of other well-timed alternatives, like taking a shower. Not everyone who plays these games is burned out—but chronic shirking of responsibility can indicate an unhealthy attitude toward the job.

- **Threatening to quit.** Some people try to cope with distress by constantly talking about quitting. Stress is easier to bear when it appears to have a fixed time frame. For example, a person with a fractured leg can handle the pain better if she knows she can have a shot for the pain after the x-rays are done. If a situation is distressful, a prehospital worker may, then, persistently verbalize intentions to quit, say, "in six months," "after the summer," or "soon." Such talk becomes a source of distress for those who have to listen to it all the time. Other people on the ambulance service begin to question their own decisions to stick around when they are constantly reminded of another person's plans to leave.

Healthy Remedies

There is a saying that an oyster's response to sand in its shell is to make a pearl. Why not make positive things out of irritants? It takes effort to adjust a burned-out outlook. But it is worth it! One of the first things is to reexamine what you are doing. Are you really suited for EMS? Many people realize that, in fact, they are not, and they often quit at this time. Those who remain convinced that EMS is right for them have good options for overcoming the effects of cumulative stress. The commitment to change things is in itself a positive step. Stressors are automatically less fearsome when you decide to face them head-on. Following are strategies and techniques.

Vacation

A vacation may be all you need to recharge depleted emotional batteries. One paramedic who had been exhibiting clear signs of burnout for years found himself out of work for six weeks with kidney trouble. When he returned to work, his attitude had turned around. He had been so "crusty" for so long that many newer personnel did not know he was capable of being so positive and friendly! Then he admitted that he had not taken a vacation for eight years. Lesson: If you do not elect to take vacations, your body may "elect" to do so for you.

Work Fewer Hours

Many people in EMS work inhumane amounts of time. In some cases, the problem is an inordinate loyalty to EMS in the face of low staffing. The gung-ho worker, who is already highly susceptible because of extreme enthusiasm, cannot bear to see an ambulance taken out of service for lack of personnel. In other cases, overtime is the culprit. It's economic. Some people in EMS, as in every segment of our credit-card society, live beyond their means. This leads to a stressful cycle of working too many hours trying to earn the money to pay for their purchases rather than being at home enjoying them. At a certain point, the individual needs to call "time out." Without a refreshed outlook generated by working fewer hours, any chance for a balanced view of EMS is increasingly jeopardized.

Increase Exercise

Psychiatrists have known for years that depressive and overstressed people benefit from exercise (Fig. 12.5). Exercise is a great way to combat the lethargy of underload. People in EMS may sit for hours on end at times. If you push yourself out of that chair and do isometrics or calisthenics, it helps significantly without causing a big sweat and ruining your

Figure 12.5

The form of excercise you choose is less important than actually getting out and *doing* it! Usually, the days you least feel like exercising are those on which you need it most.

professional demeanor! It also keeps your muscles better prepared for sudden demands to lift heavy, awkward weights. In a survey of prehospital workers who claimed to have burned out, and then overcome it to continue in EMS, 52 percent said that an increase in exercise helped. They did everything from jogging, weight lifting, aerobics, and other strenuous sports, to darts and competitive fishing.[14]

Physical exercise has two benefits. Exercise is an excellent way to blow off the pent-up emotions of typical EMS personalities. EMS providers are by nature assertive, physically active, and energetic. Physical exercise is a great vehicle for "blowing off steam," and it also helps us stay fit enough to handle the physical demands of the job.

Develop Outside Interests

It can be very helpful to realize that the rest of the world does not live and breathe emergency medicine. It is remarkably easy to allow EMS to become all-encompassing, regardless of whether yours is a paid or a volunteer system. It helps to associate with people who have no link with the streets, or to start doing things that have nothing to do with EMS. One paramedic, during recuperation from burnout, decided he would spend no off-duty time with coworkers at all. He developed an entirely separate group of people as his leisure-time friends. Many people plunge into completely untried territory—perhaps taking up gardening or learning about the stock market. Others return to former, neglected interests.

Quit for Awhile

Some people find that it is helpful to quit EMS for some time, ranging from several months to several years. A leave of absence lets you regain objectivity about EMS, and provides enough perspective to help you remember the good parts. Although it may be more difficult to leave a paid position than a volunteer one, the solution has worked well for some people.

Meditation

What is meditation? Some people do meditate in the stereotypical way, sitting in uncomfortable positions, burning incense, chanting, and listening to music unfamiliar to the Western ear. There are actually innu-

---

[14] Private research by the author.

merable ways to meditate. For some, the words "reflection," "contemplation," and "introspection" come to mind. The point is to take some time—say, 20 minutes a day—for yourself. Take time to stop and be quiet, inside and out. For my grandmother, prayer was meditation. For others, it is sitting quietly with the eyes closed, repeating a sound that helps clear the mind of thoughts. Others do yoga or deep-breathing exercises. There is another technique called "deep relaxation." Any style of meditation has beneficial results—even for doubters. One paramedic told the story of how she started doing transcendental meditation, and continued with it (20 minutes morning and evening) for several years. Without her knowledge, both her mother and best friend (neither one a likely candidate for this sort of thing) learned it. They were drawn to it because of its dramatic positive effect on the paramedic.

There are different styles of yoga and many kinds of meditation. High-quality instruction gives you the best chance of finding agreeable results. Check with your YMCA or YWCA, community recreation centers, or community college for locally-available classes.

Learn to Think Positive

Many people in EMS become callous, crusty, and cantankerous—in other words, if they are not burned out, they are certainly not fun to be around, or optimally effective in their interpersonal communication. Their attitudes are negative. Sometimes you would just like to shake some sense into them about how destructive those attitudes are, not only to themselves, but also to coworkers, patients, and even the public. But change has to be self-motivated. A person has to decide it's worth the effort to self-reprogram. This is the process of switching from a negative to a positive attitude. It is fun because it has a domino effect. One large urban agency went from being mostly negative to mostly positive over the course of 18 months. As the beneficial effects of a positive attitude grew in one person, others became "infected" until a magical transformation had occurred.

Actually, it is not magic at all. Self-reprogramming demands a conscious effort and the all-important ingredient of self-awareness. If you cannot objectively hear the things you say, and visualize the things you do, you cannot evaluate and rephrase them more productively. Simply, negativity can be broken by a commitment to think positive. It is actually self-induced behavior modification, the same as quitting smoking, effective dieting, or elimination of other bad habits. Even the crustiest old-timer can change.

Start positive thinking by making yourself hear the things you say and see the ways you behave. Use the "detached observer" technique described in chapter 2. When something you do looks or sounds negative, alter those statements and actions on the spot, until being positive becomes a habit. If you say, "I hate rainy days," let your next statement be, "and let me think of something good about them. Well, at least I won't have to water the lawn." (Fig.12.6).

HOW TO TRANSLATE FROM NEGATIVE TO POSITIVE

Look at some comparisons:

Negative Thought: "This jerk is certainly overreacting to the pain. What a wimp. . ."

Positive Thought: "A dislocated shoulder is one of the most painful kinds of injury. This guy's not directing his abrasive statements at me personally; it's the pain."

Negative Thought: "You should have had this looked at three days ago." ("...so why did you have to get me up at 3:00 a.m. to help you?" say your thoughts!)

Positive Thought: "Let's take you in and have this looked at."

There is no gain in scolding strangers about the way they are handling their emergency. If you want to say something, use the chance to educate, not to belittle.

Figure 12.6

Your "detached observer" also has access to what you are thinking. Negative thought patterns are even more insidious than negative verbal patterns because they reinforce negativity where no one else knows about them: the interior of your mind. You have to routinely correct negative thoughts if you want to become truly positive-minded.

Extend the process of learning to be positive beyond prehospital encounters. Let it infuse every aspect of daily life. For example, take time to surprise a harried cashier at the supermarket with some pleasantry, and see for yourself how nice it is. Being around a positive person really cheers people up.

Negative statements have no positive purpose. Most negativity is an unnecessary expenditure of energy. Once you stop being negative, there is a double benefit; you will no longer exhaust yourself with ineffective and unappreciated interpersonal interactions, and you will feel good, too. Be careful, though. A too-positive outlook can be as unrealistic and detrimental as a negative outlook. It can be dangerous to view the world through rose-colored glasses. Your ultimate goal is to have a positive outlook that blends appropriately with reality.

Thus the next concept in reprogramming provides balance. It is called "even-keeling" (Fig. 12.7). Like a sailboat, which uses a keel to remain upright in the water, our minds need to maintain emotional and intellectual balance. Even-keeling works on the pendulum principle. Most people who are working to change are coming from a very negative point of view. When initially seeking a positive outlook, they swing like a pendulum too far into being positive, then back to being negative, a little less into the positive extreme then, back and forth in progressively smaller increments. Eventually, equilibrium is reached and the person is on an even keel.

Figure 12.7

This woman looks pretty relaxed! Her life is on even keel. Let your mind find the same peace through mental "even-keeling."

Let Things "Roll Off Your Back"

It's a relief to learn to let verbal abuse "roll off your back." Verbal assaults on the streets (and maybe in your home) are frequent. At least on the streets, they may not be directed at you personally. You are a convenient target, that's all. Accept it. To react negatively only confirms the angry suspicions of the person shouting at you. Many of these people are influenced by alcohol or other drugs. To refuse to be drawn into such a meaningless game as arguing with a drunk can be very gratifying.

This is an important point. Many prehospital workers, by virtue of their own aggressive or assertive personalities, have become involved in fights because they let verbal assaults escalate into the physically painful kind. Fights are almost always unnecessary. They can be avoided simply by letting the verbal abuse, like a heavy load, roll off your back. There's a definite psychological sense of feeling less burdened.

Rational Concern

A promise to practice rational, rather than detached, concern is a nice gift to yourself. "Detached concern" involves remaining objective, which isn't all bad. But sometimes people are so "objective" that they forget to have any compassion. This cheapens the human component of our work. Rational concern allows permission to have and express feelings while maintaining the ability to make decisions. Rational concern alleviates (or eliminates) the emotional drain that results from giving your help impersonally. From a burn-out point of view, author Stephen Levine expressed it this way:[15]

> Burn-out occurs when we give from the little self, the small mind. We give from who we think we are. We become "helpers." Because the little mind, the little personality, doesn't have much room, we don't have space enough for the suffering of others. We feel isolated and struggle to keep from being submerged in our separate suffering. It's like trying to give water to someone dying of thirst. You can either wring the fluid from your cells to give them something to drink, thereby becoming dry and wizened in the process. Or you can go to the well, the great source of sustenance, and carry buckets of clear water to those who need it, finding there's plenty to drink for yourself. Those who give from themselves burn out. Those who give from the source are nourished in the giving. Approaching the well, they enter intuition, sensing the subtleties of another, responding from the heart, not the mind.

Rational—not detached—concern is a professional approach to the troubles other people have, balanced realistically with your ability to

---

[15] Stephen Levine, *Who Dies?" An Investigation of Conscious Living and Conscious Dying* (New York: Anchor Press/Doubleday, 1982), 170–171

help them. With it, you can lend a sense of genuine concern to the people you encounter, and still remain disengaged enough from the situation to make good decisions and preserve your emotional well-being. The patient perceives a level of support which you can channel from a place other than your own private reserve. Everyone benefits.

Critical Incident Stress

EMS is sometimes overwhelming, even for people accustomed to handling major crises. In the 1980's, the myth of "toughing out" the aftermath of unsettling events was shattered. Rescuers are now routinely educated that it is unrealistic to expect to cope well with *everything*. Certain experiences transcend everyday tragedy and horror to a point that even rescuers consider abnormal. Those events can generate a response known as critical incident stress (CIS).[16]

CIS generates specific signs and symptoms in the aftermath of a powerful emotional event. There are specific interventions, the most noted being critical incident stress debriefing (CISD), that *work*. These interventions must not be implemented casually or improperly. To do it right, they require a clear understanding of the process, backed up by specific training. The processes for critical incident stress identification and intervention described here are known as "Mitchell-model" processes. Beware! There are others, and the applicability and reliability some of them is questionable. Rescuers are cautioned to seek Mitchell-model CIS information if they want the one most widely recognized and used internationally. Do not assume everything you read about CIS is referring to Mitchell-model information.

There are a number of major types of emergency calls that can precipitate CIS. Basically, these are powerful abnormal events which generate a normal response in normal people. They include:

- Traumatic death or serious injury to children
- Line-of-duty death or serious injury of a coworker
- Suicide of a coworker
- Events that draw unusual media exposure
- Prolonged events, particularly when they end badly

---

[16] Jeffrey Mitchell, Ph.D. and former paramedic/firefighter, has devoted his career to critical incident stress education. The material in this section stems from his work. He is the acknowledged industry leader in CIS and its management.

- Symbolic events (such as Kennedy's assassination and the space shuttle explosion)
- Personally significant events (such as having a cardiac arrest go sour on the anniversary of your father's death, or dealing with a patient you know)
- Mass-casualty situations

There do not have to be a lot of patients to generate a critical incident stress response. What may bring it on in one person may not do so in another. Situations that fit these categories will not inevitably stimulate a critical incident stress response. For example, some mass-casualty situations were handled very well because of a well-planned disaster system. Pride and a sense of accomplishment, not devastation, were the over-riding emotions. (However, according to Mitchell, such events inevitably trigger a stress response in at least some of the people involved, and help for CIS should still be available.)

Sometimes, seemingly insignificant events may precipitate critical incident stress in a responder. If this problem is not recognized, rescuers may be left to cope alone in the aftermath. For example, when a patient took pot shots at close range to two paramedics, it was three days before anyone in the administration thought to ask how they were doing.

Signs and symptoms of critical incident stress are *normal* responses by *normal* people to *abnormal* events. They are most likely to start within 48 hours after the event, but this may vary. Physically, a person is likely to feel excessive fatigue. Exhaustion comes not only from the sleep disorders that can commonly begin (such as too much or too little sleep, nightmares, etc.), but also because the event is so all-consuming. A person may have flashbacks, vividly reliving the scene over and over (which interrupts concentration and the ability to attach importance to anything but the event), or may have complete amnesia for the event. Vague health complaints such as headache and gastrointestinal upset may arise. Hyperactivity, underactivity, anxiety, or depression may occur. A person may be oversensitive and have "hair-trigger" anger. There may be strong feelings of guilt or fear—or, conversely, feelings of helplessness or even emotional numbing. An affected person may withdraw and seek isolation. There is often an inability to concentrate or make decisions (which obviously has an impact on subsequent patient care).

One of the best self-help activities is to reach out and talk with others. Coworkers are likely to feel just as rotten. If no one is available, "talk" to a journal by writing down your thoughts. Physical exercise is another great way to help blow off steam. Pamper yourself, go easy, and maintain a normal routine. Try to stay busy enough that you cannot dwell on the pain—but not so busy that it means you are trying to avoid it. Also, be careful not to drown your sorrows in a beer stein or by abusing other drugs.

It is worth emphasizing again: these reactions are normal and a person is normal for having them. Make all the regular daily decisions (what to wear, what to eat) even if it seems uninteresting. This imparts a sense of control over daily life.

Critical Incident Stress Interventions

According to the processes developed since 1983 by Mitchell, critical incident stress management (CISM) works within a framework of ten basic interventions. Note that specific training is important; many well-meaning people with some knowledge of critical incident stress and its interventions have caused additional emotional harm at a time when emergency providers needed and deserved the *right* kind of support.

A *critical incident stress management team* (CISM team) is a carefully selected blend of Master's degree-level, or higher, mental health professionals and peer support personnel drawn from local emergency service organizations.[17] A CISM team, to be most effective, is multi-jurisdictional, nonpartisan, regional, and apolitical. The regional nature of a CISM team is important so that the members get enough—but not too much—opportunity to provide interventions. The multi-jurisdictional framework matters, according to Mitchell, because "the emotional dangers of serving one's own people are considerable to both the helper and the person being helped. The practice of debriefing or providing a defusing to one's own people should generally be avoided."[18]

The purpose of critical incident stress management is to educate emergency personnel about how to manage work-related stress (both before and after an event) and to assist personnel in the wake of an unusually stressful event. Following are some of the interventions that have been developed:

---

[17] Important: do not try to form a CISM team from the information provided here. This is simply a primer to a complex topic. Done wrong, interventions can cause harm to emergency personnel. For more information, contact the International Critical Incident Stress Foundation, in Maryland, at 410-730-3411. (The hot line number, 410-313-2473, is for emergencies only.)

[18] Jeffrey Mitchell and Grady Bray, *Emergency Services Stress* (Englewood Cliffs, NJ: Brady, 1989)

- *On-scene support services* are done *during* an event, such as a mass-casualty situation or prolonged event. After checking in with command staff, peer support personnel identify rescuers demonstrating acute reactions to the event, speak with them briefly, provide immediate support to the individual, and advise command staff as the situation warrants. Those needing it are given a break. Some victim and family assistance may also be rendered. This service may be done in conjunction with an Emergency Incident Rehabilitation command at larger incidents.

- *Demobilization services* are intended to give rescuers a transition point (away from the scene) between the intensity of a large-scale situation and going off-duty or back to regular duty. There, emergency personnel can rest and regroup physically and emotionally, and ventilate their feelings (if they wish). They also can receive basic information about normal signs and symptoms for rescuers after such an event, and the most effective methods to deal with them.

- *Initial discussion* about an incident is a spontaneous sort of intervention that emergency crews and agencies often do somewhat automatically after a "big" call, while equipment is cleaned and ambulances are put back in service. The talk should be positive, and criticism or critique should be saved for later. Personal attacks and excessive negative humor may signal the start of a critical incident stress response. A formal intervention is probably indicated.

- *The defusing* is usually begun within one to four hours after an event and should *not* be done more than twelve hours post-event. Defusings are shorter (30 to 45 minutes), less formal, and not as structured as a full-blown CISD. Here, the crew is assisted in a small-group setting to ventilate their reactions to the event. An initial defusing is usually conducted by a peer support member of the CISM team, although sometimes one of the team's mental health workers may also be included. Those affected are also given a quick lesson in the normal signs and symptoms of CIS and ways to work through them. A well-run defusing may have the effect of either eliminating the need for a CISD, or enhancing its effectiveness should one become necessary.

- Formal *Critical Incident Stress Debriefing* (CISD) was the founding intervention of the critical incident stress movement. Someone experiencing signs and symptoms of critical incident stress after a profound event may feel really bad—until finding out that others feel the same way. This is the purpose of a debriefing: to teach rescuers that their responses are normal, other potential responses to watch for, and how to deal with them in a healthy way. CISD is done optimally 24 to 72 hours after an event. Any earlier and people are still too close to it; too much later and emotional defenses begin to solidify, making successful debriefings more difficult to achieve. (Fig. 12.8).

- *Follow-up intervention.* This is integral with a CISD, and begins within 24 hours afterwards. Follow-up services are extremely important for providing referrals and general advice to command officers about how best to help distressed personnel. Violations of confidences are carefully avoided. Good follow-up intervention will help pinpoint when, or whether, a subsequent CISD is indicated.

ANATOMY OF CISD

A CISD is led by two to four people. The leader must be a trained and qualified mental health worker, assisted by one or more peer support person(s) intimately familiar with emergency service. A formal CISD usually takes two to three hours and should involve *only* the people directly involved with the case. This is not a time for extraneous personnel. Format of a CISD is, generally:

1. **Introduction.** This includes a promise of confidentiality and setting of certain rules. Open discussion occurs only in an environment perceived to be safe by those attending.

2. **Fact phase.** Reconstructing the event, intended *not* as a critique, but to reintroduce the situation and its associated feelings.

3. **Thought phase.** Helping participants tap into personal aspects of the situation. The group leader asks them to relate their first thoughts during the event to help separate their thoughts from the facts of the situation.

4. **Reaction phase.** Allowing each person to express the feelings he or she had during the event and in the aftermath.

5. **Symptom description.** Those that occurred immediately and those that have come on since. Hearing others' symptoms may be the first time some people realize they are not alone.

6. **Teaching phase.** Informing the gathering about normal stress responses and how varied they can be.

7. **"Reentry" phase.** Gathering loose ends and giving logistical information (such as how to call for additional help, when a follow-up debriefing might be, etc.).

Figure 12.8

- *Individual consultation.* When an incident affects just two or three people, there is no need for a complete CISD. Instead, intervention by a trained mental health worker and peer support person from the CISD team may be provided for these individuals, alone or in a small group.

Other interventions, notably spouse support and special services (for non-EMS groups hit by critical incident stress, such as corporations or schools hit by mass-murderers or terrorists) also have been developed by critical incident stress specialists.

The CIS processes are most powerful when not overused. Because EMS personnel expect difficult calls, they usually have excellent coping mechanisms. Reserving these interventions only for events that are extraordinary even from an EMS perspective is best. Do not dilute their effectiveness by conducting defusings or debriefings more than necessary.

With properly conducted intervention, most people will find their signs and symptoms gone in six to eight weeks. Many feel "whole" much sooner than that. But when an EMS agency ignores the need for critical incident stress education and intervention, lives can be completely altered—to the point of quitting EMS, wrecking significant relationships, and worse. Indeed, many people still carry the scars of critical incident stress from the days before CISM was brought to the EMS community. Thankfully, this is no longer necessary.

Summary

Wellness is the new twist on self-care. Life should not be about avoiding illness. Rather, it should be about grabbing for the "gusto," living fully and well. There is so much that any person can do to promote wellness. Physical fitness and nutrition, life-long learning, seeking to grow as the operative word in the phrase "grow old" instead of focusing on the word "old." All of these things are part of wellness.

As a group, EMS providers are not noted for their attention to their own personal wellness. It's time to start. Begin with understanding the forces that threaten wellness. Stress, for example, is essential to life; distress is not. Burnout is the end result of living with distress too long without managing it adequately. Each person is affected differently by stress, and it is invalid to compare your ability to cope with stress to the abilities of others. Some people will find EMS too stressful to do on a continuing basis. They will leave it behind for other kinds of stress. This is the natural way that people find their niches in life.

There is little emphasis in EMS literature on the positive emotions, yet clearly they exist. We often feel satisfaction, a sense of helping. The good feelings come, not during calls, but during times of reflection. As one EMT put it: "EMS isn't fun, but it is something you can feel good about." If EMS is what you want, yet you feel the signs and symptoms of distress (or burnout) building, acknowledge the situation and deal with it effectively. The important thing is to manage whatever stress you have—not to let it manage you. By doing that, along with other wellness strategies described in this chapter, your chances of remaining well for many years will be happily increased.

This is a court of law, young man, not a court of justice.

—Oliver Wendall Holmes

Chapter Overview

This chapter addresses the insidious risks that we face in prehospital care, the ones that can come back to haunt us long after we have provided care. These risks can involve the legal concerns that can have profound effects on our lives if something goes awry out there.

Avoiding legal risk depends once again on the basic premises of this book. If you are self-aware, have a candid understanding of others, and connect the two with effective communications, your risks can be reasonably well controlled. This chapter examines risk management in three parts. The first part describes the common risks that exist, such as accusations of malpractice and negligence, accusations of theft, consent, refusals, and traffic hazards. The second section discusses ways to fend off those risks with documentation, malpractice insurance, and good public relations. The last section gives you some clues about the legal system and how to survive it if you need to.

The risks of being a prehospital worker do not end when you arrive back at the station safely. No one ever knows when news of client dissatisfaction (deserved or not) will arrive in the form of a legal complaint. Being slapped with any accusation of wrongdoing is so contrary to our goals of helping others that it stings like a slap in the face. To be accused of actions that are not in the best interests of our patients is emotionally devastating. That devastation can seep, if the plaintiff wins, into another painful spot: our pockets.

The risks discussed in this chapter warrant just as much management on your part as does a person who is threatening you with a knife. The discussion is necessarily general, because local rules and practices often vary widely. It is impossible to state definitively "how it is" everywhere. Be sure to discuss questions and issues raised here with someone in your EMS system who understands your local medicolegal complexion.

Legal Risks in EMS
Malpractice and Negligence

None of us ever likes to think that we deliver bad care. Yet that is exactly what "malpractice" means: *mal* is Latin for "bad." It is a catch-all term for improper, unskilled, or injurious medical care. Obviously, there are times when the delivery of care is not of peak quality. We are human, too, and the middle of the night is, after all, the middle of the night. We get tired, frustrated, angry—all the things this book has cautioned against. We make mistakes. Unfortunately, no one gets much of a margin for error in medicine. Everyone hopes that the mistakes they make or witness will be minor, resulting in no injury to the patients. No matter what kinds of mistakes happen, try to benefit from them. Make it a point to learn from them, and teach others about them, so they will not happen again.

The likelihood of being accused of malpractice has less to do with the physical care you give than it does with the impressions you make emotionally. Of course, an obvious failure to provide appropriate physical care, such as improperly applying a traction splint, is also a medical malpractice problem. But in many instances, people file suit because of a breakdown in interpersonal relations. Basically, do you *look* and *act* competent? Are you nice to your patients? Are you fair, and do you give the best care you can? Does your concern show? Whether it is right or wrong, the medically incapable prehospital worker who answers "yes" to those questions probably has a much lower risk for being sued than the most capable and competent worker whose honest answer is "no" or "not always." The issue of attitude is pervasive in this book because it is a benchmark of streetsense. Technical and medical knowledge is essential, of course, but a good attitude can be just as important out there—and it also will help ward off legal hassles.

We have all witnessed the boom in malpractice suits against physicians and lawyers. One researcher cites studies that indicate that "a breakdown in the physician/patient relationship may indeed be a major cause of malpractice suits."[1] People who are arrogant, apparently uncaring, pushy, condescending, or just plain negative should watch out! You can honestly care, but if it doesn't show, it doesn't count. An upbeat interpersonal style may deter accusations of malpractice. People who feel they were treated fairly, honestly, and with genuine compassion are not likely to turn around and sue you (assuming appropriate and adequate physical care). "As ye sow, so shall ye reap."

Negligence is the first thing most people think of when the topic of conversation turns to malpractice. There is a technical difference between the two.

- Malpractice indicates a failure to conform to a standard of care.
- Negligence infers a duty to act and is defined as the failure to render the degree of care that a person of reasonable prudence and similar training would have exercised given the same circumstances.

The difference is that a professional, acting within the standard of care of that profession, commits malpractice if he or she does not conform to that standard. "Negligence is based on the reasonably prudent person standard, and thus is applicable in non-professional matters. The negligence case may or may not require an expert; a malpractice almost always does, so that the standard of care is put into evidence. Conceivably, a plaintiff could have difficulty showing a breach of the standard of care (or not be able to establish malpractice because of the absence of a standard in a particular situation) but be able to prove negligence, based on foreseeability of harm and prudence."[2]

Accusations of negligence and malpractice are the forms of legal action most likely to come back to haunt us. The prehospital track record shows that negligence suits are on the rise. There is a trend that people who have sustained a tragedy somehow deserve a remedy. Negligence suits have been filed against prehospital workers for:

- *Failure to heed the input and advice of family.* In one case, the EMTs mistook the indwelling nasogastric tube for oxygen tubing

---

[1] Lewis Bernstein, *Interviewing: A Guide For Health Professionals* (New York, Appleton-Century-Crofts, 1980), 8.

[2] Personal correspondence with C.J. Shanaberger, attorney-at-law and paramedic, July 1988. Now deceased, C.J. was an internationally-renowned EMS resource for legal matters. This chapter is dedicated to her memory. She is missed.

and ignored the family's warnings. The patient's stomach was oxygenated until it ruptured.

- **Failure to start CPR.** A declaration of death is serious. It is more serious, obviously, when your perception of a patient's viability is inaccurate.

- **Loss of function, especially paralysis.** Regardless of the quality of care, plaintiffs tend to seek any remedy they can get for such an absolute loss. This is why you should carefully document neurological status at each stage of an extrication.

Fortunately, being accused of negligence and having a jury agree are two separate things. The burden of proof lies with the plaintiff (the person bringing the suit to the courts), and there are four elements to be proved before a finding of negligence can be made:

1. A duty to act
2. Breach of that duty
3. Injury
4. Causation, which means that the injury was related to the breach of duty (sometimes among other concurrent causes). Causation is usually the difficult part to prove. Was the person paralyzed before or after you moved her from the wreckage? If the plaintiff cannot prove all four elements of the negligence charge, no liability by the defendant is allowable. It's all or nothing.

Two inherent parts of the malpractice and negligence concepts to understand are "standard of care" and the "reasonable man" idea. Standard of care has to do with the criteria used to define what care is given and how it should be done.

The important thing to recognize is that the parameters of standards of care are constantly being updated. Once it was considered progressive to have oxygen on board an ambulance; now you could be held liable for not having it. Standard of care is no longer defined by what the guys in the next township are doing. Because national legislative and policy making bodies (such as the U.S. Department of Transportation), along with a national EMS registry, exist, there are now national standards of emergency medical care. If a person in one locale can expect a certain minimum standard of care from EMTs and paramedics, should someone somewhere else have to settle for less? This has important implications for EMS systems that are not keeping up.

The "reasonable man" concept means that the actions you take in a specific incident should be the same ones that a person with similar training would take to handle reasonably the same or very similar circumstances. If your case involved immobilizing a trauma patient in a howling snowstorm at two in the morning with one other person to assist, your case will be judged according to those circumstances. You would not be judged by the way you would immobilize someone in a warm, dry, well-lit classroom with plenty of help.

One area of negligence potential that warrants special mention lies in the mandatory child abuse reporting laws in every state. One doctor, in fact, was charged with negligence for failure to report a case of child abuse. Although prehospital workers are not specifically named as having a legal duty to report in every state, the moral duty is obvious. Report child abuse when you suspect it.

Abandonment

This law protects the public from being left in the lurch by medical professionals. Abandonment is a *unilateral* termination of a relationship where medical treatment is needed, without provisions for that treatment being made. (If an angry patient kicks you off his property and you leave prudently, this is not abandonment.) You may be liable for abandonment by establishing a helping relationship that you later leave without delivering the patient to the care of someone with at least your level of training. The plaintiff would have to show that provable damage occurred as a result. This includes the emergency department hand-off. Be careful not to leave a patient with a volunteer or a ward clerk because the nurses and doctors are busy. The family's lawyers will be knocking at your door very quickly if a patient is subsequently found dead in a quiet corner of the emergency department.

Use your common sense and good judgment about the best way to help the patients.

Another potential source of abandonment charges could occur if you were to discover an accident in the proverbial "middle of nowhere." When you realize you could be there for hours waiting for another car to go by, you may decide that it is more appropriate to leave the scene to get help. Use your common sense and good judgment about the best way to help the patients. If you leave, explain what you are doing and that you will be back with help. Then follow through. Return to the scene to be sure that the patients are actually found and that they received help.

Consent

Prehospital workers encounter the issue of consent constantly. We have to obtain implied or express consent on every call. Usually, consent is readily apparent because most people are seeking help and are grateful for it. Should they eventually decide that you did not explicitly inform them of what you were doing, it is valid to say that they never objected to receiving your care.

Minors cannot consent to or refuse medical care. Consent for them has to come from a parent or legal guardian. Exceptions (depending on your state) may include people who have been "emancipated," or legally released by their parents into adulthood, are in the armed services, or are married. There are certain medical situations for which minors can consent on their own, such as treatment for venereal disease and unwanted pregnancy, and for AIDS testing. Consent is implied for a minor with a true medical emergency, if the parents or guardians cannot be found.

When a third party calls for help that is legitimately needed but the help is vigorously declined by the patient, the situation can get downright sticky. If you are willing to persist at a difficult problem in effective communication without resorting to coercion, you can often end up with a patient's consent to medical care; you can then legitimately proceed.

Implied consent, fortunately, is easier. Unconscious people are not in a position to discuss options for treatment. You can safely assume that they want your care, on the principle that the unconscious party would ask for help if they were able.

Consent is an intricate issue. One ideal model for informed consent, is that "when information is disclosed to a competent person, that person will understand the information and make a decision to accept or refuse the recommended medical procedure."[3] While the intent of informing patients is to safeguard personal rights, anyone with some street time well appreciates that many patients cannot cope with true "informed" consent. How much information satisfies the requirement? Do you have to list the eight potential complications of IV therapy every time you start one? How can we, in the short time we have, judge the abilities of people who are frightened by a medical crisis to understand

---

[3] Alan Meisel and L.H. Roth, "What We Do and Do Not Know about Informed Consent," *JAMA* 246 (November 27, 1981), 2473.

our advice? How much alcohol does it take to impair competency? We do not carry the tools to measure inebriation quantitatively. And what is acceptable disclosure of information? "I'm starting an IV because it's important"? Besides, does anyone document exactly what was said in the process of informing a person? It is easy to see how the issue of consent can be a real thorn.

The most obvious risks we regularly face occur when patients do not want treatment, yet are not clearly judgmentally impaired. Is the belligerent, abusive person on the scene of the auto accident "just" drunk, head injured, angry about wrecking his car, or is he always like that? If you haul him away, kicking and screaming, you could end up with charges of false imprisonment. How aggressively to intervene is an on-the-spot decision, depending on the specifics of the case and local laws. But when in doubt, act. Be tactful and diplomatic, but act. It is easier in court to defend acts of commission than acts of omission.

> **When in doubt, act. Be tactful and diplomatic, but act. It is easier in court to defend acts of commission than acts of omission.**

Refusals

There are basically three kinds of refusals. One is when your patient refuses even to let you near enough to make an assessment. Assuming that you have made a genuine and appropriate effort to interact with someone like this, your only option in the end is to leave. Another kind of refusal is when a patient lets you make an evaluation, and your findings are that hospital treatment is indicated, but the patient refuses to go with you. The last kind of refusal is when a situation does not warrant ambulance transfer, and alternative arrangements for further care (medical or otherwise, such as detox) are made. Obviously, it is important to document each encounter carefully, in case legal hassles arise.

The topic of refusals is full of pitfalls. Many patients are in a gray zone, at the hazy rim of risk to themselves for not going with you, and a risk to you if they decide later that you did not perform your duties reasonably. If someone is drug- or alcohol-impaired, admits it, and acts like it, it is easy to defend your decision to insist on transport. Their judgment was legitimately questionable. Unfortunately, many people do not act or look drunk or drug impaired when, in fact, they are. That leaves the detective work up to you. In one such case, a young man had fallen through an unstable floor and landed on his rear end on the landing below. He was still sitting where he had landed, but was not complaining of any pain. He denied alcohol or drug ingestion. (That is the first question to ask when you see a definite mechanism of injury and no complaint of pain!) His girlfriend concurred. The incredulous paramedic did a complete physical exam twice before letting the patient stand up. Standing and moving around caused him no pain. He refused ambulance transport, and subsequently walked six blocks home and went to bed.

The following afternoon, the paramedic arrived at work and found the patient's girlfriend waiting in the day room. "Just thought you might like to know," she said (in a friendly voice—three cheers for positive patient interactions!), "that my boyfriend is up in ICU with a spinal fracture and a shoulder injury." (This case occurred before treatment standards related specifically to mechanism of injury had been named.)

There are various ploys to try to get people to change their minds about being examined or going to the hospital. First of all, try to play to a friendly audience. If you can get the crowd on your side, peer pressure can make the difference. Appeal to friends and family. Explain that you are legally powerless simply to load 'em and go. Explain the hazards of delay. Lacerations should not wait too long before being stitched. Heart attacks can get worse. Cut heads on alcoholics can mean internal cranial bleeding.

One of the worst things to do is ask this question: "Do you want to go to the hospital?" If you say this and then turn around and leave as soon as a patient says

One of the worst things to do is ask this question: "Do you want to go to the hospital?"

"no," watch out. The poor phrasing and even poorer display of tolerance and patience is ample demonstration of poor communication. Few people ever *want* to go to the hospital! Accepting a refusal is risky until you are completely comfortable that the patient understands the possible consequences of not going. Juries are not sympathetic later when you were not sympathetic to begin with.

How can you insulate yourself against refusals that come back to haunt you? Aside from meticulous documentation, which will be addressed later, the most important thing is to "clear" *every* patient refusal by speaking with a higher authority at the hospital on a tape-recorded radio or telephone system. Some EMS systems adhere rigidly to this policy, but many do not. If your system does not, consider having the policy changed. Even when the patient does not let you near, document the encounter by calling it in to the base station. That way, should trouble loom, you will have some company at the defendant's table. Besides, we work as extenders on the licenses of physicians. It seems only fair that they should have a voice in these potentially risky decisions.

Signed Refusal Forms

The value of signed refusal forms is questionable. You are asking for trouble if you rely on them alone. First, the signature is seldom a good sample of a patient's legal signature. The line to sign is often at the bottom of the page, so when the patient is balancing the clipboard on a bent knee, in the rain, at night, there is not a firm surface for his hand to rest against. When that signature is compared to the last hundred checks he signed, "It's obvious," says his lawyer, "that Mr. Jones was under too much stress to sign his own name normally. How could he have been in any condition to competently refuse medical care?" Signed refusals for medical care are better than nothing, but use them only as an adjunct to the rest of your documentation.

Occasionally, people who need a doctor's attention are left behind because, despite it all, you could not find a way to get them to agree to transport. One completely lucid woman had dangerous arrhythmias but refused transport. "I'm 94 years old," she said. "I've lived a good life. If it's my time to die, I'm ready to do so. But I intend to die at home. Thank you."

People have the choice to refuse. Don't feel badly when someone does not choose what you consider to be the correct solution.

Another 36-year-old had crushing chest pain but refused transport. Every effort was made to inform him about the risks of that decision. The paramedics called the hospital, and the doctor spoke with the patient, to no avail. The only thing they could do was discontinue the IV, pack up the monitor, and tell his wife to call back if he changed his mind or lost consciousness. People have the choice to refuse. When that is what they really want to do, there is little we can do about it. Don't feel badly when someone does not choose what you consider to be the correct solution.

Vicarious Liability

Have you ever considered the implications of your partner's actions on your liability? What if your partner makes a finding of death in someone who is subsequently resuscitated without brain function? What if your partner allows a patient to refuse treatment who was later found to have a subdural hematoma and a blood alcohol level of 3.55? What if your partner makes threats against an abusive patient who later decides to sue?

You do not actually have to be the wrongdoer to be held accountable. All you need is a relationship with the wrongdoer. When a suit is filed, the plaintiff's lawyer will go for all the "pockets" that are associated with the case. That includes your partner, your medical director, the doctors who gave in-hospital care, the hospital—and you. You can be drawn into a mess that you would never have caused had you been in charge of that scene.

The way to try to avoid a problem due to vicarious liability is to speak up! Say something when you see substandard care, when you feel your partner's actions are inappropriate and could jeopardize both of you. This is difficult, especially for people without enough seniority or experience to have the "right" to a say-so, according to the rules of peer pressure. But if you speak diplomatically, honestly, and with legitimate concerns, you may help yourself avoid real problems later.

Accusations of Theft

There is little so frustrating as working your hardest to save a life, only to have the phone ring 15 minutes later and have the deceased's wife ask about "the two thousand dollars Henry had in his wallet." Maybe there are a few dishonest prehospital workers, but the majority no doubt find such accusations infuriating.

The items of value that we most commonly deal with are watches. Most people wear them on the left wrist, which is the arm of choice when you start an IV in the ambulance. Before you touch a patient's watch, tell her what you are planning to do, or ask her to remove it for you. An excellent place to put a watch is on the patient's other wrist, because objects tend to fall out of pockets when people are lying down on the stretcher. The second-best place is to put valuables in the custody of an accompanying relative or friend.

Verbalize everything: "I'm taking off your watch. Let's put it on your other wrist so that you will still be able to watch the time." (Emergency

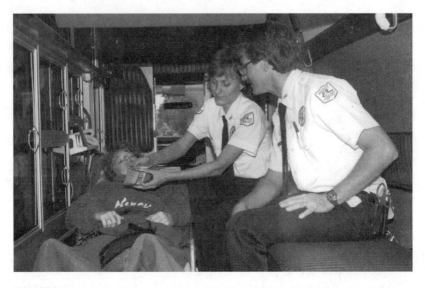

Figure 13.1

Handle someone else's valuables carefully. Conduct wallet searches in plain view of witnesses to minimize the hassle of wrongful accusations of stealing. Notice that this patient's purse has been placed between her legs. She can see that it is safe, and it is unlikely to drop and spill its contents.

departments can be so slow. . . .) "I'm taking off your watch, but Mrs. Jones will have it. Here, Mrs. Jones, will you please hold on to your husband's watch?"

If you have to do a wallet search for identification or medical information, make sure that someone you trust watches you for backup. Hold the wallet high in the air so that everyone can see that you are not pocketing anything (Fig. 13.1). When you put the wallet back, say, "Mr. Smith, I'm putting your wallet back in your pocket now." Use verbalization even if the patient is unconscious. Many of the things that are said around patients are for the benefit of the bystanders.

Purses and other medium-sized items of value (such as bags containing patient medications) can often be kept visible and secure, yet out of the way, by placing them between the patient's legs. If that is impossible for some reason, a second-best place is between a leg and the stretcher railing. Placing them there will protect you from leaving them in the ambulance when you take the patient into the hospital, and will keep them constantly in view of suspicious patients.

Your final action in preventing the risk of theft accusations is to document in writing the final disposition of valuables. Write down the name of the person who took them at the ED, and be sure they know what they are receiving: "Here are Mrs. White's valuables, including her watch and wallet."

Risks in Emergency Driving

Emergency driving poses a great degree of legal risk. It requires a lot of skill to drive a heavy, bulky vehicle. More than skill, it requires consistent caution. Whether yours is a rural, suburban, or urban service, volunteer or paid, your self-protective radar has to be out and operational whenever you are in a moving ambulance, whether or not you are driving. Not only is the trajectory often rapid, it also transcends the usual rules of the road. We are allowed (by privilege, by the way, not by right) to drive in empty oncoming lanes, the wrong way on one-way streets, in breakdown lanes, even on sidewalks. We go through red lights. We travel faster than posted speed limits. Abuse of these privileges is not uncommon. A lot of people view driving the ambulance as the fun part, as a power trip. People with that mind set are immature and irresponsible, and they erode the credibility of our profession with their roadway antics and cavalier attitudes. Abuses of driving privileges are often contributing factors in intersection crashes and give emergency drivers a bad reputation.

Hogging the road and bullying your way through traffic skyrockets your risks for accidents.[4] People often panic when they realize they have been daydreaming while a lit-up emergency vehicle was behind them. Some of them simply jam on their brakes, which makes their tailgate a bad place to be. You have no margin for error. It is safer to hang back and let oblivious drivers notice your presence while everyone still has the time and space to react appropriately.

Risk management includes proper use of the lights and sirens. Don't "run hot" without just cause. Emergency services that still condone (or mandate) running hot for advertising purposes, when returning to the station after a call, and for the purpose of getting back in service more quickly are asking for trouble. These are inappropriate uses of the equipment. Another bad idea is to try to allay patient anxiety about the lights and siren by saying that the emergency equipment is being used "because we have another call waiting." What would such a person say after the crash (if he survived)? He would be justified in suing on the

---

[4] Howard Handler, "Underwriting The Ambulance Industry," *JEMS* 13 (July 1988), 6.

basis that you were using the lights and sirens inappropriately. This is not a good reassurance ploy!

Protection Against Risk

There are two major categories of risk protection. They can provide an umbrella of protection when a real threat to personal security arises. The first is developing strong documentation habits. The other is malpractice insurance. Why should you insure yourself against assets you don't have? There are some compelling reasons. Finally, you and everyone in your service should strive for a positive public image in the community. No one likes to see a respected group's reputation besmirched.

Documentation

Documentation falls into two broad categories. First are tape-recorded radio transmissions. In most places, these are saved for at least one month. Few places save tapes much beyond three to six months, so if you know a taped conversation may be needed in a legal case, be sure to copy it before the spool is recycled. Written reports are the second category of documentation (Fig. 13.2). (In addition, you may be asked now and then to write a statement for the police about a criminal situation.)

> Good documentation contains four elements. When would-be plaintiff's attorneys review a record that displays all these characteristics, they may well be dissuaded from pursuing the case at all.

Good documentation contains four elements. When would-be plaintiff's attorneys review a record that displays all these characteristics, they may well be dissuaded from pursuing the case at all. The report has to be:[5]

- Accurate
- Complete
- Legible or audible
- Free of extraneous or nonprofessional information

If the plaintiff's lawyers start finding holes in your report, you dug them yourself. If, when giving a radio report on a patient refusing trans-

---

[5] Kate Boyd, "Trip Reporting: The Power of Paperwork," *JEMS* 5 (July 1980), 21.

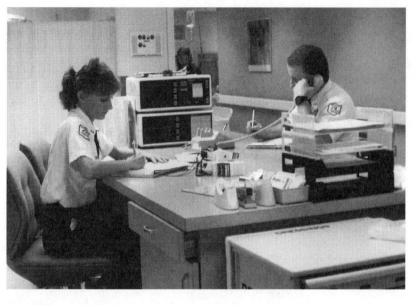

Figure 13.2

Take the time to do your paperwork carefully, legibly, and completely.

port after a bar fight, you indicate that he can stand up without mentioning that he is being almost completely supported by his buddies, your report is inaccurate. You are asking for trouble. If he collapses later for any reason, watch out! One 20-year veteran paramedic (dubbed "Dr. Death" by his peers) was convicted of felony charges for falsifying two reports to make it appear that he had examined an alcoholic man (twice the same day!) who later died. This case involved the classic scenario of responding repeatedly to a man prejudged a "scumbag" (according to his partner's testimony). After their third visit, the patient stopped breathing. The paramedic pleaded guilty to charges that he had falsified the two reports to make it appear that he had taken the patient's vital signs. He faced a maximum of three years in prison and a $10,000 restitution order.[6]

It matters a lot that you be compulsive about filling in *every* single box on every trip form. Without such scrupulous attention to detail, you will be unable to prove that you knew (for example) that the blood pressure was within normal limits. On the other hand, your report will

---

[6] *Los Angeles Times*, July 23, 1988, 1.

demonstrate irreproachable completeness and accuracy if you record values such as how much fluid you gave in the fluid challenge, and the height of the balcony from which the patient jumped. If you write "patient extricated," you have not stated specifically whether or not a cervical collar was applied. The rule of thumb in law is that if it is not written down, it was not done.

The same principle applies to legibility and audibility. If your report cannot be understood, it can shed no light for your defense. People with poor handwriting and soft voices can avoid this trap just by being aware of the problem and generating the self-discipline to overcome it. Trying to identify an anonymous voice is difficult, and is often related to audibility. When making a radio report, be sure to state your name and to get the name of the person to whom you are speaking. If a case takes several years to come to trial, it will be a lot easier to remember who was speaking if the name is stated on the tape.

We do see a lot of very funny things in the day-to-day delivery of prehospital care. It is fine to have a good belly-laugh about the man who thought he would die of an "overdose" of five over-the-counter pills intended to prevent drowsiness. "Caffeine," he said, when asked. "Renal failure!" But extraneous and unprofessional comments have no place on documents and in reports that may end up in court. Juries have the benefit of hindsight; it was not so funny when the "crazy" woman's case went to court (after she died of a subdural hematoma) and the trip report said that she had been left at home to call an exorcist. In cases where the patient's verbal messages are significant, such as when someone is suicidal, let the patient's own words and actions do the talking. Instead of writing "emotionally out of control and suicidal," describe the behavior and quote the patient's words: "Patient was thrashing about and stated, `Leave me alone, I just want to die.'" When patients require restraints, explain why in the trip report; for example, "kicking and scratching patient was restrained for the protection of self and others."

Sometimes, EMS services are canceled en route, or situations turn out not to need an ambulance. It is incomplete to write "no ambulance needed" or "canceled en route." It is always possible that there was a dispatch error or some other misunderstanding. You could end up in trouble for never showing up at the scene of a legitimate emergency. Always note at least who canceled you, and why: "canceled by first responders—no such address," or "police advise no injuries" or "closer ambulance came in service."

Some people use a catch-all phrase such as "no ambulance needed" to avoid the hassle of properly documenting a refusal. Certainly, it can be tempting to do this on routine calls when there was no meaningful injury or the situation is nonmedical (a scuffle that the police are handling), but be careful! Your definition of "no ambulance needed" may be woefully inadequate when you later discover that what appeared to be a benign situation is going to land you in court. It also provides you no clues to jog your memory about the incident. For example, if someone wants to speak to you about a canceled call to 14th and Washington three years later, chances are better that you might remember something if you note why you were called, plus the information noted above. In fact, one study of malpractice claims found that inadequate reporting was a major problem, and that "a properly completed rescue run report is the best defense in a malpractice allegation." That study found many reports to be too brief and skimpy, contradictory, and/or poorly worded. It noted the difficulty in building a strong defense without a good report when the time lapse between an incident and filing a claim was anywhere between four months and 1.6 years.[7] You might have some recollection about a call if you give a brief synopsis of the circumstances. It could make a big difference to your future to discipline yourself to do good, thorough, accurate reporting.

> It could make a big difference to your future to discipline yourself to do good, thorough, accurate reporting.

Malpractice Insurance

The average EMT or paramedic can't believe that malpractice insurance is necessary. After all, most of us don't have enough assets for someone else to take! The truth, though, is that "going bare," as it is called, exposes you to the cold winds of legal risk. Lawsuits, although relatively rare, are on the rise for prehospital workers. The claim rate was 1 per 24,096 runs in 1985,[8] and it has only increased since. You think it can't happen to you? They can't get blood from a turnip, you say? Want to bet?

First of all, "they" don't have to win a lawsuit to put you in debt. It can cost thousands of dollars just to defend yourself. Even if a pending action never gets to trial, you will incur legal expenses that can destroy any savings you happen to have. Protect yourself, especially if

---

[7] J.M. Soler et al., "The Ten-Year Malpractice Experience of a Large Urban EMS System," *Annals of Emergency Medicine* 14:10 (1985), 983.
[8] J.M. Soler, et al., "The Ten-Year Malpractice Experience of a Large Urban EMS System."

you have any appreciable personal assets. It is foolish to put everything you have at risk. Your current assets may not be much, but future assets can change remarkably, through hard work, inheritance—or even winning the lottery! An insurance policy can cover it, usually relatively inexpensively.

If a successful lawsuit is brought against you, and a monetary settlement announced, your investment in malpractice insurance will be worth every premium. Malpractice settlements can be very large—into the millions of dollars. Plaintiffs will still get the money if you do not have insurance. It will be taken from you little by little—for the rest of your life, if that's what it takes. Wages will be garnisheed. Credit may be impossible to get, which effectively eliminates major purchases such as a home or car. Every dime not judged essential for basic expenses will go toward paying off the settlement.

Every state, plus the District of Columbia, now has immunity legislation for people in the emergency services at all levels. The laws vary from state to state, but in general they exempt rescuers from civil damages or other elements of the law unless the offenders were "willful and wanton," (which is conduct showing a reckless disregard for safety) or were "grossly negligent," (which are actions that are a severe violation of the standards of reasonable care).[9]

Volunteers should also consider having professional liability coverage. Good Samaritan and immunity laws don't pay legal expenses, and they don't guarantee a positive court outcome. Yet EMS providers covered by Good Samaritan legislation often operate under the misconception that they do not need malpractice insurance. Don't be lulled into a false sense of security, especially if you are the designated EMS provider in your community. If you think that no one can sue you because you provide prehospital care without remuneration, understand that "remuneration" may have many shapes. Does the ambulance service supply your uniform? Do you get a token amount of money for running calls to cover gas expenses? Is there an educational fund for the volunteers' training? There is also some question about the constitutionality of a law that prevents a plaintiff from suing someone who was not being paid to do a job when they could have sued had that person been paid for the work.[10]

---

[9] Stephen A. Frew, *Street Law: Rights and Responsibilities of the EMT* (Reston, Va.: Reston Publishing Company, Inc., 1983), 41–42.

[10] Interview with Howard Handler of The American Agency, Overland Park, Kansas, April, 1996.

Besides, if a claim of malpractice is brought, savvy lawyers will open the lawsuit with charges of "willful and wanton" or "grossly negligent" care, to bypass the Good Samaritan or immunity laws. Malpractice attorneys know how to approach these cases in the manner most likely to result in success for them and their clients.

Another thing to consider is the malpractice insurance carried by the company with which you are affiliated. Does it honestly have your best interests in mind? Find out not just whether insurance exists, but also what kind and exactly whom it covers. Some companies are not particularly employee-minded. Their insurance policies protect the company, not the individuals working for it. Don't be timid about this crucial issue; ask your administrator whether the malpractice policy does, in fact, include you. Better yet, ask to read it for yourself and have it reviewed by a competent insurance agent.

Don't be timid about this crucial issue; ask your administrator whether the malpractice policy does, in fact, include you.

Be aware, too, that companies and municipalities can find loopholes when they want to wriggle free of a sticky lawsuit. Your role in a situation that precipitates a lawsuit will be scrutinized. If there is evidence that your actions exceeded the scope of your duties, you may be left to your own defense. If you did not call in a refusal, how can the doctor and hospital be expected to share the liability when the patient's grieving family arrives, lawyer in tow?

To be positive that you are adequately covered, you can purchase your own malpractice insurance. You can even get together with co-workers and buy group malpractice insurance through state or local EMS associations, or if your EMS agency is large enough, in-house. Information about malpractice insurance is available through insurance agents and through the EMS industry's magazines.

One important distinction to make when you buy is between "claims-made" policies and "occurrence" policies. Occurrence policies cover actions made during the policy period even after the insurance is terminated. Say that you work in EMS for five years and then quit. The statute of limitations, which varies from state to state, may run for several more years. (In fact, the statute of limitations for minors does not begin until they reach the age of majority.) Lawsuits could be filed long after you have left the business. It is nice to know that your coverage will still be there. Claims-made insurance covers you only while the policy is still in effect. This means that if you want to keep your assets protected, you have to keep a policy paid up for years after you quit, or purchase an "extended reporting period endorsement."[11] This is an endorsement which, as long as the premium is paid, covers claims made for situations that occurred while the original policy was in effect.

One last important detail is that your insurance agreement may legally require you to notify the insurance company whenever even a remote chance of being slapped with a lawsuit occurs. We often hear angry people use the words, "I'm gonna sue you!" But occasionally you get the feeling they may really follow through. Tell your insurance company right away, or you may find it has a legal basis to avoid the policy agreement for failure to notify it of the possibility of a lawsuit. Read the fine print, and understand what you are buying.

Public Relations

One very good risk management technique is to develop a positive local image. Most small-town emergency medical services are already popular because people know how hard people work to provide the service. They appreciate and are proud of the ambulance corps. Fund-raising events such as bake sales are common and well-supported.

> **Most people want to believe EMS personnel are the "good guys." However, we earn that positive image day by day.**

Most people want to believe EMS personnel are the "good guys." However, we earn that positive image day by day. We have to take care to maintain it. Good public relations hinges on the hallmark qualities of professionalism and unceasing consideration of others. Your appearance is your first statement of professionalism, and it is one of your best PR ploys. People who see a neat, clean, proudly worn uniform on someone who looks capable automatically will get a positive impression. The same goes for a shiny, clean ambulance. You demonstrate consideration by being polite to the people you see both on and between emergency calls. This includes the way you drive the ambulance around town. Obey the same traffic rules that everyone else has to, and when appropriate, yield willingly to other drivers.

Another excellent public relations technique is to give "mini-classes" in first aid. If you have a frightened family member sitting in the cab

---

[11] Personal correspondence with Howard Handler, The American Agency, April 1996.

while you drive to the hospital, talk about what has happened. Explain your understanding of the apparent medical problem. This is a good opportunity to help someone realize that although the seizure was frightening to watch, it was not as life threatening as it seemed. Explain the basics of first aid so that the person can react more appropriately if it happens again someday. For example, you can teach that person not to shove anything in a seizing person's mouth. You can draw from the situation at hand to help the bystanders benefit somewhat from the experience. By being sensitive about how you "teach" so that you don't sound belittling about whatever first-aid efforts were made, you can have a positive impact. That's difficult when the 2-year-old who pulled the boiling water onto himself is now covered with butter, or when the patient's mouth is bleeding because someone shoved a dandelion digger between her teeth during the seizure. But by providing some accurate instruction, you can feel more confident that they'll do better next time—and they will think well of the care given now, too.

Other, more formal, public relations efforts include public education about emergency medicine. We are the obvious goodwill ambassadors to go out and teach first aid and CPR. The better we present ourselves, the more positive our public image will remain—and that is an important thing to have to our credit when things go awry and the chips are down.

Dealing With the Legal System

It is downright uncomfortable to find that the legal dragon has raised its head and is breathing down your neck. No one likes the feeling that someone out there believes that they have done something badly enough to bring a lawsuit against them. It feels shameful and accusatory even when you know the accusation is wrongful (Fig. 13.3). But one of the risks in helping others is that the stranger who thanks us today may feel differently tomorrow. Anyone can sue anyone else for anything. The real issue is whether the suit is warranted. Fortunately, the sort of encounter prehospital workers are much more likely to have with the legal system is to testify at someone else's court case. You may be asked, for instance, to tell the judge or jury what you saw and heard at the scene of a shooting or vehicular homicide.

No matter whose side you are on, going to court is stressful. It is an alien and uncomfortable place for most people. You are asked to swear to tell the truth, but the case happened three years ago (again—the value

Figure 13.3

As this mock-up shows, going to court is *not* fun, whether or not you are the accused. (Photo courtesy of JEMS Communications.)

of iron-clad documentation!). You hate speaking in public, and the witness chair puts all eyes on you. Big decisions hinge on what you say.

Lawyers

It is relatively uncommon for a case to go all the way to trial. The road to obtaining a judgment from the bench or the jury is as long and unpredictable as was the road to the Wizard of Oz. That is why having a lawyer is worth it. Lawyers can help you prepare, explain what to expect at court, and teach you how to present yourself optimally. Our system does not require having a lawyer, but lawyer jokes aside, it is advisable to retain a guide through the legal labyrinth.

Many people are spooked by the mystique of both lawyers and doctors. Most EMS providers understand doctors pretty well, but still don't know how to relate to lawyers. According to the American Bar Association, there were 896,140 lawyers in the United States in 1995 (and according to projections there will be more than one million by the year 2000!). That leaves room for both good and bad lawyers. Do not be reluctant to view the relationship as a business deal. Your lawyer works for *you*. It is important to feel comfortable and confident with your lawyer. Find a lawyer whose interpersonal style suits yours; just because a person has a law degree does not mean that you will work well together. Also, be sure to discuss fees openly and come to an agreement at the outset.

> Find a lawyer whose interpersonal style suits yours; just because a person has a law degree does not mean that you will work well together.

The Subpoena and the Summons

There are two basic ways of being called into court. One is when you are the defendant in the case. The more common (you hope!) is when someone involved in a case thinks you can shed light upon it and wants your testimony. In either case, you are likely to receive a subpoena, which is a court-enforceable demand to appear. The frustrating thing about being subpoenaed is that the court date is inevitably in the middle of your vacation, or causes some other conflict. After you readjust your schedule, you then discover that the case has been continued for six months. Nonetheless, if the subpoena is requesting your testimony in someone else's case, you have to heed it or risk being found in contempt of court for not showing up. Many of the subpoenas prehospital workers receive are generated by the district attorney's office. We are often in a position to support a case being made by "The People" against the accused. Whether the defendant stabbed someone, or was driving drunk and killed someone that way, we have the chance to help see justice served. That opportunity is reason enough, despite the inconveniences, to cooperate whenever we are asked to testify.

If you are served with a summons, you are looking at a different situation. A summons requires you to answer to a complaint. When served with one, heed it. Legally, your responsibility to answer it is very clear. You usually have 20 to 30 days to answer. If you do not, the court may find a "default judgment"—usually against you, since you did not bother to try to defend yourself. There is little, if any, recourse against a default judgment.

Settling out of Court

Say that you have been named a codefendant in negligence litigation. The plaintiff has a relatively small claim of $50,000. There is no way that you did what the plaintiff claims you did. You are sure you can win the case. But the next thing you know, your lawyer informs you that the case is being settled out of court. What about justice? Your reputation has been besmirched and you want it exonerated!

The fact is that insurance companies will view the situation with an eye for whether it will be less expensive to pay the claim than to try it in court. The fine print in many insurance policies gives insurers that option. Justice has nothing to do with it. Unfortunately, they do not care much about the embarrassment the whole thing has caused you.

On the Witness Stand

Your involvement in EMS could certainly land you on a witness stand someday. There are certain things you should do from the moment you are potentially in view of the jurors. Even as you arrive at the court-house, let your behavior emote your professionalism. Back to first im-pressions. Look sharp. If appropriate, wear your uniform. Be polite. Speak respectfully, and use eye contact on the audience you are addressing. (If the opposition's lawyer tells you to look somewhere, though, be careful that you are not being manipulated!)

Be honest. Being under oath is a serious matter. A perjury charge is not worth the discomfort of having to admit something you might rather not. Choose your words carefully. The legal system is an adversarial system; each lawyer is out to represent clients to the best of his or her abilities, even if it embarrasses you. Answer only the question that has been asked; do not volunteer unrequested information.

Prepare to testifying by reviewing the written records of the case and trying to refresh your memory of the incident. Whenever a situa-tion makes you suspect it could end up in litigation, write a complete statement of every detail. Do this the day it happens. Otherwise, you will not remember which hand the gun was in when you get to the witness stand years later. Details as seemingly insignificant as that have turned out to be crucial.

Summary

It is no fun to be dragged into legal waters when you would much rather be swimming in the medical mainstream. Thankfully, very few patients are out to get you. When discussing risk management, it can be easy to forget that perspective! There is a lot to do on our own behalf to guard against these legal risks. Incorporate the principles discussed in this chapter into your daily practice of prehospital care. If everyone in your department works at it, the "good guy" view of the prehospital team can be preserved intact. If you don't tarnish the image, you won't have to pay for it to be polished.

Scene Control and Scene Choreography 14

Efficiency of a practically flawless kind may be reached in the struggle for bread. But there is something beyond—a higher point, a subtle and unmistakable touch of love and pride beyond mere skill; almost an inspiration which gives to all work that finish that is almost art—which is art.

—Joseph Conrad

Chapter Overview

Good scene control is an aspect of prehospital care that is difficult to describe in words. When a scene is well-controlled, things get done seemingly by magic. It is far easier to detect poor scene control, because nothing seems to go right. Leadership on a scene may change hands one or more times as waves of increasingly qualified people arrive; along with other tasks, each leader assumes responsibility for scene control. Scene control does not end until *after* patient hand-off at the emergency department.

Normally, scene control is best done by the person in charge of the patient, because that person most clearly knows what must happen, and in what order. The communication skills and interpersonal flexibility of the scene leader tend to define the degree of scene effectiveness. There are good scenes and rotten scenes, but an unwavering constant of prehospital medicine is that there is always a scene of some type. Your goal is to control it, not let it control you.

This chapter strives to address control of the circumstances that are common to everyday scenes. It does not refer to other elements of control that are related either to unusual circumstances (such as disasters or haz-mat incidents) or to medical control (where a system's protocols and medical philosophies are defined by a medical advisory system).

In the final part of the chapter, the concept of scene choreog-

323

raphy is discussed. Scene choreography is the ultimate refinement of scene control. The term has been coined to represent the fine art that comes with putting all the elements of streetsense together at once. Scene choreography is like the "caller" at a square dance, who keeps the circles of people moving in intricate patterns until the music stops. From the beginning to the end of an emergency call, an EMS provider who wants the experience to outshine plain mechanics should strive for smooth and timely completion of all tasks. That is the essence of scene choreography.

Scene control is a science. It is the coordination of the unlikely mix of people, their emotional and physical conditions, the physical setting, and all the other aspects of the scene into a coherent plan. In a way, doing scene control is a lot like playing the game of backgammon. It is easy to learn to do, but it is difficult to learn to do well. Done well, it is smooth and scarcely noticeable. Done poorly, it can be a mess.

There is always a scene. Each is unique, and in need of some facilitation by you, the expert. Scene control is an important part of every prehospital situation, even interfacility transfers. As with many other aspects of EMS, the best expertise comes from hands-on experience. Learning to control a scene is the same as anything else: Practice makes (more) perfect. Therefore, this chapter speaks in the sort of generalizations that will provide a solid framework for you to build upon. At first, directing how and when various tasks are done, and by whom, requires conscious thought. Eventually, scene control becomes more innate. You will no longer notice handling details that once required specific concentration.

Personal style accounts for many of the differences in the way scene control is done. Many people are excellent at it. Others are not. Working under somebody with poor scene control capability is a source of real frustration for many prehospital workers.

Some prehospital workers do not have the luxury of much apprenticeship before finding themselves in charge. One brand-new EMT was plunked onto a 9-1-1 response ambulance two days after being hired to her first job in EMS. The more experienced partner (who had to drive) was of some assistance, but for the new EMT, those first few days were full of anxiety, frustration, and poor scene control. Preferably, the climb to the honor and responsibility of being the one to control a scene is less abrupt for most people.

Power

Power is a curious thing. Control is power. When you are in control of a prehospital medical scene, you are responsible for the well-being of the patient(s), the bystanders, and other rescue personnel around you. That can include anything from you, your partner, and one patient to dozens of people.

Sometimes power is diffused, and it is unclear whose orders to follow. This is especially common when law enforcement concerns are not blending with those of the EMS providers. For example, parking at a motor vehicle accident can become an issue. Also, it has happened that EMS providers have been ordered by the people with the guns not to go near the "victim" because the police made a presumption of death—only to discover otherwise later. On the other hand, EMS providers sometimes interfere unnecessarily with legitimate concerns of the police, such as criminal evidence. Emergency personnel from all agencies need to try to understand the concerns of the others, and establish good working relations and general policies. That way, power struggles will fade away.

EMS providers have power because people want our advice and defer to our judgment. We have a palpable impact on their destiny. Heady stuff. The next aspect of power, then, is knowing how to employ it well. This means having a realistic, mature view of power. We all have a place in the pecking order. As the saying goes, the boss berates the husband, who berates the wife, who berates the kid, who hits the dog, who goes and bites someone. More graphically, there were two EMTs at the bottom of their pecking order who took their frustrations out on a skid row drunk. They were the ones who decided to give him a ride he'd never forget. If you remember from chapter 2, it killed him.

Misuse of power happens more than it should. Many people bestowed with power have subsequently discovered that they were unprepared to handle it. They went on "power trips." They alienated coworkers and angered the public. Some have nearly destroyed the organizations they were asked to lead. Misuse of power tends to occur when people misunderstand the implications of power-tripping, both on the individuals at a single occurrence and on the overall EMS system. When you are in charge of scene control, you set the example. It is important to use power wisely, responsibly, and judiciously. Understand how easily power can turn against you, so you can try to use it well—not let it use you.

EMS is suffused with power in many ways. We use lights and sirens to cut through traffic. We have the implied and express consent of people to tell them what to do during a crisis—whether to go to the hospital or not, how to get there, which hospital can best serve their needs. There are different sources of power, and people in EMS have access to several:[1]

- Expert power. The people who dialed 9-1-1 couldn't manage, so they called in the "experts."
- Informational power. The information we can impart is influential and persuasive. "Your EKG is showing me that a trip to the hospital would be a good decision."
- Legitimate power. The public's trust in the concept of EMS is what gives us authority at emergency scenes, and by extension, to do interfacility transfers.
- Sanction power. At times, we have the ability to interfere with someone's ability to pursue their own interests, such as when we transport a suicidal person to the hospital.
- Nuisance power. One strategy for helping some people decide to go to the hospital is to be a gentle nuisance. That patient might say, "OK! I'll go with you! Just stop buggin' me!"
- Reward power. Sometimes, the use of such interpersonal strategies as verbal approval, encouragement, and praise give us power to accomplish what others could not. It may mean getting a patient to decide to go to the hospital, or it may mean getting a coworker to feel motivated to keep the ambulance clean.

Each individual has a measure of power in every situation. Every participant has at least some power. If nothing else, we are each empowered to maintain our own self-control.

The Leader

Although we collectively share the responsibility for the outcome of every call, the person in charge, the scene leader, has ultimate authority (and thus power) at a scene. This person should ideally handle primary patient interaction and care, since the medical needs of the situation should drive the overall tone of the call. There are specific attributes common to good leaders, but the hallmark is excellent interpersonal capability. Without this, achieving and maintaining scene control is a real struggle.

---

[1] Conflict Resolution Workshop, *Council of Michigan Foundations*, November, 1995.

The other most influential person is the patient attendant's partner (usually the driver). This person acts as the patient attendant's "stage manager," assuring scene safety on the large scale, gathering peripheral information (such as mechanism of injury reports, medications, and patient history from relatives), and checking for follow-through on assigned tasks (such as getting the stretcher positioned, etc.)

> There are specific attributes common to good leaders, but the hallmark is excellent interpersonal capability.

Problems of leadership come up for many reasons, and they are often the cause of poor scene control. When there are many other people on a scene besides the patient attendant and driver, the scene control challenges will increase. On some scenes there may be eight or more people, some in the capacity of "first responder," others in law enforcement or fire suppression, and so on. Many EMS services have three or more people on the ambulance. One thing that must not happen is "control by committee." One, and *only* one, person should be in charge. When that is the primary patient attendant, medical needs can remain the most influential factor in decision making. "Just as no teacher can be effective unless he or she has some control over the classroom, no health professional can be effective without some control over the therapeutic situation."[2]

In systems with a high degree of formal rank structure, someone with high rank may be in charge while the EMTs and paramedics try to deliver prehospital care. It can be a problem if someone who does not have the training and experience required to appreciate the practice of prehospital care is trying to direct the show. Things may not go well—and may get downright dangerous. One group of EMTs and paramedics worked in an EMS system where prehospital care was politically controlled by the large volunteer fire department. The commercial ambulance service that employed these EMTs and paramedics was awarded the lucrative city contract. The fire chiefs had old-fashioned ideas about how a medical call should be run, but the paramedics had liberal standing orders. Therefore, on many calls, there was an undercurrent of tension because the fire chiefs preferred the old scoop-and-run method, yet the paramedics had an obligation to provide appropriate care. Sometimes, the only way to "control" the scene was to load the patient quickly, leave, and stop a few blocks away to render care. That was suboptimal,

---

[2] Mark King, Larry Novik, and Charles Citrenbaum, *Irresistible Communication: Creative Skills for the Health Professional* (Philadelphia: W.B. Saunders Company, 1983), 15.

but it was the only way to balance the delivery of necessary prehospital care with the political realities. No contract, no job. Fortunately, this type of scenario is changing as EMTs and paramedics achieve higher rank in their organizations.

Problems are quick to arise, too, when too many people are vying for the leadership role. There is a control conflict. This tends to occur in areas where ambulance services are in direct competition for patients. On-scene squabbles erupt when one crew wants to do things differently from another crew. Once a system matures, many of these problems iron out. But poor patient care has been the result too often when local EMS politics have prevented appropriate scene control.

Finally, some leaders do not command the respect of those they lead. Either they are just learning to lead and have the excuse of inexperience, or they have been doing it badly for years. Administrators of EMS systems that have leadership troubles need to look objectively at rank dissension and determine if it stems from poor leadership.

> **Like everything else in streetsense, many of the attributes of leadership can be learned.**

Like everything else in streetsense, many of the attributes of leadership can be learned. All rely on superior interpersonal communication skills. Good communication skills are obviously an important quality of an effective leader. Scene control is hard to attain when you cannot explain your needs in a way that gets people moving. Most of the necessary skills have been addressed in other chapters. Four additional attributes to be discussed here are presence, tact and diplomacy, imparting impressions of both reliability and compassion, and building a good reputation among your EMS colleagues.

Presence

More than anything else, your ability to display scene presence will highlight you as a leader (Fig. 14.1). "Presence" is an elusive quality to describe, but you can tell when someone has it because others always look to that person for direction. Basically, presence is "the ability to project a sense of ease, poise or self-assurance, especially the quality or manner of a person's bearing before an audience."[3] It is different from

---

[3] *The Random House Dictionary of the English Language* (unabridged), 2nd ed. (New York: Random House, Inc., 1987).

Figure 14.1

There is something about a good leader's physical presentation that says "I'm it." This leader is pointing out a task for the firefighter to handle.

charisma, because people are either endowed naturally with charisma or not. Presence can be consciously developed if you want to work at it. It takes practice to be poised in the face of chaos, at ease in the face of death, and self-assured in the face of complex problems demanding rapid solutions. But it can be done.

Presence is in many respects a loud nonverbal statement of self-confidence. It includes an erect, shoulders-back, head-up posture and a directness of gaze. It is saying, "I'm here, I'm capable, there's a job to do, and together we can get it done." It has nothing to do with either size or gender. Some very small women have impressive presence, and some very large men lack it completely. It has a great deal to do with the way you carry yourself and the genuine confidence you exude.

It is easy to mistake presence for a style that is actually cocky, aggressive, or even belligerent. This is the swaggering, bigger-than-life, "I'm great" mentality—a far different thing than presence. It may seem similar, to a point, but a person with presence has real staying power—intellectually and emotionally—to hold things together when the going gets tough. Obviously, people who have good presence command a lot of respect.

When attempting to build an image that projects good presence, remember to use good eye contact. Eyes can send powerful messages (even when you are busy with your voice and hands) that prompt others to calm down, regain self-control, listen to directions, and accomplish tasks despite chaos and confusion. They can also be powerful touch-stones. For example, imagine that you are in charge. You are kneeling on the floor trying to start an IV when the time comes to ask someone to go for the stretcher. You say, "Could someone please get the stretcher?" without looking up. The job may not get done in time, all because you didn't take a moment to make eye contact with someone, an act which causes others to feel personally responsible for the task.

The nonverbal nature of presence cannot be overstressed. Many people forget that there are aspects of vocal dynamics that are, in fact, nonverbal. To project calmness and control with appropriate tone, pitch, rate and volume in your voice helps solidify the impression that you know what you are doing.

Tact and Diplomacy

Of course, it is not only how you say things that matters—it is also *what* you say. This is where tact and diplomacy enter the picture. Tact: "a keen sense of what to say or do to avoid giving offense; skill in dealing with difficult or delicate situations." Diplomacy: "handling people so there is little or no ill will."[4] These definitions are tailor-made to scene control (Fig. 14.2). We wear many hats in EMS. We are actors, playing roles to suit each occasion. We are detectives, ferreting out the true underlying facts about a call. In scene control, we also have to be diplomats, both to the public and to our partners and coworkers.

Someone who is poised and self-assured can be intimidating to others. Often, carefully chosen words can soften this assertiveness. Someone who barks out orders like a drill sergeant will not get much cooperation. It works better to employ the art of tactful communications and diplomatic maneuvers.

When people do a nice job, remember that a compliment goes a long way—all the way to scenes where you work with those people again. "Please" and "thank you" are great words. Often, the only differ-ence between someone with whom everyone hates to work and some-one they would do anything for, is that the latter has a knack for tact and diplomacy.

---

[4] *Random House Dictionary*

Figure 14.2

Crowds of bystanders are part of the job. While receiving a quick report from a first responder, this paramedic has a chance to survey the situation before entering the circle of attention.

Reliability

It is important to project an impression of reliability because EMS is a pursuit built largely on trust. If presence is a factor in first impressions, the aspect that carries you along is the faith that people have in your reliability.

There are certainly situations that sorely test personal ability. Can you really project steady scene presence when confronted with a man trapped by collapsed girders? The bystanders are hysterical. The nearly amputated leg and pool of blood is gruesome. You need him freed *now*, but there will be delays. Your medical intervention has to go perfectly if you want to save his life. There's a lot of chaos. Yet you must convey the impression that others can rely on you, even when you may be feeling a little out of control inside.

Imparting the impression of reliability builds trust. To do this, the leader must demonstrate good self-control and clarity of mind. These qualities help set the tone of the call. If the coworkers, the patient, and the bystanders think that your plan is unreliable, scene control is destined to fall apart. An easy way to lose clarity of mind is to become "hyper," or inappropriately excited by what is happening. If you become hyper as the scene leader, others will too. The most capable EMS providers actually become slowest and most deliberate in situations where others get the most excited.

Sometimes, as a leader, you will lose some self-control. You might be able to salvage things somewhat by admitting what is happening. For example, a flight nurse who had been on the scene of a plane crash all day finally got back to the hospital. As she rolled a patient through the emergency department doors, her first words were, "I'm a little hyper today, so bear with me." This helped everyone slow down enough to realize that she was not the only one swept up by the mass casualty incident.

A reputation for reliability is also built when you can keep from flying off the handle. There is no excuse for anyone to lose his or her temper at a prehospital scene. Sometimes you may *choose* to give the impression that you are angry—for example, with an uncooperative patient upon whom a flare of irritation might work—but that is different. Really losing your temper means losing self-control. A true professional is better than that. Avoid at all costs the temptation to vent frustration and anger on a prehospital scene.

Developing your ability to impart compassion also helps build a good reputation for leadership. Compassion can also soften the autocratic, declarative style common to prehospital leadership. Make others sense that, above all, you are concerned about the emergency at hand. On minor cases (where others might be condescending or act irritated), you are the one who can proceed professionally and with compassion. On life-threatening cases (where others might be swept up by the intensity), you are the one who can still show compassion for the patient and everyone else involved.

Do not shrink from using compassionate touch as an effective tool. It is another highly effective method of control. Touching is an anchoring act. It helps anchor words and actions so that people around you feel a sense of control. Even while walking onto a scene, as you see things that need to be done, you can squeeze a first responder's elbow as you pass and say something like: "Hi. It looks like we'll be needing our stair chair. Could you get it, please?" Touching is a tremendously powerful tool because others feel your control as well as hearing and seeing it.

Another good way to "touch" people individually is to use names. Try to get to know the other people in your EMS system. People on EMS squads in small towns and rural areas usually know each other, but in bigger EMS systems, it can be difficult to keep up with the faces, much less the names. You will more readily be acknowledged as a leader, though, when you can arrive on a scene and greet people by name. On chaotic scenes, this capability also helps you get others' attention when you need it quickly.

Reputation

Some people discover that, because of the professional reputation earned by the company or agency they work for, other EMS organizations readily view anyone wearing that uniform positively. They are willing to give new employees a chance to live up to that agency's reputation. Eventually, though, each EMS provider earns a reputation based solely on his or her individual abilities.

If you are unfortunate enough to have developed a bad reputation, ask yourself, "Why?" Do people think you are unreliable? Tactless? On a power trip? Maybe you get hyper, or are chronically preoccupied with thoughts unrelated to the task at hand. Maybe people think you are apathetic or complacent. Maybe you get distracted too easily. With self-awareness (see chapter 2), a bad reputation can be turned around, but expect to give it a lot of time and effort. People in our field do not give second chances very easily.

On the other hand, if you consistently demonstrate the qualities of presence, tact, diplomacy, reliability, and compassion, you will earn an excellent reputation among your peers. This makes a scene easier to control—not to mention personally rewarding and fun.

Problem Solving

An ability to solve problems quickly and accurately is a necessary aspect of good scene control. Prehospital care is a process of making continual decisions. Things to consider on every call, regardless of the complaint, are:

- The presence of threatening environmental hazards
- The presence of other hazards, such as people who mean you harm
- Whether the patient is life-threatened and, if so, whether the nature of the situation indicates "scoop and run" or, as with cardiac arrest, on-scene stabilization
- Whether there is space enough to work efficiently, and if not, whether to move the impediment or move the patient

- Whether there are enough human resources on hand to handle the task or whether a call for more help is best
- The best ways to put the available resources to work
- The level of attention that bystanders will require, and how much

This section describes two aspects of inefficient problem solving—mono-approaches and tunnel vision—which can generate unnecessary problems. It also discusses the value of knowing your helpers' capabilities and how to use bystanders in a positive and useful manner. Finally, it considers the value of making amends when the stresses of a call cause interagency and interpersonal relations to wear thin.

Mono-Approach

Being in charge demands flexibility in style and approach. "Mono-approach" is a term coined to describe the narrow-minded philosophy that there is only one way to do things. There are people in EMS who approach every call with the same phrases, tone of voice, body language, and hands-on care. These people do not appreciate the variation among humans, and insist that strangers involved in a crisis adjust to their approach regardless of the patient's current intellectual, emotional and behavioral ability or needs (Fig. 14.3).

Mono-approaches are unrealistic, rigid, and arrogant. There is no room for any of these traits in EMS. A sensitive EMS provider can understand the value of a flexible approach for building rapid rapport and trust with patients and bystanders. Those with a mono-approach will risk generating ill will, misunderstanding, obstinacy, even belligerence when patients miss the compassion and willingness to meet their needs.

Prehospital leaders who use a mono-approach also risk losing the respect and cooperation of coworkers. Mono-approach is a great way to miss perceiving other, possibly better, ways to get the job done. Although some people have always worked the streets this way, the question is—how effectively? It is obvious that some scenes need a strict, businesslike leader. Others will not work unless a looser, more casual approach is adopted. Still others—for example, with children—need a calm and soothing atmosphere. Molding the ambience of a scene is the responsibility of the leader.

Prehospital situations often include rapid-fire stimuli. The best way to stay on top of the barrage is to be like a surfer, riding the crest of the wave of information. You have to learn to anticipate the things that will happen before they occur. This requires an attitude of offense instead

Figure 14.3

A mono-approach is the worst thing you can do if you are in charge of scenes. The more flexibility you have in interpersonal relations, the better.

(boring & ineffective)

of defense. In defense, you are in the flustering position of having to react to what is happening. You are not in control. With an offensive frame of mind, you can anticipate activities and events, and stay ahead of them. This promotes calm, and helps you maintain a sense of being in charge. For example, when you know it will take five minutes to get the stretcher, it is best to send someone for it as soon as you know you will be transporting the patient. (Wait until you know you will need it, though, because it makes no sense to put someone to the trouble if the patient refuses transport.) On the other hand, there will be an unnecessary delay if you wait to finish the entire physical exam, history gathering, and hands-on care before asking for the stretcher. Similarly, if an elderly spouse or friend is planning to go along to the hospital and you notice that she does not move very quickly, start her toward the ambulance early. That way, departure delays are minimized and she avoids the additional pressure of having to rush.

Troubleshooting each step of a call is important to overall call efficiency. For example, you can be watching for access problems at the same time that you are assessing for safety threats during the initial scene approach. When you know the dimensions of your equipment so well that you can accurately judge that the stretcher will not fit into the patient's room, you can ask for the stair chair. This sidesteps having to choose between forcing the stretcher into the patient's room (and the embarrassment of marring walls) and the indignity of an unnecessary arm-and-leg carry to the stretcher in the hall. It also helps minimize on-scene time and makes you look very efficient.

Tunnel Vision

Tunnel vision is that state of mind where you are concentrating solely on what's in front of you, as if you're looking down a tunnel and that's all you can see. One of the basic rules of prehospital medicine is to avoid tunnel-visioning into the medical demands of the call. That is the quickest way to lose sight of the overview. It is a very dangerous practice. Its opposite state—the ability to attend to the patient *and* remain aware of the other elements of the scene—is exciting to develop. The ability to anticipate all that is required to problem-solve does not happen overnight, but once you obtain it, good scene control is easier too.

Scene control can be destroyed by tunnel vision. When a scene threatens to fall into that trap, avoid it by taking a deep breath, letting it out, then STOP-ing. STOP means:

S   stop

T   think

O   observe

P   plan

Without a game plan, you cannot foresee the unique aspects of each call and deal with them as they come up. You cannot make a plan if your concentration is solely on the patient and medical care. Tunnel vision kills the ability to coordinate the details of the scene comprehensively.

Task Delegation

Another important key to good problem solving is knowing how to delegate tasks, and to whom. First you have to assess the available resources. Good scene controllers know how best to use the available resources. Assess how many hands there are to do the work. Call for more people immediately if you think you will need them.

In many cases, you can delegate people to find solutions to certain problems. A good leader welcomes reasonable suggestions by others when there is time. Once a task is delegated, though, trust that person's judgment. Some "leaders" resist input from others because they think the meaning of their role is to make every decision. In some cases, this may be true, such as when an explosion is imminent and there is no time to do anything but react. But in the normal course of things, some give and take can affect the quality of patient care positively. Two (or more) heads are better than one—as long as the leader retains the final "say-so." For example, you may ask someone to figure out the most efficient way to get out of a convoluted building.

Be sure the person you have asked to do something is capable of accomplishing the task you would like to give him. Be careful about making assumptions. Just because you have worked successfully with another agency in the past does not mean that the person you are specifically addressing is not on his first run. Don't say, "please take a BP," without first (tactfully) determining that the person does, indeed, know how to take blood pressures. Some people are too proud or shy to admit they lack a skill that you obviously think they ought to know. If you ask someone to get your suction without being sure they know what suction is and where to find it, you may end up waiting longer for it. One paramedic finally went to the ambulance to get it himself—and discovered a first responder, screwdriver in hand, disassembling the in-house suction unit! Some people will try to bluff their way through a task. This can throw your overall scene timing out of synch.

On the other hand, if you know another responder was just cleared to start IVs, for example, and is dying to have a chance at it, you can build the learning opportunity into your choreography plan if the patient's condition warrants.

Using Bystanders

Another effective scene control strategy that can solve a host of problems is to use bystanders when possible. Someone who is made to feel essential, especially in the eyes of the neighborhood, will feel special. This can completely change a hostile attitude. If you can isolate the leaders of the crowd and put them to work controlling "their scene" (i.e., doing crowd control), your time is well invested. A group for whom this works especially well are youth gangs; if you can identify gang leaders, they may be especially well-suited for this purpose.

Delegate tasks to bystanders. There are many things they can do, and they are often thrilled to be asked (Fig. 14.4). In a multi-victim accident, if there is a patient with apparently minor injuries, a bystander might be capable of staying with that person with instructions to let you know if anything changes. Having someone to talk to helps both the patient and the bystander. This frees you to get essential tasks done, you've done some public relations, and the entire situation is imbued with a more positive flavor. For example, one crowd was irritable that the paramedics seemed to take so long on the scene of a shooting. They were there only a few minutes, but the crowd's perception, as is common, was that the paramedics should "Just get him to the hospital. Hey, get going!" Things were getting hot when a member of the crowd,

Figure 14.4

One good crowd control measure is to set boundaries. Asking the crowd to stay behind the curb is highly effective in traffic situations. Have a neighborhood leader insure that no one passes the boundary you've established.

who obviously had some neighborhood authority and respect, spoke up. He controlled his crowd by shouting out, "Hey now! Leave 'em alone! Everyone knows they gots to *stabilize!*"

Making Amends

Problem-solving goes beyond individual scenes. Another good way to ensure good future working relations with others is to be willing to admit mistakes. Sometimes, things do not go as well as you would have liked. No one is perfect, and each new scene is a learning experience. You might need to acknowledge that you were curt with someone: "I'm sorry if I came off a little harsh. I was a little frustrated at that moment." Maybe you had a disagreement about treatment: "Let's find Dr. Fossel and find out what he says about this case."

Making amends may be hard on your pride, especially if you feel that the other person was wrong and ought to apologize to you. But the long-term benefit of taking the initiative to talk it over is that it's an effective way to dissipate hard feelings. This is a good thing when you need that backup on another call and the only helper available is someone who might otherwise be bearing you a grudge.

Supporting Roles in Scene Control

A good leader is made by good followers. Leaders who are surrounded by people who refuse to recognize their authority face a tough job. The role of ancillary personnel is to follow the directions of the leader.

Sometimes followers have no clear leader. This can be especially true at big, chaotic scenes where the supposed leader is ineffective. This spurs those who see the job being done poorly to try to assume the leadership role. If your leadership is not completely apparent and appropriate, your followers will not be organized, either. This is one advantage of highly rank-structured systems; no matter how bad the leadership is, the guy with the most stars, or bars, or stripes is the boss. If your role is to follow, you should:

- Advise the leader of your arrival. Do whatever tasks you are assigned without argument or delay.
- Respect the authority of the leader. Do not argue technique or policy. Arguing has no place on a prehospital scene. If the leader is new to the system and apparently does not know or understand protocols or procedures, there are ways to get the point across without arguing.
- Never undermine leadership by publicly berating and belittling the leader's efforts. The opposite is also true; the leader should not publicly berate or belittle helpers, either.
- Be helpful. If the leader appears to have forgotten something relevant, mention it. Even good leaders cannot always remember every detail, and they depend on that kind of support. Make suggestions brief, concise, and clear. As members of "the troops," followers have a responsibility to be concise and well intentioned when making suggestions to the team leader, who is busy with many details.
- Most important, if you are uncertain about any order, don't bluff. If you have been asked to spike an IV with a blood pump and you don't know how, admit it. Not only will you save everyone on-scene time, you could also avoid causing real harm to the patient.

Good Scenes, Bad Scenes

To people who are just starting out in the emergency services, every scene is a big deal. Even interfacility transfers are new. It takes time to absorb every detail. Eventually, the environment will become less alien and scenes that used to be difficult will become easier. Your sense of what comprises a challenge will change.

Scenes are easy to control when they are not really out of control to begin with, and the leader really only has to attend to the essentials. Other times, scene control is as simple as recognizing a rotten situation; your response is to "load and go," even if you only go a couple of blocks before stopping to assist with patient stabilization. Leaving the scene behind was how you could best "control" it.

But have you ever witnessed the chaos that occurs when the person in charge has completely lost scene control or never took charge to begin with? It is not a pretty sight. In some cases, there is no clearly recognizable leader; in those situations, if the group is lucky, an ad hoc leader may emerge to assume charge. In the worst scenes, though, no one takes charge. Often, these are difficult scenes to begin with, with a lot of hysteria or hostility. Bad scenes can be a real nightmare.

You can take control and prevent a situation from getting rotten by recalling some of the tips given throughout this book:

- Eliminate distractions. If the group cannot hear you, you cannot communicate. If you cannot function well because you are afraid of dogs, have them removed.
- Make room to work. Either move obstructions or, if possible, move the patient. Position yourself so that you have a good line of communication with other arriving helpers.
- Be identifiable. This is especially important when working with people you do not know well. Identification of the person in charge depends as much on the nonverbal messages of presence as it does on rank recognition or uniform.
- Be flexible. Improvisational skills are a sign that you are a thinking leader, and this commands respect.
- Use staging areas. When you have several victims, have them brought to a central staging area where you can retain control without having to be all over the scene. That also lets you carefully control their departure.

Everyone has bad days and bad scenes. Sometimes things simply don't go the way they should. Everything that can go wrong, does go wrong—that's Murphy's Law![5] If you are a good follower, you may need to loosen your expectations of the leader. If you are the leader, and you have previously earned the respect of your peers, they will tolerate a bad day. Don't be too hard on yourself.

---

[5] Then there's Robinson's Law: Murphy was an optimist. . . .

Hand-Off of Control

Tiered-Response Systems

Transition of control occurs whenever the person who has been in charge of the patient (and ideally,,then, the scene) turns the patient over to someone else. This happens usually at least once in the prehospital phase, and again at the hospital.

Hand-off is a two-way process. One person is "giving" the patient to another, who is "taking on" the patient. There are good ways and bad ways to make the exchange. The most acceptable is to maintain your professionalism regardless of what you see. Save criticism about mistakes or problems for an appropriate time and place. If they have made a mistake or missed an important detail, no matter how blatant, preserve your good working relationship by taking the criticism into private. If the first responders have done a good job, of course, do tell them in front of the family. This boosts morale a lot.

From the other side, if you are handing over responsibility for patient care to an arriving paramedic unit, keep in mind that the paramedics have a lot of things to assess. They are eager to get on with their part of the job. The first responder who has been most actively working with the patient can introduce her to the attending paramedic and give a quick report. Be concise, brief, and cooperative. Then step back and let the paramedic establish rapport.

Hospital Hand-off

The other aspect of hand-off has to do with transfer of patients to the staff at the hospital (Fig. 14.5). Hand-off technique is important, because in many places the tempo begun by prehospital personnel sets the tempo for the next phase of the patient's care. If you are concerned about the patient, express it to the emergency department staff. For example, how many times has your arrival with a hygienically distasteful person met with pained expressions and rolling eyes, even when that is not ideal? Yet in this case, you feel the patient is not just looking for a warm place to sleep for the night. He really is sick. The words you choose, your stance, and your expression of concern all tell the emergency department staff that this is not "just another drunk." On the other hand, neither do you want to over-inflate the importance of minor cases. It is just as important not to acquire a reputation for crying "Wolf!"

If you do not display your concerns adequately, you might be sorry.

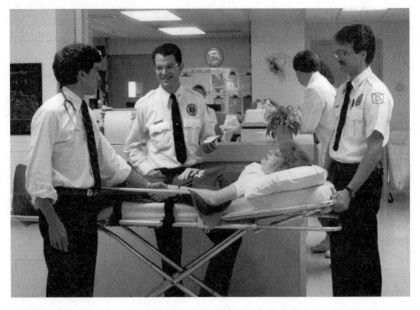

Figure 14.5

Hand-off at the emergency department is a crucial transition point for the patient. Your report sets the tempo for in-hospital response to the patient's medical condition; your introductions can help the patient feel more welcome.

That happened in one case where the patient was put into a corner bed and temporarily forgotten. Unfortunately, when the Narcan wore off, there was no one around to notice that the patient had gone into respiratory arrest.

Scene Choreography

If scene control is science, then scene choreography is art. For those who aspire to be really masters of prehospital care, it is not enough just to get the job done. The goal is to do it well, smoothly, agreeably, and with style. People with a knack for scene choreography bring a special element of capability to their scenes. Scene choreography is an ideal. It is a philosophy. It happens largely as the result of day to day, hands-on experience. It is exhilarating to do! It gives a sense of genuine pleasure when a scene comes together well.

The ties to scene control are obvious. If you cannot control the scene, you cannot hope to choreograph it. As with obscenity, it is hard to define, but you certainly know it when you see it. Everyone—coworkers and the public alike—senses the excellence associated with a well-choreographed scene.

Scene choreography requires an open mind for every detail. Employ every ounce of your awareness. It requires attaining a high degree of cooperation from others via an advanced concept of good human relations. It requires knowing how to delegate tasks appropriately. It means developing a sense of timing and knowing how to expedite things without rushing. All this is done concurrent with patient care; therefore, your medical knowledge and capabilities have to already be of first-class quality. If you do not know what to do for a supraventricular tachycardia, it is ludicrous to be practicing scene choreography. You have other learning priorities.

> For those who aspire to be really masters of prehospital care, it is not enough just to get the job done. The goal is to do it well, smoothly, agreeably, and with style.

The process of becoming an excellent prehospital medical care provider is like climbing a mountain. Once you acquire the basic skills, you strive to reach the "summit" by attaining intermediate goals along the way. You start as a first-aider, then go to EMT training, maybe get IV capability and some telemetry training along the way, and finally you go on to paramedic school. The mountain of capability you are climbing has as its reward the summit—the ability to truly choreograph a medical scene!

Timing

A sense of timing is the most important skill in scene choreography. With it, you can arrive, assess the situation, delegate tasks, and attend to the patient so that, magically, everything gets finished at about the same time. It is impressive to witness, not to mention direct, such a scene. The satisfaction generated is similar to that of having friends over for an intricate meal and having everything ready to serve at exactly the right moment.

Learn timing by paying attention to how long everything takes. Gain a sense about the "cost," in seconds or minutes, of every detail of the job. This requires some experience, but is a skill you can begin developing on your first call. Notice how long it takes to prepare an IV infusion. If you are still in the ranks of being a helper, watch the way a person adept at timing can ask questions and listen effectively to the answers while doing other tasks such as sticking electrodes on the patient. Be aware how long it takes to raise the base station on the radio, so that you can plan case notification according to your distance from the hospital. If you are close, it's a higher priority; if not, maybe the radio report can wait a few minutes.

The second part of developing a sense of timing is to learn to estimate accurately how long something will take based on the unique setting of each call. Notice when an elevator in a particular building is unusually slow. Notice that getting the stretcher into a house will take longer than usual because there are 25 outside steps to the door—which also means that two people will be needed to handle the stretcher. Notice when there are fewer on-scene helpers than usual, and prepare for things to take longer. You can even learn to estimate by the patient's condition how long it will take for the veins to stand up once you apply the constricting band. On some people, it takes extra time, so learn to apply the tourniquet before you start preparing the IV if you are spiking it yourself. Attention to such detail becomes enormously helpful in time-essential calls.

Expediting

Closely related to timing is knowing how to get a lot of things done in a short period of time. The last thing you can allow yourself to do is be in a hurry. "Haste makes waste!" The key is not to let yourself get swept up by the sense of urgency many calls generate. With good planning and task delegation, the IV tubing finishes filling just as you finish drawing the bloods. The leads are snapped onto the electrodes just when you are ready to read the monitor. The stretcher comes through the door when you're preparing the patient to load. This all happens because you combined an ability to anticipate every need with a keen sense of timing. You planned ahead and delegated tasks. These efforts brought it all together.

> The last thing you can allow yourself to do is be in a hurry. The key is not to let yourself get swept up by the sense of urgency many calls generate.

The one element that spoils choreography is when people who are otherwise cooperating well begin to rush. People make mistakes when they hurry too much. They drop the tape. They miss the vein. They forget important details, like doing up the straps on the stretcher. It is no good to have the airway pulled out because, in your haste, you forgot to tie it. Re-intubating results in an additional waste of time. Don't hurry. Instead, expedite! Use your on-scene resources so that everyone has a task they can manage in an amount of time that reasonably ensures that things will continue to run smoothly. By expediting, you can avoid the most dreaded scene of all, accurately depicted in this rhyme: "When in worry and in doubt, run in circles, scream and shout!"

Timing and expediting depend for obvious reasons on good inter-personal cooperation. That means getting along with the other people in your agency as well as having a good working relationship with the other agencies that respond to medical emergencies in your system.

EMS System Maturity

It is difficult to get anything done, much less with style, when the people on a scene are more concerned with themselves than with the scene. Ambulance wars, for example, make scene control and scene choreography nearly impossible. When the "professionals" on the scene do not have open lines of communication and cooperation, about all you can do is struggle through, hoping the patients have not suffered for it. Later, get to work on improving the local political climate.

The providers of prehospital care have to get along. We depend on each other too much to let petty rivalries get in the way. At one point, one group of paramedics could predict that the first responder who was bagging the patient would be the one to stand up and walk out to get the stretcher, bag-valve-mask device in hand, ET tube attached. He would be likely to "trip" on the IV tubing on the way. Years of effort and growing system maturity healed that terrible mess.

System maturity is ultimately what allows for the best interagency cooperation. During the upheaval of the 1970s, when prehospital care was undergoing the metamorphosis into advanced prehospital life sup-port, there was considerable resentment and turf jealousy in many places. The industry was in turmoil. Over time, though, many systems have developed admirable maturity. They have learned that it is okay to get along. Individuals learned to stand aside to let others develop their capabilities and skills.

In the nineties, managed care and increased intensity of competi-tion among providers has renewed many interagency squabbles. As competitor agencies have been swallowed into mega-ambulance com-panies, field personnel who were once rivals have found themselves on the same team, in name. Such transitions are hard, because people with rescue personalities are highly loyal and dedicated. There is some confusion about where to pledge allegiance. Once again, it is a time of turmoil in the EMS industry.

The most important thing to remember is the patient, and the mission of EMS. If everyone can keep this touchstone in mind, interagency cooperation can result.

The most important thing to remember is the patient, and the mission of EMS. If everyone can keep this touchstone in mind, interagency cooperation can result, with all the needed in improvements in scene control and scene choreography. When you know you can depend on people to do the tasks you delegate, trust and rapport can build. Whenever interagency cooperation improves, the obvious beneficiaries are the patients themselves. Isn't that why we're here?

Summary

Scene control is a science. It incorporates everything you know about streetsense. It is like taking the bands of color separated by a prism and making them whole again.

People who are particularly adept at scene control do not view it as a power trip. They are good leaders because they know how to generate good followers—and that is done by understanding human nature. It takes time and practice to be good at scene control, but the rewards are well worth the effort.

For many experienced prehospital workers who have long since lost their fascination with routine procedures, scene control is the element that holds their interest. Every time they step out of the ambulance, no matter how minor or mundane the emergency, there is a scene to control. It is always new and different.

The ability to do scene choreography is not an absolute requirement of prehospital care. But becoming adept at scene choreography can certainly make prehospital care a lot more fun. It opens up a whole new array of challenges. The best part is that those challenges never end, because no two scenes are ever alike.

Prehospital workers who honestly want to carry their care beyond basic performance to levels of greater achievement have the opportunity to try. It takes dedication and practice. Those who achieve the ability for scene control and scene choreography benefit themselves, their entire EMS systems, and the public they serve.

After the Streets 15

"You can't go home again."

—Thomas Wolfe

Chapter Overview

The purpose of this chapter is to get you thinking about the edges of life beyond EMS. First, during your EMS career, you have to link your EMS world with the off-duty world of home, family, and friends. Second, eventually, there will come an end to your lights and siren years. It may be your choice when to quit, or it may not. Either way, there are various things to consider to promote the chances of having the most fulfilling life possible. The lessons that are available compliments of the streets of EMS cannot be gained elsewhere. There are plans to make and mental attitudes to choose about your life, now and later. When it comes time to make some changes, there are strategies for making them smoothly and successfully.

The world of emergency medical services has a tendency to draw people in like moths to a nighttime lamp. We are fascinated by this turbulent world, and we often have a hard time pulling away. This is true in the everyday sense, when we finish an interesting shift. It is also true at the end of a career, upon retiring from the streets. Whether you are moving from active field duty to an office job within EMS, or leaving EMS altogether, there is a tug when you remember the good times.

The experiences a person has in EMS—volunteer or paid—are impossible to duplicate in any other field of endeavor. For many, EMS is vivid, profound, and—given appropriate perspective—personally fulfilling. Others leave EMS with a bitter taste in their mouths, and with hardened hearts. It doesn't have to be that way, but it happens. For such people, there is inner healing to do, which sometimes comes with time and distance from the intensity of EMS. Whichever it is for you, the choices for learning and growing are endless. Because of EMS, your life can be enhanced in extraordinary ways, by both the exciting "campfire stories"— and also the quieter lessons of the streets.

> Because of EMS, your life can be enhanced in extraordinary ways, by both the exciting "campfire stories"—and also the quieter lessons of the streets.

This chapter is intended as a link between being at work and not being at work. It can be read on two levels. If you are actively engaged in the field delivery of out-of-hospital medical care, you still have to go home at the end of the shift. How are you then? Does your work—both its victories and defeats— follow you, haunting your off hours and interfering with your chance to focus on more regular pursuits? If you are no longer actively engaged in delivering field care, are you able to let go of both the thrill and the harder parts?

Your EMS time and the rest of your life are unavoidably interconnected. All of life is. Like everyone, you have a time line that extends from birth, through life, to death. Some people traverse their time line without giving much thought to it. One day simply follows the next. They follow the tides of life without looking ahead, and without pausing to consider that, "if you don't know where you're going, then any port will do." Other people make a hard and fast plan for their lives. They know that they will do one thing at age twenty, another at thirty, and so on. But given its unpredictability, maybe it isn't best to have such an absolute approach to life, either. Both following the stream of life without looking ahead and pushing too hard may result in unnecessary or avoidable regrets at the end of life.

A helpful strategy is to take time now and then to gain perspective. Say you're 28 years old. Take time to reflect. Use the fruits of that reflection to chart the upcoming phases of your life, so that you have some idea how to avoid uncharted and uninteresting territory. You've had 28 years of life experience and you've learned a lot. Celebrate the successes! And acknowledge the failures. There's a saying that it's OK to make mistakes, but it's not OK to make the *same* mistakes.

How to find time to reflect is a personal choice. On a daily basis, it might be part of a ritual such as prayer or meditation. It could happen during a commute to or from work. Solitary exercise, such as walking

Figure 15.1

Make a point of getting into the habit of taking time to refresh, reflect, and recreate—preferably with loved ones.

or running, is great for mental processing as well. Sometimes, just sitting and watching the sky is best. It depends on you. For larger doses of reflection, you might need a change of scenery. Take a weekend road trip, or a vacation. Include reflection among your plans. Take an afternoon's fishing trip, or even a whole day, just for thinking about your life. Writing in a journal is an excellent, hard-copy place for private dialogue, if you are so inclined. No matter how you find the chance to reflect, the more important message is: do it!

Finding time to reflect upon your life seems daunting in this era of fast-paced living. You have the choice to make it a priority. Think about your goals with a global frame of reference. There are many elements: your career, family, other relationships, financial condition, physical wellness, spiritual being, hobbies, home and hearth (Fig 15.1). Are these in balance? Are your affairs blending in a way you like? How does your work in EMS impact the other elements? This should be considered because EMS tends to overshadow everything else for many of us.

Often, if there is an imbalance, it is due to an overcommitment to EMS at the expense of the other elements of life. At first, this is understandable. It is human nature to spend a lot of energy rising up the initial learning curve of any new interest. There is a lot to learn to become involved in the emergency services. You need to know about bodies, what can go wrong, and what you can do about it at your training level. You also need people skills, interpersonal communication abilities, self-awareness and awareness of others. After initial education comes the learning curve of the streets, the part that comes from time in the trade. This book can provide beginners with a better start than others have had historically. But after those two initial, steep learning curves, the rate of learning flattens. While there is always an up slope, the rate of change never seems as exhilarating. It must be how astronauts feel after the booster rockets are jettisoned. They're still traveling really fast, but the G-forces have disappeared.

Yet as the rate of change slows, the degree of involvement remains as intense for many EMS providers. Those who are unaware of or refuse to heed the signals sometimes find themselves burned out, cynical, negative—and hating what they set out to love. It's a classical imbalance. The relevance of stopping to reflect comes again to the forefront. Becoming conscious of the vast array of choices available when you remove the blinders is a key to entering life after the streets in a healthy, balanced manner.

The Take-Home Lessons of the Streets

EMS providers have a unique opportunity to live life better and more fully as a result of the things they see out on the streets. No one else is a witness to life as unrehearsed and unplanned as we are. We go into the deep recesses of strangers' homes, where polite company would never go. The only others to routinely see those places—real estate people—are at least expected. Things are usually straightened and cleaned before they arrive. Not so with EMS! We are summoned upon a moment's notice, and no one usually cares what the house looks like. We go to outbuildings of farms, elevator shafts, and high-rise basements. We burst past whatever socioeconomic backgrounds we come from and go to the mayor's house, the CEO's office, the skid row flophouse, and the suburban home. We are invited to parts of town we'd normally never enter safely otherwise.

Because of these experiences, we are bestowed precious lessons about life without having to live the tragedies ourselves. We can learn from the experiences of others and take those lessons home, to live our lives differently in hopes of avoiding some of the mistakes and misfortunes. If nothing else, we can make better choices about how we live with those we love—if we stop to reflect, and then heed the lessons.

People generally do not expect bad things to happen to them. Yet the disdain of some EMS providers during interfacility transfers is perhaps cavalier, when so many still smoke, drink to excess, and refuse to take the opportunity to alter their own pathways to poor physical health. Others are making other choices, though—ones that could result in vibrant instead of decrepit old age. The difference boils down to a philosophy about "intention" versus "expectation." Those who don't expect bad things to happen, but don't engage in healthful living might be disappointed. They've heard of "life expectancy" tables, and expect to live into their 70's or 80's. Chronic illness may occur, or premature death. Each is more shocking when you were expecting something else. Sometimes, bad things happen and it's not even your doing: For example, a couple who are "expecting" a child can imagine birthing a healthy, full-term infant. Anything less is a blow to their expectations.

Perhaps rather than expecting so much of life, a person could choose to have intention. If you're intending to live to be very old (rather than expecting it as a birthright), you might try now to promote the likelihood that old age will be accompanied by robust health. These are choices that are available to anyone willing to stop and reflect on the impact of how they're currently living on their overall lifeline. We know, because we've handled the scenes repeatedly, that life can be snuffed out or snatched away in a heartbeat. We know we cannot expect a natural end to our lifelines. So maybe it helps to intend to live long and well, but not to expect to be alive tonight. Doesn't that promote an interest in living this day as well as possible?

Another area of rich learning comes from working with difficult people. Many patients are less than pleasant. So are bystanders, relatives, even coworkers! They are difficult for many reasons. They may be in pain, angry, or frustrated. They may be negative people to begin with. They may be in a bad mood. They may be burned out. It doesn't matter—as professionals, we are mandated (at least morally) to work with them as effectively as possible. The skills you have, and the information available in places like chapters 3, 4, and 5 in this book, travel far beyond the streets. They go to the store with you, when you come across a harried cashier. They go to the ticket lines for concerts, to the airports and into the neighborhoods of your life—wherever other difficult people cross your path. Handling them well, with humor or the ability to let their negativity roll off your back, is a gift from EMS to your life after the streets.

EMS has abundant other lessons. For example, our lives are filled with boundaries and territories. Some of these boundaries are logistical. They occur between one response district and the next, or between one EMS agency and another. Within the agency, there is hierarchy and rank, both formal and by tenure. Junior partners are often at the mercy of their senior partners. There are "us versus them" feelings, too, between genders. In the high-pressure world of EMS, there is a good reason to smooth the boundaries and learn to work well with others. When we get home, those skills will remain valuable in terms of building a strong local community and getting along with the neighbors.

Some of the boundaries in our lives are within each of us. If you are a shy person, what can you bring from the assertiveness you have to muster on the streets to your personal life? If you are afraid to dance, because of a limit set by your parents in junior high school, what freedom there is in busting out of that boundary! If EMS is your whole life, you might see it as another sort of boundary. If you like your life that way, that is one thing; however, if it is interfering with other elements of your life, there are choices to make in the interests of personal development. Try regarding emotional baggage as something as burdensome as too much luggage on a trip. After carrying the luggage from the car to the ticket counter, you feel so light when you set it down! Similarly, letting go of emotional baggage can lighten your psychological load. If there is any emotional baggage holding you back from being as complete as you'd like to be, you are ahead of many others just by acknowledging its existence. In your work as an EMS provider, watch for patients or coworkers who struggle with the same limits. What can you learn from those persons? The keys to your own personal development are in your hands—if you learn to recognize them.

Blocks to the Change Process

Growth along your lifeline implies change. A baby changes from an infant to a toddler by learning to walk. "Big kid" pants mark another glad change! Finishing each school year culminates, eventually, in graduation from high school and perhaps college. First licenses, first jobs, first loves—each is part of the life process, and each marks a transition. Passages from one stage of life to the next are stressful no matter how joyous they are. And some are not joyous at all.

On a daily level, changing from work to home also requires adjustment. Some people rely on their commute homeward as the time to adjust appropriately. Others never let go of their day, and it carries forward, often affecting after-work relations with people. Which seems more fun? More effective?

Stopping to reflect is an important key to deciding whether or not you like your path. If you do not, you can then ponder what you'd like to change. It might be your physical body, your mental outlook, your relationship with your spouse, your time with your children or parents, your lawn. Whatever it is, the decision to change something implies a willingness to take the time and make the effort to alter the course of your life—either a little or a lot, depending on the task.

There are attitudes and preconceived notions about change. It's frightening to many people, because that's the nature of the change process. Some common blocks to change are:[1]

- We are bound by habits. People choose the familiar over what might be better or best. The antidote: replace habits, become aware, and take the risks to change. Understand that trying something once or twice will not work. It requires 21 consecutive days of doing a new thing to make it a habit.[2]

- You don't have 100 percent of your time or energy to make a change. Fine! Focus on key areas and change one percent at a time.

- There are filters that interfere. For example, a person with poor self-esteem (a common filter) has difficulty hearing compliments. The antidote is to change the interfering filters through the self-modification of behavior. There are numerous self-esteem courses and audiotapes available. Use them.

- The "I should" message is poison. Every time you say, "I should," your sub-conscious mind answers, "Oh yeah? *Make* me!" Guilt is an ineffective change strategy. An antidote is to use more flexible language, such as, "I'd really like to . . ." instead. Also, assess your demands. Are they realistic?

- Judgment of the self versus others focuses attention on the wrong thing. Comparing yourself with others is unrealistic. Others will always be thinner or richer. The only true enemy in your life is yourself. Don't worry about other people—they have struggles of their own. Accept yourself, and forgive yourself. Without forgiveness, you will stay stuck in your old ways.

- Fear is a potent block to change! Whether you are fighting fear or ignoring it, you're still in reaction to it. Accept the fear, and transcend it. That is the only way to move past it. Take a deep breath, then take the plunge into the risks that are inherent to change.

- Self-hate is also poison. Do you know people who self-sabotage

---

[1] Used with permission of publisher, CareerTrack, Inc. Material originally obtained from a CareerTrack workshop on self-esteem. For more information about CareerTrack programs, call 800-325-1202 (Colorado).
[2] Mike Taigman, "Get A Life," *EMS Today*, March 15, 1996.

their own successes? Somewhere along the line they got the message that they do not deserve the good stuff in life. If this block fits you, rescue yourself! Alter your world to be more self-nurturing and loving. It can be done.

- There is no environment of support. Those who choose to change often threaten the *status quo* of others they might leave behind. A classic is the person who decides to stop drinking so much. Drinking buddies will try everything to entice their friend to stay with their habit. "What's the matter, aren't we good enough for you anymore? You used to be so much fun." Such situations can be very difficult to change, but you can do it if it's important enough to you. Find (or create) a positive support group. It's there. Look for it!

- People have a lack of understanding for the change process. The operative word in the phrase "grow old" is "grow." As you move along your life line, are you growing in the way you wish? If not, educate yourself about how to seek the life you want. Read. Listen to audiotapes. Education does not have to come from a traditional classroom. Remember, this life is *not* a dress rehearsal! It may as well be as close to perfect as you can make it. The choice is yours.

Some people live their lives in the past. Others are constantly looking to the future. There is nothing wrong with either—unless it prevents a person from noticing the "now." In the end, "now" is all there is. Take the pulse of your life and be sure it's robust here-and-now. This is how you can stay fully in the present moment. Working on changes, and honoring the past are nice, but if you really want to shift the course of your life, the time to be most aware of is now.

Letting Go

After the last emergency run, what then? A person who has dedicated him or herself to the streets dislikes thinking about it, but the time will come sooner or later. Sometime you will have to put the word, "former" in front of your EMS qualification. How does it feel to be a former paramedic? It could happen after only a few months, or after many years of emergency service. For anyone who has experienced the satisfaction (and trepidation) of being an EMS provider, stopping entails a significant identity adjustment that can be both wrenching and emotional. Not only are you letting go of the licenses and certificates you sweated so

Figure 15.2

Gaining perspective on life, and living in a conscious and deliberate fashion, brings meaning and depth to your experiences that might not be there otherwise.

hard to earn, you are deciding to close the door on an era of your life that was rewarding and thrilling in ways no other pursuit will be able to match.

Guaranteed, the sound of a siren will always evoke a response in your gut and you will vicariously share the intensity you can imagine in the emergency vehicle going by. Keep in mind, though, that many EMS skills cross over handily to other activities in life. If you go into sales, for example, you will be talking people into buying a product, similar to the way you helped people on the streets see the wisdom of ambulance transport. If you choose construction, think how it takes tremendous patience to see a project through from start to finish, similar to the patience you needed to approach each new scene with a fresh slate in your mind. Teachers, should you become one, need to know effective crowd control to retain orderliness in the classroom. At-home, parenting demands enormous flexibility,

> The lessons learned on the streets can *always* be applied to the rest of your life. Therefore, can we say that we ever truly leave the streets?

since children require you to be many things: cook, laundry worker, driver, toy repairperson, nurturer, and so on.

EMS training and experience clearly blend into life in general. The lessons learned on the streets can *always* be applied to the rest of your life. Therefore, can we say that we ever truly leave the streets?

CHIEF TECUMSEH
CHIEF OF THE SHAWNEE INDIANS
"VIEW OF THE ETHICAL LIFE," 1810

So live your life that the fear of death can never enter your heart.

Trouble no man about his religion—respect him in his views, and demand that he respect yours.

Love your life, beautify all things in your life, perfect your life.

Seek to make your life long and of service to your people.

Always give a word or sign of salute when meeting or passing a friend, or even a stranger, if in a lonely place.

When you arise in the morning, give thanks for the morning light, for your life and strength. Give thanks for your food and for the joy of living. If you see no reason for giving thanks, the fault lies in yourself.

When your time comes to die, be not like those whose hearts are filled with the fear of death, so when their time comes they weep and pray to live their lives over again in a different way. Sing your death song, and die like a hero going home.

Whatever you go on to do, be a life learner. Seek win-win situations in the conflicts that inevitably arise in life. Both these approaches to life can enrich it beautifully. They allow you to make the most of each day. By having the interest to notice how your lifeline is proceeding, you might eventually see the many elements begin to weave themselves into a beautiful tapestry, one of which you deserve to feel proud. Live life well! And enjoy.

Summary

The world of prehospital care gives us many things. For some, sadly, those "gifts" are not as positive, such as permanent disabilities or serious illnesses. But for most, the streets give abundant lessons about all kinds of things— mostly about ourselves. We see all ranges of humanity, from down-and-out to elite, in the most vulnerable moments of their lives. They depend on us for capable, competent, quick, compassionate care.

Streetsense is part of it all. The exciting thing is that each prehospital practitioner has a unique way of applying the concepts of streetsense to their practice of prehospital medicine. It comes from the experiences of your formative years and your previously acquired sense of the world, blended with the new knowledge gained on every new call. You add a flavor to EMS that is all your own. Trust your own instincts. Acknowledge the abilities you already have. If you embrace the ideals set forth in this text and combine them well with your own good values and ideals, you will find EMS a rewarding experience. Good luck, and stay safe.

3rd Edition Acknowledgments

My grateful thanks to the following for their advice, contributions, reviews, and support in preparation of the second edition:

- Cynthia Osborne (Chicago), for making me do it.
- Jim and Melody Dernocoeur (Michigan), for their continued love and tolerance, and for Jim's computer wizardry!
- Alison Taggart (California), MBFITWWW and photographer extraordinaire.
- Mike Taigman (Planet Earth), for two-plus decades of friendship, and for bringing Elaine into my life too.
- Steve McGervey, Paul Kasson, and Lyn Morgan of the Eagle County Ambulance District (Colorado), for help with art/photos.
- John Becknell (California), for encouraging the writer in me.
- Mike Smith (Washington), for taking it on the road so long, so well, and so often.
- Keith and Heidi Griffiths (California), for Grindle Lake and beginning it all for me in 1979.
- Kathy Lastas (Michigan), for hours of work putting in the editing changes.
- Jana VanderGoot (Michigan), for artwork and friendship.
- My editor! Elaine Yoder. Awesome. Thanks!
- Norm Bolotin (Washington), production and marketing.
- My producers, especially Laura Dickinson, Sandi Harner, and Kelly Rush at Laing. Also awesome! Thanks!

For Their Respective Expertise—Thanks!

- Charly Miller (Denver) for material on restraining.
- Shannon Gwin (Howard County CIS Team, Maryland), critical incident stress.
- The International Critical Incident Stress Foundation and Jeff Mitchell, as always.

- Douglas A. Miller, University of Illinois at Chicago, guns and ballistics.
- Doug Smith, Kent County EMS, (Michigan), elderly people.
- Nancy Manix, M-P.T. (California), back safety and safety in lifting.
- Denis Meade (Colorado), gang-related material (chapter 6)—plus a new chapter quote!
- Dave Maatman (Michigan), gang information.
- Mercy Ambulance (Michigan), assistance with artwork.
- Marilyn Smith (Michigan), The fabulous photos in the second edition (belatedly!).
- Carolyn Jaffe (Colorado), hospice nurse, death and dying.

Suggested Readings

Generally Recommended Reading

BERRY, CARMEN. *When Helping You is Hurting Me.* New York: Harper Paperbacks, 1988.

DASS, RAM, and MIRABAI BUSH. *Compassion in Action.* New York: Bell Tower, 1992.

DICK, THOM. *Street Talk: Notes from a Rescuer.* California: Jems Communications, 1988. An EMS classic, filled with Thom's insightful essays about the streets.

EMS Safety: Techniques and Applications FA-144 (Washington, D.C., FEMA, 1994) An outstanding reference on EMS safety from soup to nuts.

GOLEMAN, DANIEL. *Emotional Intelligence.* New York: Bantam Books, 1995.

IVY, PAT. *EMT:Rescue.* New York: Ivy Books, 1993.

KUBLER-ROSS, ELISABETH. *On Death and Dying.* New York: Collier Books, 1969. This is the book that started the revolution for death and dying awareness.

MITCHELL, JEFFREY, AND GRADY BRAY. *Emergency Services Stress.* New Jersey: Brady, 1989. Essential reading about a topic of universal concern to EMS providers.

MOYERS, BILL. *Healing and the Mind.* New York: Doubleday, 1993.

NEELY, KEITH. *Street Dancer.* California: Brady, 1990. A novel which captures much of the flavor of the prehospital world and those who live in it.

PAGE, JAMES. *The Magic of 3 A.M.: Essays on the Art and Science of Emergency Medical Services.* California: Jems Communications, 1986. Another historical EMS classic.

PAGE, JIM et al. *The Best of JEMS: Timeless Essays from the First 15 Years.* St. Louis: Mosby Lifeline, 1996.

RICHARDS, EUGENE. *The Knife and Gun Club: Scenes from an Emergency Room.* New York: Atlantic Monthly Press, 1989.

TANNEN, DEBORAH, PH.D. *You Just Don't Understand: Men and Women in Conversation.* New York: William Morrow and Company, Inc., 1990. This book is guaranteed to help you understand why confusing inter-gender miscommunications happen!

Chapter 2: Know Yourself

BRANDON, NATHANIAL. *The Power of Self Esteem.* Florida: Health Communications, 1992.

HELMSTETTER, SHAD. *What to Say When You Talk to Yourself.* New York: Pocket Books, 1982.

SHAPIRO, PAUL. *Paramedic.* New York: Bantam Books, 1991.

TRACY, DIANE. *Take this Job and Love It: A Personal Guide to Career Empowerment.* New York: McGraw-Hill, 1994.

Chapter 3: Understanding Others

BECKNELL, JOHN. "Cultural Perspectives." *JEMS*, 13 (April 1988).

BECKNELL, JOHN. "Marriage and the EMS Experience." *JEMS*, 13 (June 1988).

BERNE, ERIC. *Games People Play.* New York: Ballantine Books, 1964.

BOYD, KATE. "The Public Inebriate: Assessing a Complex Problem." *JEMS*, 5 (April 1980).

DICK, THOM. "Anxiety in the Street: Understanding Yourself and Relating to Your Patients." *JEMS*, 5 (June 1980).

DICK, THOM. *Street Talk: Notes from a Rescuer.* Solana Beach, California: *JEMS* Communications Publishing Company, 1988.

FISHER, ROGER, and WILLIAM URY with BRUCE PATTON. *Getting to Yes: Negotiating Agreement Without Giving In.* New York: Penguin Books, 1981.

IZARD, CARROLL E. *Human Emotions.* New York: Plenum Press, 1977.

KUSHNER, HAROLD. *When Bad Things Happen to Good People.* New York: Avon Books, 1981.

LYNCH, DOROTHEA and EUGENE RICHARDS. *Exploding into Life.* New York: Aperature, 1986. About the battle one woman waged against her cancer and public sentiment toward her as a cancer patient.

MACDONALD, JOHN and DAVID MICHAUD. *The Confession: Interrogation and Criminal Profiles for Police Officers.* Denver, Colo.: Apache Press, 1987.

MAGID, KEN, and CAROLE A. MCKELVEY. *High Risk: Children without a Conscience.* New York: Bantam Books, 1987. A chilling book about one cause that people are growing up without a sense of conscience.

REES, W. LINFORD, ed. *Anxiety Factors in Comprehensive Patient Care.* New York: American Elsevier Publishing Company, Inc., 1973.

SHANABERGER, C. J. "The Legal File: Beyond Personal Injury (The Trauma of Emotional Distress)." *JEMS*, 12 (July 1987).

SOMERS, SUZANNE. *Keeping Secrets.* New York: Warner Books, Inc., 1988. The story of growing up the child of an alcoholic.

STORR, ANTHONY. *Human Aggression.* New York: Atheneum Publishers, 1968.

TAVRIS, CAROL. *Anger: The Misunderstood Emotion.* New York: Simon and Schuster, 1982.

WEISSBERG, MICHAEL. *Dangerous Secrets: Maladaptive Responses to Stress.* New York: W.W. Norton & Company, Inc., 1983.

Chapter 4: Effective Interpersonal Communication

ASHCRAFT, NORMAN and ALBERT E. SCHEFLEN. *People Space: The Making and Breaking of Human Boundaries.* New York: Anchor Press/Doubleday, 1976.

BERNSTEIN, LEWIS. *Interviewing: A Guide for Health Professionals.* New York: Appleton-Century-Crofts, 1980.

BROWN, CHARLES T. and CHARLES VAN RIPER. *Communication in Human Relationships.* Skokie, Ill.: National Textbook Company, 1974.

COLLINS, MATTIE. *Communication in Health Care: The Human Connection in the Life Cycle.* (2nd ed.). St. Louis, Mo.: The C.V. Mosby, Company, 1983.

DICK, THOM. *Street Talk: Notes from a Rescuer.* Solana Beach, Calif.: *JEMS* Publishing Company, 1988.

FAST, JULIUS. *Body Language.* New York: Pocket Books, 1970.

KENDRICK, S. BRYANT and OZIMEK, DAN. "Is Talk Cheap? Communication Skills for the EMS Professional." *JEMS*, 17 (February 1992), 49–53.

KING, MARK, LARRY NOVIK, and CHARLES CITRENBAUM. *Irresistible Communication: Creative Skills for the Health Professional.* Philadelphia: W.B. Saunders Company, 1983.

MACDONALD, JOHN, and DAVID MICHAUD. *The Confession: Interrogation and Criminal Profiles for Police Officers.* Denver, Colo.: Apache Press, 1987.

MARSH, PETER. *Eye To Eye: How People Interact.* Topsfield, Mass.: Salem House Publishers, 1988.

MITCHELL, JEFF and GRADY BRAY. *Emergency Services Stress.* Englewood Cliffs, NJ: Prentice-Hall, Inc., 1990.

SOREFF, STEPHEN M. and ROBERT T. CADIGAN. *EMS Street Strategies: Effective Patient Interaction.* Philadelphia: F.A. Davis Company, 1992.

SWAN, THOMAS H. "Effective Communication, So To Speak." *JEMS,* 17 (July 1992), 78–81.

TAIGMAN, MIKE and SYD CANAN. "Recognition of Acute Myocardial Infarction." *JEMS,* 12 (October 1987).

TANNAN, DEBORAH, PH.D. *Talking From 9 to 5.* New York: William Morrow and Company, Inc., 1994.

TANNEN, DEBORAH, PH.D. *You Just Don't Understand: Men and Women in Conversation.* New York: William Morrow and Company, Inc., 1990.

TUBBS, STEWART L. and SYLVIA MOSS. *Human Communication: An Interpersonal Perspective.* New York: Random House, Inc., 1974.

Chapter 5: Death and Dying

BRIDGES, WILLIAM. *Transitions: Making Sense of Life's Changes.* Massachusetts: Addison-Wesley, 1980.

COLLINS, MATTIE. *Communication in Health Care: The Human Connection in the Life Cycle.* 2nd ed.. St. Louis, Mo.: The C. V. Mosby, Company, 1983. (Good section on grief and mourning.)

DUBIN, W. and J. R. SARNOFF. "Sudden Unexpected Death: Intervention with the Survivors." *Annals of Emergency Medicine.* 15, (January 1986).

GLASER, BARNEY G. and ANSELM L. STRAUSS. "Awareness Contexts and Social Interaction." *American Sociological Review,* 29 (1964) 669–679. (An interesting interpersonal model.)

KUBLER-ROSS, ELISABETH. *On Death and Dying.* New York: Macmillan Publishing Co., Inc., 1969. (A classic, must-read book about this topic.)

LEVINE, STEPHEN. *Who Dies? An Investigation of Conscious Living and Conscious Dying.* New York: Anchor Press/Doubleday, 1982.

ROSEN, PETER and BENJAMIN HONIGMAN. "Life and Death." in *Emergency Medicine: Concepts and Clinical Practice,* ed. Peter Rosen. St. Louis, Mo.: The C. V. Mosby Company, 1983.

SCHULTZ, RICHARD. *The Psychology of Death, Dying, and Bereavement.* Reading, Mass.: Addison-Wesley Publishing Company, Inc., 1978.

SHANABERGER, C. J. "The Legal File: The Moment of Death." *JEMS,* 13 (September 1988).

VENINGA, ROBERT. *The Gift of Hope: How We Survive Our Tragedies.* New York: Ballantine, 1985.

VICTOROFF, VICTOR. *The Suicidal Patient: Recognition, Intervention, Management.* Oradell, N. J.: Medical Economics Books, 1983.

WEISSBERG, MICHAEL. *Dangerous Secrets: Maladaptive Responses to Stress.* New York: W.W. Norton & Company, Inc., 1983. (Good chapter on suicide.)

ZUNIN, LEONARD, and HILARY STANTON ZUNIN. *The Art of Condolence.* New York: Harper Perennial, 1991.

Chapter 6: Special Populations, Special Challenges

ALEXANDER, MARY and MARIE SCOTT BROWN. *Pediatric History Taking and Physical Diagnosis for Nurses.* 2nd ed. New York: McGraw-Hill Book Company, 1979. (Ways to work with children.)

BARTON, RICHARD THOMAS. *Religious Doctrine and Medical Practice.* Springfield, Ill.: Charles C Thomas, Publisher, 1958. (About Jehovah's Witnesses and Christian Scientists.)

BERNSTEIN, LEWIS. *Interviewing: A Guide for Health Professionals.* New York: Appleton-Century-Crofts, 1980. (Sections on cultural considerations.)

DERNOCOEUR, KATE. "Maltreatment of Children, Part I: Recognition and Care in the Prehospital Setting." *JEMS,* 8 (February 1983), 22–27.

DERNOCOEUR, KATE. "Maltreatment of Children, Part 2: Understanding the Problem." *JEMS,* 8 (March 1983), 40–44.

DERNOCOEUR, KATE. "Prejudice: Spoiling the Melting Pot Brew." *JEMS,* 13 (April, 1988).

DERNOCOEUR, KATE. "Southeast Asians: A Cross-Cultural Medical Challenge." *JEMS,* 6 (May 1981), 38–39.

DICK, THOM. *Street Talk: Notes from a Rescuer.* Solana Beach, Calif.: JEMS Publishing Company, 1988.

DIERKING, BRENT. et al., "The Stress of Trauma: Psychological Response of the Pediatric Patient." *JEMS,* 13 (February 1988).

GRATZ, R. R. "Children's Responses to Emergency Department Care." *Annals of Emergency Medicine,* 13 (May 1984).

HENSCHEL, MILTON G. "Who Are Jehovah's Witnesses?" in *Religions in America,* ed. Leo Rosten. New York: Simon and Schuster, 1963.

HOGAN, TERESITA M., M.D. *Geriatric Emergencies: An EMT Teaching Manual.* Turlock, California: Medic Alert Foundation, 1994.

MEADE, DENIS M. "When Colors Kill." *Emergency Medical Services,* 21 (January 1992).

REES, W. LINFORD, ed. *Anxiety Factors in Comprehensive Patient Care.* New York: American Elsevier Publishing Company, Inc., 1973.

SCHWARTZ, MARILYN. *Guidelines for Bias-Free Writing.* Bloomington, Indiana: American University Press, 1984.

SHANABERGER, C. J. "The Legal File: Children's Rights and EMS." *JEMS,* 12 (February 1987).

WEISSBERG, MICHAEL. *Dangerous Secrets: Maladaptive Responses to Stress.* New York: W.W. Norton & Company, Inc., 1983. (Chapter on child abuse.)

Chapter 7: Service Orientation and The Nature of Routine

FISHER, ROGER and WILLIAM URY. *Getting to Yes Negotiating Agreement Without Giving In.* Viking Penguin, 1991.

GILLIGAN, CAROL. *In a Different Voice.* Cambridge, Massachusetts, 1993.

GREENLEAF, ROBERT K. *Servant Leadership: A Journey into the Nature of Legitimate Power and Greatness.* Mahwah, NJ: Paulist Press, 1977.

KLOPF, DONALD W. *Interacting in Groups: Theory and Practice.* Denver: Morton Publishing Company, 1989.

LEONARD, GEORGE. *Mastery: The Keys to Success and Long-Term Fulfillment*. New York: Penguin Book, 1991.

LESTER, JOAN STEINAU. *The Future of White Men & Other Diversity Dilemmas*. Emeryville, Calif.: Conari Press, 1994.

PAGE, JIM et al. *The Best of JEMS: Timeless Essays from the First 15 Years*. St. Louis: Mosby Lifeline, 1996.

PETERS, TOM and AUSTIN, NANCY. *A Passion For Excellence: The Leadership Difference*. New York: Random House, 1985.

PETERS, TOM and WATERMAN, ROBERT H. *In Search of Excellence: Lessons from America's Best-Run Companies*. New York: Harper and Row, Publishers, 1982.

RECK, ROSS R. and LONG, BRIAN G. *The Win-Win Negotiator*. Kalamazoo, Michigan: Spartan Publications, Inc., 1987.

TANNEN, DEBORAH, PH.D. *Talking from 9 to 5*. New York: William Morrow and Company, Inc., 1994.

TANNEN, DEBORAH, PH.D. *You Just Don't Understand: Men and Women in Conversation*. New York: William Morrow and Company, Inc., 1990.

WHYTE, DAVID. *The Heart Aroused: Poetry and the Preservation of the Soul in Corporate America*. New York: Doubleday, 1994.

Chapter 8: Prior To Arrival

CHILDS, BRADFORD J. and DONALD J. PTACNIK. *Emergency Ambulance Driving*. Englewood Cliffs, N. J.: The Brady Company, 1986.

CLAWSON, JEFF J. and KATE DERNOCOEUR. *Principles of Emergency Medical Dispatch*. 2nd edition (Salt Lake City: MPC, 1996 [release pending]). The definitive text on priority dispatching, by the originator of the concept.

FREW, STEPHEN A. *Street Law: Rights and Responsibilities of the EMT*. Reston, Va.: Reston Publishing Co., Inc., 1983. Sections on how and why to maintain both a proper attitude and adequate equipment.

MCCALLION, RUSS and FAZACKERLEY, JIM. "Burning The EMS Candle: EMS Shifts and Worker Fatigue." *JEMS*, October 1991.

Chapter 9: The Scene

ADAMS, RONALD J., THOMAS M. MCTERNAN, and CHARLES REMSBERG. *Street Survival: Tactics for Armed Encounters*. Northbrook, Ill.: Calibre Press, 1980. (Available only to people actively involved in emergency medical services and law enforcement; not available to the lay public.)

COWAN, PHIL. "Tunnel Vision!" *Emergency* (January 1988).

NORDBERG, MARIE. "The Bystander Mindset: Where EMS Goes, Crowds Follow." *Emergency Medical Services*, 17 (January/February 1988).

REMSBERG, CHARLES. *The Tactical Edge: Surviving High-Risk Patrol*. Northbrook, Ill.: Calibre Press, 1986. (Available only to people actively involved in emergency medical services and law enforcement; not available to the lay public.)

STANFORD, TODD. "Eliminating Complacency." *Emergency* (January 1988).

Chapter 10: In The Ambulance

CHILDS, BRADFORD J., and DONALD J. PTACNIK. *Emergency Ambulance Driving*. Englewood Cliffs, N. J.: The Brady Company, 1986.

FENICHEL, DOUGLAS. "Stop Skidding Around." *Emergency*, 20 (May 1988).

LUEDTKE, GLENN. "Could You Please Speak Louder?: Coping with Hearing Loss in EMS." *JEMS*, 13 (May 1988).

PEPE, PAUL, et al. "Accelerated Hearing Loss in Urban Emergency Medical Service Firefighters." *Annals of Emergency Medicine*, 14 (May 1985).

SHANABERGER, C. J. "The Legal File: Running Hot." *JEMS*, 12 (April, 1987).

Chapter 11: Guns, Knives and Other Weapons

ADAMS, RONALD J., T. M. MCTERNAN and C. REMSBERG. *Street Survival: Tactics for Armed Encounters.* Northbrook, Ill.: Calibre Press, 1980. (Available only to people actively involved in emergency medical services and law enforcement; not available to the lay public.)

BERG, STANTON O. "The Forensic Ballistics Laboratory." in *Forensic Medicine*, Vol. 1, ed. C.G. Tedeschi, William G. Eckert, and Luke G. Tedeschi. Philadelphia: W.B. Saunders Company, 1977.

CAMBELL, JOHN EMORY. *Basic Trauma Life Support for Paramedics and Advanced EMS Providers.* Englewood Cliffs, New Jersey: Prentice Hall, 1995.

CARTER, WALLACE A. "Arming Yourself to Treat Gunshot Wounds." *JEMS*, 15 (September, 1990).

GORDON, I., and H. A. SHAPIRO. *Forensic Medicine: A Guide to Principles.* New York: Churchill Livingstone, Inc., 1975.

KNIGHT, BERNARD. "Firearm Injuries." in *Forensic Medicine*, Vol. 1, ed. C. G. Tedeschi, William G. Eckert, and Luke G. Tedeschi. Philadelphia: W.B. Saunders Company, 1977.

NORDBERG, MARIE. "Assault & Pepper." *Emergency Medical Services*, (March 1996).

ORDOG, G. J., J. WASSERBERGER, and S. BALASUBRAMANIUM. "Wound Ballistics: Theory and Practice." *Annals of Emergency Medicine*, 13 (December 1984).

VOLLRATH, RICHARD C. "Crime Scene Preservation: It's Everybody's Concern." *JEMS*, 20 (January 1995).

WARNER, KEN, ed. *Gun Digest.* Northbrook, Ill.: DBI Books, Inc., 1984. (Lists every kind of gun there is.)

WILSON, JAMES. "Wound Ballistics." *Western Journal of Medicine*, 127 (July 1977), 49–54.

WILSON, JAMES. "Shotgun Ballistics and Shotgun Injuries." *Western Journal of Medicine*, 129 (August 1978), 149–155.

Chapter 12: Stress and Wellness

ALBRECHT, KARL. *Stress and the Manager.* Englewood Cliffs, N. J.: Prentice-Hall, Inc., 1979.

ARMSTRONG, KEVIN. "EMS Psychology 101." *JEMS*, 18, (January, 1993).

BAILEY, COVERT. *Smart Exercise.* New York: Houghton Mifflin Company, 1994.

BAKER, J. L. "What Is the Occupational Risk to Emergency Care Providers from the Human Immunodeficiency Virus?" *Annals of Emergency Medicine*, 17 (July 1988).

BOURN, SCOTT and MICHAEL G. SMITH. "Pay Now or Pay Later: A Look at Substance Abuse in EMS." *JEMS*, 13 (May 1988).

CANFIELD, JACK and MARK VICTOR HANSEN. *Chicken Soup for the Soul.* Deerfield Beach, Florida: Health Communications, Inc., 1993.

CHERNISS, CARY. *Staff Burnout: Job Stress in the Human Services.* Beverly Hills, Calif.: Sage Publications, Inc., 1980.

CLARK, CHARLES. "Stress Varies from Job to Job, Person to Person," *Congressional Quarterly*, (January, 1996).

CLAWSON, J. J. and J. A. JACOBSON. "Prevalence of Antibody to Hepatitis B Virus Surface Antigen in Emergency Medical Personnel in Salt Lake City, Utah." *Annals of Emergency Medicine*, 15 (February 1986).

CROW, SUE. "Much Ado About Nothing." *Infect Control Hosp Epidemiology,* 9 (May 1988).

COVEY, STEPHEN R. *First Things First.* New York: Simon and Schuster, 1994.

CULLIGAN, M. J. and K. SEDLACK. *How to Kill Stress Before It Kills You.* New York: Grosset & Dunlap, 1976.

DERNOCOEUR, KATE. "Are we Getting the Help we Need?" *JEMS*, (August, 1995).

FEDERAL EMERGENCY MANAGEMENT AGENCY. *A Handbook on Women in Firefighting: The Changing Face of the Fire Service.* FA-128. Washington, D.C., 1993.

FREUDENBERGER, HERBERT J. and GERALDINE RICHELSON. *Burnout: The High Cost of Achievement.* New York: Anchor Press/Doubleday, 1980.

HAWKS, STEVEN R. "Rating Stress in EMS: A Responder Survey." *JEMS*, 15 (September 1990).

INTERNATIONAL ASSOCIATION OF FIREFIGHTERS. *Developing Fire Service Labor/Employee Assistance Programs.* Washington, D.C., IAFF, 1992.

KOOP, C. EVERETT. *Understanding AIDS: A Message from the Surgeon General.* HHS Publication CDC HHS-88-8404 Rockville, Md.: U.S. Department of Health and Human Services, 1988.

KROHNE, HEINZ W. and LOTHAR LAUX. *Achievement, Stress, and Anxiety.* New York: Hemisphere Publishing Corp., 1982.

LaCOMBE, David M. "What'd He Say? How To Effectively Communicate via Radio Reporting." *JEMS,* 20, April 1995.

LAMAR, ERIC. "Gun Incident Shows Firehouse Stress." *The Fairfax Journal*, (January 1993).

LAZAR, RICHARD A. and ROBERT J. SCHAPPERT III. "Presumed Insufficient: The Importance of the Prehospital Care Report." *JEMS*, January 1991.

MARKOWITZ, ELYSA. "Eating on the Run: Finding 'Fast Food' That Feeds your Health." *JEMS*, 18, (January, 1993).

MASLACH, CHRISTINA. "The Client Role in Staff Burn-out." *Journal of Social Issues*, 30 (January 1974), 111–124.

MITCHELL, JEFFREY T. "When Disaster Strikes: The Critical Incident Stress Debriefing Process." *JEMS*, 8 (January 1983).

MITCHELL, JEFFREY T. "The 600-Run Limit." *JEMS*, 9 (January 1984).

MITCHELL, JEFFREY T. and GRADY P. BRAY. *Emergency Services Stress.* Englewood Cliffs, N. J.: The Brady Company, 1989.

O'REAR, JOYCE. "Post-Traumatic Stress Disorder: When the Rescurer Becomes the Victim." *JEMS*, 17, (January 1992).

PALMER, RONALD. "Authoritarianism, Inner/Other Directedness, and Sensation Seeking in firefighter/Paramedics: Their Relationship with Burnout." *Prehospital and Disaster Medicine,* 11, (January–March, 1996).

PEPE, P. E. et al. "Viral Hepatitis Risk in Urban Emergency Medical Services Personnel." *Annals of Emergency Medicine,* 15 (April 1986).

"Prevention and Control of Stress among Emergency Workers: A Pamphlet for Team Managers." DHHS Publication (ADM) 88–1496. Rockville, Md.: U.S. Department of Health and Human Services, 1988.

SELYE, HANS. *Stress in Health and Disease.* Woburn, Mass.: Butterworth Publishers, 1976.

SELYE, HANS. *Stress without Distress*. Philadelphia: J.B. Lippincott Company, 1974. The classic text on stress.

SHEEHY, GAIL. *Passages: Predictable Crises of Adult Life*. New York: E.P. Dutton, Inc., 1976.

SHELTON, RAY, and JACK KELLY. *EMS Stress: An Emergency Responder's Handbook for Living Well*. California: Jems Communications, 1995.

SIEGEL, BERNIE S. *Love, Medicine & Miracles*. New York: Harper & Row, Publishers, Inc., 1986. (Excellent book for helping formulate a healthier approach to patient care and for developing your own human potential.)

WEST, KATHERINE H. *Infectious Disease Handbook for Emergency Care Personnel*. Philadelphia: J.B. Lippincott Company, 1987.

Chapter 13: Managing Legal Risks

BERNSTEIN, LEWIS. *Interviewing: A Guide for Health Professionals*. New York: Appleton-Century-Crofts, 1980. (Section on malpractice.)

BOYD, KATE. "Trip Reporting: The Power of Paperwork." *JEMS*, 5 (July 1980), 20–27.

FREW, STEPHEN A. *Street Law: Rights and Responsibilities of the EMT*. Reston, Va.: Reston Publishing Co., Inc., 1983.

MEISEL, ALAN and L. H. ROTH. "What We Do and Do Not Know about Informed Consent." *JAMA*, 246 (November 27, 1981) 2473–77.

SHANABERGER, C. J. "The Legal File: So You Want to Be a Good Samaritan." *JEMS*, 12 (May 1987).

SHANABERGER, C. J. "The Legal File: The Trip Report *Is* Important." *JEMS*, 12 (October 1987).

SHANABERGER, C. J. "The Legal File: Equipment Failure Is Often Human Failure." *JEMS*, 13 (January, 1988).

SHANABERGER, C. J. "The Legal File: Why Releases Are Ineffective." *JEMS*, 13 (February 1988).

SHANABERGER, C. J. "The Legal File: The 'Black Letter Law'." *JEMS*, 13 (March 1988).

SHANABERGER, C. J. "The Legal File: No Apparent Injuries." *JEMS*, 13 (April 1988).

SHANABERGER, C. J. "The Legal File: Look Before You Leap." *JEMS*, 13 (July 1988).

SOLER, J. M. et al. "The Ten-Year Malpractice Experience of a Large Urban EMS System." *Annals of Emergency Medicine*, 14 (October 1985), 983.

Chapter 14: Scene Control and Scene Choreography

FREW, STEPHEN A. *Street Law: Rights and Responsibilities of the EMT*. Reston, Va.: Reston Publishing Co., Inc., 1983. (Chapter on interdepartmental relations and scene control.)

NEELY, KEITH. "Staying in Control." *JEMS*, 9 (December 1984).

Chapter 15: After The Streets

BECKNELL, JOHN. *Medic Life*. St. Louis: Mosby Lifeline, 1995.

BLANCHARD, KENNETH and SPENCER JOHNSON. *The One Minute Manager*. New York: Berkley Books, 1981.

BLANCHARD, KENNETH and ROBERT LORBER. *Putting the One Minute Manager to Work*. New York: Berkley Books, 1984.

BRANDON, NATHANIEL. *Honoring the Self*. New York: Bantam Books, 1983.

COVEY, STEPHEN. *The Seven Habits of Highly Effective People.* New York: Simon and Schuster, 1989.

DERNOCOEUR, KATE. "The 'We Save Lives Myth'." *JEMS,* 11 (March 1986).

DICK, THOM. *Street Talk: Notes from a Rescuer.* Solana Beach, Calif.: *JEMS* Publishing Company, 1988.

FRANKL, VIKTOR. *Man's Search for Meaning.* New York: Washington Square Press, 1985.

LEIDER, RICHARD. *The Power of Purpose.* New York: Ballantine Books, 1985.

MANDINO, OG. *A Better Way to Live.* New York: Bantam Books, 1990.

MILLMAN, DAN. *The Way of the Peaceful Warrior.* California: H.J. Kramer, 1980.

NAVE, JEAN, and LOUISE NELSON. *Mid-Career Crisis.* New York: Perigee Books, 1991.

NEELY, KEITH. *Street Dancer.* Solana Beach, California: JEMS Publishing Company, 1990.

PECK SCOTT. *The Road Less Traveled.* New York: Simon and Schuster, 1978.

PETERS, THOMAS J., and ROBERT H. WATERMAN. Jr. *In Search of Excellence.* New York: Harper & Row, Publishers, Inc., 1982.

ROGER-JOHN, and PETER McWILLIAMS. *Do It!,* Los Angeles: Prelude Press, 1991.

SCHOR, JULIET. *The Overworked American: The Unexpected Decline of Leisure.* New York: Harper Collins, 1991.

SHANABERGER, C. J. "The Legal File: Not Just an Ambulance." *JEMS,* 12 (March 1987).

SINETAR, MARSHA. *Do What You Love and the Money Will Follow.* New Jersey: Paulist Press, 1987.

SINETAR, MARSHA. *Living Happily Ever After: Creating Trust, Luck and Joy.* New York: Villard Books, 1990.

Index

About the Author

Kate Boyd Dernocoeur worked as a paramedic for the City & County of Denver Paramedic Division between February 1979 and January 1986, with breaks to travel overseas for a year and write the first edition of *Streetsense*. Her involvement with emergency medical services stems back to 1973, when she was a member of the Vail Mountain Rescue Group. In 1976, she worked for seven months as a police/fire/EMS dispatcher for the Town of Vail (Colorado). After becoming an EMT in 1977, she worked for a year for a private ambulance service in metropolitan Denver (mostly running transfers!).

She has lectured extensively in the United States and Canada on EMS topics, and has written for EMS journals since April, 1980, when she wrote the cover story for the second issue of *JEMS*. She is also the co-author (with Jeff J. Clawson, M.D.) of *Principles of Emergency Medical Dispatch,* 2nd edition.

In private life, she is known as Melody's mom and Jim's wife. Jim—now a PA-C at St. Mary's Hospital's Emergency Department and still an EMS leader and lecturer—is also the computer wizard of Team Dernocoeur. As of 1996, the Dernocoeur family was still living in Michigan.